THE STRATEGIC DEVELOPMENT OF TALENT

A Completely Revised and Updated Second Edition of
Human Resource Development: A Strategic Approach

D1294625

WILLIAM J. ROTHWELL ✧ H. C. KAZANAS

HRD Press, Inc. • **Amherst, Massachusetts**

HRD Press, Inc.
22 Amherst Road
Amherst, MA 01002-9709
800-822-2801 (U.S. and Canada)
413-253-3488
413-253-3490 (Fax)
www.hrdpress.com

The Strategic Development of Talent

Editorial Coordinator: Suzanne Bay

Cover Designer: Eileen Klockars

Printed in the United States of America. Second Edition 2003.

ISBN 10: 0-87425-752-2
ISBN 13: 978-0-87425-752-2

CONTENTS

List of Exhibits xiii
List of Activities xv
Preface xix
   The Audience for the Book xix
   The Importance of the Topic xix
   The Purpose of the Book xxi
   The Organization of the Book xxi

Part I   **The Background and Purpose of Talent Development** 1
Chapter 1 **Background Issues** 3
   Strategic Business Planning 5
      Using History to Understand Strategic Business Planning 5
      Using Metaphor to Understand Strategic Business Planning 7
      Using Questions to Understand Strategic Business Planning 8
      A Model of Strategic Business Planning 8
      Key Assumptions of Strategic Business Planning 15
      The Value of Strategic Business Planning 16
      Levels of Planning 17
      Methods of Planning 19
   Human Resource Planning 21
      A Model of HRP 22
      Key Assumptions of HRP 23
      The Value of HRP 25
      Levels of HRP 25
      Methods of HRP 27
   The Strategic Development of Talent: A Definition 28
      A Model of SDT 30
      Key Assumptions of SDT 31
      The Importance of Strategic Development of Talent 33
      Competency Identification, Modeling, and Assessment and the Strategic
         Development of Talent 34
      Leadership Development Programs for the Strategic Development of Talent . . 40

Chapter 2 **The Vision and Purpose of the Talent Development Effort** 49
What Is Vision? 49
What Is Purpose? 50
How Important Is Purpose? 54
Relationships with Strategic Business Plans and HR Plans 54
   The Top-Down Approach 56
   The Market-Driven Approach 57
   The Career Planning Approach 59
   The Futuring Approach 60
   The Artificial Experience Approach 61
   The Pulse-Taking Approach 62
   The Performance Diagnosis Approach 63
   The Educational Approach 64
   The Interpersonal Approach 65
   The Rifle Approach 67
   Choosing an Approach. 68
Clarifying the Purpose of a Talent Development Effort 68
   Formulating the Purpose of the Talent Development Effort 68
   Changing the Purpose Statement. 71
The Effects of Organizational Philosophy and Culture on the
   Purpose of the Talent Development Effort 72
   The Philosophy of Talent Development 72
   Organizational Culture. 72

Part II **Assessing Needs and Scanning the Environment** 87
Chapter 3 **Comprehensive Needs Assessment** 89
Comprehensive Needs Assessment: Definition and Description 90
Needs Assessment: Background Issues 91
Steps in Comprehensive Needs Assessment 93
Identifying Learners 94
Classifying Learners by Market Segment. 95
   The Job Market. 96
   Individual/Career Market 98
   The Work Group or Department Market 99
   The External Market 100
Comparing Actual to Desired Knowledge and Skills 101
   Levels of Assessment and Assessment Strategy. 102
   Data Collection Methods 103
   Selecting Data Collection Methods 110
   Involving Others in Data Collection and Analysis. 111
Identifying Present Learning Needs by Market or Market Segment. 112

Chapter 4   Environmental Scanning 119
Environmental Scanning: Definition and Description 120
The State of the Environmental Scanning Art in Business Planning 122
Environmental Scanning for Talent Development 124
Definition 124
Importance 124
Environmental Scanning and Curriculum Needs Assessment 125
Steps in Environmental Scanning for Talent Development 125
Classifying the External Environment...................................126
Deciding on a Time Horizon...126
Examining Environmental Sectors......................................129
The Economic Sector...129
The Political Sector 130
The Technological Sector 131
The Social Sector..132
The Market Sector 134
The Geographic Sector 135
The Supplier Sector..136
The Distribution Sector 136
Anticipating the Effects of Environmental Changes 136
Identifying Future Learning Needs 140
Key External Stakeholders and Their Future Learning Needs 143
The Organization and Its Future Learning Needs 144
The Individual and Future Learning Needs 145
Jobs and Future Learning Needs 146
Sources of Information for Talent Development Scanning...................148
Methods for Carrying Out Environmental Scanning for Talent Development 150
Reassessing Learning Needs by Market or Market Segment 155

**Part III   Choosing and Implementing Organizational Strategy
for the Development of Talent** 161
Chapter 5   Choosing Organizational Strategy for the Development of Talent 163
Organizational Strategy for the Development of Talent: Definition
and Importance...163
Definition 163
The Importance of Choosing Organizational Strategy for the
Development of Talent 164
Suggestions for Choosing Organizational Strategy...........................165
Advice..165
Issues of Concern 166
Choosing Organizational Strategy for the Development of Talent: The Process...166

Step 1: Find the problems 167
Step 2: Formulate the problems.. 169
Step 3: Identify a way to look at the problems........................ 170
Step 4: Consider possible solutions................................... 174
Step 5: Choose organizational strategy for the development of talent 175
Special Issues to Consider in Choosing Organizational Strategy.............. 182
Past Strategy 182
The Degree of Environmental Uncertainty 183
The Degree of Dependence on Key Groups 183
Attitudes about Risk... 184
In-House Politics 184
Timing 185
The Need for a Special Focus 185
Available Skills 187
Relationships to Other Plans 187
Planning for Contingencies 190
Choosing Organizational Strategy for Talent Development: The Product 191
History 192
Curriculum Design... 194
Curriculum Development... 194
Approaches to Curriculum Planning....................................... 196
The Curriculum Planning Process...................................... 196
Alternative Approaches to Curriculum Planning 199
Results of Curriculum Planning and Choice of Organizational Strategy for the
Development of Talent... 213

Chapter 6   Implementing Organizational Strategy for the Development of Talent 219
Steps in Implementing Organizational Strategy for the Development of Talent... 220
Establishing Operational Objectives for the Talent Development Effort 220
Creating, Reviewing, and Revising Talent Development Policies............... 224
Examining Leadership 226
Reviewing Structure.. 227
Reviewing Reward Systems 233
Types of Rewards 233
Learning and Rewards 234
Reviewing Rewards and Changes in Organizational Strategy for the
Development of Talent.. 234
Getting Necessary Resources... 236
Communicating about Strategy 237
Meetings 238

Training. 239
Advisory or Oversight Committees 240
Developing Functional Strategies for the Development of Talent 243

Part IV   **Functional Strategies for Talent Development** 255
Chapter 7   **Organization Development** 257
Definition of Organization Development. 257
How Is Organization Development Distinguishable from Other
Change Methods? 258
What Is the Relationship between Organization Development and
Organizational Learning? 258
The Work Group 259
Organizational Learning. 261
Methods Associated with Organization Development 263
Action Research 263
OD Interventions 265
Problems Associated with Traditional Organization Development Interventions . . 275
Recent Themes in OD and How They Impact Strategic Talent
Development. 276
Strategic Organization Development. 277
Conceptualizing Strategic OD 277
Identifying Norms that Should Exist 278
Assessing Future Pressures Favoring Change 279
Assessing Existing Pressures that Impede Change 280
Comparing Pressures Favoring and Impeding Change. 280
Carrying Out OD Interventions. 280

Chapter 8   **Nonemployee Development** 285
Steps in Nonemployee Development. 286
Creating Classification Schemes 287
The General Public 287
External Stakeholders. 287
Analyzing Relationships between and among the Corporation, Its Public,
and Its Stakeholders 291
Analyzing Present and Future Criteria. 294
Pinpointing Discrepancies 296
Separating Instructional from Noninstructional Needs 296
Deciding What Changes Should Occur 299
Designing Instruction Consistent with Desired Changes 300
Selecting Content and Delivery Methods 301
Following up on Instructional Needs. 304

The Relationship between Organizational Strategy for the Development of
Talent and the Talent Development Effort Planned for Groups outside
the Organization 305

Chapter 9 **Employee Development** 323
Definition of Employee Development 323
Identifying ED Needs. 324
Step 1: Identify each work group. 325
Step 2: Clarify the group's purpose, activities, and responsibilities 325
Step 3: Plan changes in group purpose, activities, and responsibilities 326
Step 4: Determine how many and what kind of people are available 326
Step 5: Plan how many and what kind of people are needed 327
Step 6: Compare desired to available HR supplies. 327
Step 7: Establish action plans. 328
Specialized Methods for Employee Development. 328
Long-Term, Informal Mentoring Programs. 328
Long-Term, Formal Mentoring Programs 329
Long-Term, Formalized Transfer Programs. 330
Short-Term Rotation Programs 333
Special Job Assignments 335
Action Learning Projects 336
Field Trips 337
Professional Conferences 338
Behavior Modeling. 339
Think-Tank Experiences 340
Other Development Experiences. 342
Problems with Traditional Employee-Development Programs. 343
Strategic Employee Development 345
Conceptualizing Strategic Employee Development 345
Specialized Employee Development Methods for Meeting Long-Term
Organizational Needs 346
Long-Term Planning of Related Experiences 346
Select Experiences 347
Plan Each Developmental Experience. 347
Follow up Each Experience 348

Chapter 10 **Employee Education** 361
What Is Employee Education? 361
The Relationship between Employee Education and a Career Program 362
The Two Components of Career Programs. 362
Key Terms. 363
Career Planning: Some Considerations. 363

Career Planning in Organizations 364
Steps in Establishing a Formal, Organizational Career Planning Program 365
   Developing a Climate Conducive to Career Planning 365
   Establishing Career Policy 366
      Employee Education and Strategic Business Plans 368
      Employee Education and HR Plans 369
      Employee Education and Career Plans 369
      Employee Education and Organizational Strategy for the Development
        of Talent 369
   Analyzing the Work 369
      Career Path Analysis 370
   Analyzing the Workforce 373
      Workforce Analysis by Individual 373
      Workforce Analysis by Position 374
      Workforce Analysis by Occupational Group 375
      Workforce Analysis by Department, Division, or Work Group 375
   Identifying Future Needs for Work and the Workforce 376
Career Planning: Individual Issues 378
   Purposes of Career Planning 378
   A Model for Individual Career Planning 378
   Clarifying Personal Values and Identity 379
   Making Decisions 379
   Assessing Personal Strengths and Weaknesses 379
   Scanning the Future Environment 379
   Establishing a Long-Term Career Strategy 380
Employee Education 380
Planning Educational Efforts: The Organizational Component 381
   By Occupational Group 381
   By Special Group or Needs 382
   By Stage of Individual Socialization or Career 383
Planning Educational Efforts: The Individual Component 384
   By Employee Appraisal 384
   By Individual Learning Contract 385
   By Organizational Offering 386
Kinds of Employee Educational Programs 386
   Adult Basic Education 386
   Career Education 387
   Continuing Education 388
   Occupational Education 388
Methods of Delivering Employee Educational Programs 389
   In-House, Formal Group Instruction 389
   In-House, Informal Group Instruction 390

In-House-Sponsored, Externally Developed Instruction 390
External Instruction Sponsored by Universities 391
External Instruction Sponsored by Community Colleges 391
External Instruction Sponsored by Vendors 392
External Degree Programs 392
Other Delivery Methods 393
Tuition Reimbursement Programs 394
Tying Employee Education to Organizational Strategy for the Development
of Talent 395

Chapter 11   Employee Training 401
What Is Employee Training? 401
What Is Job Performance? 402
Definition 402
What Is the Relationship between Training and Job Performance? 402
How Is Training Related To Planning? 402
Training and Organizational Strategy for the Development of Talent 403
Training and HR Planning 403
Training and Strategic Business Planning 403
A Model for Designing and Delivering Training 403
The Model 403
Identifying Occasions to Use the Approach 404
Assessing Learner Needs 408
Clarifying Key Characteristics of Learners 410
Analyzing the Setting 412
Carrying Out Detailed Work Analysis 413
Preparing Training Objectives 414
Creating Tests 415
Arranging Objectives in Sequence 417
Philosophy of Sequencing 418
Identifying Appropriate Delivery Methods 418
Lecture 419
Independent Reading 420
Panels 421
Buzz groups 421
Exercises 421
Case Study 422
The Incident Process 422
The Role Play 423
Behavior Modeling 424
Demonstration 424
Simulations/Games 425

Choosing a Delivery Method to Present Instruction 426
Preparing or Selecting Content 427
Problems with the Traditional Model of Training........................... 432
Strategic Training.. 434
   How Is Strategic Training Related to Planning? 434
   Strategic Training and Organizational Strategy for the Development
     of Talent 434
   Strategic Training and HR Planning 435
   Strategic Training and Strategic Business Planning 435
Strategic Training vs. Traditional Training 436
A Model for Strategic Training 436
   The Model 436
   Step 1: Identify occasions to use the approach..................... 437
   Step 2: Assess strategic training needs. 439
   Step 3: Clarify key characteristics of future learners.............. 441
   Step 4: Analyze the future setting. 443
   Step 5: Carry out future-oriented work analysis..................... 443
   Step 6: Prepare strategic instructional objectives. 444
   Step 7: Create strategically oriented tests. 444
   Step 8: Arrange objectives in sequence............................. 444
   Step 9: Select and use appropriate delivery methods................ 445
   Step 10: Prepare and select content for strategic training.......... 453
   Step 11: Deliver the training. 453

Part V   **Evaluating Talent Development** 465
Chapter 12 **Evaluating Talent Development** 467
What Is Evaluation?... 467
Why Are Values Important?.. 468
Why Is Evaluation Worthwhile? 469
What Are Some Ways of Thinking About Evaluation?.......................... 469
   Stakeholders 469
   Evaluator... 470
   Content... 471
   Timing 471
   Purpose... 471
   Method 474
Evaluating Training 477
   What Should Be Evaluated? 477
   Front-End Evaluation: The Traditional Approach 477
   Front-End Evaluation: The Strategic Approach 479
   What Then? 479
   Testing: The Traditional Approach.................................... 480

Testing: The Strategic Approach. 481
Formative Evaluation: The Traditional Approach. 482
Formative Evaluation: The Strategic Approach. 482
Summative Evaluation: The Traditional Approach. 484
Summative Evaluation: The Strategic Approach. 485
Concurrent Evaluation: The Traditional Approach 485
Concurrent Evaluation: The Strategic Approach 487
Post-Instructional Evaluations: Traditional Approaches. 487
Post-Instructional Evaluations: The Strategic Approach 490
Comprehensive Reviews of Training 490
Evaluating Employee Education 491
What Should Be Evaluated? 491
Front-End Analysis (FEA) for Employee Education. 492
Evaluation of Educational Sources 492
Advance Counseling. 493
Concurrent Evaluation 494
Post-Educational Follow-up 494
Comprehensive Reviews of Employee Education 494
Evaluating Development 496
What Should Be Evaluated? 496
Front-End Analysis of Development 497
Field-Testing Development 498
Concurrent Evaluation of Development 499
Post-Development Follow-up 499
Evaluating the Talent Development Effort. 499
Definition of Strategic Evaluation 499
When Is Strategic Evaluation Appropriate? 500
Strategic Evaluation Prior to Strategic Choice 500
Strategy Review 501
Summative Evaluation 502

Appendix I   A Template to Formulate Organizational Strategy for the Development
              of Talent 511

Appendix II   An Instrument to Assess the Competencies of Stakeholders in the
              Talent Development Effort 514

References   519

About the Authors 539

Index   543

LIST OF EXHIBITS

Exhibit 1-1:   Key Terms Associated with Strategic Business Planning 9
Exhibit 1-2:   A Model of the Strategy Business Planning Process 10
Exhibit 1-3:   Selected Web Site Resources to Support Strategic Business Planning. . 11
Exhibit 1-4:   A Simplified Representation of the Structure of a Large, Diversified
               Corporation 17
Exhibit 1-5:   Levels of Planning. 19
Exhibit 1-6:   A Simplified Model of Human Resource Planning (HRP) 24
Exhibit 1-7:   Selected Web Site Resources to Support Human Resource Planning . . 25
Exhibit 1-8:   A Simplified Representation of the Relationships between
               Organizational Structure, Organizational Plans, and Human
               Resource Plans 26
Exhibit 1-9:   One Possible Relationship between Business Plans, HR Plans,
               and Talent Development 29
Exhibit 1-10: A Simplified Model of the Process for the Strategic Development
               of Talent 32
Exhibit 1-11: Selected Web Site Resources to Support the Strategic Development
               of Talent 33
Exhibit 1-12: Relationships between a Unified Plan for Talent Development
               and Other Talent Development Plans 34
Exhibit 2-1:   Web Resources for Visioning 51
Exhibit 2-2:   A Summary of Relationships between Strategic Business Plans, HR
               Plans, and Talent Development 55
Exhibit 2-3:   A Simplified Model of Steps in the Top-Down Approach 58
Exhibit 3-1:   Recurring Instructional Needs Stemming from Movements of People. . 97
Exhibit 3-2:   Approaches to Instructional Needs Assessment 104
Exhibit 4-1:   Relationships between Environmental Sectors and the Organization . 127
Exhibit 4-2:   Visioning for the Future 128
Exhibit 4-3:   The Environmental Context of Any Department, Division,
               or Work Group inside the Organization 138
Exhibit 4-4:   Resources for Finding Information About the Future. 149
Exhibit 5-1:   Selected Web Site Resources to Support WOTS-UP/SWOT Analysis 168

Exhibit 5–2:   Relationships to Consider in Choosing Organizational Strategy
                for the Development of Talent 168
Exhibit 5–3:   A WOTS-UP Analysis Profile 173
Exhibit 5–4:   A Grand Strategy Selection Matrix 176
Exhibit 5–5:   Meanings of Different Grand Strategy Choices for Organizations
                and for Talent Development. 177
Exhibit 5–6:   Corporate Talent Development Issues. 188
Exhibit 5–7:   Business Talent Development Issues 189
Exhibit 5–8:   HRP Issues Related to Talent Development Issues 190
Exhibit 5–9:   Curriculum Matrix 200
Exhibit 5–10:   Steps in a Strategic Course-Centered Approach to Curriculum
                Planning 203
Exhibit 5–11:   Organizational Structure of the Texarkana Office of the Auditor
                General 217
Exhibit 5–12:   List of Job Titles and the Chief Responsibilities of Each Job
                in the Texarkana Office of the Auditor General 218
Exhibit 6–1:   Talent Development Advisory Committee 242
Exhibit 7–1:   Appropriate Group Development Efforts by Phase of Group 262
Exhibit 7–2:   The Steps in the Action Research Model 264
Exhibit 8–1:   Relationships between the Organization's Hierarchy of Authority,
                Geographical Scope, and the Primary Groups with which Managers
                Come in Contact. 289
Exhibit 8–2:   Systematic Methods for Assessing the Needs of Various Groups. 298
Exhibit 11–1:   Key Issues to Consider about Learner Characteristics 411
Exhibit 11–2:   The Relationship between Work Tasks and Instructional Objectives . 415
Exhibit 11–3:   The Relationship between Instructional Objectives in Training,
                Employee Education, and Employee Development 416
Exhibit 11–4:   Job Groupings for Training Curricula 429
Exhibit 11–5:   Relationships between Organizational Strategy for the Development
                of Talent and Training Curriculum, Job Curriculum, Course Plans,
                Lesson Plans, and Instructional Activities 430
Exhibit 11–6:   Differences in Focus between Traditional and Strategic Training 433
Exhibit 12–1:   Interests of Stakeholders 470
Exhibit 12–2:   Content Issues for Evaluation 472
Exhibit 12–3:   Methods of Conducting Formative Evaluation 483
Exhibit 12–4:   Donald Kirkpatrick's Evaluation Hierarchy. 488

LIST OF ACTIVITIES

Activity 1–1:   A Checklist on Organizational Strategy for the Development of Talent 41

Activity 2–1:   The Purpose of the Talent Development Effort 75

Activity 2–2:   Improving Relationships between a Strategic Business Plan, an HR Plan, and a Talent Development Effort 79

Activity 2–3:   A Culture Audit 81

Activity 2–4:   A Case Study on the Purpose of the Talent Development Effort 85

Activity 3–1:   Information for Talent Development 114

Activity 3–2:   Job Groupings 116

Activity 3–3:   Classifying Individuals 117

Activity 3–4:   A Case Study on the Strengths and Weaknesses of the Organization's Talent Development Effort 118

Activity 4–1:   A Worksheet to Collect Information on Future-Oriented Needs 157

Activity 4–2:   A Case Study on Environmental Scanning for the Talent Development Effort 159

Activity 5–1:   A Worksheet for Problem Framing 215

Activity 5–2:   A Case Study on Organizational Strategy for the Development of Talent 216

Activity 6–1:   Objective-Setting for Implementing Organizational Strategy for the Development of Talent 245

Activity 6–2:   Evaluating the Comprehensiveness of an Organization's Talent Development Policy 246

Activity 6–3:   Leadership and Implementation of Organizational Strategy for the Development of Talent 248

Activity 6–4:   Rewards of Implementation of Organizational Strategy for the Development of Talent 249

Activity 6–5:   Budgeting and Organizational Strategy for the Development of Talent 250

Activity 6–6:   Communicating about Organizational Strategy for the Development of Talent 251

Activity 6–7:   A Case Study on Implementing Organizational Strategy for the Development of Talent 252

Activity 7-1:   A Worksheet for Identifying Forces Favoring Change in an
                 Organization 282
Activity 7-2:   A Worksheet for Identifying Forces Impeding Change in an
                 Organization 283
Activity 7-3:   A Worksheet for Comparing Forces Impeding and Favoring
                 Change 284
Activity 8-1:   Pinpointing Key Institutions and Issues at the Community Level 306
Activity 8-2:   Pinpointing External Stakeholders 307
Activity 8-3:   The Relationship between the Corporation, General Public,
                 and External Stakeholders 308
Activity 8-4:   Collecting Information 309
Activity 8-5:   Clarifying the Role of the Corporation in Society 310
Activity 8-6:   A Worksheet for Social Monitoring 311
Activity 8-7:   Pinpointing Weaknesses and Threats in Relationships between
                 the Corporation and External Groups 312
Activity 8-8:   Pinpointing Strengths and Opportunities in Relationships between
                 the Corporation and External Groups 313
Activity 8-9:   Types of Change Sought through a Talent Development Effort 314
Activity 8-10:   Providing Instruction to External Groups through Innovative
                 Approaches 315
Activity 8-11:   Establishing Instructional Objectives for External Groups 316
Activity 8-12:   Deciding What Instruction to Offer to External Groups 317
Activity 8-13:   Deciding How to Deliver Instruction to External Groups 318
Activity 8-14:   Deciding on Evaluative Methods 319
Activity 8-15:   Integrating Corporate Grand Strategy and Instruction for External
                 Groups 320
Activity 8-16:   Integrating Organizational Strategy for the Development of Talent
                 and Instruction for External Groups 321
Activity 9-1:   Developing a Formal Mentoring Program in Your Organization:
                 A Brainstorming Exercise 349
Activity 9-2:   Designing a Short-Term Rotation Program for New Employees 350
Activity 9-3:   Critical Incidents 353
Activity 9-4:   Assessing the Developmental Climate 354
Activity 9-5:   Identifying Problems, Issues, or Challenges Confronting the Work
                 Group 355
Activity 9-6:   A Worksheet for Identifying/Summarizing Present and Desired
                 Future Competencies of an Organization 356
Activity 9-7:   A Worksheet for Identifying/Summarizing Work Group/Department
                 Competencies in Your Organization 357

Activity 9–8:   A Worksheet for Identifying Appropriate Employee-Development
                 Efforts in an Organization 358
Activity 9–9:   Pinpointing Resources to Meet Strategic Employee-Development
                 Needs 359
Activity 9–10:   A Case Study on Employee Development........................ 360
Activity 10–1:   Continuing Education 396
Activity 10–2:   Occupational Education...................................... 397
Activity 10–3:   Tying Employee Education to Organizational Strategy for the
                 Development of Talent.. 399
Activity 11–1:   A Structured Form for Analyzing Human Performance Problems 455
Activity 11–2:   Alternatives to Classroom-Based Training..................... 457
Activity 11–3:   Carrying out a Needs Assessment 458
Activity 11–4:   An Activity on Learner Characteristics 459
Activity 11–5:   The Work Setting and the Instructional Setting 460
Activity 11–6:   Designing a Traditional Training Curriculum................... 461
Activity 11–7:   A Checklist for Creative Reconsideration of Work Activities and/or
                 Job Tasks.. 462
Activity 11–8:   A Case Study on Employee Training............................ 463
Activity 12–1:   Importance of Goals in Instructional Evaluation............... 504
Activity 12–2:   Fundamental Issues to Consider in Instructional Evaluation 505
Activity 12–3:   Strategic Front-End Analysis of Training 507
Activity 12–4:   Reviewing Organizational Strategy for the Development
                 of Talent 508

PREFACE

This book applies the principles of strategic business planning to the field that has had a variety of names: Training and Development, Human Resource Development (HRD), Human Performance Improvement, and Workplace Learning and Performance (WLP). Earlier versions of this book focused on strategic planning as applied to HRD. This edition has been completely revised and updated to move beyond HRD to apply the principles of strategic business planning to talent management, knowledge management, and the newest generation of what was once called HRD—Workplace Learning and Performance (WLP), as described by Rothwell, Sanders, and Soper in a 1999 work. To underscore this change, the book has been retitled *The Strategic Development of Talent*.

The Audience for the Book

The possibility of integrating Talent Development with organizational strategy has long fired the imagination of CEOs, operating managers, HR practitioners, HRD practitioners, and WLP professionals (see Rothwell, Prescott, and Taylor 1998; Rothwell, Lindholm, and Wallick 2003). This newest version is written for anyone who wishes to find a way to use talent to support organizational strategy. These days, that can include just about anyone.

The Importance of the Topic

For a while, strategic planning was out of fashion (Campbell and Alexander 1997), and even today only some graduate programs in the HRD or WLP field address it (Kuchinke 2002). The key reasons why strategic planning fell out of favor have to do with the slowness and formality of traditional approaches to it, which have increasingly been at odds with a demand for shorter cycle times (Grant and Gnyawali 1996). Additionally, traditional approaches to strategic planning limited the role of the strategic planning process to senior executives or corporate planners (Mintzberg 1994), but the idea of only involving senior leaders in the strategic planning process has yielded to a new approach that includes many groups and stakeholders (Wall and Wall 1995).

Strategic planning re-emerged in a new form sometime in the mid-1990s (Byrne 1996; Galagan 1997). There are good reasons why: First, we live in a time when nothing is constant except change, and those unwilling to change will not survive for long. Learning is a form of changing, and planned learning in organizations is important for formulating and implementing strategic business plans. It might even be the key to competitive success for organizations and individuals alike (Rothwell 2002). And, of course, the strategic development of talent is synonymous with efforts to facilitate planned and unplanned learning in organizational settings. It is a means of cultivating intellectual capital and thereby enhancing the pool subject to knowledge management (Booth 1998; Nerney 1997). Human resources play a key role in achieving sustained competitive advantage (Lado and Wilson 1994).

Second, managers around the world are frequently accused of shortsightedness. Shortsightedness has been cited as the culprit in recent scandals involving major corporations. It has also been shown as a factor leading to the derailment of executives who never quite reach the top or otherwise realize their potential.

Farsightedness is something we learn. Managers, and indeed all employees, must learn to adjust to change and even to anticipate it in their work, their careers, and their organizations. The strategic development of human talent can contribute to this learning by basing organized training, education, and development on present and future organizational needs. But developing talent should be guided by a comprehensive, unified plan for learning in the organization. We call this plan the *organizational strategy for the development of talent*, which is really a term for the strategy for organizational learning.

The Purpose of the Book

Three tasks are undertaken in this book.

The first task is to present a model to guide the process of formulating and implementing organizational strategy for the development of talent. It differs from traditional and past-oriented approaches to developing talent. The strategic development of talent (SDT) is neither past-oriented nor reactive; rather, it is future-oriented and proactive.

The second task is to show decision-makers how to unify planned and unplanned learning activities intended to

1. Change organizational culture and work group norms.
2. Improve relations between an organization and its general public and key external stakeholders.
3. Match up the collective competencies of a work unit with its present or expected future responsibilities.
4. Help individuals realize their career objectives.
5. Match the competencies of those who do the organization's work with the expectations of customers, clients, and other relevant stakeholders.

The first activity is associated with organization development; the second is associated with nonemployee (stakeholder) development; the third is associated with employee development; the fourth is associated with employee education; and the fifth is associated with training.

The third task is to provide managers, HRD or WLP professionals, HR practitioners, and others with activities and case studies to help guide their thinking. If practitioners use the activities, they will be better equipped to formulate and implement a unified organizational strategy for the development of talent.

The Organization of the Book

This book is organized into five parts and 12 chapters.

Part I provides important background information about strategic business planning, HR planning, and the strategic development of talent. It also explains how to establish a vision for Talent Development for an organization and formulate a purpose or mission to articulate the rationale for an organization's Talent Development effort.

> The strategic development of talent is the process of changing an organization, stakeholders outside it, groups inside it, and people employed by it through planned and unplanned learning so that they will possess the competencies needed to help the organization achieve and sustain competitive advantage at present and in the future.

To understand the strategic development of talent, practitioners should understand strategic business planning, HR planning, and various approaches to developing talent. Chapter 1 deals with these issues.

A unified organizational strategy for the development of talent stems from a sense of purpose that deals with the means by which SDT contributes to meeting organizational and individual needs. Chapter 2 establishes this framework. It dramatizes the range of possible purposes for a comprehensive SDT effort.

Part II covers analysis of present strengths/weaknesses and future threats/opportunities affecting groups, individuals, and jobs.

To formulate an integrated organizational strategy for the development of talent, the stakeholders—senior managers, operating managers, people developers, and others—require information about present learning needs and future environmental conditions confronting

I   Groups outside the business
I   Groups inside the business
I   Individuals
I   Jobs

Chapter 3 focuses on comprehensive needs assessment. It identifies broad learning needs, and thus underscores significant, strategic weaknesses. It also identifies unique talents (strengths). If it is used in formulating organizational strategy for the development of talent, comprehensive needs assessment will be geared to the present. It examines the collective capabilities or competencies of the organization's talent.

Chapter 4 focuses on environmental scanning. It explains how to pinpoint possible future needs and, thus, underscores threats or opportunities affecting human performance. When it is used in formulating organizational strategy for the development of talent, environmental scanning can be applied broadly to all planned or unplanned learning events, or applied narrowly to specific events.

Part III focuses on choosing and implementing organizational strategy for the development of talent. Choosing the organizational strategy for the development of talent means selecting one or more comprehensive plans to guide learning in an organization. The strategy can come out of a process of comparing strengths (present talents/competencies), weaknesses (present learning needs), threats (possible future learning needs), and opportunities (possible future talents/ competencies). Alternatively, it can result from a whole-system effort to discover change, perhaps building appreciatively on the existing strengths of the organization. The process of choosing a strategy for Talent Development will in itself provide the integrated direction needed to guide learning in the organization.

Implementing the strategy means transforming plans into actions. It activates learning plans and sets the stage for unifying such learned efforts as organization development, nonemployee development, employee development, education, and training.

Part IV explains the various functional strategies for learning that can be used to implement a comprehensive organizational strategy for the development of talent. These functional strategies serve different purposes:

I Organization development is intended to change the culture of an organization, division, department, or work group.

I Nonemployee development is intended to improve relations between an organization and groups outside it with which it deals.

I Employee development is intended to match up the collective competencies of a work unit and the responsibilities assigned to the unit by the organization.

▮ Education is intended to help individuals achieve their career objectives.

▮ Training is intended to furnish people with knowledge and skills needed to perform their work.

Each component of organizational strategy for the development of talent can be viewed separately or together. In addition, development, education, or training can be treated from a past, present, or future orientation.

Part V closes the circle, describing evaluation methods for each component of the Talent Development effort and assessing the overall process. Evaluation means placing worth on something. Evaluating Talent Development closes the circle on strategic decision-making and action, providing useful feedback when it is time to

▮ Define the purpose of the Talent Development effort.

▮ Assess comprehensive learning needs.

▮ Scan the environment.

▮ Choose organizational strategy for the development of talent.

▮ Implement organizational strategy for the development of talent.

▮ Implement functional strategies such as organization development, nonemployee development, employee development, education, and training.

It is worth noting that each chapter concludes with one or more activities to help readers apply what they have read. That should encourage transfer of learning.

There are two appendices: The first provides a simple template to guide readers through the process of formulating an organizational strategy for the development of talent. The second provides a self-assessment instrument for those readers who would like to reflect on how well-prepared they are, through the competencies they can demonstrate, to formulate, implement, and evaluate organizational strategy for the development of talent.

This book can also be used effectively with William Rothwell's 1998 work, *In Action: Linking HRD and Organizational Strategy*, published by the American Society for Training and Development. It provides 17 in-depth case studies to show how organizations have effectively integrated organizational strategy and Talent Development.

William J. Rothwell
State College, Pennsylvania

H. C. Kazanas
Champaign, Illinois and Naples, Florida

PART I

THE BACKGROUND AND PURPOSE OF TALENT DEVELOPMENT

The chapters in Part I lay the foundation for the book.

Chapter 1 provides important background information on strategic business planning and human resource planning. It also provides background on the strategic development of talent, Talent Development, and the role of Human Resource Development and Workplace Learning and Performance professionals.

Chapter 2 focuses on the vision and mission (purpose) statement that will guide a comprehensive, long-term effort to develop the human talent of the organization systematically. The chapter defines *vision* and *purpose*; lists and describes ten specific ways by which strategic business plans, HR plans, and Talent Development can be integrated; explains how the purpose of the Talent Development effort is clarified; lists occasions when it is appropriate to change the purpose statement of Talent Development; and discusses the key role that organizational philosophy and corporate culture play in Talent Development.

BACKGROUND ISSUES

Over the past 20 years, many books and articles have been written about the need to strategically develop and manage human resources. These writings have focused attention on the importance of having a strategic orientation before trying to develop and manage human talent in organizational settings. There are works that focus on the role of senior or operating managers (Rothwell, Lindholm, and Wallick 2003) and works that focus on the role of HR or training practitioners (Caster 2001; Manzini and Gridley 1986; Rothwell, Prescott, and Taylor 1998; Gilley and Maycunich 1998 and 2000; Wright 1998). Others focus on the need to establish a learning culture (McCracken and Wallace 2000) or the need for individuals to think beyond immediate learning needs for their own long-term development (Rothwell 2002). Writers have also explored the relationship between knowledge and strategy (Cross and Israelit 2000; Zack 1999), building on a venerable tradition that first related experience/learning curves to winning competitive strategy, and then looked at the extent to which intellectual capital and knowledge management contribute to competitive success (Blancett 2002; Earl 2001; Ghemawat 2002).

Some confusion on relating talent management and development to organizational strategy is understandable. Since learning and development can occur on-the-job, near-the-job, and off-the-job, many different groups have roles to play in the strategic management and development of human talent. But if each group focuses solely on its unique role, the result is often a disjointed, fragmented approach to Talent Development; some efforts will actually conflict with others, rather than contribute to the synergy that stems from a unified approach.

> The strategic development of talent (SDT) is the process of changing an organization, stakeholders outside it, groups inside it, and people employed by it through planned and unplanned learning so that they possess the competencies needed to help the organization achieve and sustain competitive advantage.

SDT focuses on what was once called the "Human Resource Development" effort, now referred to as "Workplace Learning and Performance" (Rothwell, Sanders, and Soper, 1999): the coordinated learning activities undertaken by HR practitioners, operating managers, and employees to support business and HR plans. The strategic development of talent uses an organizational strategy for Talent Development, placing special emphasis on leadership development because this has a significant impact on competitive success (Gratton 2000; Ireland and Hitt 1999). SDT is a comprehensive, coordinated plan that describes how an organization's managers and individuals intend to meet business and staffing objectives through learning. By implication, learning is the key process by which talent is developed (Rothwell 2002). It is also central to what distinguishes high potentials from fully successful performers (Lombardo and Eichinger 2000). Talent Development enhances an organization's intellectual capital—generally understood to mean the estimated worth or value of an organization over its liquidation value (Booth 1998). Talent Development increases the pool of capabilities for *knowledge management*—what some refer to as "a conscious strategy of helping people share and put knowledge into action by creating access, context, infrastructure, and learning cycles" (Grayson and O'Dell 1998, 25).

To understand SDT, practitioners should first learn about strategic business planning and HR planning, because SDT is only a tool for helping to implement these plans, and the quality of an organization's competitive strategy will only be as good as the talent of the strategists who formulate and implement it. This chapter provides this necessary background information. It describes strategic business planning, HR planning, and the strategic development of talent. Further, it clarifies how they can support each other.

Strategic Business Planning

In the most fundamental sense, strategic business planning involves choosing how an organization will compete. Oliver defines *strategy* as "understanding an industry structure and dynamics, determining the organization's relative position in that industry, and taking action to either change the industry's structure or the organization's position to improve organizational results" (Oliver 2001, 7). The strategic plan has traditionally been considered a chief concern of top-level corporate executives, and it should command the highest priority of corporate top managers. It requires consideration of an organization's present internal strengths and weaknesses, as well as future external threats or opportunities.

Using History to Understand Strategic Business Planning. Until the 1950s, managers tended to worry more about coordinating the internal operations of their businesses than about dealing with changes occurring outside their businesses. The reason for that focus was simple enough: Businesses operated in defined geographical areas, marketed products or services to distinct customer groups, and restricted their range of products and services. In such settings, managers separated the world outside the business (the external environment) from the world inside (the internal environment). *Long-range planning*, sometimes called *first-generation planning*, was regarded as sufficient to examine the external environment. Managers assumed that the future would be like the past. Planning concentrated on building from past successes and cultivating existing markets for the firm's products or services. Handled by staff specialists who prepared reports for top managers, long-range planning did not command much attention. The main focus was on the internal environment, because coordination within the organization was needed. Without coordination, such classic functions as production/operations, marketing, finance, and personnel worked at cross-purposes. Top managers used *policies*, understood to mean guidelines for action, to coordinate organizational functions. Often it was during the annual budgeting process that conflicts between long-range plans and internal policies were resolved. This process was not systematic.

In the 1960s, managers found themselves facing conditions unlike those of the past. The external environment was growing increasingly unpredictable.

The government passed laws, created regulations, and handed down court rulings that affected hiring, employee appraisal, training, financial matters, health and safety, and much more. There were shortages in raw material—the first since wartime. Technological innovation became more important as the gap narrowed between basic and applied research.

At the same time, organizations became larger and more complex. Businesses expanded into overseas markets, new industries, and multiple product or service lines. Consumer preferences and expectations of business began to change faster. It became harder to manage the businesses themselves (Ghemawat 2002).

Amid these more dynamic external and more complex internal environments, three things were changing:

I   Managers found it inappropriate to separate examinations of external and internal environments without making greater efforts to integrate them.

I   They did not extend their assumptions about a certain past into an uncertain future.

I   They did not want to use identical policies to coordinate operations across autonomous businesses in different industries operating under one corporate banner.

First-generation planning proved inadequate for dealing with this complexity. *Strategic planning*, also called *second-generation planning*, emerged at this time. It supplanted first-generation planning and became a tool that top corporate executives used to manage amidst growing complexity and environmental turbulence. Initially, plans of this kind were rather inflexible.

Strategic management, also called *third-generation planning*, added consideration of contingency plans in the event that the environment changes as a strategic plan is implemented. Scenario analysis grew in popularity as a means of preparing for these contingencies. The growing uncertainty of the external environment also pushed the need for strategic decision-making to lower levels, as middle management underwent wholesale downsizing and as organizations adopted technological advances that permitted faster responses to customers or clients.

As the business environment grows dramatically more complex, strategic management is yielding to real-time strategic thinking (Liedtka 1998). This *fourth-generation view of planning* is more appropriate for a world in which time horizons have shrunk, profit margins have narrowed, quality and customer service issues have grown into competitive necessities, markets have expanded, and organizations have had to deal with the upheaval created by continuing mergers, acquisitions, takeovers, and such large-scale change as widespread downsizing and the implementation of Enterprise Resource Programs (ERPs). At the same time, employer-employee relationships have also undergone radical change (even the players change frequently). Additionally, the advent of e-commerce has led to a growing need to integrate strategic thinking into real-time decisions. Jacobs and McKeown say that *strategic thinking* means "bringing your preferred future into the present — thinking and acting as if the future were now." Strategy is often reduced to following simple rules of engagement in order to guide real-time decisions and actions (Eisenhardt and Sull 2001).

Current thinking about the strategy formulation process stresses the key value of time as a consideration in achieving competitive advantage (Ghemawat 2002; Oliver 2001; Stonich 1990). Traditional approaches to strategy formulation and implementation are especially inappropriate in so-called "fast cycle" environments (Camillus, Sessions, and Webb 1998). Human talent is often regarded as central to this ability to meet the time challenge (Krell 2001). Indeed, learning and innovation have been combined as one issue to consider in formulating strategy based on a *balanced scorecard approach* (Kaplan and Norton 1996), understood to mean the application of four performance measures for organizational oversight. (Those measures are financial performance, customer satisfaction, process efficiency, and innovation.) Using the balanced scorecard, leaders are accountable for their ideas based on how they answer one important question that is related to these four measures: *"Does [the organization] have the competencies to drive the processes needed to produce the value that will render your financial expectation?"* (Dalton 2002, 54).

Using Metaphor to Understand Strategic Business Planning. Apart from history, another way to understand strategy is to look at the metaphors that have driven it (Oliver 2001). Metaphors are equated with creativity. They provide important clues to the way managers view the world. In the earliest periods of the Industrial Revolution, strategy was equated with waging war. As the

Industrial Revolution advanced, strategy gradually became associated with machines, the dominant symbol for the machine age and assembly lines. In more recent times, strategy has been equated with networks (i.e., computers), biology (i.e., living systems, DNA, and genetics), and most recently with complexity theory that has grown from a new scientific view about the nature of the universe as exhibiting order within disorder (Oliver 2001).

Using Questions to Understand Strategic Business Planning. A third way to understand strategic business planning is to look at the answers to some important questions. Phrased in terms of the famous "journalistic questions" of *who, what, when, where, why,* and *how,* strategic business planning focuses on the answers to these important questions:

- Who does the organization serve?
- What results does it seek, and what does it do to serve its customers?
- When does the organization serve its customers?
- Where does the organization serve its customers?
- Why is the organization in business?
- How will the organization achieve its purpose on a continuous basis?

The most important questions on which to focus, however, center on the measurable results to be achieved (*What are the organization's strategic objectives?*) and how they will be achieved (*How will the organization pursue achievement of its objectives?*). Strategy is a means to an end. Strategic objectives are the ends sought.

In recent years, strategic business planning has almost become a discipline in its own right. In fact, those not familiar with the subject need a primer to understand all the specialized terms associated with it. Exhibit 1–1 provides a list of these terms and their definitions.

A Model of Strategic Business Planning. Think of strategic business planning as a process. Managers or others should

1. *Clarify purpose.* What is the purpose of the organization? What should it be?

2. *Select goals and objectives.* What is the organization trying to achieve? How can achievement be measured?

Exhibit 1–1: Key Terms Associated with Strategic Business Planning

Term	Brief Definition
1. Analysis of business definition	What is our business?
2. Core competency	The term refers to the essence of what the organization does better than any other organization. Alternatively, it can also mean "an analysis of core systems, processes, skills, techniques, and technologies" (Oliver 2000, 9).
3. Critical success factors	The process of asking and answering this question: What three to five things must the organization do to outperform its competitors?
4. Customer analysis	An examination of customer perceptions about the organization that comes from the customers themselves
5. Environmental scanning	Examining what trends or issues might affect the organization in the future—and the likely impact of those trends on the organization, which (in turn) will create opportunities and threats
6. Financial analysis	An examination of financial ratios
7. Seven Ss of Strategic Readiness	"An evaluation of staff, style, skills, structure, systems, shared values, and strategy" (Oliver 2000, 10).
8. Strategic question	"What drives the organization to success or failure?" (Oliver 2000, 9).
9. Sustainable competitive advantage	What does analysis reveal about how the organization competes, the foundation of what makes it competitive, the means by which the organization competes, and what other organizations or groups this organization is competing with?
10. SWOT analysis	An assessment of the organization's strengths, weaknesses, opportunities, and threats (SWOT)
11. Timeline assessment	An examination of the organization's history. An examination of various financial ratios commonly used
12. Value chain analysis	What is the impact of the organization's structure and activities on profit margins?
13. Value system analysis	How does this organization relate to the chain of suppliers who end up providing something of value to clients or customers?

3. *Identify present strengths and weaknesses.* What is the organization doing well now? Not so well now?

4. *Analyze future threats and opportunities.* What opportunities or threats will the external environment pose to the organization in the future?

5. *Compare strengths/weaknesses to threats/opportunities.* How can the organization take advantage of future opportunities and avert future threats posed by the environment, considering its present internal strengths and weaknesses?

6. *Decide on long-term strategy.* What should be the long-term direction (strategy) pursued by an organization so that it can take advantage of opportunities and avert threats posed by the environment?

7. *Implement strategy.* What changes need to be made inside the organization so that its chosen strategy can be pursued with the greatest likelihood of success?

8. *Evaluate strategy.* How well do decision-makers think the strategy will work? How well is it working? How well has it worked?

These steps outlined by Glueck and Jauch in 1984 are depicted in Exhibit 1–2. Selected Web site resources for strategic business planning are shown in Exhibit 1–3.

While these steps appear to be sequential, they need not be. Any step can be taken in any order. Any step can also be taken at any time. And any step can also

Exhibit 1–2: A Model of the Strategic Business Planning Process

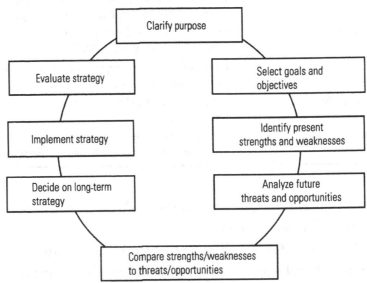

Exhibit 1–3: Selected Web Site Resources to Support Strategic Business Planning

Link	Brief Description
1. http://www.planware.org/strategy.htm	A comprehensive Web site with many tools and shareware to support strategic business planning.
2. http://coba.shsu.edu/JBS/vol13/no1/13-1-1.htm	Journal of Business Strategy Javad Kargar John A. Parnell North Carolina Central University Durham, North Carolina *Strategic Planning Emphasis and Planning Satisfaction in Small Firms: An Empirical Investigation*
3. http://www.fastcompany.com/online/resources/strategy.html	Many articles are available from Fastcompany on strategic business planning
4. http://bbasicsllc.com/sp.htm	An online webinar on strategic business planning
5. http://www.paloalto.com/ps/bp/?ac=findwhat,businessplanfind	The Web site for Business Plan Pro software to support strategic business planning
6. http://pages.prodigy.com/EYWU79A/m&a2a.htm	A Web site with many Web links for strategic business planning
7. http://www.work911.com/management/planning.htm	A Web site with many online articles about strategic business planning

be taken at any level—from the top of the corporation all the way down to one worker carrying out her work and serving a customer or client.

It is worth emphasizing that the model is a way to help managers and workers who are otherwise not entrepreneurial to think like entrepreneurs. Indeed, entrepreneurs progress through these steps intuitively, often not even knowing that they are doing so; it comes naturally. They sometimes identify worthwhile initiatives through a flash of insight without even knowing how they chose them. The model can help guide managers and workers to think like entrepreneurs so that they can discover which opportunities will be most profitable to the organization and lead to sustained competitive advantage. In short, strategic advantage can be as much art as science (Schrage 2001).

The earliest models of strategic business planning tended to emphasize the value of management, organizational experience, and quantitative analysis in order to discover sources of competitive advantage. The emphasis now is on using intuition to formulate strategy (Agor 1989; Eisenhardt 1999). It is not blind intuition devoid of experience that matters, however: Instead, the insight and leaps of logic that lead to breakthrough thinking are often key (Ghemawat 2002)— the essence of entrepreneurial thinking. This underscores the true value of *talent*:

The intellectual capacity of the organization's people to discover new products or services, identify new markets or niches, find new ways to meet or exceed client expectations, learn collectively and individually, and outpace competitors through agility by moving faster and more deliberately. Unique competencies are associated with successful strategic thinking (see Linkow 1999).

Creating a *vision* is often considered necessary before beginning any strategic business planning process, though a vision is also needed to establish the organization's purpose, goals, and objectives. A *vision* is a compelling view of what an organization or its components should be in the future (Horan and Shaw 1997; Thompson 1997). *Visioning* is a process. It is a province of *leadership*— the ability to influence others in positive ways. Case studies on the importance of leadership dramatize the crucial role it can play in strategic success. One key to devising a winning strategy is to start with the customers and focus on *their* changing needs and expectations (Webb and Gile 2001).

The first step in strategic business planning is to clarify the organization's purpose. A *purpose statement* clarifies beliefs and assumptions. When written down and communicated, it is a rallying point and a stimulant for action. At the same time, it also helps strategists create a vision of what the organization should be like in the future. This vision should be concrete and understandable by others. It should also excite their enthusiasm, motivating everyone in the organization to make this ideal view of the future a reality.

A purpose statement can also be the economic rationale for an organization's existence. To address this issue, decision-makers should ask several questions.

1. In what areas should the organization operate?
2. How much opportunity does an activity offer the organization in terms of growth? Flexibility? Stability? Return on investment?
3. What does it take to succeed?
4. What are the organization's capabilities?
5. How well do the organization's capabilities match up to what is needed to succeed?
6. What is the organization's likelihood of success in the business activity?
7. What methods of doing business can be considered?
8. How do these choices compare on the basis of feasibility?
9. How do these choices compare on the basis of potential profitability?
10. What business activities should the organization enter in the future? What should be its purpose?

More than just an exercise in paper work, clarifying purpose is an essential starting point in formulating a strategic business plan.

The second step in strategic business planning is to select objectives and goals. Objectives and goals operationalize purpose. *Goals* identify broad areas in which action is to be taken. *Objectives* state what measurable results are desired over a specific time period. However, some writers reverse the terms: the word *objectives* is used to refer to broad activity statements, and *goals* refers to measurable counterparts.

Goals are usually timeless; objectives are not. In fact, it is possible to think of levels of objectives—some long-term, some intermediate-term, and some short-term.

The third step in strategic business planning is to identify organizational strengths and weaknesses. Strategists ponder what the organization is doing especially well at present and what it is not doing so well. Strengths and weaknesses are often viewed in competitive terms. In other words, top managers think of their organization's strengths and weaknesses relative to competitors or relative to customer or client expectations. To this end, they should first identify key factors leading to success in a business or an industry, and then assess how well their organization compares to key competitors on those factors. Strategists should also monitor customer or client perceptions of how well the organization is meeting or exceeding customer/client expectations.

The fourth step in strategic business planning is to analyze future threats and opportunities posed by the external environment. Strategists consider what events or trends outside the immediate control of the organization are likely to affect it in the future, and what resulting threats or opportunities these events/trends will pose to the organization. An *event* is a one-time occurrence. A *trend* is a gradual tendency toward change—change in economic conditions, social mores, technology, laws and regulations, consumer preferences, and even within an entire industry. Any change in the external environment can pose threats to an organization's survival or profitable opportunities worth pursuing.

The fifth step in strategic business planning is to compare organizational strengths and weaknesses to environmental threats and opportunities. Strategists ponder how well-prepared the organization is to cope with expected future environmental changes, and what managers have to do to turn expected future opportunities to advantage or avoid expected threats created by environmental conditions.

The sixth step in strategic business planning is to decide on long-term strategy. Decision-makers ponder what actions should be taken to achieve organizational goals and objectives and realize competitive advantage, given present internal conditions and expected future external conditions. Of course, one approach that is quite popular is to do a SWOT analysis (**S**trengths, **W**eaknesses, **O**pportunities, and **T**hreats). They can then select a long-term plan to ensure that these actions will be taken over time. Strategists then decide on a long-term direction for the organization. Chief executive officers usually bear primary responsibility for strategy selection, since they are the highest-level officials of management and are accountable to the corporate board of directors.

The seventh step in strategic business planning is to begin implementation. This has frequently been the weakest link in SBP, because top managers too often change strategy without making adjustments to support the change within the organization. Common problems in implementation usually stem from a failure to align duties, reporting relationships, leadership talent, employee talent, incentives, and/or policies with desired strategy.

The eighth and final step in strategic business planning is evaluation. Strategists ponder:

1. What is the likelihood that a given SBP will produce desired results? (This question is addressed prior to implementation.)
2. What has been the progress to date? (This question is addressed during strategy-review meetings.)
3. What were the overall results? (This question is addressed at the time a new SBP is first contemplated.)

Many approaches to strategic evaluation have been proposed. Perhaps the simplest is to compare results to the intentions expressed through goals and measurable objectives.

A model is helpful in conceptualizing the strategic business planning process. However, it is only a model—literally, a simplified depiction of a more complicated process. In the real world, strategists skip steps in the model, reorder them, call them by different names, drop some steps, or perform several steps concurrently.

Key Assumptions of Strategic Business Planning. Authors writing about strategic business planning traditionally make assumptions about it. These assumptions are worth reviewing in order to clarify what SBP can and cannot do.

The first assumption: *Strategy making begins with clarification of organizational purpose.* Strategists should agree on organizational purpose as a starting point for planning. Since many people have a stake in what the organization is or should be, strategic managers function as arbiters of organizational purpose against a backdrop of conflicting interests. Important stakeholders include owners or shareholders, consumers, employees, managers, and members of the general public. Each group has its own expectations about what the organization is and what it should be.

The second assumption: *Strategy making is based, in part, on identification of organizational strengths and weaknesses.* Traditionally, writers on strategic business planning assume that managers are capable of identifying the present status of the organization. However, managers face a difficult time examining their organizations as critically as good strategy making requires. After all, managers made the decisions initially. Rarely can they step back and attack their own logic and results. In any case, there are enough examples of organizations in which top management strategists are less, not more, aware of operational problems than front-line employees. One reason is that top managers may receive distorted information because people reporting to them are interested in looking effective and competent.

The third assumption: *Strategy making is based on an examination of the future and the external environment.* Strategic business planning assumes that managers can identify important trends or events likely to affect the organization in the future and then draw accurate inferences about the effects of those trends or events. These assumptions are not always valid. Strategists seldom possess all relevant information about trends or events. Nor can they predict all the consequences of trends or events, even if they are identified. And rarely do strategists enjoy a free hand to change an organization to anticipate future external trends or events. About the best that can be hoped for is that major trends or events will be identified, their major ramifications will be anticipated, and some changes will be made in the organization.

The fourth assumption: *Strategy making is about future implications of present decisions, not future decisions.* Strategists should first identify future conditions, and then step back to the present and establish plans to take those future conditions into account.

The fifth assumption: *Strategy making is a mental activity that requires holistic thinking.* Hence, creativity and problem-solving skills are essential to the process.

The Value of Strategic Business Planning. How much, if any, does strategic business planning improve organizational performance? Numerous academic studies have sought answers to this question. The issue is a complex one, since there are actually different ways by which to conceptualize and measure "performance" or "results" (Venkatraman and Ramanujam 1986).

A 2002 study examined "the profitability results of more than 10,000 distributors in 40 different lines of trade" and concluded that "despite the importance of strategic actions, operational issues have the most effect on profitability" (Bates 2002, 61).

Despite that finding, it seems reasonable to assume that any effort to anticipate the future would be superior to dependence on mere luck, chance, good fortune, or efforts to handle otherwise unexpected crises in real time. An old saying states the case succinctly: "The organization with a plan beats an organization without a plan every time." Organizational failures are sometimes attributed to strategic planning processes that ceased to function, as was the case with Bausch and Lomb in the early 1990s (Picken and Dess 1997). Of course, it is also true that no strategy is sometimes better than a bad strategy (Campbell 1999).

Levels of Planning. There are several levels of strategic business planning in most large corporations. There are also other types of planning.

Consider Exhibit 1–4, which illustrates the simplified structure of a large, diversified corporation. Grand Strategy is established at the highest corporate level. However, each business possesses its own enterprise or business unit strategy. In each enterprise, functions such as operations/production, finance, marketing, and human resources have their own functional strategies. Each should be related to and should support the organization's Grand Strategy.

Exhibit 1–4: A Simplified Representation of the Structure of a Large, Diversified Corporation

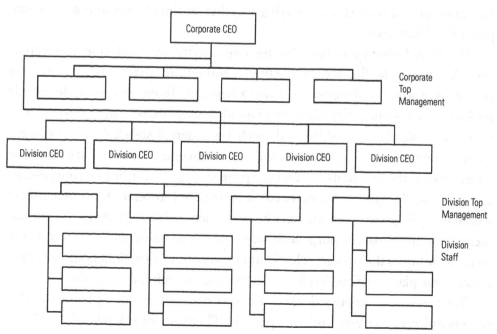

Grand Strategy is ultimately the responsibility of the corporate chief executive officer and the corporate board of directors. Recent thinking, however, suggests that employees and other stakeholders should also have a role in the process (Bennett, Ketchen, and Schultz 1998; Guffey and Nienhaus 2002), and successful companies like Microsoft often use a highly participative approach to strategic planning (Fuller 1998). *Grand Strategy* defines the overall character of the corporation, the ways it competes, and the means by which corporate goals and objectives are to be achieved. Grand Strategy ties together all other plans so that they do not work at cross purposes.

Enterprise strategy is the plan for a single business within the corporation. An enterprise is often called a strategic business unit (SBU) to emphasize its relative autonomy. A diversified corporation, by definition, is engaged in various businesses. At the level of SBU, decision-makers focus on a single organization in one industry. They consider such questions as: (1) What products or services are offered by the SBU? (2) Who are the customers? and (3) How can this SBU compete most effectively? These questions are quite different from those considered at the corporate level, where Grand Strategy necessarily focuses on overall corporate mission and on methods of tying together distinct SBUs into a corporate portfolio of businesses.

Functional strategy is the plan for one activity area within an enterprise. Functions include finance, marketing, production/operations, and human resources. Any major department is also a function. To cite one example outside business: A large university will have a Grand Strategy that defines its overall purpose and desired relationships with such key external stakeholders as government, community, alumni, business, and other segments of society. Each school or college within the university has an enterprise strategy that defines its purpose, its services, and the groups whose needs it is intended to serve. Each department within the college or school will have its own functional strategy that defines a segment of the enterprise, its purpose, its services, its programs, its service users, and its relationship to the college, school, and university. Hence, "functional strategy" refers to the planned direction for key activity areas within an organization.

Enterprise and functional plans are also part of a planning hierarchy that reflects differing concerns and time periods. There are three levels (Huse 1982):

Exhibit 1–5: Levels of Planning

Strategic Plans	▪ The concern of top management
	▪ Long-term time horizon
	▪ Encompasses the entire organization
	▪ Primary focus: External
Coordinative (Tactical) Plans	▪ The concern of middle managers
	▪ Immediate-term time horizon
	▪ Encompasses only part of the organization
	▪ Primary focus: Internal
Operational Plans	▪ The concern of supervisors
	▪ Short-term time horizon
	▪ Encompasses only a small segment of an organization's full range of activities
	▪ Primary focus: Internal

(1) strategic, (2) coordinative or tactical, and (3) operational. They are illustrated and briefly summarized in Exhibit 1–5.

Strategic planning has traditionally been the chief concern of top-level managers. It is used to achieve long-term results. Strategic plans are uncertain and involve high risk, but they help decision-makers anticipate changes in a largely uncontrollable external environment and play the high-stakes game of organizational success or failure.

Coordinative planning is intermediate-term. It is primarily the concern of middle-level managers. Less risky than strategy making, coordinative plans involve the deployment of resources to implement strategy.

Operational planning is short-term. It is the primary concern of first-line managers or supervisors. Annual budgets are expressions of operational plans. Less risky than strategic or coordinative plans, operational plans involve scheduling and moving needed resources. These plans are tied to their longer-term strategic and coordinative counterparts.

Methods of Planning. Some organizations have relatively formal planning processes; others have less-formal processes. Large diversified corporations obviously face conditions somewhat different from those confronting medium-sized or small, single-product organizations. Methods match conditions. In large corporations, planning is likely to be quite complicated: A full-time, professionally trained corporate planning staff conducts studies for top managers. Top corporate executives concentrate on evaluations of overall corporate mission, goals, objectives, environmental conditions, and internal strengths and weaknesses across the corporation's portfolio of SBUs, and they also concentrate on resource acquisition and allocation. Middle-level managers operate within broad corporate objectives, but devise their own specific objectives and allocate resources by priority area. Lower-level department heads in each division establish objectives in line with middle-managers, and devise corresponding action plans. Budgets usually follow planning.

Medium-sized companies with a single line of products or services can copy the structured planning approach of larger organizations or the less structured approach of smaller organizations, or devise some combination. External consultants can be used instead of a full-time planning staff. Top executives can solicit ideas from managers of functional departments such as finance, marketing, production/operations, and human resources about appropriate initiatives for the organization, information about competitors, and legal issues. This information provides the basis for planning.

In small companies, a team approach to strategic planning might suffice. A formal committee, headed up by the chief executive, develops plans. Meetings are vehicles for the process.

Much has been written about the planning process. Several points about it are clear. First, the planning process should be highly innovative, creative, and experiential. Second, formal planning encompasses only a tiny fraction of strategic decision-making. Most planning is informal, falling outside formal processes and meetings. Third, planning has to do with managing organizational culture, because any strategic business planning activity involves cultural change. Fourth and finally, people are essential for formulating and implementing strategy. Strategic plans stem from human values, beliefs, decisions, and problem-solving. Likewise, successful implementation of strategic business plans depends on the availability and application of intellectual capital, appropriate knowledge management, and the identification and cultivation of individual competencies.

Human Resource Planning

Human resource planning means making sure that the right numbers and types of people are available to apply the right skills needed to realize a strategic business plan. HRP is sometimes synonymous with workforce planning or talent planning (Rosse and Levin 2001). The outgrowth of HRP is a Grand Strategy to help the organization achieve its mission. Managers rarely worried about HRP until the 1950s or 1960s. Most work involved physical, not mental, labor. It was easy enough to find warm bodies on short notice to do work that was largely physical and often menial.

The earliest efforts to plan for labor were tied to financial forecasting and budgeting, as noted in a classic treatment by Alpander (1982). It was readily apparent to managers in the early 1900s that labor was a major production expense. It is not surprising, then, that the first fitful attempts to plan for labor stemmed from the need to estimate product demand and schedule production levels. In this pioneering period, budgeters—not HR practitioners—handled estimates of labor needs (Alpander 1982).

During the 1960s, manpower planning first appeared on the scene. It focused on forecasting supplies of personnel by examining movements into organizations and through various jobs. Forecasting demand for labor was another matter: Distinct from supply forecasting, its focus is directed to the numbers and kinds of people needed to produce goods at a desired level of output. If it was done at all, it was generally handled by corporate planners and budgeters (Alpander 1982).

During the 1970s, managers began to devote more attention to the human side of their enterprises. Manpower planning was gradually supplanted by human resource planning (HRP) to denote a comprehensive approach to forecasting personnel supplies and demands and planning HR initiatives to help meet organizational needs (Alpander 1982). The HR function became the means by which to operationalize activities that would source, retain, and develop talent that was aligned with business needs.

Since the 1970s, more and more organizations are recognizing that human beings are the only real source of competitive advantage. However, that viewpoint—while often given lip service—actually flies in the face of custom and practice in the United States. Until recently, labor has always been plentiful in the

United States and generally productive. When organizations face increasing demand for products or services, they "staff up" by hiring and by tapping additional sources of talent by outsourcing work, relying on external consultants, using temporary or contingent workers, or using a host of other strategies. If the existing population is insufficient to meet demands, then immigration restrictions are relaxed.

But in recent times, labor has become less plentiful. In the United States, employers complain that workers are not prepared for employment at the time they leave school. Immigration restrictions have been tightened for various reasons ranging from (at this writing) a war on terrorism and, in Europe, a backlash of citizens who think that immigrants are taking the best jobs. At the same time, the world is experiencing a succession crisis as workers approach retirement in developed and in developing economies (Kinsella and Velkoff 2001; Young 2002). That has prompted growing recognition of the need for succession planning and management as part of a larger HRP strategy that is designed to ensure the continued stability of talent sufficient for organizations to function (Rothwell 2000).

A Model of HRP. Think of human resource planning as a process in which decision-makers

1. Link the purpose, goals, and objectives of the HR plan to the purpose, goals, objectives, and competitive strategy of the organization.

2. Assess the present status of HR in the organization by analyzing the work performed, the competencies of the people who perform it, and the HR department.

3. Scan the environment to assess how work will probably change over time, how the talent requirements of the people will probably have to change over time to keep up with work changes and competitive requirements, and how the HR department will probably be affected over time by changes inside and outside the organization.

4. Compare present work being done to expected future work, and compare the present competencies of people doing the work to those competencies needed in the future.

5. Consider unified, long-term HR strategies that will help close planning gaps in the work and workforce (the one selected becomes an HR Grand Strategy).

6. Implement HR Grand Strategy through coordination of such HR practice area efforts as career management programs, succession programs, work management efforts, work design, organization development, labor relations, employee assistance programs, and compensation/benefits.

7. Manage HR activities so that they are effective at helping implement HR Grand Strategy by changing people and jobs.

8. Evaluate HR Grand Strategy before, during, and after implementation.

(Rothwell and Kazanas 2002; Rothwell and Sredl 2000)

These steps are illustrated in Exhibit 1–6, and selected Web site resources to support HRP are shown in Exhibit 1–7.

Those who are curious about this model are advised to see our book-length treatment (Rothwell and Kazanas 2002). For now, it is sufficient to note that *human resource planning (HRP) is a long-term activity intended to identify an organization's future talent needs and to change jobs, people, the department, and other stakeholders so that they support implementation of strategic business plans.* HRP can be synonymous with what Bechet (2002, 7) calls *strategic staffing*: "the process of identifying and addressing the staffing implications of business strategies and plans."

Key Assumptions of HRP. Authors writing about human resource planning have traditionally made several assumptions about it. First, they assume it should be handled from the top down. There is a distinct tendency in the literature to suggest that the HR needs for an entire corporation should be forecast by those at the top, and that programs should be established and implemented from the top. Much evidence suggests it is a rare organization that develops a comprehensive HR plan, despite years of academic and business writing about the need for one. More often than not, action is taken to fill immediate vacancies as needed.

The second assumption is that writers on the subject have traditionally assumed that a comprehensive HR plan should integrate the many different programs and activities of the HR department (Rothwell, Prescott, and Taylor 1998). Few authorities in HRP dispute the importance of integrating HR programs so that they are mutually supportive, but there is little evidence that such integration is being done.

Exhibit 1–6: A Simplified Model of Human Resource Planning (HRP)

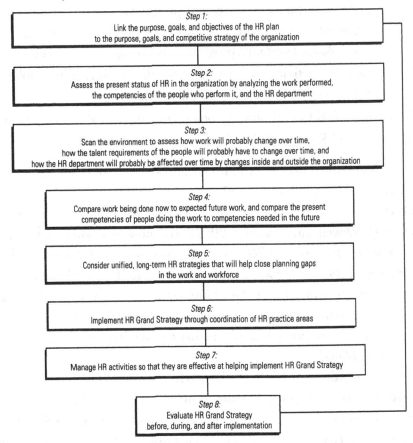

Third, authorities assume that HRP should support but be distinctly different from strategic business plans. We believe that HR plans should not merely be driven by strategic business plans; rather, HR planning should be interactive, at once influencing strategic business plans, and being influenced by them. The people presently available have an important influence on which strategies an organization can or should undertake, and even on which strategies are chosen. If a new venture is contemplated, one question to ask is this: Does the organization now employ people with the requisite competencies to make the venture successful? If not, the venture is handicapped from the start. HR strategy must support business strategy.

Exhibit 1–7: Selected Web Site Resources to Support Human Resource Planning

Link	Brief Description
1. http://www.hrps.org/home/index.shtml	The Web site of the Human Resources Planning Society
2. http://www.wimlaw.com/Humres.htm	The Human Resource Executive's Desk Reference
3. http://www.shrm.org/Hrmagazine/Search.html	The Web site of the Society for Human Resources Management. Enter "Human Resource Planning" in the box and see the articles that come up.
4. http://www.workforce.com/Cgi-Bin/ Archive.cgi?content_type_ids=0:0"	The Web site of *Workforce Magazine*. Enter "Human Resource Planning" and see the articles that come up.
5. http://www.hrprosgateway.com/ www/listserv.html	A Web site of listservs in HR for participation.

HR practitioners have long desired a seat at the table of organizational strategy formulation, but they do not always get it. For instance, the results of one HR practices survey showed that only one third of the 540 respondents indicated that they play a role in their organization's strategy-making efforts (Orr 2002).

The Value of HRP. How much does HRP contribute to successful organizational performance? This question is difficult to answer. Definitions of HRP vary. Not all organizations even attempt it.

Levels of HRP. Traditionally, writers have not discussed different levels of HRP; the usual assumption is that there is only one. However, there are obviously different HR needs for corporate, enterprise, and functional levels. Perhaps it helps, then, to speak in terms of different levels of HR planning. Of course, this idea is based on analogy with corporate planning.

Consider the simplified relationship between organizational structure, plans, and HR initiatives depicted in Exhibit 1–8. Comprehensive, corporate-wide HR Grand Strategy is established at the highest levels. Each autonomous strategic business unit, however, devises its own HR plans in keeping with broad corporate guidelines. Within each enterprise, functional HR plans guide and integrate HR practice areas such as career management, recruitment, training, organization development, job redesign, employee assistance, labor relations, and compensation/benefits.

Exhibit 1–8: A Simplified Representation of the Relationships between Organizational Structure, Organizational Plans, and Human Resource Plans

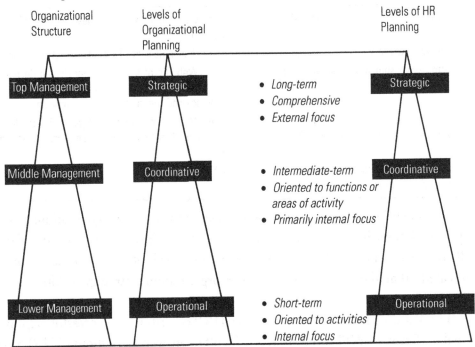

HR Grand Strategy, like its corporate planning counterpart, is ultimately the responsibility of the top HR executive, the chief executive officer (CEO), and key line executives. The HR Grand Strategy establishes the relationship between the corporate HR function and corporate Grand Strategy.

HR enterprise strategy is more detailed, encompassing the HR plan for only one business in the corporation. At this level, the highest-ranking HR executive works with the CEO and key line managers to address such questions as:

1. What are the chief products/services of HR? What should they be?
2. What are the major responsibilities of HR practitioners, line managers, and employees in working toward realization of HR plans? What should they be?
3. What HR initiatives are desirable in light of enterprise strategy? What resources are available to pursue those initiatives?

4. Who is the chief client or customer of HR activities? Line managers? Top managers? Employees? Who should be the chief client or customer?
5. Given the major responsibilities of the HR department, how can it best serve its chief client? Other clients?

The answers to these questions should help link the purpose, goals, and objectives of HR to those of the enterprise.

HR functional strategy is more specific than enterprise or corporate HR strategy. Its focus is on providing guidelines for HR practice areas within the HR department at the enterprise level. These HR practice areas can include recruitment/selection, training, organization development, and compensation/benefits (see Rothwell, Prescott, Taylor 1998). Any division or subcomponent of the HR department is a function. Another way to look at it is that any HR activity, with or without someone assigned responsibility for it, is a function. Each function has its own purpose, goals, and objectives; each function operates in its own environment; each function possesses its own strengths and weaknesses; and each function can establish its own strategies.

The notion of HR functional strategy is important because many efforts to conduct planned Talent Development are often coordinated from HR.

Methods of HRP. Some organizations use sophisticated computer simulations and models to forecast HR demands, movements between job categories, and available HR supplies inside and outside the organization. Much of what is known about HRP comes from published case studies about methods. Large, diversified corporations often employ HRP specialists.

Forecasting HR demands and supplies is often referred to as the "heart" of human resource planning. Various advanced quantitative techniques are used in forecasting (see Rothwell and Kazanas 2002).

Despite sustained academic interest in HRP—long enough for academic research efforts to direct practitioner attention to this area—actual practices lag far behind theory. There are several reasons for this gap. As Stella Nkomo (1986) pointed out in a classic treatment, people tend to pay lip service to HR, rather than actively support it. Second, managers often assume that the right people for the right jobs are always available. Third, HR practitioners too often lack the credibility and skills to lead an effort to predict the organization's future talent needs. Lastly, managers rely more on informal than formal HRP methods. One sign of that problem is, of course, a practice of only hiring to fill vacancies, without coordinating across the organization about its use of talent.

The Strategic Development of Talent: A Definition

We are using this definition of the Strategic Development of Talent (SDT):

> **The process of changing an organization, stakeholders outside it, groups inside it, and people employed by it through planned and unplanned learning so that they possess the competencies needed to help the organization achieve and sustain competitive advantage at present and in the future.**

SDT helps implement strategic business plans and HR plans by building the competencies of people inside the organization or changing the knowledge and skills of stakeholders outside it. One possible relationship between strategic business plans, HR plans, and SDT is illustrated in Exhibit 1–9.

SDT is more holistic than traditional efforts to develop people. The outgrowth of SDT is an organizational strategy for talent that guides, unifies, and provides direction to learning that occurs in the organization. In SDT, the focus of planning centers on the roles and responsibilities of everyone who shares responsibility for developing the talents of people in the organization—line managers, participants, and HR practitioners. This focus on planning for talent differs from mere department planning for a corporate training department or corporate university or planning for isolated learning events such as one-shot training courses.

Traditional efforts to develop human talent provide individuals who otherwise lack the present or future competencies they need with structured opportunities to receive the fruits of distilled organizational experience. Those advocating this view think in much the same way that John Dewey's critics in 1938 thought of education: "the subject-matter of education consists of bodies of information and skills that have been worked out in the past; therefore, the chief business of the school is to transmit them to the new generation" (Dewey 1938, 17).

Exhibit 1–9: One Possible Relationship between Business Plans, HR Plans, and Talent Development

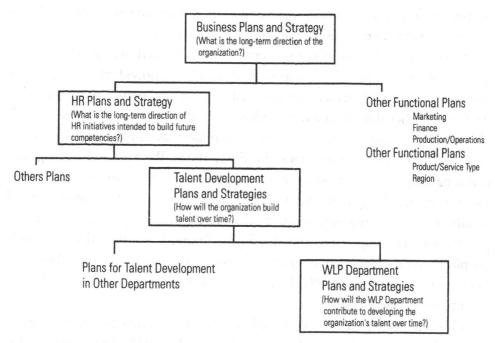

When viewed in this traditional way, Talent Development is a *maintenance subsystem* as Katz and Kahn (1978) defined it: a system intended to improve organizational efficiency by increasing routinization and the predictability of human behavior. It facilitates the socialization of newcomers into the corporate culture, work group, and job. In a sense, traditional efforts to develop people are rites of passage that furnish newcomers with ideas, techniques, and approaches worked out in the past.

It is appropriate to rely on experience if future events and situations are similar to or call for knowledge and skills derived from the past. If future problems are much like problems faced in the past, then few should question the wisdom of relying on what has been learned in the past as the basis for learning.

The trouble is that experience is not always appropriate in preparing for the future. There are many reasons why this is so: New knowledge is created faster today than it was in the past. Computers increase the speed with which information can be processed, but not the speed at which human beings can absorb it or use it. Organizations face more competition and must anticipate competitive challenges if they are to survive and thrive. The same principle applies to individuals who are competing with others for career success.

A new approach to developing human talent is needed to cope with a future that is not like the past. This approach should help individuals anticipate the *competencies* or the characteristics essential to successful performance needed in the future, rather than react after problems become apparent. SDT does this. It can aid in planning one-time learning experiences as much as a sequence of longer-term learning experiences. In SDT, those Workplace Learning and Performance practitioners who coordinate people development do not spend as much time distilling past experiences; rather, they facilitate organizational members in a continuing, creative process of discovery so that they can prepare for the competencies needed in the future. More than that, they help people become competent workplace learners who take charge of their own development (Rothwell 2002). In that way, SDT helps to organize and unify Talent Development efforts.

This is not to say that developing talent is always a creative process for the discovery of new approaches or information. It is not. But SDT places more emphasis than traditional approaches on generating creative approaches, and thereby facilitates strategic thinking.

A Model of SDT. SDT resembles strategic business planning and HR planning. According to Rothwell and Sredl (2000), WLP practitioners work with operating managers and individuals to

1. Clarify the vision and purpose of the Talent Development effort. Why is the organization undertaking the effort, and what does it hope to gain from it?

2. Assess present conditions. What are the strengths and weaknesses of the organization in terms of human skills and competencies?

3. Scan the external environment. What threats and opportunities affecting human performance are likely to result from changes outside the organization? Department? Work group? Occupation? Job?

4. Compare present strengths and weaknesses to future threats and opportunities.

5. Choose a long-term organizational strategy for Talent Development that is likely to help prepare individuals and the organization for the future.

6. Implement organizational strategy for Talent Development through such approaches as

   I Organization development
   I Nonemployee development
   I Employee development
   I Employee education
   I Employee training

7. Evaluate the organizational strategy for Talent Development.

These steps, illustrated in Exhibit 1–10, are the basis for the structure of this book. Selected Web site resources to support SDT are provided in Exhibit 1–11.

With slight modifications, this model can also guide WLP practitioners or an operating department in planning for Talent Development. After all, both a WLP department and operating departments should support a unified strategy for the development of talent (see Exhibit 1–12).

Key Assumptions of SDT. Generally speaking, an organization's Talent Development efforts can be effectively aligned with strategic business plans and human resource plans when several conditions are met.

First, there should be an overall purpose statement for the organization, and the purpose of the Talent Development effort should be clearly related to it. It is important to link the organization's mission to the learning that is sponsored by the organization. In this way, few critics can challenge the value of Talent Development, unless they also question the value of the organization.

Second, every major plan of the corporation should be weighed in terms of its talent requirements. Planned learning efforts are not the only ways to build essential competencies. Talent can be obtained through external recruitment, contracting for talent, internal transfers, worksharing, telecommuting, job redesign, or reliance on part-time employees. Nevertheless, any plan implies that talent will be

Exhibit 1–10: A Simplified Model of the Process for the Strategic Development of Talent

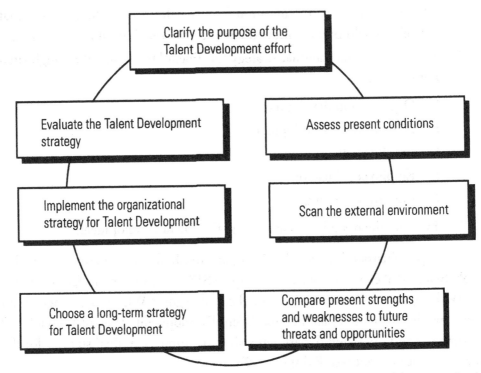

needed to formulate it, implement it, and evaluate it. Where and how to obtain these talents should be explicitly considered.

Third, people at all levels in the organization's chain of command share responsibility and accountability for developing talent. *Learning is an important part of the job of every supervisor and every employee, and talent is the outcome of effective learning.* It is not enough to give lip service to it. Supervisors and employees should be evaluated, in part, on how well they develop themselves and contribute to the development of others. Decisions about pay, promotions, and transfers should be based in part on how well people are contributing to the development of their talent and the talents of others.

Fourth, there should be a systematic, holistic planning process for developing talent. It is difficult for WLP practitioners to coordinate Talent Development if nothing is planned. This is why formal planning is best. It furnishes opportunities

Exhibit 1–11: Selected Web Site Resources to Support the Strategic Development of Talent

Link	Brief Description
1. http://www.businesspotential.com/	A connection to resources that are intended to build specific competencies
2. http://trgmcber.haygroup.com/ Products/competencies/mcqus.htm	The managerial competency questionnaire from Hay/McBer
3. http://www.amanet.org/research/ pdfs/mang_skl_comp.pdf	A report from the American Management Association on top-ranked management competencies
4. http://www.hrnext.com/content/ subs.cfm?subs_id=120	A Web site with many resources and information about job analysis
5. http://www.job-analysis.net/	A Web site with much information about job analysis
6. http://www.hr-guide.com/ data/G012.htm	HR Guide to the Internet: Job Analysis; Methods of; Questionnaire
7. http://www.hr-guide.com/ data/010.htm	Comprehensive list of Web resources on human resource management

for information-sharing among the stakeholders and participants in the Talent Development effort. Unlike informal planning, formal planning calls for a deliberate, systematic approach to specifying what should be done, when it should be done, and who should be accountable for the results.

The Importance of Strategic Development of Talent. SDT is important for several reasons. First, it makes Talent Development efforts proactive rather than reactive. The organization commits to developing talent. Second, SDT ties learning to a comprehensive planning process for talent that aligns it to strategic business plans and HR plans. Third, organizations known for their excellence in productivity improvement handle their human resources strategically. Talent Development efforts such as training have been shown to serve as retention tools, as well as a means of building internal bench strength. Finally, those who coordinate Talent Development must increasingly think strategically if they are to enjoy long-term career success.

But it is also true that SDT is no panacea. It *can* serve to anticipate and build the competencies needed for future competitive success. In this respect, it can support strategic business plans and individual career plans. But it cannot

Exhibit 1–12: Relationships between a Unified Plan for Talent Development and Other Talent Development Plans

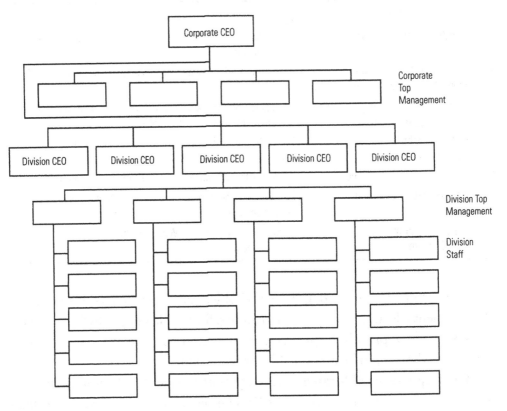

anticipate all future problems or even head off the sometimes-unknown consequences of current trends.

Competency Identification, Modeling, and Assessment and the Strategic Development of Talent. It is, of course, critically important to have a blueprint of what talent to develop. Competency models serve that purpose, and many authorities believe they are essential for the process of developing talent (Zenger, Ulrich, and Smallwood 2000). Much has been written on competency modeling. (See, for instance, Boyatzis 1982; Dubois 1993; Dubois 1996; Dubois 1998; Dubois and Rothwell 2000; Rothwell and Lindholm 1999; and Spencer and Spencer 1993.)

A *competency* is any characteristic related to successful performance. Competencies are tied to individuals, not to the work they do.

Competencies should not be confused with job descriptions or job specifications. Job descriptions delineate the work that must be done by a job incumbent. Job specifications list the essential education, experience, and other bonafide occupational requirements necessary to qualify for a position. Neither job description nor job specification is necessarily tied to results, but competencies *are* tied to work results.

Competency work has a lexicon all its own. Individual competency models are about people who do work. The following key terms are associated with these models:

I   *Competency identification* is the process of discovering what competencies are essential to success in a unique corporate culture and in a unique position.

I   *Competency modeling* is the process of describing which competencies have been identified. A competency model indicates which characteristics should be demonstrated by a successful performer.

I   *Competency assessment* is the process of comparing an individual to the competency model usually through an assessment center or by a 360-degree assessment.

Organizational competence is about what sets an organization apart from its competitors. What key competitive strength keeps an organization in business, and what is distinctive about that business? If decision-makers answer that, they are beginning to define *organizational core competencies* (Prahalad and Hamel 1990; Hamel and Prahalad 1994), understood as the essence of what makes an organization successful in its competition with other organizations (Mascarenhas, Baveja, and Mamnoon, 1998).

Talent Development is done by narrowing gaps between competency models and assessment results, usually through individual development plans (IDPs) that stipulate the activities in which individuals should participate to build their competencies in line with the model (Dubois and Rothwell 2000). Leadership competence is particularly important. As Hagen, Hassan, and Amin (1998) note,

"A survey conducted among American CEOs found that they rank the following six-core leadership competencies in the following order of importance: (1) determining strategic direction, (2) developing human capital, (3) exploiting and maintaining core competencies, (4) sustaining effective corporate culture, (5) emphasizing ethical practices, and (6) establishing strategic controls" (1998, 39).

Competency models can be past-, present-, or future-oriented. *Past-* or *present-oriented competency models* describe the characteristics that have made some people successful. *Future-oriented competency models,* based on the organization's strategic business plan and on future trends expected to influence that plan, describe which characteristics should be demonstrated by performers in order for them to be successful in that future.

Competency models can also be distinguished by what level of performance they are intended to identify. *Derailment models* pinpoint the most common causes for performers to fail. *Occupational models* usually show the general competencies required for average performance in an occupation. But most competency models are usually intended to underscore what characteristics distinguish *exemplary* (best-in-class) performers from *fully-successful* (average) performers in a job category, department, or occupation. Since exemplary performers are dramatically more productive than their fully-successful counterparts, many decision-makers are trying to determine how to make all or more of their workers as productive as the best-in-class workers. If they can do that, they can realize quantum leaps in productivity and will likely outcompete any other organization. Of course, not all competencies can be developed. Some competencies must be hired for.

There are many ways by which to identify competencies. Dubois (1993) has listed many approaches. Spencer and Spencer (1993) provide a cookbook that essentially focuses on one approach.

The most rigorous approach to identifying competencies for any job category, department, or occupation is to do these things:

1. Identify the most-productive, successful performers in the target group.

2. Identify average performers in the target group.

3. Conduct behavioral-event interviews with both groups, asking people to describe the most difficult situation that they have ever encountered in their work in the target group in the organization.
4. Videotape or audiotape the interviews.
5. Transcribe the results.
6. Apply content analysis to the transcriptions, identifying common themes.
7. Subtract the themes shared by both groups, leaving only those that are shared by the most-productive, successful performers.
8. Draft a narrative competency model that describes the competencies identified in statement #7.
9. Identify behaviors associated with the most-productive, successful performers in the target group.
10. Establish behavioral anchors for the competencies so as to render them measurable, and involve the most-productive, successful performers in the process.
11. Ask the organizational superiors of the target group to review, comment, and refine the competencies and behaviors identified for the target group.

The result of this process should be a competency model that isolates the characteristics shared by the most-successful, productive performers. Note that this approach identifies the past or present competencies associated with exemplary performance. After all, the behavioral-event interviews are based on experience, a product of the past.

An alternative approach is to focus attention on the future. (For an example, see Rothwell, Prescott, and Taylor 1998.) To carry out this approach, you should take these actions:

1. Identify the key trends facing the organization and industry through a process of environmental scanning.
2. Clarify for each target group in the organization:
   I How the trend can be defined for that group in the organization.
   I What causes the trend.
   I What consequences are likely to stem from the trend.

I   How best-practice organizations are preparing to deal with the trend.

I   What competencies will be necessary for each target group in the organization to deal with the trend.

3. Draft a narrative competency model that describes the competencies identified in statement #2.

4. Identify behaviors that are likely to demonstrate the competencies by productive, successful performers in the target group.

5. Establish behavioral anchors for the competencies so as to render them measurable.

6. Ask the organizational superiors of the target group to review, comment, and refine the competencies and behaviors identified for the target group, based on how well they align to the organization's strategic business plans.

There are other ways to identify competencies. The simplest, least-expensive and least-useful approach is to find published competency models from the Web or from print sources, and adapt them to the organization's corporate culture. While that approach is quick and inexpensive, it is also most likely to create a blueprint that is not very precise or well-aligned to the organization's future challenges.

Of course, once the competency model has been prepared and approved for each job category, or department, or occupational group, it can provide the basis for individual assessments of job incumbents to see how well they measure up to the model. Such evaluations can be carried out by 360-degree assessment, assessment centers, or other means. Whether assessing individual talent for the future or assessing individual performance in the present job, 360-degree assessments have proven to be very popular in many organizations today. According to one authority, 90 percent of the Fortune 1000 firms have used some variation of 360-degree assessment (Atwater and Waldman 1998), which is also known as *multisource assessment*. It is thought by some that good feedback sufficient to guide coaching and developmental planning is the weak link in multisource assessment (Wells 1999). To be most successful, 360-degree assessments must be carried out in organizations where the culture has been managed to make the assessments most useful (Jackson and Greller 1998).

Gaps between the competency model and the individual's assessment should be narrowed through an individual development plan (see Dubois and Rothwell 2000; Rothwell 1999). An IDP should typically spell out

- Who should learn
- What the individual should learn
- When the individual should learn it
- Where the individual should learn
- Why the individual should learn
- How the individual should learn
- How any successful learning will be evaluated

Much recent attention is being paid to the delivery methods for Talent Development, such as e-learning. However, delivery methods should not be selected without the goals in mind. Strategy is even needed for e-learning (Pope 2002). Since 62 percent of all learning occurs on the job and informally, rather than off the job, it makes sense to integrate "learning while doing" with "doing while learning" (Verespej 1998). *Informal learning* occurs during work, and *incidental learning* occurs as a result of learning from experience. Both are likely to grow more important in the future. So, too, is situated learning in which learning is embodied in the work process itself (Robin 2000). However, learners can be directed toward which competencies to build, through various methods, on their IDPs.

Individual competencies can be aligned with organizational strategic objectives by making concerted efforts to assess which competencies are essential to achieve strategic objectives, and how well workers in each group perceive their competencies to be aligned with the organization's strategic objectives (see Sensenig 1998).

The strategic development of talent is the process of building the collective individual competencies of everyone in the organization. In that way, the organization becomes a community of practice and a learning organization. Learning becomes a means of individual and organizational progress toward continuous improvement.

To be most useful in realizing strategic objectives, competency models must be aligned with the future direction of the organization. Then individuals should be assessed against those models. This is no easy chore, of course. It often requires the creation of competency models for each department and/or each job category in the organization. Then individuals must be compared to those models and learning plans established to narrow any gaps. But doing that is a means by which to align Talent Development efforts to strategic objectives, thereby transforming Talent Development to a strategic focus.

While individual and organizational competencies are important, they don't always go far enough. They only focus on results alone, and don't always take ethical issues related to values far enough. That has prompted writers such as Dahlgaard, Dahlgaard, and Edgeman (1998) to discuss core values—the ethical beliefs that are essential. The message here is an important one: Remember that results alone are not enough, and play by the rules of morality. Attention to values can help you do that.

Leadership Development Programs for the Strategic Development of Talent. Many companies have established leadership programs in an effort to develop their talent and build the competencies of leaders (see Rothwell and Kazanas 2000). This is especially important in a time of crisis, which some experts believe we are now in (Weiss 2002). Many case studies have been written about these leadership program. For examples, refer to the description of the U.S. Postal Service program (Delahoussaye 2002), the description of the program at Texas Instruments (Moser 2001), the description of the program at Johnson & Johnson (Fulmer 2001), the description of the program at Xerox (Pulley, Sessa, and Malloy 2002), the description of the program at Ford (Friedman 2001), the description of the program at TRW (Neary and O'Grady 2000), and the description of the program at GE (Tarley 2002). Much has also been written about using maps, models, or graphics to show the linkage between strategy and training or Talent Development efforts (see, for instance, Kapp 2000). The CEO's role in the process is critically important, as Larry Bossidy, formerly CEO of Allied Signal, emphasizes. CEOs themselves need special preparation as they take charge (see Arthur 2000). To be successful, leadership programs should be competency-based and linked to organizational strategy (Zenger, Ulrich, and Smallwood 2000). Winning companies invest in leadership development, as Hewlett-Packard and other companies demonstrate (Fulmer, Gibbs, and Goldsmith 2000; Phillips 1999).

Activity 1–1: A Checklist on Organizational Strategy for the Development of Talent

Directions: This checklist is intended to serve two purposes. First, it introduces the complete model for the strategic development of talent (SDT) described in the text. In this sense, it is an overview of SDT and an advance organizer for the book. Second, this checklist can aid Workplace Learning and Performance (WLP) practitioners and operating managers who are brave enough to fight the tendency toward short-term, crisis-oriented planning for SDT that prevails in many organizations. Think of it as a "to-do list" for creating and implementing Organizational Strategy for Talent Development. For each activity listed in the left column, check an appropriate response in one of the middle columns: "yes," "no," or "not applicable." Write remarks to yourself in the right column. Since organizations vary by culture, you may need to add or subtract steps and activities in the SDT process so that the steps will apply to your organization.

In formulating and implementing a comprehensive organizational strategy for Talent Development, have HR, WLP, and operating managers together:	Yes ☒	No ☒	N/A ☒	Remarks

Clarifying the purpose of the Talent Development effort

1. Worked to clarify the purpose of the Talent Development effort in the organization?	☐	☐	☐	
2. Worked to create a purpose statement for the effort that is aligned with the organization's strategy?	☐	☐	☐	
3. Worked to prepare a purpose statement that describes	☐	☐	☐	
a. the role of Talent Development in the organization?	☐	☐	☐	
b. the part to be played by Talent Development in each part of the organization?	☐	☐	☐	
c. how Talent Development helps meet needs of people inside and outside the organization?	☐	☐	☐	
d. how Talent Development is related to the organization's philosophy of doing business?	☐	☐	☐	

Activity 1–1: *(continued)*

In formulating and implementing a comprehensive organizational strategy for Talent Development, have HR practitioners, WLP practitioners, and operating managers together:	Yes ☒	No ☒	N/A ☒	Remarks

Assessing present needs

	Yes	No	N/A	
4. Worked to assess present strengths and weaknesses of talent in the organization?	☐	☐	☐	
5. Worked to identify learners to be served by the Talent Development effort over time? More specifically, is it clear	☐	☐	☐	
a. who the learners are?	☐	☐	☐	
b. where they are located?	☐	☐	☐	
c. how many there are?	☐	☐	☐	
d. how they can be reached for carrying out the development process?	☐	☐	☐	
e. how intense is their motivation to learn?	☐	☐	☐	
f. when they are most interested in learning?	☐	☐	☐	
6. Worked to classify learners into broad "market segments" to be served by the Talent Development effort?	☐	☐	☐	
7. Worked to compare actual to desired competencies at present in each market segment of learners?	☐	☐	☐	
8. Worked to identify present	☐	☐	☐	
a. strengths (competencies) in each market?	☐	☐	☐	
b. weaknesses (learning needs) in each market segment of learners?	☐	☐	☐	

Activity 1–1: *(continued)*

In formulating and implementing a comprehensive organizational strategy for Talent Development, have HR practitioners, WLP practitioners, and operating managers together:	Yes ⊠	No ⊠	N/A ⊠	Remarks
Scanning the environment				
9. Worked to classify the external environment into discrete sectors or components for analysis?	☐	☐	☐	
10. Worked to decide on a time horizon appropriate for scanning for Talent Development?	☐	☐	☐	
11. Worked to examine environmental sectors for expected changes over the time horizon that has been chosen?	☐	☐	☐	
12. Worked to infer effects of environmental changes on	☐	☐	☐	
a. the public?	☐	☐	☐	
b. key external stakeholders?	☐	☐	☐	
c. departments/work groups inside the organization?	☐	☐	☐	
d. individuals and career prospects?	☐	☐	☐	
e. work requirements?	☐	☐	☐	
13. Worked to identify future	☐	☐	☐	
a. threats affecting each market segment of learners?	☐	☐	☐	
b. opportunities affecting each market segment of learners?	☐	☐	☐	

Activity 1–1: *(continued)*

In formulating and implementing a comprehensive organizational strategy for Talent Development, have HR practitioners, WLP practitioners, and operating managers together:	Yes ☒	No ☒	N/A ☒	Remarks

Comparing present strengths/weaknesses to future threats/opportunities

	Yes	No	N/A	
14. Worked to compare present strengths/weaknesses to future threats/opportunities relative to	☐	☐	☐	
a. interactions with external groups?	☐	☐	☐	
b. interactions between groups within the organization?	☐	☐	☐	
c. competencies needed by departments and work groups in the organization?	☐	☐	☐	
d. competencies needed by individuals in order to achieve career goals?	☐	☐	☐	
e. competencies needed by individuals to improve present performance in their work?	☐	☐	☐	

Choosing organizational strategy for Talent Development

	Yes	No	N/A	
15. Worked to choose an organizational strategy for Talent Development, such as these:	☐	☐	☐	
a. *grow* (by increasing developmental activities)?	☐	☐	☐	
b. *retrench* (by decreasing developmental activities)?	☐	☐	☐	

Activity 1–1: *(continued)*

In formulating and implementing a comprehensive organizational strategy for Talent Development, have HR practitioners, WLP practitioners, and operating managers together:	Yes ☒	No ☒	N/A ☒	Remarks
c. *diversify* by changing the learners who are served, the needs addressed, the emphasis placed on potential markets of learners, etc.?	☐	☐	☐	
d. *integrate* by establishing closer ties to other functions inside the firm or to groups outside it?	☐	☐	☐	
e. *turn around* by retrenching and then pursuing another organizational strategy for Talent Development?	☐	☐	☐	
f. *combine* by pursuing two or more strategies at the same time?	☐	☐	☐	

Implementing organizational strategy for Talent Development

	Yes	No	N/A	
16. Worked to implement organizational strategy for Talent Development by coordinating Talent Development efforts?	☐	☐	☐	
17. Worked to establish operational objectives for the Talent Development effort so as to unify the developmental efforts?	☐	☐	☐	

Activity 1–1: *(continued)*

In formulating and implementing a comprehensive organizational strategy for Talent Development, have HR practitioners, WLP practitioners, and operating managers together:	Yes ☒	No ☒	N/A ☒	Remarks
18. Worked to review and revise all organizational policies in light of a new strategy for Talent Development?	☐	☐	☐	
19. Worked to examine leadership in the organization relative to the new organizational strategy for Talent Development?	☐	☐	☐	
20. Worked to review structure for Talent Development relative to the organization and to groups/departments with responsibilities for Talent Development?	☐	☐	☐	
21. Worked to review reward systems relative to the organizational strategy for Talent Development?	☐	☐	☐	
22. Worked to budget for the resources necessary to implement the organizational strategy for Talent Development?	☐	☐	☐	
23. Worked to establish the means to communicate about organizational strategy for Talent Development?	☐	☐	☐	
24. Worked to develop functional strategies for Talent Development in line with the organizational strategy for Talent Development? (Examples include employee development, employee education, and others.)	☐	☐	☐	

Activity 1–1: *(continued)*

In formulating and implementing a comprehensive organizational strategy for Talent Development, have HR practitioners, WLP practitioners, and operating managers together:	Yes ☒	No ☒	N/A ☒	Remarks
Evaluating organizational strategy for Talent Development				
25. Worked to clarify . . .	☐	☐	☐	
a. who wants information from evaluation of Talent Development efforts?	☐	☐	☐	
b. who will do the evaluating?	☐	☐	☐	
c. what the primary focus of interest is?	☐	☐	☐	
d. when evaluation should be carried out?	☐	☐	☐	
e. why evaluation is necessary?	☐	☐	☐	
f. how evaluation will be conducted?	☐	☐	☐	
g. how each Talent Development functional area will be evaluated, including organization development, nonemployee development, employee development, and employee education and training?	☐	☐	☐	
26. Worked to clarify when there is a need to change organizational strategy for Talent Development?	☐	☐	☐	

Remarks:

CHAPTER 2

THE VISION AND PURPOSE OF THE TALENT DEVELOPMENT EFFORT

The vision leaders have for the Talent Development effort is an important starting point for the strategic development of talent (SDT). The outcome of a visioning process is a purpose statement that puts the organization on record about the reasons for the Talent Development effort, the goals and objectives for that effort, and the ways in which the effort aligns with the organization's competitive goals and strategic objectives.

Just as strategists should first identify in what business they are operating before they formulate a strategy to succeed in that business, so too must key stakeholders of the Talent Development effort decide why they are undertaking the effort. A purpose (mission) statement is as important for the strategic development of talent as it is for strategic business planning. It provides the rationale for why the organization is developing talent, justifies why the organization's leaders support it, and clarifies what results the organization's leaders hope to gain from it.

What Is Vision?

A *vision* is a mental picture of an ideal situation or condition. "Visioning," writes Nickolson (2002, 52), "is about visualizing a desired future state and then working backward to develop an action plan to get to that desired state." In some cases, the term *visioning* is used to refer to the process of establishing a mission or purpose statement. In other cases, it is viewed as a preliminary step. Visioning meetings are fairly common. Nickolson creates a case study that describes one vision meeting and the process used to guide it.

The value of visioning should be apparent: Whether one is doing strategic planning for an organization or is trying to establish an organizational strategy for Talent Development, every decision-maker must reach some common understanding about what they are doing, why they are doing it, what benefits they hope to achieve from it, and how they will establish the purpose, goals, objectives, and strategy to guide the effort. The process of doing this can thus be critical (Flores and Fadden 2000).

Vision is sometimes seen as a critical element in strategy (Brown 1998), even if it is regarded somehow as separate from it. For instance, Hilton (1999, 29) cites a study that revealed that no less than 40 percent of a company's reputation is attributable to the CEO's reputation. More to the point, the most important quality of a CEO is his or her ability to "communicate a clear vision of the company's strategy."

Many writers today agree that visioning is often the key to a successful strategic planning effort. As Kim and Mauborgne (2002, 76) note: "Few companies have a clear strategic vision. The problem stems from the strategic-planning process itself, which usually involves preparing a large document, culled from a mishmash of data provided by people with conflicting agendas. Instead, companies should design the strategic-planning process by drawing a picture: a strategy canvas. The process is four steps: (1) visual awakening; (2) visual exploration; (3) visual strategy; and (4) visual communication."

Many resources are available to support an organization's visioning efforts. (See Exhibit 2–1.)

What Is "Purpose"?

Purpose refers to the fundamental reason for an organization's existence. It is often synonymous with *intention* or *mission* (Krattenmaker 2002). While the value of specifying intentions has sparked substantial debate among those

Exhibit 2–1: Web Resources for Visioning*

Link	Description of the Web site
1. http://www.nsba.org/sbot/toolkit/cav.html	Emphasizes the benefits of visioning
2. http://www.improve.org/stratpln.html	Provides a 10-step model of strategic planning
3. http://allianceonline.org/faqs/spfaq7.html	Describes how to introduce the visioning process
4. http://prosci.com/visions.htm	Tutors users in visioning
5. http://mapnp.org/library/plan_dec/gen_plan/gen_plan.htm	Supplies links and resources for nonprofit organizations—which can, of course, apply to other organizations as well—about the visioning process

*These links are based on a much more extensive list provided in Nickolson's Envisioning an Enriched Future (2002) in *Association Management*, 54(5), 52–57.

who facilitate learning, it is advantageous because it (1) helps guide design and development efforts; (2) helps learners understand what they are supposed to learn; (3) provides means to evaluate the relative success of subsequent instructional efforts; and (4) provides information worth communicating to employees and operating managers about what instruction is intended to do. A sense of purpose, whether for an organization or instruction, instills confidence. It gives people the feeling that they know "where they are going" and helps them understand "why they are doing what they are doing." And the process of developing a purpose or mission statement can build *esprit de corps* among work group members (Ishoy and Swan 1992).

Perhaps the best description of a formal purpose statement for an organization is this classic and succinct passage from Morrisey's 1976 work:

> For the total organization, the statement [of purpose] should include the broad identification of the type of operation for which it is responsible, its major areas of service, clientele or user groups, organizational approach, plus the philosophical basis for its operation (p. 25).

A purpose statement thus answers such questions as: (1) What is our business? (2) What should it be? (3) What are the major parts of the business? (4) What should they be? (5) Who are the customers? (6) Who should the organization be serving? (7) How is the business presently meeting needs of each customer group? (8) How should it be meeting those needs? (9) What do managers believe about the business, customers, and methods of operation? and (10) What *should* they believe?

In recent times, however, corporate executives use purpose statements to explain why the organization exists, but also to stress its noble purpose. But take care in doing that, note Kleiner, Roth, and Kruschwitz (2001, 18):

> We live in a post–mission-statement era. These days, the most admired companies are trying not only to develop effective strategies for profit, but to make themselves into examples of greatness. They want their companies to be like Mary Kay Inc., with its stated intention "to enrich women's lives"; or like Merck and Co. Inc., whose "business is preserving and improving human life"; or like British Petroleum, which recently announced a brand-name change to "Beyond Petroleum," signaling a leadership role in moving civilization out of the fossil-fuel era.

A similar concern has been expressed about grand vision statements that can distract strategists from the real purpose of their organizations (Langeler 1992).

Strategic business planning theorists prefer to direct their primary attention to customers or clients during the process of formulating purpose. In a classic description, Rothschild suggests pondering these questions:

I   Who are you as an organization?
I   Who are your customers?
I   How can they be classified?
I   Which classification is most important to you and your competitors?
I   Will this classification still be most important in the future? Why?
I   Why do customers buy when and as much as they do?
I   What are their objectives?
I   Which objectives are most important?
I   Are the reasons for purchasing and their ranking in importance likely to change?
I   What if . . . ?

- What could cause a change in customers' objectives?
- What information will help anticipate these changes?
- So what?
- What are the implications of change in customer behavior and objectives?
- Will the impact be positive or negative on you, relative to the impact on your competition?
- What then?
- How will this customer classification add to your understanding of the total market, size, mix, growth rate, and time? (Rothchild 1976, 29-30; reprinted with permission)

Customer analysis of this kind suggests valuable clues about the purpose of the organization—and profitable strategies for the future.

It does not require much imagination to see that these questions are applicable to developing talent. Indeed, a good starting point for long-term planning for Talent Development in any organization is to pose the same kind of questions that Rothschild (1976) suggests in his classic work. Consider:

- What purposes does Talent Development seek to attain inside the organization? Outside it?
- What part of this purpose is the responsibility of the Talent Development effort? Operating managers? Learners?
- What is known about the learners? How can they be classified? How can this classification scheme be used in planning instruction and other developmental efforts?
- How are Talent Development activities presently benefiting the organization? How should they benefit the organization?
- How are Talent Development activities presently meeting learner needs? How should they meet learner needs in the future?
- What is the organization's present philosophy about Talent Development? What should that philosophy be in the future?

By posing these questions, WLP practitioners can stimulate a meaningful dialogue about the Talent Development effort in their organizations. This information, in turn, helps to set priorities.

How important is Purpose?

Without a sense of purpose, WLP practitioners might successfully complete many projects or activities, but might never know how they are contributing to the organization or to improvements in job performance. Nor will they be able to demonstrate their value in convincing ways if asked to do so. If WLP practitioners or line managers lack purpose for the Talent Development effort, they will not be able to establish a strategy for realizing that purpose.

What are the possible relationships between strategic business plans, HR plans, and Talent Development?

There are many possible relationships between strategic business plans, HR plans, and Talent Development efforts. These can be summarized as follows:

1. Talent Development can be driven by organizational and HR plans. This is the *top-down approach.*
2. Talent Development can be driven by perceived future learning needs of managers and employees. This is the *market-driven approach.*
3. Talent Development can be driven by comparisons between individual career plans/objectives and organizational plans/objectives. This is the *career planning approach.*
4. Talent Development serves as a tool for helping top management strategists formulate business and HR plans. This is the *futuring approach.*
5. Talent Development furnishes learners with artificial experience tied to organizational and HR plans. This is the *artificial experience approach.*
6. Talent Development provides feedback about implementation of plans for use by top managers in subsequent planning. This is the *pulse-taking approach.*
7. Talent Development provides information to strategists about organizational strengths and weaknesses. This is the *performance diagnosis approach.*
8. Talent Development teaches people how to think strategically. This is the *educational approach.*

9. Talent Development serves the unarticulated needs and interests of strategists. This is the *interpersonal approach.*

10. Talent Development focuses on specific issues, problems, or projects of major strategic significance to the organization. This is the *rifle approach.*

Exhibit 2–2 summarizes all ten approaches. Note that they are not mutually exclusive. In fact, they may overlap conceptually. Each approach is worth describing in more detail because they describe how strategic business plans and Talent Development efforts can be aligned. Remember: each approach also implies a purpose for a Talent Development effort.

Exhibit 2–2: A Summary of Relationships between Strategic Business Plans, HR Plans, and Talent Development

Approach	Brief Description
1. Top-Down	The Talent Development effort is used to support implementation of organizational and HR plans, and is driven by those plans.
2. Market-Driven	The Talent Development effort is used to identify future learning needs and to convince people to meet those needs.
3. Career Planning	The Talent Development effort is a tool for helping individuals realize their own career plans.
4. Futuring	The Talent Development effort is used to provide assistance to top management strategists in formulating strategic plans.
5. Artificial Experience	The Talent Development effort is used to simulate future conditions, helping individuals identify their own learning needs.
6. Pulse-Taking	In the course of Talent Development efforts, WLP practitioners and others collect information about how well the organization's strategic plans are being implemented, and later feed it back to the strategists.
7. Performance Diagnosis	In the course of assessing Talent Development needs, WLP practitioners and others identify problems of larger scope, and provide that information to strategists for their use in strategic business planning.
8. Educational	WLP practitioners and others work to teach people how to think strategically.
9. Interpersonal	WLP practitioners and others interact with the strategists, identifying their beliefs and communicating those beliefs to others.
10. Rifle	WLP practitioners and others concentrate their attention on issues, problems, or projects of strategic importance.

The Top-Down Approach. Perhaps the most common way to think of aligning strategic business plans, HR plans, and Talent Development efforts is from this perspective. Top managers envision the organization as it exists in the future and as it is positioned relative to the external environment. This vision is embodied in a formal strategic plan (a product); however, planning is synonymous with a process.

To transform a vision to reality, human knowledge and skills are necessary. Indeed, any plan implies that knowledge and skills will be needed for proper implementation. As a matter of fact, today's organizations are in a "knowledge race" in which a key to competitive success is matching how quickly an organization can support reduced cycle time through speed to market (Krell 2001). Of course, plans also require adequate resources, money, and time. But without human qualities to mobilize and apply resources, no plan can ever be implemented.

Theorists have long argued that to implement a strategic business plan successfully, top managers should devote attention to matching appropriate leaders to the strategy. Each part of the organization should be led by someone who wants the strategy to succeed and who also possesses the skills necessary for success. Unfortunately, it is difficult to find the right person for the right leadership job at the right time if nobody worries about the issue until the need arises. This problem is a major one confronting all corporations.

Top managers consistently cite a need for better long-term planning for management talent. By virtue of position, top managers are acutely aware of how important leadership can be in implementing a business plan. Generally, top managers direct less attention to comprehensive HR planning than to leadership planning. The aim of comprehensive HRP is to match available numbers and skills of employees in different job categories to requirements implicit in strategic business plans. Unfortunately, forecasting future skill requirements has been a traditional weakness of HR planning. The reason is that the common practice is to compare numbers of people needed to fill job categories to numbers of people available. In addition, top managers do not establish overall direction for all HR programs to match them to corporate strategy. Alignment of organizational strategy and talent fails because nobody thinks about it (Weiss 2002).

In the top-down approach, a comprehensive HR plan is necessary before strategy can be formulated to guide the Talent Development effort, because the competencies essential to implement strategic business plans are available from more than one source. It is thus necessary to consider alternative ways of obtaining them. If managers need an individual who possesses unique skills, they can (1) recruit from outside the organization; (2) transfer somebody possessing the skills from a different part of the firm on a temporary or permanent basis; (3) contract for talent externally on a short-term or long-term basis; (4) use innovative techniques such as worksharing to get more than one person's talents mobilized to deal with the job's tasks; (5) simplify or change job duties; or (6) train, educate, or develop individuals within the firm. Talent Development activities are appropriate only for the last of these choices. For this reason, other methods of sourcing necessary skills have to be considered before Talent Development plans are formulated. A comprehensive HR planning process affords a means to make these choices.

To use a top-down approach, WLP practitioners have to link up Talent Development plans to plans of the HR department and the organization. Organizational and HR plans must be decided on first before Talent Development plans are formulated. The Talent Development effort is forced into a role in which it can only support these plans. It is driven by them, and thus has little impact on how they are formulated. (See Exhibit 2–3 for a depiction of the top-down approach.)

The Market-Driven Approach. A second way to think of aligning strategic business plans, HR plans, and Talent Development efforts is from a market-oriented perspective. WLP practitioners must build their efforts based on the perceived needs of their stakeholders. In short, they must sell what they do and why they do it. A major problem with the market-driven approach results from the tendency of managers and employees alike to identify learning or development needs on the basis of past problems.

Much effort must be exerted to get people to think about long-term needs that anticipate future requirements. WLP practitioners contribute to a past-oriented bias by using learning-needs assessment techniques that rely on present, rather than future, determinations about the talent needed for organizational success.

Exhibit 2–3: A Simplified Model of Steps in the Top-Down Approach

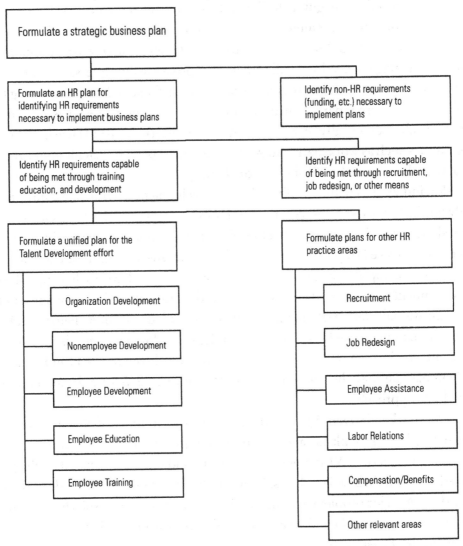

Think of this problem from another perspective: Suppose Company X creates a new product with which consumers are not familiar. At one time, most products were in this category. Consumers experience a need that the new product can satisfy, but are unaware of the need, the product, or both. Products of this kind are referred to as "unsought goods."

To promote these goods, marketing specialists suggest starting with informational advertising. Consumers have to be informed about the product and be convinced of their need for it before they will buy. This step is the beginning of a product-development life cycle. The introduction of a new product begins the cycle. As consumers learn about the product and the needs it satisfies, they purchase it. The product thus gains popularity. More firms begin manufacturing the same product or a substitute. As competition grows stiffer, firms enjoying marketplace advantage due to size, name recognition, or other strengths drive out firms not enjoying such advantages. Eventually, the number of competing firms stabilizes. The product-development life cycle is essentially a learning curve. A visionary entrepreneur begins the cycle by introducing a new product or service. Consumers and competitors learn about the product. Eventually, market factors reduce how many firms are making the product.

Consider Talent Development from this perspective. Acting like entrepreneurs, WLP practitioners can take the lead to identify learning needs before others are aware that they exist. The strategic business plan is a good source for identifying these needs, because it clarifies the firm's direction. WLP practitioners promote instruction designed to meet these unsought needs, showing learners and their superiors what the instruction is and why it will be useful to them in the future.

To use the market-oriented approach, WLP practitioners (1) classify employees into distinct groups, perhaps by job category; (2) predict what competencies employees will probably need in the future to perform in ways consistent with business strategy; (3) assess what competencies are available in each employee group at present; (4) decide how to close gaps between present and future competency requirements; (5) plan training, education, and development to close gaps over time in each group of employees; and (6) mount a promotional campaign to inform managers and employees about strategic business plans and HR plans, implications of those plans for them, and the value of Talent Development programs in preparing for the future.

The Career Planning Approach. A third way to think of aligning strategic business plans, HR plans, and Talent Development efforts is from the individual's career perspective.

Individual career plans must be taken into account if employees are to be committed to a strategic business plan. The organization's plans must be translated into terms that are directly applicable to present and possible future jobs. In order to be motivated, individuals must see "what's in it for them." They must see how they fit in at a future time and be convinced that they will benefit if strategic objectives are met and the strategic business plans are successfully implemented.

To use this approach, WLP practitioners (1) establish individual development programs to provide structure for negotiations between individuals and their superiors, (2) identify learning experiences that will help individuals achieve their career objectives and will, at the same time, help the organization implement its business and HR plans, and (3) facilitate the delivery of these learning experiences.

An individual development program (IDP) must be organized if this approach is to work. An IDP is designed to produce an individualized development plan. It is similar to employee performance appraisal except that the resulting plan is geared to achieving the individual's future career objectives in line with company staffing needs.

The Futuring Approach. A fourth way to align strategic business plans, HR plans, and Talent Development efforts is through the strategy formulation process itself. Formulation can occur formally or informally. If it is formal, then top executives come up with a written business plan. If it is informal, then executives make daily decisions consistent with a formal plan. Most strategy is informal. The essence of strategy formulation is *futuring*, defined as the ability to assess what is happening outside the organization and estimate what consequences will stem from those external trends.

WLP practitioners contribute to the strategy formulation process by facilitating effective interaction of strategists, whether in meetings common to formal planning or in daily interaction between top managers. In either case, *group process*—that is, how strategists get along with each other—is important in obtaining results. Skilled in group-facilitation, WLP practitioners are well-suited to leading creative small-group experiences—precisely what strategic planning meetings should be. WLP practitioners are also well-suited to help strategists cooperate to implement plans through daily decisions.

WLP practitioners can also contribute to strategy formulation by designing structured exercises that aid decision-making. Examples of such exercises include brainstorming, the Delphi procedure, nominal group technique, and scenario generation. Each elicits new ideas that can be important in strategy formulation.

To use this approach, WLP practitioners (1) describe elements of a creative group to strategists prior to formal planning meetings, (2) stimulate strategists to identify ways in which formal meetings could be improved so that group members work together more effectively, (3) encourage strategists to surface and deal with problems of group interaction, (4) use group facilitation skills during formal meetings to help participants interact, and (5) design experiential exercises to help group members structure their thinking on strategic issues.

The Artificial Experience Approach. A fifth way to align strategic business plans, HR plans, and Talent Development efforts is by simulating future conditions.

As noted earlier, one major problem confronts those who try to integrate planning and Talent Development activities: Managers and learners tend to associate learning needs with the problems they have experienced in the past. The trouble with this is that to bring a plan into reality, responding to past needs might not work. After all, future conditions might be quite different than those of the past.

The same problem confronts planners. Plans should not be based on the assumption that the future will be like the past. Nor should planning be a one-shot, one-time-a-year affair. It should instead be approached as a continuous process of learning and improving. Strategy formulation produces long-term objectives, but they should be considered tentative. Objectives should be revised as managers acquire experience or confront new environmental conditions. Unfortunately, most mistakes will have already been made by the time objectives are revised. The point is that most of the time, people feel the need to learn and managers feel the need to change only *after* there are problems, not before.

Is an organization's Talent Development effort doomed to be reactive, geared to meeting needs only after people recognize them? Not necessarily. One way to get around the problem is to simulate future conditions. This has been done before in planning by using *scenarios*, defined as brief narrative descriptions of a possible future. Decision-makers use scenarios to plan what to do and how to do it under future conditions.

WLP practitioners can design learning to produce artificial experience. Such learning does not produce improved skills or more knowledge; rather, it results in the discovery of possible future learning needs. Trainees and their supervisors are jolted into firsthand awareness of the competencies that will be necessary to grapple with future problems confronting them. It is the reverse of the traditional training process: learners *end up with*, rather than begin with, heightened awareness of learning needs. They create, rather than receive, information. They are then motivated to seek people, resources, and activities that help them anticipate future problems. Many computer simulations and many so-called "experiential methods" such as case studies, critical incidents, role plays, simulations, and games can be directed to anticipating future learning needs in this way. They thrust learners into a simulated future world so that they experience it firsthand.

To use this approach, WLP practitioners should (1) apply special approaches to work analysis to identify what the future holds in store for job incumbents (see Rothwell and Kazanas 2002); (2) prepare descriptions of future conditions; (3) design exercises set in the future to give learners vicarious, artificial experience; (4) lead learners through discoveries during the exercises; (5) discuss results of exercises with learners, prompting new insights; (6) guide learners to discover their future learning needs; and (7) help learners prepare action plans so that they can anticipate and meet future learning needs.

There is one major drawback to this approach: the future is not as certain nor as well-defined as the past or present. Learners might have to assess the relative probabilities of several alternative futures as they assess their needs. Their learning plans should include contingency plans to cope with unexpected changes.

The Pulse-Taking Approach. There is a sixth way to align strategic business plans, HR plans, and Talent Development efforts. Training, education, and developmental activities can be used to collect information about how well strategic business plans are being implemented. Small groups become vehicles for surfacing problems posed by the implementation of plans and for brainstorming solutions to those problems. Group instructional efforts "take the pulse" of the organization.

To use this approach, WLP practitioners focus Talent Development activities on a few key issues pertinent to organizational plans and objectives. Practitioners concentrate on helping participants (1) surface problems that impede progress on business plans; (2) define or clarify the problem; (3) consider solutions; (4) examine the value of solutions by using developmental activities for "reality testing"; and (5) devise action steps to implement solutions (Mason and Mitroff 1981).

The Performance Diagnosis Approach. A seventh way to align strategic business plans, HR plans, and Talent Development efforts is to use the needs-assessment process to examine the organization's internal strengths and weaknesses. This information is valuable to managers who are contemplating changes to strategic business plans.

Traditionally, strategists think of strengths and weaknesses from a marketplace perspective. Strengths are what organizations possess that set them apart from other organizations. A weakness is the reverse. It is anything that places organizations at a competitive disadvantage. In this sense, strengths and weaknesses exist only in comparison to competitors.

There are, however, other ways to think of organizational strengths and weaknesses. They have to do with differences between

1. *The ideal and the actual*: How well does the organization measure up to what strategists would like it to be? When it does measure up, it possesses strengths; when it does not measure up, it possesses weaknesses.

2. *The possible and the actual*: Are some divisions, work groups, or individuals performing better than others? What accounts for these differences? When differences do not exist, the organization possesses strengths; when variations exist, there are weaknesses.

3. *Desirable state-of-the-art methods and those that are less-effective, less-efficient, or less-progressive*: How well is the organization taking advantage of new ideas and technology? How well is the organization taking advantage of best practices uncovered through benchmarking? When the organization is not taking advantage of new ideas or technology, weakness exists; when it is taking advantage of new ideas, strength exists.

Assessments of strengths and weaknesses provide clues about possible strategy. There are two basic approaches to strategy formulation. The first, called the *inside-outside approach* (Huse 1982), examines strengths and weaknesses in order to determine what an organization is doing better than its competitors. Strategy is based on identifying organizational strengths and building on them. The second, called the *outside-inside approach* (Huse 1982), examines the world outside the organization to identify trends that may pose future threats and/or opportunities to the firm. The key to strategy selection is averting threats or seizing the advantages to be gained by opportunities.

When analyzing performance problems, WLP practitioners frequently encounter information of value in strategy making. Developmental efforts only solve performance problems caused by lack of knowledge or skill. Yet poor performance quite often stems from more than one cause: inappropriate reward systems, poor feedback on performance mismatches between duties and people doing them, conflicts between individuals or work groups stemming from poor organization or job design, and so on.

Information about performance problems, collected during needs assessment or during developmental activities, can be fed back to strategists for use in subsequent planning so that corrective action can be taken. This approach provides a descriptive, intuitive element lacking in the stark figures of financial reporting. This information is needed because organizational leaders are sometimes at a loss to explain why their organizations are effective or ineffective.

The Educational Approach. An eighth way to align strategic business plans, HR plans, and Talent Development efforts is to focus attention on enhancing strategic thinking skill. Many problems are attributable to short-term thinking. But focusing attention on building strategic thinking skill might help correct these problems (Kaufman 1998). And, of course, strategy making itself is a learned skill (Christensen 1997).

There are at least three ways by which to build competence in strategic thinking. The first is *education*. Participants learn generally about the theory of strategic thinking. Applying on the job what they learn in training is left up to them. The second is *education tied to training*. Participants learn generally about the theory of strategic thinking and then about the strategic plan of their organization. Then they develop action plans to relate what they do in their work to what must happen if strategic business plans are to be successfully implemented. The third is *training*. Participants are taught specific skills they will need to achieve strategic objectives. Regardless of which form is used, instruction on strategic thinking helps position the organization so that it learns through experience (Bartlett, Ghosal 1998). In today's fast-paced work settings, the ability of managers and employees to respond to customer needs in real time is a key strategy advantage. People can be taught how to do that (Wall 1997).

Off-the-shelf instructional programs can be purchased from commercial publishers for pure education. Education tied to training requires the help of WLP practitioners to design the instruction so that training content is carefully tailored to the unique requirements of the employer. Pure training may also require a great deal of tailor-made instruction.

Managers can engage in active learning to learn what they need to do to implement strategic business plans. They can then return to their respective work groups and develop joint action plans with subordinates along similar lines.

To use the educational approach, WLP practitioners should first clarify their primary purpose. Is it to help individuals become better strategic thinkers? If so, pure education is appropriate. Is it to help individuals learn generally about strategic thinking and about how to apply it in their jobs? If so, education tied to training is appropriate. Is the purpose to help those at every level of the organization learn how to translate broad strategic business plans into specific action plans to guide their work groups or jobs? If so, pure training is appropriate.

Once purpose has been clarified, it is then possible to select or design instructional materials consistent with it, deliver instruction, and follow up after instruction to see how well it is applied.

The Interpersonal Approach. There is a ninth way to align strategic business plans, HR plans, and Talent Development efforts: WLP practitioners can improve their access to top managers. A substantial percentage of corporate strategy is informal, existing only in the minds of top managers. For WLP practitioners to be aware of informal plans, they must increase interaction with and serve the interests of top managers. Few corporate planners or corporate WLP practitioners would disagree that greater access to top managers is desirable.

Increasing interaction with top managers is, of course, easier said than done. Too often, WLP managers are accorded junior rather than senior executive status. They are denied direct access to the chief executive officer and perhaps to other top managers. The HR vice president is often the only top manager to whom they have access. As a consequence, information they receive and whatever they try to communicate is filtered through a third party—the HR chief.

What can be done about this problem? The answer depends on the situation. Recently hired or promoted WLP managers might be able to take advantage of the license accorded newcomers to get a foot in the door, so to speak, with top managers (Rothwell and Sredl 2000). They can request appointments with higher-ups and, in so doing, establish the foothold denied to their predecessors. Once the foothold is established, they can take full advantage of it to gather information about the values, goals, and strategies of top managers.

For those who do not enjoy the license accorded newcomers but who wish to gain access to strategists, several approaches are possible:

1. Identify a problem that troubles people at the top. Take action on it in a highly visible way.
2. Schedule a meeting to discuss the importance of access to top managers. Ask to form a management or training advisory committee consisting of senior executives. (The worst that can happen is that the request will be denied.) Ask the CEO to help organize such a committee—and ask him or her to be a member.
3. Lobby for support from people who already have access to top managers. Use grassroots pressure in hopes that it leads to success.

Do some brainstorming if none of these alternatives seems to fit the situation. What can you do to get a foot in the door with senior executives?

Those who succeed can ask strategists this question: What Talent Development activities can help solve their problems? If that question does not produce useful answers, ask them to describe the organization as they would like to see it at some point in the future, and ask them what barriers stand in the way. Talent Development efforts can then be planned to remove the barriers.

The Rifle Approach. A tenth way to align strategic business plans, HR plans, and Talent Development efforts is to restrict the scope of training, education, and development so that they focus on just a few strategic objectives of the organization. The term "rifle" is apt to describe this approach because it connotes a highly directed, concentrated effort that is focused on a strategic issue. It differs from a shotgun approach that attempts to link Talent Development activities to all strategic objectives.

Some WLP practitioners think all their activities should be linked directly to corporate plans. That need not be the case. Instead, they can single out a few major problems impeding strategy implementation. One way is to start small with a pilot and score a highly visible success. Early success is very important in any change effort. One small success often leads to future encouragement and greater opportunities.

To use the rifle approach, WLP practitioners should identify one or two problems lending themselves to solutions through training, education, or development. These problems should also be related to the organization's strategic business objectives. WLP practitioners should then analyze the problems, consider and implement solutions, communicate results so that others will be interested in similar efforts in the future, and repeat this process. These steps can lead to incremental change in the organization through Talent Development initiatives.

It is worth emphasizing at this point that the rifle approach is, in the authors' opinion, comparable to issue-based strategic management, where decision-makers select a problem, challenge, or other issue and focus strategic thinking and planning around it. Many efforts in the field of Talent Development have tended to foster this view. Specific business problems such as "weak bench strength" is examined as an issue to be addressed. A project plan is then established to meet that need. Issues have life cycles: they become apparent, they are addressed, and then they fade away if the intervention is successful. Issues lend themselves to solutions that rely on project management to be implemented. One study of over 2,000 articles on strategic HRD issues concluded that issue-based strategy is a commonly mentioned theme in research on strategic Talent Development.

Choosing an Approach. Each approach described in the preceding sections is a way to align a strategic business plan, an HR plan, and a Talent Development effort. But when is one more-appropriate to use than another?

Generally speaking, practitioners should strive for as many linkages between Talent Development activities and business plans as possible, as long as top managers devote more than mere lip service to formal planning (the process) and are committed to implementing plans (the products of the planning process). But even when top managers are not committed to formal planning processes and products, WLP practitioners still bear responsibility to act in ways that help strategists realize their vision of the future, no matter how poorly that vision is conceptualized or communicated.

In each organizational setting, WLP practitioners and operating managers should decide for themselves what relationships should exist between strategic business plans, HR plans, and Talent Development efforts. They will then need to establish or strengthen these relationships. Finally, they have to come up with their vision of the Talent Development effort and the role of the WLP department in helping make the vision a reality. Armed with this information, WLP practitioners will find it easy to clarify the purpose of the Talent Development effort and the WLP department.

How is the purpose of a Talent Development effort clarified?

Talent Development is only a tool for identifying and meeting the learning needs of an organization and the individuals employed in it. But how is the purpose of the Talent Development effort clarified? Previous sections of this chapter have provided clues. At this point, it is appropriate to describe concrete ways to clarify the formal purpose of a Talent Development effort.

Formulating the Purpose of the Talent Development Effort. There are at least two ways to formulate a purpose statement for a Talent Development effort.

The first is perhaps easiest. Beginning with the formal purpose statement of the organization (assuming that such a statement exists), the highest-level WLP executive should break down that statement into components pertaining to the organization's business, major areas of service, customers served, methods of competition, and philosophy. Working with top managers of the organization, the WLP executive should then construct a rough-draft purpose statement for the Talent Development effort based on the organization's purpose statement, specifying how the organization's Talent Development effort and activities will contribute to the organization's purpose. It should also answer the following questions:

1. What should be the role of the Talent Development effort in the organization?

2. What should be the role of Talent Development in each part of the organization?

3. How should the Talent Development effort meet learning needs of each stakeholder group?

4. How should the Talent Development effort help the organization compete against other firms?

5. How should the Talent Development effort reflect what strategists believe about the way the business should be conducted?

This draft purpose statement should then be circulated for comment to key stakeholders of Talent Development activities. Using these comments, the WLP executive can revise the purpose statement. Finally, he or she should communicate this statement to others through new-employee orientation, budget documents, course descriptions, training brochures, and so on.

A purpose statement of this kind clarifies what the Talent Development effort is supposed to do and why. It makes explicit how the Talent Development effort contributes to the organization's purpose. It also helps guide operations, keeping WLP practitioners and operating managers on track by reminding them about appropriate areas for action. While it is possible to clarify the purpose of the Talent Development effort without obtaining comment from others, the process of circulating the formal purpose statement communicates the role of the Talent Development effort, builds support from others, and clarifies responsibilities. Generally, participation by others in this clarification process is highly desirable.

A second way to formulate a purpose statement for a Talent Development effort is to begin with possible relationships between strategic business plans, HR plans, and Talent Development efforts undertaken by the organization (and often coordinated by WLP practitioners). WLP practitioners first examine how effective the effort is at

I   Supporting strategic business plans and HR plans
I   Meeting future learning needs of managers and employees
I   Helping individuals realize their career aspirations
I   Contributing to the formulation of strategic business plans and HR plans
I   Providing artificial experiences of the future
I   Furnishing top managers with information useful for planning
I   Helping managers identify organizational strengths and weaknesses
I   Educating managers about strategic thinking
I   Serving strategists' needs
I   Contributing solutions to problems of long-term significance to the organization

As a second step, WLP practitioners and operating managers clarify what they believe to be a desirable relationship between the Talent Development effort and any number of issues listed previously. WLP practitioners and operating managers can then (1) pinpoint gaps between present and desirable relationships of the Talent Development effort to any of these issues and (2) clarify the role of Talent Development in closing the gaps. The resulting purpose statement links the Talent Development effort directly to a specific issue or group of issues. However, no explicit linkage exists between the organization's purpose and that of the Talent Development effort.

We have described two distinct ways to formulate a purpose statement for a Talent Development effort. These are not mutually exclusive, however. They may be used separately or together, depending on the preferences of those using them. It is important, though, to take time to formulate some kind of formal purpose statement for the Talent Development effort. Without it, WLP practitioners and operating managers will not be able to carry out subsequent steps in the strategic development of talent.

Changing the Purpose Statement. How much attention should be devoted to formulating the purpose statement of the Talent Development effort? When should this statement be revised or changed?

The proper amount of attention to devote to formulating a purpose statement depends on the benefits expected to result from the process. The time spent is worthwhile if it builds support among operating managers, motivates WLP staff, clarifies accountability, establishes a clearer sense of direction about the Talent Development effort among operating managers and WLP staff, and excites enthusiasm for Talent Development. The process of discussing the purpose of the Talent Development effort is probably more important than the product of these discussions. After all, the process is likely to increase the commitment of participants.

As long as the formal purpose statement guides and describes the Talent Development effort, it need not be changed. However, the purpose statement—and its underlying assumptions—should be reviewed when

1. Managers perceive that Talent Development activities are mediocre or do not meet the needs of those they are intended to serve.

2. People compare the Talent Development effort unfavorably to typical practices in the industry or to best practices in other firms, even those in other industries.

3. The organization changes its strategic business plan or undergoes a merger, an acquisition, a takeover, or a buy-out.

4. Major new initiatives are about to be undertaken in the organization's HR practices, such as compensation/benefits or labor relations.

5. A new top-management team or a new CEO joins the organization.

6. A new director of WLP is appointed.

7. External environmental conditions place new and unexpected demands on people in the organization.

In each case, new conditions might render past assumptions out of date.

What are the effects of organizational philosophy and culture on the purpose of the Talent Development effort?

Organizational philosophy and culture are important to consider in articulating the purpose of a Talent Development effort. *Philosophy* means attitudes and beliefs about "what we do and why we do it." It refers to shared values, beliefs, and norms unique to one organizational setting.

The Philosophy of Talent Development. Practitioners in any field vary in what they believe about what they do. Though "philosophy" has a vaguely abstract sound, it rests at the heart of any purposeful activity. It is a system of beliefs and values, and it is useful because it helps determine purpose, define the roles of people working in WLP departments, change Talent Development activities and strategies, and set priorities among competing alternatives. Though not as specific as a formal purpose statement, philosophy is more important because it guides daily decision-making in pervasive yet elusive ways.

What is the starting point for articulating a Talent Development philosophy? Perhaps the best place to start is to do some soul-searching. What do you believe about Talent Development? How would you describe the mission of the WLP department? What role should operating managers and individuals play in the Talent Development effort? Why do you answer as you do?

Organizational Culture. WLP practitioners are not completely free to behave in ways consistent with their own personal philosophies. After all, they function in organizational settings that have their own meanings. The meanings implicit in a setting are synonymous with *culture*, defined as "the pattern of basic assumptions that a given group has invented, discovered, or developed in learning to cope with problems . . . and that have worked well enough to be considered valid, and therefore to be taught to members as the correct way to perceive, think, and feel in relation to those problems" (Schein 1984, 3). Culture and formal purpose are related when people in an organization share beliefs and act in ways generally consistent with values implicit in a purpose statement; organizational culture and Talent Development philosophy are related when WLP practitioners share the beliefs of organizational members and act in accordance with formal and informal norms of conduct.

Strategic business planning theorists have long debated whether culture poses more of a constraint or an opportunity for planning. Some believe that changing culture is too expensive and takes too long to be useful in implementing strategic plans; others disagree with this view. It is clear, however, that too often top managers are not well-versed enough about particular strengths and weaknesses of their organization. When a firm is doing poorly, top managers are quick to suggest change. Yet problems might have less to do with the wrong culture, strategy, or goals than with poor alignment between existing goals and the organization. In some cases, strategy fails because it conflicts with corporate purpose or identity.

A formal purpose statement can be the highest expression of culture. It can encapsulate in one sentence or paragraph the official view of what the organization should be and how it should serve the needs of its consumers or stakeholders. However, the process of formulating this statement is an empty exercise when it is focused only on economic issues like return on investment, is the product of only a few executives, and is merely descriptive of what the organization has been instead of what it should become in the future.

A change in formal purpose implies a change in strategy and culture. This change should trigger a chain reaction in which the purpose of each unit or structural component is reexamined as it relates to the whole organization. At the same time, members of each unit experience a role crisis in which they are temporarily unsure of how their jobs relate to the unit and how the unit relates to the organization. For strategic change to be implemented successfully, it is important to reduce the duration of this role crisis so that individuals carry out their work in ways consistent with a new strategic business plan.

Any Talent Development effort should reflect, at least to some extent, the organizational culture of the firm. Of course, some practitioners may be interested in changing that culture or in helping others to do so. Even in these cases, it is important to begin the change effort from the standpoint of a thorough understanding of what the culture is before taking action or drawing conclusions about what the culture should be.

Perhaps the best place to start is with a *culture audit*, a systematic examination of organizational beliefs. To conduct such an audit, WLP practitioners should survey key stakeholders and others in order to collect stories and myths about the firm. (Ethnographic interviewing techniques can be very helpful for this purpose). These stories can then be used as the basis for studies and other experiential exercises of value in training newcomers or performers in "how things are done around here." Some organizations have more pronounced cultures than others, making audits of this kind all the more challenging.

Information about culture can be valuable to the process of clarifying the purpose of a Talent Development effort.

Activity 2–1: The Purpose of the Talent Development Effort

Directions: Use this activity to do some brainstorming about the purpose of a Talent Development effort in an organization. For each question in the left column, provide a response in the right column. (There are no right or wrong responses, though some will be more useful than others in some organizations.) Continue your response on additional paper if needed. At the end, prepare a rough draft statement applicable to the Talent Development effort in the organization you are examining.

Questions	Responses
1. What *is* the responsibility of the Talent Development effort in contributing to overall business objectives?	
2. What *should be* the responsibility of the Talent Development effort in contributing to overall business objectives?	
3. What *are* the organization's major areas of service? What *is* the responsibility of the Talent Development effort in each area?	
4. What *should be* the organization's major areas of service? What is the responsibility of the Talent Development effort in each area?	
5. What are the major groups of stakeholders with which the organization must deal? What *is* the responsibility of the Talent Development effort to meet the learning needs of each group?	
6. What *should be* the responsibility of the Talent Development effort to meet the learning needs of each group?	
7. What is the organization's philosophy of doing business? How do Talent Development efforts contribute to the practice of that philosophy?	
8. How should the Talent Development effort contribute to the organization's philosophy of doing business?	

Activity 2–1: *(continued)*

Questions	Responses
9. What *is* the purpose of the Talent Development effort in dealing with such cultural issues in the organization as:	
a. individual autonomy?	
b. structure?	
c. support?	
d. identity?	
e. linkages between performance and rewards?	
f. conflict tolerance?	
g. risk tolerance?	
10. What should be the responsibility of the Talent Development effort in dealing with such cultural issues as:	
a. individual autonomy?	
b. structure?	
c. support?	
d. identity?	
e. linkages between performance and rewards?	
f. conflict tolerance?	
g. risk tolerance?	

Activity 2–1: *(continued)*

Questions	Responses
11. What *is* the responsibility of the Talent Development effort in the organization for	
a. supporting implementation of strategic business plans? HR plans?	
b. meeting perceived future learning needs of managers and employees?	
c. helping individuals realize their career aspirations?	
d. formulating strategic business plans and HR plans?	
e. providing employees with artificial experiences of the future so that they can identify their own learning needs?	
f. providing top managers with information for use in strategic business planning?	
g. identifying organizational strengths and weaknesses?	
h. educating managers and employees to think strategically?	
i. serving needs of strategists?	
j. dealing with specific issues, problems, or projects of strategic importance to the organization?	

Activity 2–1: *(continued)*

Questions	Responses
12. What *should be* the responsibility of the Talent Development effort in the organization for	
a. supporting implementation of strategic business plans? HR plans?	
b. meeting perceived future learning needs of managers and employees?	
c. helping individuals realize their career aspirations?	
d. formulating strategic business plans and HR plans?	
e. providing employees with artificial experiences of the future so that they can identify their own learning needs?	
f. educating managers and employees to think strategically?	
g. serving needs of strategists?	
h. dealing with specific issues, problems, or projects of strategic importance to the organization?	

The Purpose Statement

Using the answers to the preceding questions, prepare a rough-draft purpose statement for the Talent Development effort in the organization. Try to keep it as short and concise as possible, but be sure to include the most-important areas of responsibility. Remember: Any purpose statement should answer the question "*Why are we doing this?*"

Activity 2–2: Improving Relationships between a Strategic Business Plan, an HR Plan, and a Talent Development Effort

Directions: Use this simple activity to organize your thinking. For each approach listed below in Column 1 and briefly described in Column 2, describe in Column 3 what can be done in an organization to use this approach or improve the way that the approach is being used. Continue your response on additional paper if necessary. There are no right or wrong responses.

Column 1	Column 2	Column 3
Approach	*Brief Description*	*What can be done in an organization to:* 1. Use the approach? 2. Improve the way the approach is being used?
1. Top-Down Approach	The Talent Development effort is used to support implementation of organizational and HR plans, and is driven by those plans.	
2. Market-Driven Approach	The Talent Development effort is used to identify future learning needs and to convince people to meet those needs.	
3. Career Planning Approach	The Talent Development effort is a tool for helping individuals realize their own career plans.	
4. Futuring Approach	The Talent Development effort is used to provide assistance to top management strategists in formulating strategic plans.	
5. Artificial Experience Approach	The Talent Development effort is used to simulate future conditions, helping individuals identify their own learning needs.	
6. Pulse-Taking Approach	In the course of Talent Development efforts, WLP practitioners and others collect information about how well the organization's strategic plans are being implemented, and later feed this back to the strategists.	

Activity 2–2: *(continued)*

Column 1	Column 2	Column 3
Approach	Brief Description	What can be done in an organization to: 1. Use the approach? 2. Improve the way the approach is being used?
7. Performance Diagnosis Approach	In the course of assessing Talent Development needs, WLP practitioners and others identify problems of larger scope, and provide that information to strategists for their use in strategic business planning.	
8. Educational Approach	WLP practitioners and others work to teach people how to think strategically.	
9. Interpersonal Approach	WLP practitioners and others interact with the strategists, identifying their beliefs and communicating those beliefs to others.	
10. Rifle Approach	WLP practitioners and others concentrate their attention on issues, problems, or projects of strategic importance.	

Activity 2–3: A Culture Audit

Directions: Use this activity to structure your thinking about the status of the organization's culture and the role of the HRD effort in dealing with it. While the activity can be used by members of the HRD department, it can be readily converted to a survey for use in collecting data from the organization's employees. For each question in Column 1 below, circle a code in Column 2 representing the present status of the organization, and a code in Column 3 representing the desired status. (There are no right or wrong responses.) Finally, in Column 4, briefly describe what should be the role of an HRD effort in narrowing gaps between organizational culture as it is and as it should be. There is space for remarks at the end of the activity. Use the following scale in marking your responses to Columns 2 and 3:

0 represents no amount; 1 represents a very small extent; 2 represents a small extent; 3 represents an adequate extent; 4 represents a large extent; 5 represents a very large extent

Column 1	Column 2					Column 3					Column 4
Questions about Culture	*Actual Conditions*					*Desired Conditions*					*What should be the role of a Talent Development effort in narrowing gaps between actual and desired cultural conditions in this organization?*
	No extent				Very large extent	No extent				Very large extent	
Indicate how much you agree with each statement below.	1	2	3	4	5	1	2	3	4	5	
1. Employees believe that they have responsibility for results.	1	2	3	4	5	1	2	3	4	5	
2. Employees believe that they have independence to carry out their work.	1	2	3	4	5	1	2	3	4	5	
3. Employees believe that they are free to exercise individual initiative.	1	2	3	4	5	1	2	3	4	5	

Activity 2–3: *(continued)*

Column 1	Column 2					Column 3					Column 4
Questions about Culture	*Actual Conditions*					*Desired Conditions*					*What should be the role of a Talent Development effort in narrowing gaps between actual and desired cultural conditions in this organization?*
	No extent				Very large extent	No extent				Very large extent	
Indicate how much you agree with each statement below.	1	2	3	4	5	1	2	3	4	5	
4. Employees believe that their work behavior is guided significantly by organizational rules and regulations.	1	2	3	4	5	1	2	3	4	5	
5. Employees believe that they receive adequate supervision.	1	2	3	4	5	1	2	3	4	5	
6. Employees receive adequate assistance from their superiors.	1	2	3	4	5	1	2	3	4	5	
7. Employees enjoy close interpersonal relations with their superiors.	1	2	3	4	5	1	2	3	4	5	
8. Employees feel that their primary allegiance is to the organization as a whole.	1	2	3	4	5	1	2	3	4	5	

Activity 2–3: *(continued)*

Column 1	Column 2					Column 3						Column 4
Questions about Culture	*Actual Conditions*					*Desired Conditions*						*What should be the role of a Talent Development effort in narrowing gaps between actual and desired cultural conditions in this organization?*
	No extent				*Very large extent*	*No extent*					*Very large extent*	
Indicate how much you agree with each statement below.	1	2	3	4	5	1	2	3	4	5		
9. Employees believe that there is a strong link between how they perform individually and the rewards they receive.	1	2	3	4	5	1	2	3	4	5		
10. Employees believe that significant, destructive conflict exists in relationships between their peers.	1	2	3	4	5	1	2	3	4	5		
11. Employees believe that significant, destructive conflict exists in relation-ships between work groups in the organization.	1	2	3	4	5	1	2	3	4	5		
12. People in the organization confront conflict openly.	1	2	3	4	5	1	2	3	4	5		

Activity 2–3: *(continued)*

Column 1	Column 2						Column 3						Column 4
Questions about Culture	*Actual Conditions*						*Desired Conditions*						*What should be the role of a Talent Development effort in narrowing gaps between actual and desired cultural conditions in this organization?*
	No extent					*Very large extent*	*No extent*					*Very large extent*	
Indicate how much you agree with the statement below.	1	2	3	4		5	1	2	3	4		5	
13. Employees perceive there is freedom to take risks in the organization.	1	2	3	4		5	1	2	3	4		5	
Are there are other characteristics of the organization's culture that you believe to be important? Please specify in the space to the right.													

Remarks

Activity 2–4: A Case Study on the Purpose of the Talent Development Effort

Directions: Read the scenario below and answer the questions that follow.

George P. Willis has just been hired to set up a comprehensive Talent Development effort at The Larson Trust, a large bank.*

Larson is over 100 years old, and employs 10,000 people in a large metropolitan area in the eastern United States. Larson's management has long been skeptical of planned learning activities of any kind. Though nationally known for its innovations in banking, its reputation for Talent Development is backward for the industry. The bank's senior officers have undertaken this initiative in Talent Development because of widespread complaints by middle management.

George Willis has been hired away from another large bank, where for ten years he ran a comprehensive Talent Development effort. Willis is a zealot about Talent Development. He earned an M.B.A. from the Wharton School and completed a Ph.D. in Education, specializing in instructional design, from Indiana University. Willis has a free hand to start up the Talent Development effort however he wants. His budget for the present year is negligible, but he has been told that any reasonable request will not be refused. The company management is watching Willis closely.

Questions

1.   What should Willis do to clarify the role of the Talent Development effort?
2.   If you were in Willis's position, what would you do during the first month? The first year? Why? Explain your reasoning.

* This case is fictitious, but does bear similarities to several real situations.

PART II

ASSESSING NEEDS AND SCANNING THE ENVIRONMENT

Most authorities in the strategic business planning field believe that strategy should be formulated only after an analysis is done of an organization's present strengths and weaknesses and its future opportunities and threats. A SWOT analysis (strengths, weaknesses, opportunities, and threats) is a common strategic planning tool.

A similar analysis should be done to look at talent. The chapters in Part II focus on the elements of Strengths, Weaknesses, Opportunities, and Threats for talent. Chapter 3, entitled "Comprehensive Needs Assessment," is about examining what needs (deficiencies) exist with the organization's existing talent pool. Of course, strengths should also be identified.

Chapter 4 is about *environmental scanning*, the process of identifying the possible future opportunities and threats that might stem from future environmental change. This chapter defines and describes environmental scanning as it is applied to SBP. It also discusses how the same approach can be applied usefully to Talent Development.

CHAPTER 3

COMPREHENSIVE NEEDS ASSESSMENT

Ask experienced WLP practitioners what they believe the starting point is for planning Talent Development and most will probably give the same answer: a *needs assessment*. (A few streetwise types might say *management commitment*, but let's focus on the most common answer.) If needs assessment is the starting point for planning one Talent Development experience, what should be the starting point for planning *all* organized learning events in an organization? The answer is **comprehensive needs assessment:** a broad, systematic examination of conditions conducted for the purpose of identifying general differences between what people should know or do and what they actually know or do.

Comprehensive needs assessment is the second step in the model of SDT presented in Chapter 1. It naturally follows the first step in the model—determining the purpose of the Talent Development effort. Managers and employees must be thoroughly familiar with present conditions before they can effectively plan for the future and consistently act in line with a predetermined purpose. Much strategy fails because managers are unaware of the present competitive positioning of their organization, as well as its present strengths, weaknesses, and core competencies. A map will not help you find your way if you do not know your present position, and the same basic principle applies whether attention is focused on organizational strategy or an organizational strategic learning plan.

Comprehensive Needs Assessment: Definition and Description

Comprehensive needs assessment is similar to situation analysis in strategic business planning. *Situation analysis* is an examination of company performance. Its focus is usually on present relationships between the organization and its competitors. Its purpose is to evaluate the status of the organization. Abels (2002) relates this internal appraisal step to external environmental scanning, noting that both amount to an environmental scan, but focus on different environments.

In educational settings, instructional planners sometimes undertake a similar kind of analysis. When assessing needs for a "course," they might focus on one discipline, issue, or problem. But when assessment is directed to, say, a curriculum as an instructional plan spanning all learning experiences sponsored by a school, the focus is more general. Educators typically examine the full range of human needs, and consider which ones the school should try to meet and how well they should strive to meet them.

This broad philosophical question of which needs should be addressed is one that must be considered on many levels—not just on one level. First, which needs must be addressed in order to comply with public policy and legal mandate? Second, which needs must be addressed so that the school is responsible to the community and the society it serves? Third, which needs do learners and teachers feel should be addressed? Fourth, which needs result from economic and labor market conditions, technological change, and so on?

Unfortunately, educators seldom address all these issues. Tradition, not analysis, drives most educational planning at primary and secondary school levels. Nor do WLP practitioners handle the process much better in work settings: formal needs assessment is rarely carried out there, either. When it is, no attempt is made to plan for meeting long-term learning needs. Rather, the focus is typically on solving specific problems and delivering specific training to solve them. Yet strategic business plans clearly imply a need for human skills. A formal Talent Development effort is one way to meet those learning needs through the development of skills within an organization over time.

Viewed in this context, *comprehensive needs assessment* is **the process of specifying present but general gaps between what people should know or do**

and what they actually know or do. It pinpoints not just needs *(weaknesses)*, but also significant talents, skills, or competencies *(strengths)*. It thus clarifies what people are doing well and not so well. Regarded another way, it assesses the strategists' vision of what should be to what capabilities the organization and its people presently possess.

Needs Assessment: Background Issues

A learning need is traditionally considered to be a deficiency between *what is* and *what should be,* between present conditions and present criteria. An important point to stress is this: *A need implies that the deficiency is caused by lack of learner knowledge or skill.* It is a weakness in organizational talent. Of course, needs *can* stem from root causes within the work environment that, unlike individual needs, fall under management control (Rothwell and Sredl 2000). Examples would include lack of supervisory planning or lack of proper tools and equipment. Needs stemming from such root causes, of course, cannot be appropriately met through instruction. They will require alternative management action.

The history of needs assessment in Talent Development begins with the work of McGehee and Thayer, who in 1967 suggested that needs should be identified by synthesizing the results of three different examinations: First, WLP practitioners should analyze the organization and identify instructional needs stemming from production, legal, and other requirements. This is called *organization analysis.* Second, practitioners should direct attention to jobs and identify instructional needs stemming from work tasks. This is called *operation* or *work analysis.* Third, practitioners should focus on people working in the organization, and identify instructional needs stemming from individual performance problems. This is called *individual analysis.* Each analysis should be separately performed and the results compared to yield instructional needs. Sources of information vary for each type of analysis.

Traditional needs assessment is thus based on problem-solving. When decision-makers perceive that a difference exists between their expectations and actual results, they are actually detecting a problem that warrants attention. Only if the problem is caused by a lack of knowledge or skill is it properly classified as an instructional need. If the problem is caused by something other than a lack of knowledge or skill, such as poor motivation or morale, poor job structure, poor work incentives, or another cause, it is a *noninstructional need* requiring management action other than training, education, or development. Thomas Gilbert (1967) was among the first to draw this distinction between instructional and noninstructional needs. He contended that WLP practitioners should look beyond mere instructional solutions to any appropriate, cost-effective performance improvement strategy for dealing with problems. Building on this idea, Geary Rummler (1976) proposed comprehensive performance audits to identify improvement programs yielding high payoffs by making jobs more efficient and effective. Audits of this kind examine (1) job context, (2) incumbents, (3) desired actions or decisions, (4) results, and (5) feedback to incumbents on results. There are three levels of analysis: (1) *policy,* focusing on identifying performance improvement programs that yield the highest payoff; (2) *strategy,* focusing on ways of defining and improving a job; and (3) *tactics,* focusing on specific ways to make people more efficient.

In another classic treatment, Dugan Laird (1985) distinguished between two types of instructional needs. The first type he called a *microtraining need,* arising from individuals: Whenever one person or a small group faces change of any kind requiring new knowledge or a new skill, a microtraining need exists. Whenever people are hired, promoted, transferred, or temporarily reassigned to a new job, they will likely require special instruction in order to perform effectively. Microtraining needs can also be identified by reviewing individual performance appraisals, career contracts, a group's production record, and quality control reports.

The second type is a *macrotraining need,* arising from change in the organization: Whenever groups of people face change requiring new knowledge or skills, there is a macrotraining need. For example, macrotraining needs stem from changes in strategic business plans, personnel policies, organizational structure, production methods, sales policies, and government laws or regulations.

Laird's distinction between microtraining and macrotraining needs is important for several reasons. First, it positions the WLP practitioner in a role somewhat like that of an air traffic controller. To speak figuratively, the practitioner monitors a radar screen sweeping the environment (Rothwell and Sredl 2000). Changes occurring inside or outside the organization appear as blips on the screen. Some blips require action—that is, planned learning activities intended to help people cope with change. A second reason is that change differs by degree. Not all blips are the same size or are configured the same way. The scope of corrective action depends on the scope of the problem. Finally, Laird implies that some changes are predictable, even cyclical. They recur. No matter how stable the organization, some needs keep coming up. Newly hired, transferred, or promoted employees have to be oriented to new jobs, for instance. This need recurs every time an individual's duties change. On the other hand, some changes are neither predictable nor recurrent. An industry's deregulation might be apparent for years, but it will probably not unfold in any predictable way. This kind of trend might call for learning activities so that people build the competencies they need that are pertinent to the change.

From long tradition, WLP practitioners have thus viewed instruction as a means of rectifying deficiencies or solving performance problems. Needs assessment is really a form of deficiency analysis. It uncovers areas in which present conditions are not as good as desired conditions.

There is another side to performance, of course. In some areas, people excel: the organization outperforms competitors; individuals do better than the minimum standards established for them; and job results turn out better than expected. In each case, condition is better than criteria. When the cause of this favorable discrepancy stems from human knowledge and skill, it is a special talent or core competency.

Steps in Comprehensive Needs Assessment

There are several appropriate ways to carry out a comprehensive needs assessment. However, at some point WLP practitioners and line managers should

1. Identify learners to be served by the Talent Development effort over time. More specifically, who are the learners and prospective learners? Where are they located? How many are there? How can the learners be reached?

How intense is their motivation to learn? When are they most interested in learning?

2. Classify learners into broad "market segments."

3. Compare actual to desired competencies for each market segment of learners.

4. Identify present learning needs for each market and market segment of learners.

When actual knowledge and skills minus desired knowledge and skills equals a *deficiency*, then it is classified as a *weakness*. On the other hand, if actual knowledge and skills minus desired knowledge and skills equals a *proficiency*, then it is classified as a *strength*.

These steps are worth considering in more detail.

Identifying Learners

To assess instructional needs, WLP practitioners should collect as much information as possible about present and prospective learners and clients. A *learner* is one receiving and participating in planned learning activities. A *client* is one who wants and benefits directly from those activities. The distinction between learner and client is sometimes vague. There are several reasons why: (1) Learners benefit directly from instruction and are sometimes the only clients. (2) Employees' superiors at all levels are responsible for Talent Development activities and are properly considered clients. (3) Superiors might participate in design and delivery of planned learning and might learn in the process, but they are not considered learners if learning strategies are intended to meet the needs of their subordinates.

WLP practitioners are always engaged in meeting the needs of at least two markets: the learners and their organizational superiors. The strategic implications of this should not be ignored. WLP practitioners, like marketing specialists, have two basic options: (1) to satisfy perceived needs of both groups (learners and clients/supervisors) as much as possible or (2) to concentrate on satisfying the needs of one group more than the needs of the other. Most practitioners try to satisfy the needs of both groups, while gearing their efforts to meeting the needs that would be difficult for alternative sources of instruction (like external vendors, colleges, or universities) to supply. External providers of education or training are competitors to in-house WLP departments when instructional activities are not tailored to the learners' precise working conditions.

WLP practitioners are well-positioned to detect learning needs and gather detailed information. In this respect, they enjoy a competitive advantage over external providers of instruction. In short, in-house instruction is more easily tailored to the employing firm. *Specific instruction* is useful only to the one organization providing it; *general instruction* is readily transferable to other firms, and improves the employability of learners. Managers have an incentive to offer specific instruction in-house because learners receiving it are far less likely to quit and thus take personal advantage of company-funded improvement of their skills. The learners also have an incentive to participate in such in-house learning experiences because participation in organizationally sponsored training is most likely to translate into higher pay.

To identify instructional needs, WLP practitioners have to research their markets—the learners and the clients. If the Talent Development effort is geared solely to employees, then information has to be collected about them. If it is geared solely to the external consumers of company products or services, then information has to be collected about them. If the Talent Development effort is comprehensive, then information has to be collected both about learners and clients.

A written purpose of the Talent Development effort provides direction to information-gathering by clarifying targeted learners, types of instructional activities to be offered, methods of offering those services, and follow-up activities to ensure that learning is subsequently applied.

Classifying Learners by Market Segment

WLP practitioners have to assess learning needs and talents according to precise learner characteristics. Separate but comprehensive needs assessments can be focused on different learner markets and, within each market, on different segments. A *market* is an identifiable group of people. A *market segment* is a subgroup that has unique needs.

There are at least four possible markets for a Talent Development effort: (1) the job market, (2) the individual/career market, (3) the work group market, and (4) the external market. The first three are found inside an organization; the fourth is outside.

The Job Market. One way to classify learners is by their job tasks, results, and responsibilities. Employee training, a short-term change effort, traditionally focuses on jobs (Nadler 1979). It is geared to producing immediate, observable results and to socializing individuals into an organization.

When examining the job market, WLP practitioners should be familiar with certain terminology. A *task* is a discrete unit of work; a *position* is a group of related tasks performed by one person in one organization; a *job* is a group of similar positions; a *job class* is a group of related and/or unrelated jobs occupying the same level of responsibility and bearing certain similarities as a result; a *job category* or *job family* is a group of related jobs but at different levels of responsibility; and an *occupation* is a group of similar jobs existing in different organizations. A brief example will help clarify the meanings of these terms.

Harry Smith is an Accountant I in Acme Chemical Company. Harry occupies a *position* similar to other Accountant I *jobs* at Acme. Accountant II, IIIs, and IVs at Acme are in the same *job family*. Finance experts, personnel experts, and marketing experts are in the same *job class*. Accountants at other companies share a common *occupation* with Harry.

All accountants at Acme have common needs for training as they are socialized into the organization. They are hired on the basis of qualifications. For instance, every new accountant has an accounting degree. But each newcomer has to learn "the Acme way" of performing the Accountant I's job and of getting along with colleagues. The same principle holds true for all other job classes. Each job class has recurring needs arising from movement into, through, and out of the class. (See Exhibit 3–1 for a list of them.)

Job families have similarities. For example, all supervisors share common responsibilities: They oversee daily operations and are responsible for front-line activities. Similarly, professional employees are hired for their expertise, which they put to special use.

Exhibit 3–1: Recurring Instructional Needs Stemming from Movements of People

Stages	Key Issues	Instructional Implications/Needs
Pre-socialization	What learning experiences can pre-pare an individual for occupational entry?	How well does formal schooling prepare individuals for occupational entry? Job? Job class? Employer?
Recruitment	How can an organization attract quali-fied talent in line with its needs?	What do applicants need to know about the organization and job that will help them "select themselves"?
Selection	How can an organization select effec-tive performers?	What does the organization need to know about individuals applying for entry?
Job/Group Orientation	How can an individual be oriented to the position? Job? Work group?	What training focused on job tasks should be given to newcomers? When?
Stable Performance	How can deficiencies in individual performance on the job be identified and corrected?	What training will help correct problems in job performance? Help individuals keep their skills current as technology and other variables change the competencies essential for successful work performance?
Advancement	How can individuals be groomed for increased responsibility and/or for increased professional scope?	What do individuals need to know or do to be competent for increased responsibility (vertical advancement) or a broader scope of professional responsibility (horizontal advancement)?

To design a long-term learning plan to meet recurring instructional needs, WLP practitioners should look at all of their needs and impose a way of grouping together the needs. Although titles might differ, the groups are based on common duties. Training courses and/or experiences can then be focused on these responsibilities.

One way to create logical groupings is to classify job titles into the following categories and then assess recurring training needs for each group: (1) executives, (2) senior managers, (3) middle managers, (4) first-line supervisors, (5) sales per-sonnel, (6) professionals, (7) administrative employees, (8) clerical support, (9) skilled production or service workers, (10) unskilled production or service workers, (11) customer representatives, and (12) others. Several job titles can be grouped into each category.

Each category represents a different market segment. Each requires a different long-term learning plan to meet recurring training needs.

Individual/Career Market. A second way to classify learners is by individual performance and career aspiration. Employee education, an intermediate-term change effort, focuses on this market. It prepares an individual for movement to another job. It also upgrades skills and elicits new insights.

To be successful, employee education has to be based on training, education, experience, and personal characteristics equated with successful performance at each level. In consultation with supervisors, individuals can plan for career movement by gradually building the competencies essential to success in other jobs or job families.

For example, let's say "Martina Short" is an experienced welder who wants to be a first-line supervisor in the welding department. By comparing her present skills to those required for successful performance as a welding supervisor, Martina is able to devise a learning plan that will gradually bring her skills in line with those needed by a welding supervisor. To establish this plan, Martina negotiates a learning contract with her supervisor. In this process, Martina makes explicit her desire for promotion and her plans for obtaining the necessary skills needed for that promotion. The supervisor makes no promises and raises no unrealistic expectations, but does assure Martina that without the skills she plans to acquire, she will never be eligible for promotion.

It is more difficult to assess employee educational needs than training needs and more difficult to devise categories for an employee education curriculum than a training curriculum. But it is not impossible. On the basis of employee performance appraisals and other information, individuals can be classified according to how much they are worth as educational investments.

In a classic view that has been translated into practice in many organizations, Odiorne (1984, 66–67) suggested that employees can be classified as (1) *workhorses*—"people who have reached a high peak of performance but have definitely limited potential," (2) *stars*—"people of high potential who are performing at the highest level of that potential," (3) *problem employees*—"people who have great potential but who are working well below their capacity and with mixed results," and (4) *deadwood*—"people whose performance and potential are both low." Stars are ranked first for investment; deadwood is ranked last. If individuals are classified into these categories, supervisors can determine how much each individual is worthy of the cost of skill improvement, and what kind of skill improvement the individual should receive.

Another way to classify individuals is by life stage. While it is important to avoid age discrimination, people in each age bracket have central life concerns that differ from those in other age brackets, and this affects their motivation to learn. These central life concerns are worth considering when assessing their needs. They can imply what the individual is motivated to learn about.

The Work Group or Department Market. A third way to classify learners is by their placement within the organization. Long-term change efforts like organization and employee development focus on this market. Organization development is geared to changing culture. Employee development is geared to creating a collective mix of employee skills appropriate to the responsibilities of the work group or department. In this context, a *work group* means a supervisor and his or her immediate subordinates.

Work groups are or should be readily identifiable with the aid of an organization chart. Simply begin at the top and circle supervisor and subordinates in each group. The first work group consists of the chief executive and his or her immediate subordinates. Each subordinate, in turn, serves as supervisor for a group of subordinates. Continue this process from the top to the bottom of the organization to identify all work groups.

No two organizations are structured in quite the same way. Differences exist in what kinds of departments or work groups are created and in the kinds and numbers of people or jobs reporting to the same supervisor.

Regardless of structure, human skills are essential. To meet the responsibilities of each department or work group, managers need the right numbers and types of people. While staffing requirements can be met in many ways, employee development is one way to ensure that the collective skills of a group match up to its responsibilities. A long-term learning plan for each group is thus necessary to clarify when and how these skills can be obtained.

To prepare a long-term plan for employee development, each supervisor should examine (1) the purpose of the work group; (2) the differences between how the group should be performing and how it is actually performing; (3) the competencies that are essential to narrow the gap between desired and actual group results over time; and (4) the methods of acquiring those competencies or obtaining necessary skills and knowledge.

The External Market. Employees are not the only ones who can be classified as learners. Nor are employees or supervisors the only potential clients of planned learning activities. People outside an organization may also have learning needs worth addressing.

Nonemployee development, ranging from short-term efforts to long-term instructional efforts geared to meeting the learning needs of people outside an organization, focuses on the external market. It creates consumers who know how to use company products and services, suppliers who are aware of unique needs of an organization with which they transact business, distributors who are familiar enough with company products or services to market them effectively to consumers, and members of the general public or community who understand the unique needs and problems of an employer.

To develop a long-term learning plan for the external market, WLP practitioners should consider such questions as: (1) What groups outside the organization are particularly critical to sales and/or long-term survival and success? (2) What strengths and weaknesses are evident in relations between the organization and each external group? (3) How much are these strengths and weaknesses attributable to lack of knowledge or skills? (4) How much is each weakness attributable to an external group's lack of knowledge about the organization? On the other hand, how much is each weakness attributable to lack of employee knowledge about the external group? (5) What planned learning experiences can over time help correct weaknesses attributable to lack of knowledge and build on the unique strengths of the group stemming from group competencies?

Perhaps two examples will clarify these issues.

First, consider the case of a computer company that introduces a wristwatch-size computer. At first, consumers are unaware of the product's existence and capabilities. This problem can be addressed through mass media advertising.

While costly, advertising does create product demand and familiarizes consumers with general product capabilities. Subsequent instruction is necessary, however, to demonstrate to specific consumers how the product can help meet their unique needs. In fact, a whole series of seminars can be designed around different consumer applications of the product. This instruction becomes an important marketing tool and, potentially, a profit-making enterprise of its own.

Consider a different case. Managers of the Acer Corporation want to open a new plant, which will employ 720 people, on a tract of land in rural Mississippi. The plant will benefit from a very attractive incentives package that includes tax breaks and free land provided by the state. However, some local residents fear that problems will accompany the plant's opening. For example, they are concerned about toxic waste and environmental pollution, an influx of "big city types" who will bring with them a crime wave, and the possible drain on local utilities. To address these concerns, the company mounts a massive public education effort using various media: spot advertisements on local television and radio; full-page letters to residents published in local newspapers; speeches to community and school groups; and door-to-door interviews with residents. The result of this effort is that the learning needs of the community are met, and strong community support for the new plant is secured.

Planned learning experiences can also be directed to satisfying the learning needs of critical suppliers, distributors, government regulatory agencies, and other key groups that can affect the business. In each case, WLP practitioners examine problems between the organization and a specific external group, and design planned learning activities that satisfy learning needs and thus help improve relationships with that group.

Comparing Actual to Desired Knowledge and Skills

Most books and articles on Talent Development devote considerable attention to data methods used in needs assessment. Few writers distinguish between short-term and long-term needs assessment. Most writers, like most practitioners, assume that needs assessment is focused on the short-term *training* needs of an identifiable learner group. That does not have to be the case, however.

Levels of Assessment and Assessment Strategy. Learning needs can be viewed on three levels, much like corporate plans:

1. *Strategic needs* are most general and comprehensive. They require the longest time to satisfy. By meeting strategic learning needs, WLP practitioners create cultural change. Organization development, employee development, and much nonemployee development are focused on this level.

2. *Coordinative needs* are not as general nor as comprehensive as strategic needs. They do not take as much time to deal with. Meeting these needs produces change in line with individual career plans. Employee education is focused on this level.

3. *Operational needs* are the most specific, yet they require the least time to deal with. Meeting these needs produces immediate change in job performance. Employee training is focused on this level.

Comprehensive needs assessment requires an integrated approach so that needs can be assessed on all three levels at once. Integration is important so that short-term, intermediate-term, and long-term instructional efforts are coordinated and unified.

What is necessary, then, is a strategy for needs assessment that ensures this integration. Generally, there are three possible strategies: (1) *top-down,* (2) *bottom-up,* and (3) *negotiated.* If a top-down strategy is chosen, needs assessment is carried out by a handful of people at the top. Quite often they are the same decision-makers who formulate strategic business plans. The participation of many people builds commitment for subsequent learning and helps tie the resulting learning plans to other kinds of plans. A bottom-up strategy results from a compilation of numerous separate assessments carried out by first-line supervisors or employees. A negotiated strategy is quite literally negotiated between top managers and other people in the firm.

There is no right or wrong strategy for needs assessment. However, there may be a right or wrong approach in one organizational culture. A good clue is how strategic business plans are formulated. Are they formulated at the top and imposed downward? Are they compiled from separate plans formulated at the bottom, and forwarded up the hierarchy? Is some form of negotiation used?

Whatever the pattern used in formulating strategic business plans, needs assessment should be carried out in a similar fashion—if not as part of the strategic business planning process itself.

Data Collection Methods. The essence of needs assessment is doing a comparison between *what is* and *what should be. Condition* is the same as *what is; criterion* is the same as *what should be.* Instruction is an appropriate way of narrowing the gap between condition and criteria when the deficiency is caused by lack of knowledge or skill; taking action is consistent with the purpose of the Talent Development effort. Instruction can also be used to build on *proficiencies*—exceptional competence or talent. The same principle applies whether the focus is organization development, nonemployee development, employee development, education, or training.

Different data collection methods can be used to compare condition and criteria in needs assessment, and thus uncover deficiencies (weaknesses) and proficiencies (strengths). These methods include (1) interviews, (2) surveys, (3) observation, (4) task analysis, (5) performance/productivity measures, (6) employee performance appraisals, (7) assessment centers, (8) group discussions, (9) critical incident techniques, (10) Delphi procedures, and (11) nominal group techniques. (There are more; see Exhibit 3–2.) Not every method is appropriate for a comprehensive needs assessment. Some are appropriate only for identifying specific training, education, or development needs. However, interviews are widely applicable and are probably the most commonly used data collection method.

An *interview* is essentially a conversation. Interviews can be formal or informal. A formal interview relies on a planned series of prepared questions that have been tested in advance. WLP practitioners are not free to vary the wording or the sequencing of questions. They record responses directly on a form (called an *interview schedule*). Informal interviews rely on an outline of subjects, topics, or issues. WLP practitioners can vary the wording or sequencing of questions. They record notes directly on the form (called an *interview guide*). Formal interviews preserve consistency across respondents but they sacrifice the potential for intensive probing. Informal interviews, on the other hand, sacrifice consistency across respondents for the potential to probe for additional information.

Exhibit 3–2: Approaches to Instructional Needs Assessment

Approach	Brief Description
Advisory Committee	An advisory committee is a group of employees and/or line supervisors who provide advice to WLP practitioners and others about Talent Development needs.
Attitude Survey	An attitude survey is not conducted solely for the purpose of assessing developmental needs; rather, it is intended to identify problems in the organization, some of which may be corrected through planned or unplanned developmental efforts.
Exit Interviews	An exit interview is administered to terminating employees to explore reasons for their departure and methods for improving developmental efforts.
Management Requests	Any request for developmental efforts from a supervisor, manager, or executive is regarded as a management request.
Performance Documents	A performance document is a record of individual or group productivity.
Skill Tests	A skill test is administered to employees in the work setting to identify performance strengths/weaknesses of job incumbents for purposes of identifying developmental needs.
Assessment Centers	An assessment center is a process, not a place. It usually consists of realistic, job-related activities on which individual performance is observed and rated by trained, skilled, and experienced raters.

Interviews are flexible enough to be used in identifying training, education, and development needs. The difference between them depends on *who is interviewed* and *what they are asked about.* Experienced job incumbents and their supervisors are appropriately interviewed to plan training or education; supervisors are interviewed to plan employee development; many people are interviewed to plan organization development; and members of external groups are interviewed to plan nonemployee development. In each case, they can be questioned about deficiencies (weaknesses) and proficiencies (strengths). Of course, interviews can be conducted in person, over the phone, or by videoconference. Interviews can be with one person or many. An interview of many people in a group setting is a *focus group.*

Surveys are also flexible, just as interviews are. Most people associate surveys with written questionnaires, but they can be conducted over the telephone or (increasingly) by e-mail or on the Web. A survey is essentially an interview reduced to writing. Open-ended surveys call for essay responses; closed-ended surveys require respondents to mark a choice such as *yes* or *no, agree* or *disagree,* or *important* or *unimportant.* Scaled surveys ask respondents to indicate how much they agree or disagree, or how they feel about specific issues.

Surveys are cheaper than face-to-face interviews and are quite useful in collecting a lot of information from scattered locations in a short time. But they do not allow for extensive probing or easy follow-up, as interviews often do. Open-ended surveys yield essay responses that are difficult to analyze; closed-ended surveys yield numerical responses that provide an illusion of certainty.

Surveys are sufficiently flexible to be used in identifying training, education, or development needs. Surveys on job requirements help identify training needs; surveys on education or experience in preparation for promotion help identify educational needs; surveys on work-group skills help identify employee development needs; surveys on intragroup or group feelings help identify organization development needs; and surveys of consumers, stockholders, suppliers, distributors, and the general public help identify nonemployee development needs. Like interviews, surveys can focus on uncovering deficiencies (weaknesses) and proficiencies (strengths).

Observation is not as flexible as surveys or interviews. It is appropriately used in identifying the training and sometimes the educational needs of manual laborers. It is rarely appropriate for identifying employee or nonemployee development needs, nor for identifying the training/educational needs of white-collar workers.

Observation is simple enough to do. WLP practitioners watch experienced or exemplary performers while they work. Practitioners then record the frequency of work behaviors on specially designed behavioral observation forms that resemble interview schedules, except that WLP practitioners use them during observation.

Task analysis is the term used to describe a whole range of methods that involve structured observation. It is appropriate for assessing the training and educational needs of manual workers. In some rare cases, it is used to identify the instructional needs of consumers using products. To analyze tasks, WLP practitioners (1) identify what tasks are performed in a job; (2) observe how tasks are performed in terms of work results, methods of carrying out work activities, who or what received the action, and why the task is performed; and (3) rate task importance for instructional purposes. For example, which tasks are most important for successful job performance? Which ones are most difficult to learn? Which ones are changing?

To design a training program, WLP practitioners reassemble and act out the tasks to ensure that the analysis represents a complete description of work activities.

Performances or *productivity measures* are unobtrusive. Employees are unaware that their work is being scrutinized. WLP practitioners compare actual work group outputs to (1) *work standards*—minimally acceptable levels of scrap, downtime, or product rejects; (2) *objectives*—pre-established targets for producing quantity or quality; or (3) *exemplars*—individuals or groups who produce far more or who make far fewer errors than other individuals or groups.

Performance or productivity measures help WLP practitioners identify proficient or deficient performance, but do not reveal the cause(s). Differences in group performance might occur because the group or team lacks an appropriate skill mix. WLP practitioners need only compare the prior training, education, and experience of high-performing to low-performing groups. Differences can reveal employee development needs in low-performing groups and unique competencies in high-performing groups.

Employee performance appraisals are especially appropriate for identifying individual training and educational needs. After all, an appraisal is intended to determine how well an individual is performing his or her job. Information from appraisals is used to assess an individual's need for Talent Development opportunities.

Appraisals serve a two-fold purpose. First, they furnish employees with feedback on past performance. Second, they provide a starting point for planning future performance improvement. These two purposes might not be balanced equally. Deficiencies stemming from the lack of individual knowledge or skill are appropriately used to identify traditional training needs; proficiencies are traditionally used to plan employee educational activities leading to promotion or other future career moves for individuals.

There are different kinds of employee performance appraisals. Perhaps least useful are so-called *trait ratings*, which evaluate individual performance on characteristics such as "ambition," "dependability," and "output." When paired up with a scale that uses "exceeds expectations," "meets expectations," and "falls below expectations," trait ratings will be too vague to be very helpful for identifying specific deficiencies or proficiencies.

Behaviorally anchored rating scales (BARS) are more concrete and thus more effective in providing supervisory feedback on individual behavior. The approach is based on short narratives describing behaviors that are solicited from experienced, exemplary supervisors, or job incumbents. These incidents are clustered into five to ten performance dimensions, which are then ranked in order from most to least preferable by a second group of exemplary, experienced performers. The resulting behavioral anchors become a foundation for employee appraisals, job descriptions, and training curricula. Research on BARS indicates that the approach does not work as well in organizations facing turbulent external environments as in more stable environments.

Management by Objectives (MBO) is also an employee appraisal method. Supervisors and employees meet at the beginning of an appraisal period to negotiate future goals, methods of measuring goal achievement, and times to review progress. This process of negotiating goals begins at the top of the organization when the CEO negotiates goals with subordinates, who in turn negotiate goals with their subordinates, and so on.

Management by Objectives is more than just an appraisal method. It is also useful in business planning and in changing a culture from authoritarian to participative. It is forward-looking, because measurable employee performance objectives are established up front. While MBO has been criticized on numerous counts, it is one way to plan for employee training, education, and development.

Assessment centers are not strictly used in collecting information to identify instructional needs. In fact, an assessment center relies on a standard form of appraisal, multiple raters, and multiple ways of appraisal. Individuals are interviewed, tested, and asked to participate in various individual or group exercises. The exercises are based on the activities of a job as identified through work analysis (see Guidelines 2000). Performance is assessed by trained evaluators who are also seasoned managers. The independent assessments of these evaluators are then compiled and fed back to individuals who use them to plan training and education. Theoretically, an assessment center could be used to assess the skills of a work group and thus help identify employee development needs. In the same vein, an assessment center could be used to assess the skills of customers using the products, and thereby identify nonemployee development needs. In more practical terms, assessment centers are commonly used in making selection, promotion, and transfer decisions (Spychalski et al. 1997). They have also been used in assessing individual training needs and even as developmental processes in their own right.

Group discussions are general enough to be used for almost any purpose. They range from *group interviews,* in which WLP practitioners question job incumbents about work tasks, to *open forums,* in which supervisors openly explore employee development needs with members of a work group. They can also be useful in developing a general training or talent plan by job class, and in identifying employee educational needs or nonemployee development needs.

The *critical incident technique* structures experience. A panel of knowledgeable people—supervisors, experienced job incumbents, or exemplary performers—is assembled. They are then asked to reflect on their experience and describe situations that exemplify extremely proficient or deficient performance. These situations are categorized to describe behaviors leading to job success or failure.

Critical incidents are highly flexible. They reveal (1) *training needs,* if focused on job behaviors; (2) *educational needs,* if focused on career, promotion, or transfer matters; (3) *employee development needs,* if focused on important, recurring problem situations that emerge in work groups; and (4) *nonemployee development needs*, if focused on past company dealings with suppliers, customers, distributors, stockholders, or members of the general public.

However, critical incidents have drawbacks. Their value is heavily dependent on who is chosen to research problems. Slight differences in the instructions given to participants may produce radically different results across expert panels. Data collection is time-consuming and thus potentially expensive. Finally, critical incidents reveal more about exceptions from norms than about norms themselves.

The *Delphi procedure,* named for the ancient Greek oracle of Apollo, was developed by the Rand Corporation and has been widely applied to research problems. Typically, Delphi participants are chosen for their special expertise. Participants remain anonymous and never assemble as a group. Instead, information is solicited from them by written survey. The results are compiled by researchers and are fed back to participants accompanied by more questions, and this process continues until participants agree on key issues.

To apply this approach to assess Talent Development needs, WLP practitioners begin by clarifying purpose. They decide (for example) to assess recurring training needs of job incumbents, career or educational interests of people facing different central life concerns, career routes through an organization, developmental needs of a work group, or nonemployee development needs. Whatever the purpose, WLP practitioners begin by developing a questionnaire. They can do so by themselves (without the help of others), or they can interview people and use the interview results as the basis for survey questions. The participants should be chosen with care and should be knowledgeable about the subject. WLP practitioners then contact participants, secure their cooperation, explain the Delphi procedure to them, finalize questions on the Delphi survey, send the survey to participants, receive completed surveys, compile the results, send the results back to participants for comment and critique, and continue this process until participants agree on key responses.

The Delphi technique's chief advantage is that participants are not pressured, as they sometimes are in meetings, to conform to the ideas expressed by articulate or respected group members. Chief disadvantages include the cost and time needed to carry out a Delphi. Moreover, separate Delphi studies must be carried out to identify job training needs, career educational needs, and work group developmental needs.

The *nominal group technique* (NGT) takes its name from the way the process itself works. People are assembled in a small group. However, they usually submit information without discussion, and so the group exists in name only—that is, *nominally.* In many ways similar to the Delphi, NGT has been applied to strategic business planning, HR planning, training needs assessment, and futures research.

NGT can help assess training, education, or development needs, depending on what issues are examined. WLP practitioners (1) select one or more panels of experienced, exemplary performers; (2) assemble group members in one place; (3) explain NGT to participants; (4) ask participants to generate ideas, identify performance problems, assess needs or problems, assess needs or prioritize instruction, and record their ideas on slips of paper, one idea to each slip; (5) have participants hand in their slips to the group facilitator (the WLP practitioner); (6) record each idea on a blackboard, flipchart, or overhead transparency so that all group members can see it; (7) encourage discussion following the generation of ideas; and (8) rank ideas by majority vote.

NGT is advantageous for two reasons. First, the silent generation of ideas prevents group pressures for conformity from affecting individuals. Second, ideas stem from participants, rather than WLP practitioners or others.

NGT is disadvantageous for three reasons. First, voting on ideas forces individuals to set priorities when they see no need for action. Second, individuals can be subtly pressured to conform to group opinions during discussion or voting. Third, it is difficult to follow up on the many ideas that can be generated in NGT, with the result that good ideas are lost and participants are sometimes frustrated.

Selecting Data Collection Methods. What specific data collection method should be used in assessing an organization's talent needs and instructional needs? Answering this question is not always easy.

More than one writer in the WLP field has addressed this subject. In choosing a data collection method, these writers suggest that WLP practitioners consider issues such as

1. *Employee involvement.* Should the assessment process build learner commitment to meeting needs once they are identified? How important is learner commitment?

2. *Time required.* How much time is available to carry out the assessment process? When are results needed?

3. *Cost.* What are the expected costs of alternative data collection methods? What financial constraints exist?

4. *Relevance.* Will a given data collection method produce useful results in a form capable of being used?

5. *Practitioner skills.* How capable are WLP practitioners to use alternative data collection methods? For instance, do practitioners possess the necessary skills to prepare a survey, conduct interviews, or carry out task analyses?

6. *Respondent skills.* Do intended respondents possess the necessary skills to provide useful information?

7. *Relations between assessors and respondents.* How dependent is a data collection method on good relations between the needs assessor and respondents? For example, it can be difficult to schedule interviews or carry out surveys when respondents distrust the motives of the assessor or when trust is lacking in an organization. In these cases, people are reluctant to speak their minds, much less commit themselves to writing, for fear of repercussions.

8. *Level of awareness.* How important do prospective learners or clients view a specific need area? When their awareness level is high, data collection efforts are easier, because people readily see benefits in responding.

9. *Management preferences.* Do supervisors or managers prefer one data collection method over others? For instance, obtaining needs assessment information from attitude survey results might be difficult if supervisors fear that poor morale in their work groups will reflect on their competence. In any given situation, one data collection method may well be more appropriate than others.

Involving Others in Data Collection and Analysis. WLP practitioners should give careful thought as to who should be involved in collecting data and determining instructional needs. There are several key issues to consider. First is *the importance of the need area.* If widespread commitment is important, it is worthwhile to take more time to arrive at decisions. The second consideration is *other constraints.* What are the constraints on time, money, and staff? When constraints are tight, then the number of people to involve in data collection or analysis should be reduced to hold down costs.

As a general rule, practitioners should involve as many interested parties as possible in data collection and analysis. The reason is that greater involvement in the needs assessment process tends to produce greater commitment to subsequent learning activities carried out to satisfy learning needs. Participation in identifying instruction needs may well be a key factor in integrating Talent Development and planning activities.

Identifying Present Learning Needs by Market or Market Segment

Strategic business planners have long noted the existence of strengths and weaknesses in organizational performance. Strengths lead to success against competitors. Weaknesses, if not handled carefully, lead to competitive failure. Generally, strategists can choose either to build on strengths or correct weaknesses. The analysis of corporate strengths and weaknesses furnishes valuable information about what business to enter or leave, what resources to allocate to what activities, and how to manage interactions between business units. The analysis of business unit strengths and weaknesses helps strategists decide what products or services to offer, what resources to concentrate on each product or service, and how to manage relations between functions. The analysis of functional strengths and weaknesses provides insight into what contributions each function should be making to the organization, what resources each should receive, and how to manage the activities of each function. Sweeping examinations of organizational strengths and weaknesses aid decision-making and unify subsequent action.

The same principle applies to learning needs assessment. Broad analysis of strengths and weaknesses of job incumbents yields valuable information to plan job training and socialization efforts spanning many related learning experiences. It is worth emphasizing that these can help build the bench strength and the collective talents of the organization's human assets. Broad analysis of individual strengths and weaknesses yields valuable information to plan employee education. Analysis of the strengths and weaknesses of each work group yields information to plan employee and organization development. Finally, broad analysis of strengths and weaknesses in an organization's relations with its product or service users, suppliers, distributors, and the general public yields information to plan nonemployee development.

Instructional needs assessment traditionally focuses on specific problems facing identifiable learners at one time. Results of assessment are then used to plan one-shot training courses to correct these problems. That makes training a "fix-it" tool. However, assessment can also be used to focus on the general strengths and weaknesses of job incumbents, individuals, work groups, or external groups. *Sweeping examinations of strengths and weaknesses make the Talent Development effort a tool for long-term and continuous improvement with a unified direction.*

A *training curriculum* can thus be planned for each job class or job category. Working with others in the organization, WLP practitioners analyze the strengths and weaknesses of each job class or category. From the result of this analysis, an organized but generalized sequence of learning experiences can be designed to orient and socialize newcomers to each job class or category. They can also be designed to identify important competencies worthy of development for the future.

An *educational curriculum* can also be planned to prepare individuals for promotion or other career moves, to upgrade skills, and to elicit creative solutions to problems. An educational curriculum stems from the analysis of present strengths/weaknesses of individuals compared to the requirements for success in possible future jobs. Employee education helps individuals achieve their career objectives.

A *development curriculum* results from comparison of present work group strengths and weaknesses. It consists of planned learning experiences designed to build a collective pool of group skills adequate for tasks facing a group. A *nonemployee development curriculum* consists of planned learning experiences intended to correct deficiencies or build on proficiencies between an organization and external groups relevant to it.

However, the world changes. Jobs, individuals, work groups, and groups outside organizations do not remain static. Consequently, analysis alone of past or present strengths and weaknesses is not sufficient to plan for meeting future learning needs. Further analysis is necessary. The next chapter deals with this issue. In it, we focus on anticipating environmental changes that change training, education, and development needs.

Activity 3–1: Information for Talent Development

Directions: Use this activity to structure your thinking about the need to develop talent in your organization. For each question in the left column below, provide a response in the right column. Use additional paper if necessary.

Question	Response
1. Who are the learners served by the Talent Development effort? Are some of them particularly important? If so, which ones? Why are they important?	
2. Who are the clients served by the Talent Development effort? Are some of them particularly important? If so, which ones? Why are they important?	
3. What is known about present learners served by the Talent Development effort? (Describe common characteristics.)	
4. What is known about prospective future learners to be served by the Talent Development effort?	
5. What is known about present clients served by the Talent Development effort?	
6. What is known about prospective future clients to be served by the Talent Development effort?	
7. Are some learners concentrated in some locations more than in others? If so, which locations and what learners?	
8. What are the major work activities of targeted learners?	
9. What are the major work activities of the clients?	
10. What do other people say about the targeted learners?	
11. What do other people say about the clients?	
12. What problems have historically faced the learners?	
13. What problems have historically faced the clients?	

Activity 3–1: *(continued)*

Question	Response
14. How motivated are learners to learn? What accounts for this level of motivation? Is it likely to change?	
15. How motivated are clients to encourage learners to learn? What accounts for this level of motivation? Is it likely to change?	

Activity 3–2: Job Groupings

Directions: Use this activity to create job groupings in your organization. For each group listed in the left column, list job titles that fall into the grouping in the organization and the major responsibilities of the jobs. If the organization is small, some groupings might not have corresponding jobs. If that is the case, write "not applicable" in the column. Use additional paper if necessary.

Job Grouping	Job Titles in the grouping in your organization	Major responsibilities common to jobs in this grouping
1. Executives		
2. Senior Managers		
3. Middle Managers		
4. First-Line Supervisors		
5. Sales Personnel		
6. Professionals		
7. Administrative Employees		
8. Clerical Support		
9. Skilled Production or Service Workers		
10. Unskilled Production or Service Workers		
11. Customer Representatives		
12. Others		

Activity 3–3: Classifying Individuals

Directions: Use this activity to classify individuals. List life stages in the left column. List individuals in a work group in the center column. Finally, in the right column, describe the implications of the individual's life stage on their likely learning interests. Use additional paper if necessary. (A separate analysis for each work group in an organization is necessary for a comprehensive analysis.)

Life Stage	Individual	Implications of individual's life stage on their likely learning or developmental interest
1.		
2.		
3.		
4.		
5.		
6.		
7.		
8.		
9.		
10.		
11.		
12.		

Activity 3–4: A Case Study on the Strengths and Weaknesses of the Organization's Talent Development Effort

Directions: Read the case below and answer the questions that follow.

Rhesus is a giant retail corporation—one of the largest in the retail industry.* Rhesus stores sell a wide selection of goods and are found in just about every medium- to large-sized city in the United States.

However, Rhesus is not exactly an industry leader in terms of Talent Development. Several years ago, the corporate-level HRD department at Rhesus was completely eliminated in the midst of downsizing. Recently, it was revived. At its helm is Harold Anderson, a five-year company employee destined for higher-level responsibilities at Rhesus. His one-year-old department is staffed with six long-time company employees. (The company will not hire professional WLP practitioners.) Anderson is to set up a department servicing the corporate office only. The corporate office employs several hundred people. Anderson has a free hand, more or less, to establish the purpose of the department and offer planned learning activities of value to Rhesus's corporate employees and managers.

The retail industry is hotly competitive. Like other retailers, Rhesus plans a major program to change its stores. This program will eventually change just about every fixture in most stores—including product display, advertising, inventory control, and even store layout and staffing. Within ten years, the plans will be a reality. In the meantime, Rhesus will continue as it always has, and continue to be a dominant force in the industry.

Questions

1. What should Anderson do to analyze the present strengths and weaknesses of the company's effort to develop its talent?

2. What problems will Anderson encounter in his start-up effort? What can he do to avert them? What can he do to minimize their effects?

* A fictitious company.

CHAPTER 4

ENVIRONMENTAL SCANNING

Try an experiment. Select several managers, at random, and ask them this question: "*What are the future Talent Development needs of your employees, and more specifically, what training, education, and development do you believe they need?*" If your organization is like most, this question should elicit some interesting responses, such as these:

I   "First explain the difference between training, education, and development."
I   "Our work is so diverse that anything will help."
I   "I just don't know."
I   "They have no needs at all."

Ater you get the answers, ask another question: "*How do you know that your answer is correct?*" Managers who feel that their employees do have needs will then recount anecdotes about past problems they have experienced.

The point of this exercise will not be lost on perceptive practitioners. All too often, managers perceive learning needs as stemming from major problems experienced in the past, anecdotal evidence, and specific people or events. Managers are thus like most people: they remember more significant events than insignificant events; they color their memory with interpretations; their memories are anecdotal; and they find it easier to think in specific rather than in general terms.

You can also bet that, when confronting an immediate problem, managers are sure to grasp at any possible solution—including Talent Development. It is probably not unreasonable to assume that managers, like most adults, are highly motivated to learn about problems they are presently confronting. They probably identify Talent Development needs on the same short-term basis. Since WLP practitioners rarely conduct any systematic needs assessment, they are likely to believe the managers.

It is easy to see what happens as a result. Instructional programs are designed on the basis of faulty memory, interpretations of special cases that took place in the past, or problems confronting people at present. Not surprisingly, the short-term focus of these instructional programs—not to mention their weak foundation—is at odds with the necessity (1) to deal with real performance issues, rather than perceived ones; (2) to anticipate future requirements of the organization; and (3) to tap individual motivation to learn by dealing with matters concerning employees. In any case, past or present problems might not stay the same under changing future conditions.

Managers, learners, and WLP practitioners alike must therefore look beyond traditional approaches to instructional needs assessment, which are too often focused on the past and limited to major problems. They should recognize the increasing value of taking a future orientation in their thinking. It is important to anticipate future learning needs and work backward to meet them in the present, and then go beyond short-term to long-term perspectives of Talent Development.

How is this possible? One answer is to do environmental scanning. But what is it, generally? How is it applied to Talent Development? What specific methods can be used to carry it out? This chapter addresses these questions.

Environmental Scanning: Definition and Description

Any organization functions in an external environment consisting of two broad components: (1) *the general public*, consisting of everyone not directly involved in or affected by the organization, and (2) *external stakeholders*, consisting of everyone directly involved in or affected by the firm but who are not working inside it. Strategists determine their organization's environment when they establish business purpose and identify the markets they choose to serve. However, changes in the external environment over time create unique threats and opportunities for a firm (Lang, Calantone, and Gudmundson 1997). Managers may approach business as usual and wait for environmental changes to affect the business. This is a *passive strategy*. If external trends are favorable, business conditions improve without requiring any effort to change the organization. Of course, if trends are unfavorable, business conditions will get worse and bankruptcy might be the result. As an alternative, managers can try to anticipate changes outside their firms and then adjust products or services beforehand so that they are attuned to change before it occurs or as it occurs. In other words, managers can spot opportunities for improving the business before they arise, or else head off external threats before they create problems. This is an *active strategy*. Generally speaking, the more information that managers receive about changes in the external environment, the more competitive the organization can be (Abdalla and Amin 1995; Ahituv, Zif, and Machlin 1998; Khandwalla 1977). It may be that it is not so important how often scanning is conducted as what is examined and interpreted (Beal 2000). Environmental scanning practices may well vary across international settings (Ghosal 1988) or by the volatility of the industry and the external environmental conditions that the industry faces (Boyd and Fulk 1996; Sawyerr, Bahman, and Thibodeaux 2000).

A simple example should illustrate these principles. Think of the funeral business. (It might be somewhat morbid, but the funeral industry is involved in business.) When people die, business flourishes; when people continue to live, business is not so good. Now consider this: On the whole, the U.S. population is growing older. If long-term demographic trends remain unchanged, the majority of the U.S. population will at least reach retirement age by the year 2020. Although medical science continues to advance and thereby increases average life expectancy, people will eventually die. What, then, are the long-term prospects for the funeral industry? Based solely on population trends, the long-term future looks bright indeed. Barring contrary trends such as a dramatic medical breakthrough that prolongs life, funeral directors can choose a passive strategy and grimly reap the rewards of increasing business.

This general principle holds true for any business: Changes taking place externally create unique opportunities and threats. Managers may conduct business as usual and remain helpless pawns of external conditions beyond their control, or they can take active steps to position their organizations so as to anticipate favorable conditions or avert problems stemming from external environmental and global change. This ability to anticipate opportunities or threats is the essence of the entrepreneurial spirit.

Environmental scanning is the name for a structured examination of the future external environment. Choo (1999, 21) defines it as "the acquisition and use of information about events, trends, and relationships in an organization's external environment, the knowledge of which would assist management in planning the organization's future course of action." It is a deliberate process for examining the outside world, discovering trends, and drawing conclusions about what consequences to the organization will stem from those trends. At the heart of modern planning, it is quintessentially anticipatory rather than reactive.

Some writers on the subject prefer to break it down into two parts: environmental analysis and environmental diagnosis. *Environmental analysis* identifies the most important sectors of the external environment and systematically monitors them. *Environmental diagnosis* tries to anticipate what will happen as a result of the trends. Obviously, analysis is far easier than diagnosis, which draws conclusions about the consequences that are likely to stem from external environmental change. After all, predicting the effects of change is not as simple as recognizing that change might occur. But research has shown that aggregating the opinions of experts about the future increases the likelihood of precision in predictions, though the methods used to do that may not be too important (Fischer 1981).

The State of the Environmental Scanning Art in Business Planning

The environmental scanning art is quite advanced in theory, if not in practice. A review of the research on its impact on organizational performance generally supports the view that effective environmental scanning can improve an organization's competitiveness (Kumar, Subramanian, and Strandholm 2001). Jain (1984) conducted a two-year study of corporate environmental scanning practices. Basing his conclusions on interviews with 37 executives in 11 large corporations and a survey of chief executives in Fortune 500 firms, he classified scanning into four categories: (1) primitive, (2) ad hoc, (3) reactive, and (4) proactive. These categories represent a continuum through which corporations progress as their size, complexity, and environmental transactions increase. Jain found that all participating firms in his study with annual sales exceeding $1 billion use a category 4 (a proactive) approach to scanning. Typically, scanning of this kind is carried out *formally* at corporate and business unit levels. In this context, *formally* means in a deliberate, structured, and systematic way.

The focus of environmental scanning varies, depending on the phase in the corporate planning process in which the information is used. Each management level faces different environmental demands. As a consequence, each level of management faces its own need for environmental analysis. Lower-level managers require more information from inside the firm than their top management counterparts. Yet every manager should keep an eye peeled on what is happening outside the organization.

Generally, environmental scanning is a highly subjective and creative process. It is likely to become more important as the future grows less like the past and present and as factors external to organizations become more critical to management decision-making. Numerous studies, both theoretical and empirical, have been conducted about environmental scanning, and numerous practical guides have been published about it (see Choo 1998a and 1998b; Fahey and Randall 1998; Fuld 1995; Kahaner 1996).

Organizations that are most successful in applying environmental scanning make it a formal process rather than leaving it to mere chance or to the irregularities of idiosyncratic intuition (Choo 1999). They use "domain experts" to interpret the information and make it available as needed. Often the biggest danger to environmental scanning is not what is observed and interpreted, but what is somehow missed (Sherman and Schultz 1999).

Environmental Scanning for Talent Development

Definition. Environmental scanning for Talent Development is the process of monitoring trends, issues, problems, or events that might create the need for future talent as a result of environmental changes.

These changes often require new competencies among people affected by them. Environmental change can affect the competency requirements and learning needs of the general public, external stakeholders, members of each work group, individuals preparing for career advancement, and the incumbents of each job class.

Importance. The basic purpose of Talent Development is to prepare people to deal with the future. In fact, a chief distinction between training, education, and development is *how far into the future* they equip people. Training is traditionally intended for short-term application back on the job. Education prepares people for intermediate-term advancement and career movement. Development is long-term and helps individuals become instruments for group or organizational change and learning.

When based on traditional methods of needs assessment, Talent Development really prepares people only to rectify past performance deficiencies. Traditional needs assessment methods "rely heavily on the examination of past deficiencies or past behaviors as a basis for planning instruction intended to equip learners for meeting future conditions" (Rothwell 1984, 19). But conditions change, rendering instruction superfluous. Experience, a product of the past, is appropriate for improving future performance only when the future will be like the past.

Of course, there are always situations and problems when the past will be the best foundation for instruction. That is particularly true in industries facing relatively stable external environments. Heavily regulated industries and government agencies, for instance, often exist in such environments. In short, environments vary widely in how dynamic or volatile they are.

It is increasingly inappropriate to base instruction solely on past problems or on solutions worked out in the past when the environment is unstable or is becoming more unstable. What is needed is a way to anticipate future talent requirements and future learning needs.

Environmental Scanning and Curriculum Needs Assessment

A curriculum is a *long-term instructional plan.* It is based on a concrete, operational vision of what the future will be like. Comprehensive needs assessment identifies long-term, holistic learning needs of various groups, based on differences between actual and desired competencies in the past and present. When comprehensive needs assessment results are compared to environmental scanning results, future long-term learning needs can be identified. By addressing these needs, managers and employees can avert problems before they arise. They may also pinpoint unique opportunities for improving the performance of job incumbents, achieving individual career objectives, changing the competency mix represented in a work group consistent with future demands facing the group, improving relations between an organization and external groups, or changing cultural norms of an organization.

Steps in Environmental Scanning for Talent Development

Environmental scanning for Talent Development comprises several distinct steps:

1. Classify the external environment into sectors.
2. Decide on a time horizon appropriate for their scanning efforts.
3. Examine environmental sectors for expected changes over the time horizon they have chosen.
4. Try to anticipate the effects of environmental changes on
   - the general public
   - external stakeholders
   - departments or work groups in the organization
   - individuals
   - job requirements.
5. Identify future learning needs of
   - the general public
   - external stakeholders

I departments or work groups

I individuals

I job requirements.

6. Reassess learning needs by market segment from a future orientation.

Let's consider each step.

Step 1: Classify the external environment.

Analysis is the first step in environmental scanning for Talent Development. It is a process of breaking down the external environment into "sectors" for analysis. The *economic sector* has to do with local, national, and international economic conditions. The *political sector* has to do with government operations at all levels. The *technological sector* has to do with machines, tools, work methods, and other applications of knowledge. The *social sector* has to do with beliefs, attitudes, and values. The *market sector* has to do with the consumers to whom the company sells its goods or provides services and competing firms marketing similar products or services. The *geographic sector* has to do with the movement of key consumers, suppliers, or distributors. The *supplier sector* has to do with firms that supply raw materials or provide essential services. The *distributor sector* has to do with wholesale/retail outlets that sell the organization's products or through which its services are offered to consumers. Strategists may also wish to analyze other sectors focused on the U.S. population, the industry, or the WLP field. Exhibit 4–1 illustrates the relationship between external environmental sectors and the organization.

Step 2: Decide on a time horizon.

How far into the future should the environment be scanned? The second step in the environmental scanning process thus addresses *time horizon,* which is the time encompassed by a plan.

Deciding on a time horizon is important for several reasons. First, the accuracy of predictions declines over time. When strategic thinkers try to peer far into

Exhibit 4–1: Relationships between Environmental Sectors and the Organization

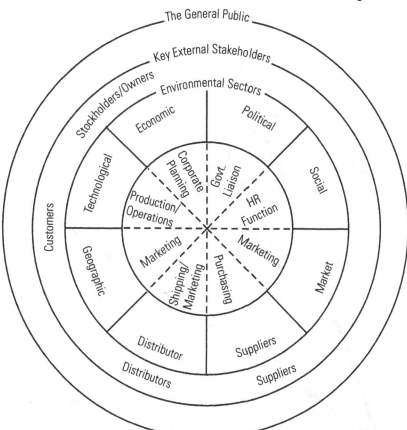

the future, they are less accurate in predicting problems and identifying trends or issues. Second, it is easier to set goals when the time period is clear. Managers can then envision where they want to be at a future point and step backward to examine what has to be accomplished in the meantime and how environmental conditions are likely to affect them (see Exhibit 4–2). Third, when the time horizon is distant, there is less need to pay attention to details; when the horizon is close, there is more need to consider details.

Top corporate managers should generally adopt the longest time perspective. They should be most strategic in their orientation and focus on the whole organization and environment rather than on specific business functions or work groups.

Exhibit 4–2: Visioning for the Future

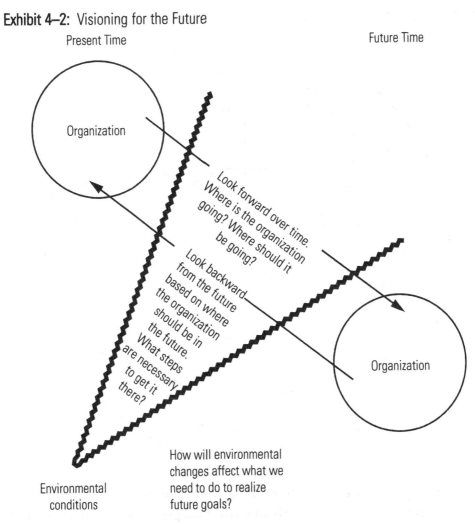

Present Time   Future Time

Organization

Look forward over time.
Where is the organization
going? Where should it
be going?

Look backward
from the future
based on where
the organization
should be in
the future.
What steps
are necessary
to get it
there?

Organization

Environmental   How will environmental
conditions   changes affect what we
                       need to do to realize
                       future goals?

Lower-level managers should adopt shorter time perspectives in keeping with their responsibility for achieving shorter-term results. They should focus on functions, work groups, individuals, and job requirements.

Although most writers on strategic business planning usually stress the top management perspective, the basic principles of environmental scanning can be applied at any level and even include front-line employees. These principles apply over any time horizon—overnight, one month, 30 years, and so on. Supervisors tired of fighting fires will surely see the value in applying forethought and training even nonsupervisors to apply it. In many respects, environmental scanning is just a fancy name for applying forethought systematically and deliberately.

There is no absolutely right or wrong time horizon. It depends on who is scanning and for what reasons. Top managers need environmental scanning results to conduct corporate or business-level planning. Lower-level managers need scanning results to help them anticipate the future consequences of their present actions, as well as trends, issues, or events that can affect goal achievement for their departments or work groups.

Step 3: Examine environmental sectors.

Strategists brainstorm about future trends or events once they decide what environmental sectors to examine and over what time horizon. At this point, they should consider what issues or trends will become more important over time. Let's briefly discuss the economic, political, technological, social, market, geographic, supplier, and distributor sectors. Not every organization needs to be concerned about every sector. Appropriate sectors to examine depend on the organization's purpose.

The Economic Sector. For the most part, businesses deal in free markets. Fluctuations in the business cycle affect sales of company products, the number of people hired or laid off, the willingness of executives to invest in new equipment, and the availability of funds for expansion. However, changes in economic climate are not felt evenly across all industries. Some areas, such as government, are relatively immune from economic influence, but not entirely. Others are dramatically affected by shifts in interest rates or currency values.

Consider: (1) What are the prospects for recession, depression, recovery, or prosperity over a given time? (2) What is the inflation or deflation rate expected to be? (3) How much will banks and other thrift institutions charge for funds necessary for business expansion and for the purchase of new, updated equipment? (4) Will the U.S. dollar remain stable against foreign currencies? and (5) How much are consumers expected to spend over a given time? What is the aggregate load of consumer debt?

Changes in any of these areas vary in their influence on different firms, and even on work groups or job categories within those firms. In addition, economic conditions affect the demand for (or supply of) labor. Consider: What will the economy probably do over a given period? What trends, events, or issues are likely to become important to a firm? Why are they likely to be important?

Researchers differ in their views about the importance of economic trends or events. Based on an extensive research project of 358 cases over a 45-year period, Glueck (1980) found that economic conditions are always a major area of concern to strategic business planners, regardless of industry or stage in the business cycle. Other researchers have not reached the same conclusions. For instance, Wall (1974) found that economic conditions are least important in scanning.

Writers in the WLP field have identified many trends that they believe will become more important in the future (see, for instance, Bierema, Bing, and Carter 2002; McLagan 1999; Marquardt, King, and Koon 2001; Salopek 2002; Van Buren and Erskine 2002). What trends will probably become more important for your organization over time? Why are they likely to be important? How are they going to create pressure for change on each work group, in career patterns, and in job requirements?

The Political Sector. The political sector encompasses the actions of government at all levels. Government action in the United States of America and in other countries affects business action. And this influence is not one-sided. Business has a strong influence on the elections and voting patterns of legislators and the actions of other elected officials through sophisticated lobbying efforts.

Think for a moment about the pervasive influence of government on business in each of the following areas:

I Government regulation/deregulation of industry
I Court decisions
I Government in competition with business
I Government regulation of safety, environmental pollution, products, and services
I Government purchases of goods and services

- ❙ Tax incentives
- ❙ Actions of the Federal Reserve Board
- ❙ Actions of the Securities and Exchange Commission
- ❙ Platforms of political parties
- ❙ Investment incentives, antitrust law, and enforcement policies
- ❙ Federal, state, county, and municipal government laws/pending legislation
- ❙ Tariffs
- ❙ Trade policy
- ❙ Welfare reform and workfare policy
- ❙ Workforce development
- ❙ Economic development efforts

How many areas will probably be important to one firm over the next few years and the next decade? What other trends in government can affect a firm? How are these trends likely to exert pressure for change on or within groups outside the firm, on work groups inside the firm, on individuals aspiring to career moves, or on job requirements at each level and in different categories?

How many of these trends are likely to exert pressure for change on or within your organization in the future? Why do you think so?

The Technological Sector. *Technology* refers to equipment used in production or service delivery, as well as the know-how to use it. The introduction of new machinery or tools greatly increases production efficiency, making it less costly to manufacture goods or deliver services. But know-how is by far the most important component of technology. It is embodied in human skills, plant layout and design, computer software, and procedures used in laboratories.

Technology is not equally important to all organizations. However, scanning for technology change, while it might be the most important sector to examine at present (Rothwell, Prescott, and Taylor 1998), is fraught with difficulty (Scott 2001). In competitive, high technology firms such as Intel, it can be crucial to success. In labor-intensive organizations such as government agencies, machine- or tool-related technology will not be as important as it is in other settings.

Take into consideration these things: (1) *State-of-the-art developments* in new equipment and new work methods; (2) *research and development efforts* and their results; (3) *new markets created by new products* derived through research and development; (4) *new applications of existing technology;* and (5) *the changes required for technological innovation to be applied* in the firm and/or by consumers using new products. How much are these and other technological issues likely to affect specific work groups in a firm, individuals seeking advancement, and job requirements in different job categories? *Why* are these issues likely to be important? How are they likely to affect learning needs?

Researchers in Talent Development have identified several technological trends worth thinking about. The most obvious is the increasing application of *e-learning,* understood to mean electronically supported instructional efforts. Of course, not all organizations or individuals are ready for that (Haney 2002). Many organizations are finding that *blended learning*—the combination of technologically delivered instruction with other approaches—is most effective (*The Business of Training* 2002). Technologically oriented approaches to Talent Development place increased responsibility on learners for taking charge of their own learning, making their learning competence key to their success (Rothwell 2002).

Some jobs requiring only moderately specialized competencies will disappear with the advent of user-friendly software requiring less technical user knowledge. The pressure to become computer literate is now so strong that it affects nearly everyone.

Ask yourself: What technological trends will grow in importance for your organization in the future? How many will create different learning needs for various work groups, for individuals preparing for career advancement, and for incumbents in different job categories?

The Social Sector. The social sector encompasses the values, beliefs, and attitudes of (1) *the general public* about all businesses, the industry of which the organization is part, and the organization itself; (2) *external stakeholders* about the organization, its management, and its employees; and (3) *employees and managers* of the organization. Clearly, attitudes and expectations can influence sales of a firm's products or services and management practices. To cite one example: employee unionization is, in part, a result of attitudes about company management.

Consider future trends relative to

I   *Corporate social responsibility.* What does the public expect from business? How are attitudes changing about the role expected from business in society and the industry of which one organization is part?

I   *Company responsibility to consumers.* What do customers expect?

I   *Company responsibility to investors/stockholders.* What do investors or stockholders expect?

I   *Work.* What do people think about work? How much is work considered an economic necessity? An outlet for creative expression? Something to be balanced with personal life?

I   *Leisure.* How do people play? How do they find recreation?

I   *Marriage.* How do people view marriage? When do people marry? Remarry? Divorce? What prompts marriage? What prompts divorce?

I   *Family life.* How many children are couples having? When?

I   *Women working.* How many women are working? How many are heading single-parent families?

I   *Attitudes about government, companies, politics, the environment, regulations, discrimination in employment, drug abuse, and many more issues.* What do people think about these issues? How does it affect their behavior in the marketplace? In the workplace?

Which of these trends will probably become more important to one organization over time, to specific work groups, to individuals preparing for advancement, and to different job categories? How many other trends will also be important?

Research in Talent Development has identified several important social trends, as well as these future trends:

I   The organization's responsibility for an employee's physical, emotional, and psychological well-being will be increasingly emphasized.

I   Employees will demand more satisfaction from job and career.

I   People will live longer, the workforce will grow older, the typical retirement age will increase, the pool of entry-level workers will shrink, and a new baby boom might occur.

- Pregnancy will be delayed more often as the number of women in the workforce increases and the number of dual-career couples will increase.

- The proportion of minorities, especially Hispanics, will increase in the U.S. population and workforce, and higher numbers of new immigrants will enter the United States.

- Illiteracy will become more pervasive among some groups at the same time that formal education will increase among other groups in the workplace. Lack of adequate preparation for work will be evident.

- Job skills will become rapidly obsolete, as manufacturing declines and information and service jobs increase. The workplace will become robotized and automated.

- Middle management positions will decrease, while the proportion of white-collar jobs will increase.

- Mid-life job or career transitions will be more common, as will incidents of burnout.

- More scientists will be employed by the military.

- Businesses will continue to migrate to certain geographic areas.

Which trends do you think will become more important to your organization, to specific groups within your organization, to individuals seeking advancement, and to successful performance in different jobs? What learning needs will these trends create? Which trends will create the most important learning needs?

The Market Sector. The market sector overlaps with the social sector. It encompasses customers and competitors. Most managers appreciate the value of finding out about the people who purchase company products or services, because this information proves useful in designing products and marketing them. They also want to identify key competitors in the current business or in a different business they contemplate entering and gather information about a competitor's entry to (or exit from) a given market or changes in a competitor's products, advertising methods, or pricing methods. And good managers understand the importance of beating competitors by gaining special relationships with key suppliers, consumer groups, and shippers. Research indicates that competitive analysis may be the single most important ingredient in successful environmental scanning (Wall 1974; Aguilar 1967; and Keegan 1974).

Michael Porter, a familiar name in strategic planning, listed key issues or trends to consider in this section: (1) *Customer loyalty:* How loyal are customers to a given brand name? (2) *Costs:* What are the relative costs of two or more firms in producing goods/services, distributing, and advertising? What changes are likely? (3) *Strategies:* What are the present strategies of competitors? How are competitors likely to react to increased competition, to entry into new markets, and to changes in production, pricing, distribution, and promotion? (4) *Experience:* Who knows the industry better? Who has the known talent? and (5) *Financial matters*: What is the financial status of key competitors? How much evidence is there that their market share can be eroded? (Porter 1980).

How important are these issues likely to become for your organization in the future? What learning needs will these trends create in each company work group? What will be the needs of individuals seeking career advancement performance and success in each job?

The Geographic Sector. This sector of the environment has to do with the present geographical placement and future movements of consumers, competitors, suppliers, and distributors. There is at least one good reason why this sector is worth considering: a firm geographically closer to consumers, suppliers, and distributors is likely to enjoy a significant advantage over competitors in shipping and transportation costs.

When scanning this sector, ask these questions: (1) Are suppliers pulling up stakes to move? If so, where? Are any special trends evident? If so, what are they? (2) Where are distributors heading? Are wholesale and retail outlets opening faster in some areas than in others? Why? (3) Are competitors moving to new locations? Are they looking for sites abroad, where labor is often substantially cheaper than in the United States of America, or are they opening in domestic population sites of concentrated growth? Are any special trends evident? If so, what are they? (4) Where are consumers heading? What markets in the United States and abroad have the highest concentration of consumers to whom a particular company markets its products or services? Are changes evident? Are they expected? Which trends might become important to one organization? Why do you think so? What new learning needs will these trends create for people in the organization?

The Supplier Sector. This sector encompasses organizations that provide raw materials. Clearly, the higher the cost of supplies, the higher the cost of finished goods. Strategists should thus be concerned about any changes in the availability of supplies. They should consider several questions. First, what trends are evident in the availability of supplies? How many companies produce subassemblies, mine needed ores, or manufacture essential machines? Second, what trends are evident in the cost of supplies? Will suppliers face new costs of production as a result of increased regulation and declining availability of *their* supplies? Third, what trends are evident in the organization's relations with its suppliers? Fourth, what companies produce key supplies that are absolutely critical to production? What is their status? Of these trends, which ones will be most significant to one organization in the future? How might they create new learning needs? What makes you think so? Are other trends in this sector worth watching? If so, why are they important?

The Distribution Sector. This sector focuses on organizations that relay products to ultimate users. For instance, wholesale and retail stores are distributors for manufacturers. Strategists in any organization should ask themselves several questions about distributors. First, which are the key organizations distributing their products or delivering their services? What organizations are likely to be more important in the future? Second, what trends are evident at the wholesale or retail level? Third, what trends are generally evident in a firm's relations with its distributors? Fourth, what are the chances that a key distributor is open to takeover by others? Are any of them hostile? Are substitute distributors available? What trends do you believe will be important in this environmental sector for one organization in the future? Why do you think so? How might these trends create new learning needs for work groups in your organization, for individuals seeking career advancement, and for performance requirements for different job categories?

Step 4: Anticipate the effects of environmental changes.

What will happen as a result of changes in the external environment? This question is very difficult to answer, for at least two reasons: Any trend can exert multiple influences, and managers can choose to either act in anticipation of an environmental change, or choose to do nothing. About the best that can be hoped for is some educated guesswork about the likely effects of external changes.

Most discussions of environmental scanning usually focus on the effects of external trends on an entire organization. The perspective is appropriate to top management. Little or no attempt is made to deal with the influence of trends on relations with external groups, different work groups, skill or competency requirements in work groups within the organization, skills or competencies needed in different job categories, or the special preparations necessary for individuals seeking career advancement in a changing environment.

The trouble with this viewpoint is that it tends to limit strategic, entrepreneurial thinking to a handful of people at the top. As a consequence, the grand vision presented by corporate planners rarely stays long with mid-level managers. Yet neither strategic thinking nor action should be limited to top managers. Others need to think and act strategically, too.

The effects of environmental change are not limited solely to the organizational-environmental interface. Each work group, each job category, and each individual is affected by external change, even though change is not felt in the same ways by all. A key distinction between lower-level managers and top managers is that the former group is more heavily affected by what is happening *inside* the organization. In some important respects, that makes their jobs more challenging than their top management counterparts. They have to scan *two* environments (Rothwell and Sredl 2000): (1) the environment *outside the organization*, particularly sectors most pertinent to activities of their work units or departments; and (2) the environment *inside the organization but outside the departments they head*, particularly strategic business plans imposed from the top and internal policies or procedures affecting their operations. Consider Exhibit 4–3, which illustrates these two external environments.

Who occupies a better position to assess the effects of external environmental change on activities in one part of the organization than managers and employees working in that part? Top managers have a broad perspective, important in its way but not necessarily helpful for nitty-gritty operations.

Exhibit 4–3: The Environmental Context of Any Department, Division, or Work Group Inside the Organization

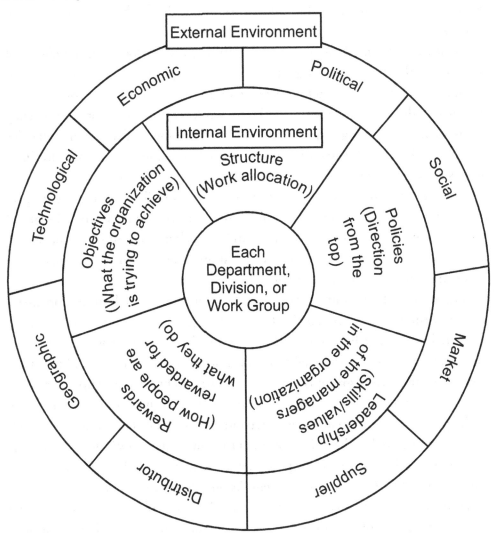

Numerous forecasting methods are often suggested for predicting the effects of external trends, but training people to think strategically might be more useful than forecasting. Training helps people spot and anticipate threats and opportunities to goal achievement, whether originating inside or outside the organization. A good place to start is with environmental scanning, as it can be applied to managing departments, careers, and job activities. Of course, the Talent Development effort can and should play a central role in this training. At the same time, of course, the Talent Development effort is subject to external environmental trends, (particularly those having to do with Talent Development practices), as well as policies, procedures, and other constraints on Talent Development inside the organization.

If managers resist planned learning activities and do not see the need for anticipatory thinking, it might take some effort just to get them to feel the need. Once they understand its importance, how do WLP practitioners design instruction on scanning? One approach: Introduce everyone in the organization to the basic principles of scanning and provide them with structured opportunities to identify pertinent trends and project likely effects of those trends in the future. They should then be given an opportunity to establish action plans for anticipating those trends.

Some managers will object, arguing that training on environmental scanning is not necessary because it is essentially idle crystal-ball gazing. But the following arguments might convince them:

1. The more information collected and applied in strategic decision-making, the more likely it is that performance will be effective.
2. As managers increase their awareness of the environment and its effects, their performance improves.
3. The greater the differences in perceptions about the environment among managers, the better the organizational performance is likely to be. Conflict breeds creative solutions to problems.
4. There is a strong correlation between organization's success and an appropriate amount of environmental scanning, given the nature of the environment in which the firm is or will be operating.

It might be risky to extend these assumptions to a Talent Development effort, but there is an intuitive appeal to unlocking the creativity of individual employees and encouraging them to *anticipate* rather than just *react to* future threats and opportunities. Training in environmental scanning is one step in this direction.

Step 5: Identify future learning needs.

The fifth step in environmental scanning for Talent Development is to anticipate future learning needs based on present trends. Let's begin with a broad overview of the traditional approach to needs assessment, and then switch to an overview of future-oriented needs assessment. We'll then show how future-oriented needs assessment can be applied to *external groups* such as the general public, consumers, suppliers, and distributors, and *internal groups* such as people in work units, individuals seeking advancement, and job categories.

The traditional approach to instructional needs assessment is based on answering four basic questions:

1. *What should be?* This question focuses on *criteria*—desired present knowledge or skills.
2. *What is?* This question focuses on *condition*—present knowledge or actual performance.
3. *What are the differences between the actual and the desirable?* This question is usually intended to pinpoint *deficiencies* (poor performance), but it is also capable of pinpointing proficiencies (exceptional performance).
4. *How much are these differences attributable to lack of knowledge/skills or to some other cause?* This question separates issues that can be appropriately addressed by Talent Development from those that cannot.

These four questions are appropriate to ask when action will be taken to deal with past or present performance strengths and/or weaknesses in a stable environment. They are not appropriate by themselves when the environment is unstable, because changing environmental conditions will likely produce new and different threats to performance and opportunities for improving it.

Future-oriented instructional needs assessment is a modification of the traditional approach. WLP practitioners and line managers pose five questions that differ from the four questions on which traditional needs assessment is based. First, *what should be in the future?* This focuses on a vision of the future and on desired *future criteria*. What should be the future relationship between the corporation and the general public or key external stakeholders? What skills have to be available in the work group to meet future responsibilities? What do people have to be able to do to prepare for career advancement and future job requirements? Second, *what is the present status?* This question focuses on present conditions. Third, *what will probably be the differences between future criteria and present conditions?* The answer to this question underscores a planning gap between present and future *and* between actual and desired conditions. Fourth, *how much will these differences be attributable to lack of knowledge or skill?* This question helps sort out instructional from noninstructional needs. Fifth and finally, *what learning experiences are necessary to meet future knowledge and skill requirements?* If discrepancies between present and future needs are not attributable to lack of knowledge or skills, then noninstructional strategies will have to be used to deal with them. These strategies include changes in job design, work, methods, and organizational structure.

How is future-oriented needs assessment applied? One way to anticipate future problems and opportunities is to devote attention to the future learning needs of the general public. What does the public need to know about the corporation in the future so that relations will be good? If WLP practitioners choose to address this area, they have to add sectors to their analysis during environmental scanning. More specifically, they should consider

1. Trends in *public and/or private education at all levels.* What are the prospects that young people in elementary and secondary school will receive adequate training in basic skills? How adequate are programs in community colleges, universities, and highly specialized technical schools for meeting the future labor requirements of an organization?

2. Trends in *economic development.* What prospects exist for effective vocational programs for building the competencies of the economically disadvantaged and the technologically displaced? Will government retraining funds be available? What requirements have to be met in order to qualify for them?

3. Trends in *attitude about the industry, organization, or business in general.* How does the public feel about business, about an industry, about one organization? Are there special-interest groups opposed to an

organization's interests? Are these groups likely to gain popular support and capture media attention?

It can be very worthwhile for an organization to sponsor future-oriented instruction as a means of winning long-term public support or averting long-term public disapproval for its products or services. Some organizations do this by adopting schools, for example, and contributing funds and management talent to their improvement. Other organizations establish closer ties with colleges and provide them with funds, talent, and access to equipment and facilities. Still other organizations champion economic development in communities in which their facilities are located. They establish ties with public sector economic developers and work toward improving the quality of life in the community. Some organizations sponsor programs for training the disadvantaged or retraining those displaced because of changes in family structure, automation, or plant shutdown.

How do WLP practitioners know whether all this is necessary? They should ask these questions:

1. *What is the present status of an organization relative to the general public?* What do members of the public know about the organization? How does this knowledge—or lack of it—affect behavior?

2. *What should be in the future?* What should the public know about a corporation and its products or services?

3. *What differences are likely to develop over time between what is and what should be?*

4. *How much will these differences be attributable to general public knowledge about an organization?* When the public lacks knowledge about the organization, this is a future threat and a learning need. On the other hand, public awareness of an organization can be a future opportunity, as well as an indication of unique talent or competency.

5. *What instructional events sponsored by the organization can help avert likely threats and seize future opportunities?*

Efforts of this kind increase what representative members of the general public know about an organization, its products, its services, and its operational requirements.

Key External Stakeholders and Their Future Learning Needs. Increasingly, Talent Development activities are directed to investors, suppliers, distributors, and customers, as well as to employees. Customer training is growing more important.

Why bother meeting the future learning needs of key external stakeholders? The more that investors, suppliers, distributors, and customers know about an organization, the more likely they are to act in ways beneficial to it. There are other benefits as well: Talent Development activities directed to external groups are likely to be run on a profit basis, which can in turn fund Talent Development activities directed to company employees.

It is easy to point to examples of externally directed Talent Development activities. Hospitals run wellness programs to help potential clients avert illness. Accounting firms offer training to clients on how to handle the accounting function. These firms meet the needs of external groups while marketing their services through instruction. Computer companies are just now discovering what most everybody has long suspected: lack of customer knowledge about computers is a major barrier to computer sales. The same principle applies to all high-technology firms. Automobile and heavy equipment manufacturers have long offered training to the sales and service employees at their dealerships. To sell and service a product, dealers must know it inside and out. Government agencies sometimes train contractors and vendors about government requirements and expectations. In each case, Talent Development is anticipatory, geared to meeting the learning needs of customers and other external groups *before they arise.* If a firm is introducing new products or services, future-oriented instruction may be necessary to avert major problems later on—particularly if these new products/services will *change* management's expectations about what suppliers or distributors should do to meet the firm's needs: What should consumers know to use the product? Ask yourself these questions:

1. *What is?* Do customers now get maximum benefit from an organization's products or services? Are suppliers and distributors interacting with the organization as efficiently as possible?

2. *What should be in the future?* What behavior is desired from suppliers, distributors, or customers? In other words, what should they be doing?

How can customer knowledge about product use be improved, for example?

3. *What gaps will probably exist between what is at present and what should be in the future?* Given present trends, what is likely to happen over time?

4. *How much will these gaps be attributable to the knowledge or skills of external groups?* Lack of knowledge is a learning need and a threat; extensive knowledge about the organization's products/services among consumers or other groups is a possible future opportunity.

5. *What planned learning activities offered between present and future can help avert potential threats to an organization's sales and other activities?* What planned learning activities can help an organization seize new opportunities by offering new, potentially profitable services to the organization's suppliers, distributors, and customers, and improve efficient operations between members of external groups and the organization?

It is easy to see that major changes of any kind create needs among customers, suppliers, and distributors. As new products or services are offered, managers should consider and plan to act on the future impact of them on groups outside the organization. Talent Development is one tool that can help.

The Organization and its Future Learning Needs. An external trend may create the need for changes in the collective competencies needed by a work group to meet its responsibilities to the organization. Organized learning efforts at the work group level often take a long time to succeed, because group norms and culture militate against change. Instruction alone is rarely adequate to change culture. However, planned learning activities can ensure that the work group has the right competencies that are essential to carry out its duties.

To apply future-oriented instructional needs assessment to employee development needs at the work group level, WLP practitioners and managers should

1. *Develop a classification scheme by which to analyze the organization.* (The same one devised during traditional needs assessment can be used.) Break the organization down into work groups.

2. *Analyze present conditions and consider how they might change over time.* What skills or competencies are now available in each group? How will the group gradually change over time? What are the present duties of the work group?

3. *Clarify implications of strategic business plans on each work group.* What should each group do in the future? What skills or competencies will be needed?

4. *Identify gaps between present and desired future conditions.* What should each work group be able to do in the future? What skill or competency mix among group members is necessary?

5. *Assess how much these gaps will be attributable to the collective knowledge and skills in each work group.* If the work group is already well-positioned to carry out future responsibilities, it is blessed with an opportunity. If the group lacks adequate skills or competencies to meet future demands, it faces a future threat.

6. *Consider what instructional efforts sponsored for work groups can help avert future threats or seize future opportunities.* What learning activities can develop the work group so that skills or competencies required in the future will be available when needed?

The Individual and Future Learning Needs. The focus of most planned learning is on the individual. The major responsibility for learning rests with the person, not with supervisors or organizations. Employee educational efforts are perhaps best handled in highly individualized ways. People should have a say in experiences designed to help them achieve their own career objectives, if not the major say.

Probably the best way to assess employee educational needs is to begin with a two-fold career program. On one hand, there are present and future careers inside and outside the organization. WLP practitioners and others in the organization should pose such questions as:

1. *What are the present relationships between jobs in the organization?* What are the career paths in the organization? What education and experience are necessary to move from one job to another?

2. *What should happen to relationships between jobs if management tries to anticipate changes resulting from new technology or work methods? How should career paths change if job duties at each level are to be consistent with strategic business plans?*

3. *What gaps are likely to exist between the situations considered in items 1 and 2?*

4. *In what ways can individuals prepare themselves for changing career paths/job duties through planned educational experiences?*

On the other hand, each person should consider such questions as:

1. *What are my future career objectives?* That is, what do I want to be capable of doing at a future time?

2. *What trends inside and outside the organization are likely to affect my career progress?* How should I prepare for their potential influence on my career?

3. *What are my present strengths and weaknesses relative to my career objectives?* How well-prepared am I now to assume the future position I desire?

4. *What gaps exist between who I am now and who I want to become?* In short, what do I need to learn in order to meet my learning needs?

5. *What formal or informal learning experiences can help avert likely threats to my career progress in the future, and help me seize opportunities to further my career progress?*

Employee educational needs are identified through comparisons of individual career plans and organizational career paths.

Jobs and Future Learning Needs. Of course, jobs cannot "learn." Only individuals can learn. However, requirements in each job category can change as a result of pressures inside and outside the job. Each change in job requirements creates training needs. Future-oriented training might be necessary when environmental trends affect *work method* (how is a job done?), job *duties* (what is expected of a job incumbent?), and *desired results* (what outcomes are needed?).

Training needs should be viewed not just from the standpoint of *each job*, but also from the standpoint of *job categories*. In this way, changes in job requirements at *each* level are also considered *across* levels. To conduct future-oriented training needs assessment, WLP practitioners and operating managers should

1. *Create a classification scheme for jobs in the organization.* Job categories devised for traditional needs assessment can be used.
2. *Consider present and future job requirements.* What is the status of present performance and duties in each job category? What job duties, work methods, and results might change as a consequence of trends?
3. *Clarify implications of business strategy for each job category in the organization.* What job requirements should be established for the future if jobs are to be carried out in ways consistent with strategic business plans?
4. *Identify gaps in the future between what is and what should be.*
5. *Assess how much these gaps will be attributable to lack of knowledge or skill on the part of job incumbents.*
6. *Consider what training offered between the present and the future can avert future threats to job performance and seize opportunities to improve job performance.*

The results of this assessment produce a general, structured training curriculum that facilitates job performance for each job category. With some modifications, the same approach can be used to focus on meeting the one-time training needs for one group of job incumbents experiencing unique performance problems or opportunities.

Future-oriented training differs from other future-oriented Talent Development activities in that it is the easiest to "sell" to management. The reason is that the time between need and corrective action is relatively brief. Managers may well feel the need to avert short-term problems by offering training just prior to the installation of new equipment or the implementation of new work methods, for example. They might have a harder time feeling the need to help individuals prepare for future career advancement, develop collective skills or competencies of work groups through long-term change efforts, or change group or cultural norms.

Sources of Information for Talent Development Scanning

What sources of information are used in environmental scanning?

Perhaps the most often-used source of information is word-of-mouth. The higher a manager's placement within the hierarchy of an organization, the more likely he or she is to rely on word-of-mouth information about the environment. The effectiveness of scanning increases as more resources are relied on and more issues are considered. In larger organizations, information is solicited primarily from people inside the organization. In smaller organizations, information about the environment tends to come from outsiders. Written information is used more by lower-level than higher-level managers and more by those in stable than in dynamic industries. The most important word-of-mouth sources for strategists are personal and professional acquaintances. Information from suppliers is least important.

Of what value is this information? First, it suggests that WLP practitioners must somehow gain personal access to top managers if Talent Development is to have a greater impact on strategy formulation. It also suggests that WLP managers, traditionally lower-level managers, are more likely to rely on written sources and research studies than their higher-level counterparts.

Where can a WLP practitioner go to collect information about general trends in the external environment and specific trends affecting the field? To answer these questions, consult Exhibit 4–4.

These sources of information can be used by WLP practitioners in several ways. First, they provide a starting point for stimulating the thinking of WLP staff members, operating managers, and even top-level strategists about issues that may imply future instructional needs. Second, they serve as a starting point for future-oriented instructional needs assessments by helping pinpoint key issues or trends for subsequent analysis. Third, they stimulate learners to think about trends that can influence how they can subsequently apply what they learn amid changing conditions. Fourth, they elicit "felt needs" among managers and individuals before a problem is experienced. Fifth and finally, they help frame instructional issues for consideration by top management committees, corporate planners, and WLP managers. How environmental information is used depends to some extent on the "age" of the WLP department and organization. Small, newly formed organizations with correspondingly new WLP departments are likely to approach the environment like entrepreneurs: Specific issues will be seized and turned to advantage without much systematic analysis. WLP practitioners, as is common in newly formed departments, will tend to focus inside the organization. As the organization or the WLP department gains maturity, special-purpose committees will often be formed in response to specific problems—usually problems identified by top management. WLP practitioners gradually pay more attention to the external environment, but only to identify instructional needs within the organization. As the organization or WLP department reaches full maturity, WLP

Exhibit 4–4: Resources for Finding Information about the Future*

Link	A brief description of the Web site
1. http://www.wfs.org	The Web site of the World Future Society, which has over 30,000 members. The Web site lists issues, resources, and people that might be helpful in conducting environmental scanning.
2. http://www.hudson.org	The Web site of the Hudson Institute.
3. http://www.futurenet.org/Default.htm	The Web site of the journal YES!, which is about positive futures.
4. http://www.extropy.org/eo/index.html	A Web site of an online journal that focuses on creative views of the future.
5. http://www.lucifer.com/~sasha/refs/wfsgbc.html	A Web site that provides links to numerous other Web sites about the future.
6. http://www.naisbitt.com	The Web site of John Naisbitt, author of *Megatrends*.
7. http://www.aspeninst.org	The Web site of the Aspen Institute.
8. http://www.brainreserve.com	The Web site of Faith Popcorn, popular futurist.
9. http://www.coatesandjarratt.com	The Web site of Coates and Jarrat.
10. http://www.tfg.com/	The Web site of the Futures Group International, which posts articles about strategic planning.
11. http://www.iconoculture.com	A Web site that contains newsletters and summaries of future trends.
12. http://www.altfutures.com	A Web site of a futurist consulting firm, with summaries of the firm's findings.

*This list of resources is based on W. Conhaim's Futurist Resources article *Link Up* (1999). The article contains a more extensive list of links.

practitioners should devote more time to scanning all the environments with which they deal.

Methods for Carrying Out Environmental Scanning for Talent Development

What methods can be used to scan the environment to begin the process of future-oriented instructional needs assessment in order to head off likely future problems before they arise? What methods can be used to create future-oriented experiential exercises for use in training sessions, strategic planning retreats, problem-finding meetings, and other settings? To construct future-oriented tests to follow instruction to see how present skills or competencies will hold up during future changes? To give learners opportunities to ponder—or even artificially experience—conditions expected in the future, so as to motivate them to do forward-thinking? To create new ideas and new knowledge?

These methods include job/task analysis, future-oriented employee appraisals, future-oriented assessment centers, group discussions, future-oriented critical incidents, the Delphi procedure, and Nominal Group Technique. Many otherwise traditional data collection techniques used in needs assessment can also be modified and used in environmental scanning. Interviews are widely applied in social science data-gathering. They range from highly informal discussions to highly formal, structured surveys. We have already discussed their traditional application to needs assessment in the last chapter.

How are interviews applied to environmental scanning? There are several ways. First, they can identify possible trends outside or inside the organization that can affect external groups, work groups, individuals, or job requirements. Second, they can narrow down possible effects of these trends on work groups, individuals, or jobs. Third, they can help separate instructional from noninstructional needs. Open-ended interview questions are most appropriate for gathering data on these issues. On the other hand, closed-ended questions are appropriately used to prioritize future instructional needs or to gauge the importance of environmental trends.

One round of interviews is rarely sufficient for everything. Several rounds should be used in designing a future-oriented curriculum. As each round of interviews is completed, practitioners will find that they are learning and discovering more about future instructional needs. Where do WLP practitioners start? They should ask executives, managers, and supervisors questions such as these:

I What groups (customers, suppliers, distributors, or others) are dealt with on a regular basis?

I What changes in behaviors of these groups over the last year or two are noticeable, if any?

I Given the changes in behaviors, what should the company do now to adapt to these changes?

I What should be done in the future?

I How might these changes affect your work group in the future?

I What changes in policies or operating procedures in some work units within the company have been noticeable over the last year or two? Describe what has changed or what is changing.

I Given this change, what does your work group have to do to adapt to these changes?

I What should your work group be doing three years from now if it is to function in a way consistent with company strategic business plans?

I What should be the duties of each position in your work group three years from now? Describe how those duties are changing in each position.

I What problems stemming from environmental change over the next three years will impede desired changes in your work group?

I How will changes affecting the company influence potential for career advancement?

I What changes do you see over the next three years in the responsibilities of such categories as executives, middle managers, and supervisors?

I What organized learning experiences will contribute to heading off problems in the future for your work group and for individuals seeking career advancement?

More-detailed questions focus on specific sectors of the environment, environmental effects, or learning needs. The results of such an investigation should be useful in discovering future threats and opportunities for dealing with the environment.

Surveys can be substituted for interviews. For exploring future environmental change, they usually do not work as well as interviews, which allow follow-up questioning and detailed probing. On the other hand, they are more advantageous than interviews when managers are skeptical about the need for change, and extensive evidence is needed to change their minds. Surveys can be most useful for prioritizing future trends previously identified through interviews. Like interviews, they can dramatize specific environmental threats and opportunities facing the organization, a work group, individuals seeking advancement, or job categories.

Future-oriented job analysis is more concrete than interviews or surveys. There are several ways to analyze jobs. Traditional job analysis describes how work has been done in the past. Each traditional approach to job analysis can be reoriented to a future perspective so that decision-makers can speculate on how work will probably be done or can clarify the way they want it to be done.

Task analysis is similar to job analysis, but is more specific. WLP practitioners can use it to identify how change will affect or alter work tasks. Obviously, it is not possible to observe events that have not yet happened, but they can be simulated by (1) identifying *what* trends might affect work, (2) identifying *how* the trends might affect work, and (3) setting up conditions like those expected or desired in the future (complete with new machines, tools, or work methods) and then observing people perform under simulated conditions. In planning instruction prior to the introduction of new weapons systems in the military or new machines in industrial settings, for instance, before-the-fact task analysis is often a necessity.

Future-oriented employee performance appraisals can provide guidance to individuals in preparing for future jobs. Werther and Davis (1985) distinguish between past-oriented appraisals that assess how well people have been doing their jobs over the past year, and future-oriented appraisals that evaluate future employee potential or help individuals establish performance goals. Two future-oriented methods they describe are (1) *self-appraisals* in which individuals set their own goals for work and career achievement and (2) *management by objectives* in which individuals and their superiors negotiate goals for a coming year.

However, self-appraisal and management by objectives seldom consider future trends likely to affect individual performance. They should. In self-appraisal, the individual should apply strategic career planning to (1) establish future career goals and objectives; (2) identify personal and professional strengths and weaknesses; (3) examine the environment for trends affecting career progress; (4) compare personal and professional strengths and weaknesses to environmental trends inside and outside the organization; and (5) select a long-term career strategy.

In management by objectives, individuals and their superiors should consider external trends and events that affect performance as they negotiate annual objectives. There is no need to be fancy here. A simple list of trends should be helpful in formulating and negotiating objectives.

Assessment centers were described in the last chapter. Based on traditional job analysis, they use multiple raters and structured activities to evaluate how well people are likely to carry out job activities. Assessment centers are touted as future oriented because they assess individual potential, but in reality they are rarely future oriented: the activities are not based on conditions expected in the future, and trained evaluators (who are usually experienced managers) tend to assess performance from a past rather than a future orientation. To solve these problems, WLP practitioners should base the assessment center on future-oriented job analysis, and should rely on evaluators trained to strategically rate employee potential.

Group discussions can focus on trends in the environment, effects of those trends, instructional versus noninstructional needs, or the importance of environmental issues on work groups, individuals, and/or job categories. Any group effort is advantageous, because groups tend to be more creative than individuals as long as people can avoid the conformist pressure of groupthink and are willing to voice their true feelings in front of superiors.

Zemke and Kramlinger (1982) suggest how to use what they call "consensus groups" in traditional instructional needs assessment. The idea is to rely on a jury of experts or "experienced" employees to arrive at a consensus on criteria for assessing job tasks, importance of tasks, or any other issue.

In addition, Zemke and Kramlinger suggest there are methods that can be easily applied to environmental scanning. One particularly promising approach is the *priority matrix*: People engaged in environmental scanning list activities in a job, work group, or profession; set environmental sectors against activity areas in a matrix; and describe in each cell of the matrix any one of the following: likely trends in the environment that might affect the activity, the likely effects of trend(s), the importance of the effects, instructional needs that might emerge in this area, and the appropriate priority for the instructional need. The process of identifying future learning needs can be an iterative one.

Future-oriented critical incidents are based on (1) inferences made about trends in the environment, (2) simulations of future conditions, and (3) observation of simulations. A critical incident is important *(critical)* and is an occasion *(incident)*. To anticipate future learning needs and changes in the environment, WLP practitioners and/or operating managers should (1) call together a group of experienced supervisors or job incumbents; (2) explain what critical incidents are and why they are used; (3) provide an example of a critical incident; (4) describe for group members the nature of incidents they are to report and how they should report the incidents; (5) ask group members to describe aspects of their jobs that they believe will be most important for successful job performance at a future time; (6) solicit information about present levels of performance; (7) ask group members to elaborate on levels of performance they expect to be necessary at a future time; and (8) have group members describe what training/education will be needed from present to future. The same approach can be applied to identifying instructional needs of organizational units, customers, or others dealing with the organization.

The *Delphi procedure* and the *Nominal Group Technique* can easily be used to (1) identify environmental trends, (2) address their effects, (3) separate instructional from noninstructional needs, and (4) set priorities for planned learning. Indeed, these approaches can also be applied during instructional delivery to stimulate creative, future-oriented thinking. To apply the Delphi procedure from a future orientation, WLP practitioners should first select a panel of experts—experienced workers, superiors, or people from outside the organization. Second, practitioners should use a small "focus group"—a handful of people—to develop a questionnaire on environmental issues or trends that might affect work groups, individuals, or job requirements in the future. The written questionnaire should then be sent to the panel of experts. Third, practitioners should compile the views of panel members and feed them back. They should ask the panel members to comment on or rate the opinions. Fourth, practitioners should continue this process until the panel members' views converge around common conclusions. It might take several different iterations of this process to identify key trends, their effects, instructional needs, and priorities.

To apply the NGT from a future orientation, WLP practitioners should call together a small group of "experts" on a work group—individuals who share similar career goals/aspirations, and job activities. Practitioners should explain the purpose of the NGT to the experts. The experts should record on slips of paper ideas about any one of the following: key environmental trends/issues; effects of these trends/issues; learning versus nonlearning needs; or learning priorities over time. WLP practitioners should then collect the slips of paper; record the ideas on an overhead or flipchart so that all the participants can see them; allow group members to discuss the ideas; and call for a vote on which ideas are best, most accurate, or most appropriate. It is thus possible to reorient each traditional approach to instructional needs assessment so that it helps predict future learning needs.

Step 6: Reassess learning needs by market or market segment.

Compiling results is the final step in environmental scanning. These results should be expressed so that they can be compared to the results of a comprehensive needs assessment. Through this comparison, a long-term organizational strategy for Talent Development can be formulated to integrate and coordinate activities and provide direction.

The results of environmental scanning should address two major questions. First, what major threats and opportunities will probably be posed by environmental changes to the organization's dealings with the general public and key external stakeholders, the organization as a whole, each work group, career objectives of individuals, and job performance or job requirements? Second, what should be the future status of the corporation relative to the general public and key external stakeholders, the organization as a whole, each work group, individuals as they progress toward realization of career objectives, and job performance or job requirements? In this context, a *threat* is any expected deficiency between what is at present and what should be in the future that stems from lack of knowledge or skill. It is a future learning need—an expected deficiency. An *opportunity* is the opposite of a threat—a future talent or competency.

In Chapter 3 we discussed the importance of broadly summarizing present strengths and weaknesses. Broadly summarizing future threats and opportunities is also very important. Organizational strategy for Talent Development is established by comparing strengths, weaknesses, threats, and opportunities.

To derive a summary of threats and opportunities, WLP practitioners should simply compile the results of environmental scanning efforts and classify the results of each trend as a threat or an opportunity. Threats or opportunities can vary in scope: Some apply to the organization; some apply to specific work groups; some apply to individuals pursuing career goals; and some apply to requirements for performance in a job.

The classification of trends or their effects can be based on the opinions of WLP practitioners, the opinions of strategists, or the opinions of others—key middle managers, for example. The results of this analysis are recorded on a simple worksheet that provides a simple view of the "big picture"—long-term, broad-scale future learning needs.

Activity 4–1: A Worksheet to Collect Information on Future-Oriented Needs

Directions: Use this activity as the basis for a structured interview guide or an open-ended survey. Ask members of your panel of respondents to answer each question individually. They can continue their responses on additional paper if necessary.

Critical Area

1. What aspect of (*your job/a job category/the work unit's responsibilities and duties/customer service*)* do you believe will be most important to successful performance in *five years*? Describe it.

Reasoning

2. Explain why you believe this aspect will be most important in five years.

Present Performance

3. Describe what you believe to be *exemplary performance* on this aspect at present.

*Choose one and use it consistently throughout the worksheet.

Activity 4–1: *(continued)*

Desired Future Performance

---

4.   Describe what you believe will have to be exemplary performance on this aspect in five years if the organization's strategic business plans are being implemented successfully.

Instructional Needs

---

5.   Describe the instruction (training/education) that will be necessary to narrow whatever gaps exist between exemplary performance on this aspect at present and desired performance in five years.

Activity 4–2: A Case Study on the Environmental Scanning for the Talent Development Effort

Directions: Read the case scenario below and answer the questions that follow.

The Amorphous Corporation* is an industry leader in retail grocery sales. The corporation owns and operates over 1,000 grocery stores throughout the United States and Canada. It is strongly positioned to capture a greater market share in discount grocery sales. Most of Amorphous's stores are new, and most are located in neighborhoods where family incomes average $50,000 a year.

Amorphous has a centralized Workplace Learning and Performance department in St. Louis, Missouri that is responsible for coordinating the company's Talent Development effort. New store managers receive one month of intensive training at the new corporate training center located in a St. Louis suburb. They learn all aspects of store management through courses such as Customer Relations, Store Accounting, and Personnel Practices.

Amorphous's strategic business plan calls for rapid growth. The company will not be able to develop and train enough store managers internally using present methods. The company does not plan for human resources comprehensively, relying instead on locally hired assistant store managers as the chief source for future store managers.

Questions

1. What trends external to Amorphous are likely to affect it? Identify the trends and then describe their possible effects on Amorphous.

2. What trends external to Amorphous are likely to create new training needs for store managers? Explain your reasoning.

3. What threats and opportunities to the Talent Development effort are likely to exist in the future for Amorphous?

*A ficticious company.

PART III

CHOOSING AND IMPLEMENTING ORGANIZATIONAL STRATEGY FOR THE DEVELOPMENT OF TALENT

How does an organization select and implement a strategy for Talent Development? The chapters in Part III answer that question. There are two chapters in this part.

Chapter 5 is entitled "Choosing Organizational Strategy for the Development of Talent." This chapter describes important issues that should be considered when choosing the organizational strategy for the development of talent. It offers specific advice and addresses special issues to consider in this process. Lastly, the chapter cautions strategists about the need to plan for contingencies.

Chapter 6 is entitled "Implementing Organizational Strategy for the Development of Talent." It emphasizes how important it is to establish and align operational objectives, organizational policies, leadership, reporting relationships, reward systems, budgets, and communication strategies so that these key issues in implementation work in harmony rather than at cross purposes.

CHOOSING ORGANIZATIONAL STRATEGY FOR THE DEVELOPMENT OF TALENT

Previous chapters addressed the importance of comprehensive needs assessment and environmental scanning for Talent Development. Comprehensive needs assessment is the process of identifying present strengths (proficiencies) and present weaknesses (deficiencies) of learner categories. Environmental scanning for Talent Development is the process of predicting future threats (deficiencies) and opportunities (proficiencies). These two things must be done before organizational strategy is selected for the development of talent—the subject of this chapter.

Organizational Strategy for the Development of Talent: Definition and Importance

Definition. *Strategic choice* for developing talent resembles strategic choice in strategic business planning. It is the decision to select a long-term strategy for building the organization's future talent needs.

In strategic business planning, *Grand Strategy* usually refers to the comprehensive, holistic strategy (the means) used to pursue the ends (strategic objectives) in the future. Grand Strategy traditionally denotes direction for an entire corporation. It guides lower-level strategies of autonomous business units within a corporation and such functions as operations/production, marketing, finance, and human resources/personnel. Further, it addresses this question: *Given present internal strengths/weaknesses and likely future-term threats/opportunities, what strategy is likely to give the organization the greatest competitive advantages?* Key to an effective strategic choice is the process by which strategy is formulated (Kim and Mauborgne 2002).

The strategic development of talent integrates long-term, intermediate-term, and short-term learning plans designed to cultivate needed talent. It helps meet needs created by strategic business plans and HR plans. **Organizational strategy for the development of talent means having a comprehensive, general instructional plan—otherwise called a curriculum—that supports achievement of strategic business plans and HR plans.** "Choosing SDT strategy" means deciding on an organizational strategy for the development of talent—*a long-term direction for learning activities offered by the organization.* A strategic choice for Talent Development is thus a unified learning plan that integrates such WLP functions as organization development, nonemployee development, employee development, employee education, and employee training.

The Importance of Choosing Organizational Strategy for the Development of Talent. Organizational strategy for the development of talent positions Talent Development efforts so that they support strategic business plans, work unit plans, individual career plans, and effective job performance. It prioritizes Talent Development activities, concentrating initiatives where they are most likely to be useful to the organization in achieving sustained competitive advantage. It encourages long-term, strategic thinking among learners so that they can take charge of their own development initiatives. And it exerts pressure on top managers to consider linkages between long-term strategic business plans and shorter-term HR decisions.

There are other reasons for choosing a strategy for the development of talent. First, it helps unify top managers in their thinking about Talent Development. Second, it encourages proactive HR practitioners to align their efforts to the realization of strategic business plans. Third, it encourages WLP practitioners to think strategically, which may be increasingly important in their career success. Fourth, successful organizations in all industries deal strategically with their human resources. Fifth, an organizational strategy for the development of talent guides the management of the WLP department. Sixth, organizational strategy for the development of talent furnishes information to top managers about employee skills they should use in strategic business planning. Seventh and finally, organizational strategy for the development of talent helps implement changes in strategic business plans, HR plans, and marketing efforts.

Suggestions for Choosing Organizational Strategy for the Development of Talent

Numerous articles have appeared over the years about strategic planning for human resource development and related topics concerning how to develop the organization's talent. At this point, it is worth reviewing the advice of a few of these authors.

Advice. According to published articles on this subject over the years, WLP practitioners—by themselves or in concert with line managers—can take advantage of a wealth of accumulated information and advice about how they should pursue strategic planning. Here are some helpful suggestions:

I   Create a vision of what the WLP department or Talent Development effort should be at some point in the future (Hulett and Renjilian 1983; Pattan 1986; Ward 1982).

I   Prepare a purpose statement that clarifies the role of Talent Development in contributing to achievement of the organization's objectives and mission (Hulett and Renjilian 1983; Pattan 1986; Ward 1982).

I   Establish annual planning objectives for Talent Development, and link these objectives to the business mission (Pattan 1986).

I   Create a database about environmental changes inside and outside the organization (Harvey 1983; Pattan 1986; Ward 1982).

I   Work to develop a holistic Talent Development plan (Linkow 1985; Mirabile, Caldwell, and O'Reilly 1986).

I   Make sure Talent Development plans support strategic business plans (Harvey 1983; Linkow 1985).

I   Convince top managers that any change in business strategy implies a change in the future skill or competency needs of people in the organization (Desatnick 1984; Linkow 1985).

I Develop plans for Talent Development, even when no corporate strategic business plans exist or when the formal plans that do exist are ignored (Linkow 1985; Tregoe and Zimmerman 1984; Ward 1982).

I Establish checkpoints and periodic updates to assess whether organizational strategy for the development of talent still matches environmental conditions (Harvey 1983; Ward 1982).

Issues of Concern. Many articles on strategic planning for HRD or the strategic development of talent focus only on planning for the HRD or WLP department, and not on the role of all Talent Development activities in the organization. Talent Development planning is sometimes treated as the functional responsibility of WLP managers, rather than treated as a shared, joint responsibility of all prospective learners. While the reason for this focus is clear (most articles on HRD or WLP planning are written solely for an audience of HRD or WLP specialists), the unfortunate implication is that WLP managers should just develop plans to manage their departments, rather than coordinate organizational adaptation to environmental change through learning.

A second tendency suggested in the literature is failing to place the Talent Development strategy in the broader context of HR planning. If the aim is to marshal human talent in the future, however, developing people is not the only way to achieve that objective. Indeed, WLP practitioners should know about initiatives in process improvement and HR areas. After all, Talent Development planning is affected by other ways to source talent or to get the work done. Examples of those alternatives include outsourcing the work, insourcing (moving the work) from one department to another, and redesigning the work process. In each case, demands for talent are not changed, but are instead shifted from one place to another.

Choosing Organizational Strategy for the Development of Talent: The Process

The process of selecting organizational strategy for the development of talent resembles problem-finding in several key respects. Practitioners find problems, formulate them, identify appropriate ways to look at them, consider possible solutions, and choose one appropriate solution.

Step 1: Find the problems. The starting point for choice of strategy is to determine if a gap does exist (or will exist) between *what is* and *what should be*. It is the point when future problems or opportunities for improvement are recognized. After considering various alternative strategies or solutions, strategists decide on one they feel will help close present or future performance gaps.

In strategic business planning, a strategic choice is made after comparing an organization's present internal status and its expected future external environment. Strategic choice thus begins by doing a comprehensive review of factors affecting organizational success. There is no one widely accepted method for conducting such a review because factors affecting organizational success vary widely, depending on the organization's competitive position in the industry, how information is obtained and used, and what strategists desire in the future.

WOTS-UP analysis—sometimes called SWOT analysis—is one way to conduct this review. *WOTS-UP* is an acronym created from the first letters of four words—**w**eaknesses, **o**pportunities, **t**hreats, and **s**trengths. As used in strategic business planning, a *weakness* is whatever works against an organization in its present competitive efforts. A *strength* is a present advantage that an organization enjoys over its competitors. A *threat* is an expected future environmental change that will result in conditions disadvantageous to the organization. An *opportunity* is an expected future environmental change that will produce possibilities for gaining a competitive advantage. See Exhibit 5–1 for selected Web site resources to support SWOT analysis. Also see Exhibit 5–2 for a diagram that can help you conceptualize relationships between analysis of strengths, weaknesses, threats, and opportunities and how an understanding of those relationships can help in the selection of organizational strategy for the development of talent.

The same idea can be applied to developing the talent of the organization's people and cultivating the organization's intellectual capital. Indeed, we have already discussed strengths and weaknesses as results of comprehensive needs assessment (Chapter 3), and threats and opportunities as results of environmental scanning for Talent Development (Chapter 4). In a formal Talent Development effort, *weakness* is any past or present discrepancy between condition (what is)

Exhibit 5–1: Selected Web Site Resources to Support WOTS–UP/SWOT Analysis

	Link	Brief Description
1.	http://www.mplans.com/ot/features.cfm?id=155&ac=overture,swotanalysis	Software to support SWOT analysis
2.	http://www.mindtools.com/swot.html	An article to support individual SWOT analysis for career planning
3.	http://www.akstrategic.com/swot.html	A graphic with a brief description of SWOT analysis
4.	http://www.smartt.co.za/swot/	An interactive tool to construct a SWOT analysis

Exhibit 5–2: Relationships to Consider in Choosing Organizational Strategy for the Development of Talent

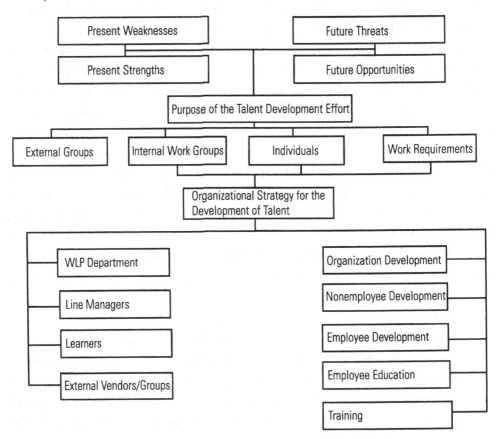

and criteria (what should be) that stems from lack of knowledge, skill, or competency. It is a *present learning need*. A *strength* is any past or present talent, proficiency, or competency. It is a state in which condition (what is) is better than criteria (what should be). An *opportunity* is a talent, competency, knowledge, or skill expected to make the conditions better than the criteria. A *threat* is the opposite of an opportunity: It is any expected deficiency, stemming from lack of knowledge, skill, or competency, between what will *probably* be and what *should be* in the future. A threat is thus an expected future learning need resulting from changes in the environment or organization.

Of course, it is also possible to use an alternative approach. Webb and Gile suggest reversing the value chain to discover what customers want as a foundation for strategic choice. It is also possible to go to the talented people in the organization to discover what they believe should be done to develop talent more effectively.

In choosing organizational strategy for the development of talent, look at and analyze four areas: (1) *external groups* such as consumers, suppliers, distributors, and the general public; (2) *internal work groups* or departments; (3) *individuals* aspiring to new positions; and (4) job requirements by job category. You are likely to find instructional needs in each area. The four markets can be separately analyzed or combined in one overall analysis of needs for the purpose of choosing a unified organizational strategy for the development of talent. The WLP department is one vehicle for meeting these needs; line departments and external vendors are other vehicles for meeting these needs.

The strategy of the Talent Development effort depends on its purpose. It is thus important to consider strengths, weaknesses, threats, and opportunities relative to purpose. Consider these questions: (1) What is the purpose of the Talent Development effort? What should it be? (2) What is the purpose of the WLP department relative to the Talent Development effort? What should it be? (3) What are the responsibilities of line managers and departments in the Talent Development effort? What should they be?

Step 2: Formulate problems. The second step in choosing strategy is to formulate problems. At this point, it is important to refine, synthesize, and prioritize problems identified in Step 1 and filter them through the purpose of the Talent Development effort. For each present or future learning need, WLP practitioners and their stakeholders such as top managers and operating managers in the organization should consider the following:

1. What is this need exactly? How precisely can it be described?
2. Why is it important now? How important is it likely to become?
3. What are the effects of this problem now? What are the expected effects of the problem likely to be over time?
4. What will probably happen if *no* action is taken to meet the need? What will probably happen by way of unintended side effects if action is taken at present or in the future?
5. How important is this need in meeting organizational objectives, individual career objectives, and job requirements?

These questions can then be applied to the raw information obtained in the previous step. The answers to these questions can then be compared to the purpose of the Talent Development effort to determine whether or not they demand action.

Step 3: Identify a way to look at the problems. Once problem areas have been prioritized, WLP practitioners and line managers are ready to look at the problem. They should

▪ *Determine cause.* What created the problem in the first place? What trends, events, or other future happenings might create new problems?
▪ *Find a way to consider a solution.* What approaches can be used in problem-solving?

Determining the cause of a problem is rarely easy, because there can be more than one cause. Does a weakness result solely from a lack of knowledge or a skill? Do threats stemming from these causes seem likely? How much do problems that seem to stem from other sources, such as outdated equipment, contribute to lack of knowledge or skill?

Cause is the reason that things have gone wrong or are expected to go wrong in the future. Here are a few examples of "cause":

1. Lack of communication
2. Negligence

3. Poor standards of performance (that is, standards that are obsolete, impractical, or unclear)
4. Lack of performance standards
5. Decisions to deviate from organizational policies or procedures
6. Lack of resources
7. Dishonesty
8. Departures from common sense or accepted methods of practice
9. Sabotage
10. Lack of motivation
11. Lack of supervision
12. Resistance to change
13. Breakdowns in equipment or automated systems
14. Lack of planning
15. Temporary changes in workflow

Finding a way to consider solutions is a link between problem-finding and solution-finding. From what standpoint do practitioners want to think about solutions? There are many. For instance, practitioners can distinguish between

I *Repetitive and nonrepetitive needs.* Every time employees enter the organization or change jobs, they have some instructional needs stemming from change. These are repetitive needs, though the content of instruction will differ, depending on changes in needs over time. Nonrepetitive needs are one-shot occurrences, resulting from the first-time introduction of change. For example, introducing an automated system to employees who have used a manual system creates a nonrepetitive learning need.

I *Long-term and short-term needs.* Some weaknesses take a long time to correct; some do not. Likewise, some threats require more time to prepare for than others.

I *Critical and not-so-critical needs.* It might be more important to the organization's strategists to focus on a handful of key instructional needs than on all needs. What do they perceive as critical now and in the future? Why?

I *Creative versus noncreative needs.* Will old ways of handling problems work well, or will it be more appropriate to create new solutions? Are creative solutions easily recognized through analytical methods like flow-charting a procedure? Or will finding a solution require more innovative methods?

I *Instructional versus noninstructional improvement efforts.* Performance of individuals, groups, and organizations can be improved in many ways, not just by instruction or training.

I *Traditional instructional methods.* Are other methods likely to be cheaper, more effective, or faster? Consider alternatives to formal instruction, such as (1) job redesign, (2) job aids, (3) feedback interventions, (4) work group redesign, and (5) reward-system redesign.

Another way to think about framing problems is to do a WOTS-UP analysis. Recall that WOTS-UP analysis, also called SWOT analysis, can be used to summarize strengths, weaknesses, threats, and opportunities of the organization, work groups, departments, individuals, job categories, or external groups. WOTS-UP analysis can also be linked to distinctive long-term strategies for the Talent Development effort, depending on which factors summarized on the WOTS-UP grid are strongest (see Exhibit 5–3).

This basic approach has been used to guide strategic choice in strategic business planning. For example, an organization enjoying substantial internal strengths and numerous environmental opportunities (Cell 1) is in a very favorable situation. The most appropriate strategy is *growth.* An organization possessing substantial strengths but facing numerous environmental threats (Cell 2) is well-advised to pursue *diversification,* branching out into new and more profitable businesses rather than trying to grow in the present one. An organization in Cell 3 faces critical internal weaknesses and numerous environmental opportunities. The most appropriate strategy is a *turnaround,* a redirection of resources from within. Finally, an organization in Cell 4 contends with internal weaknesses as well as major environmental threats. Strategists are well-advised to *retrench,* cutting back on resources and activities while regrouping forces.

In using WOTS-UP analysis as a problem-framing method, strategists address a central question that they must consider in strategic choice: *What is the key goal of the strategy?* In other words, do strategists intend to build on strengths,

Exhibit 5–3: A WOTS-UP Analysis Profile

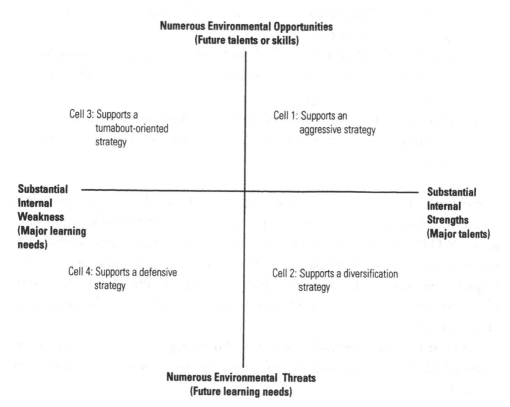

Source: Pearce, J., and Robinson, R. (1985). *Strategic Management: Strategy Formulation and Implementation* (2nd ed.). Homewood, IL: Richard D. Irwin, p. 259.

or try to overcome weaknesses? This WOTS-UP approach can yield very useful information for strategic choice.

The same idea, with slight modifications, can be applied to the problem of strategic choice for the Talent Development effort. A grid like that shown in Exhibit 5–3 can be prepared to represent

I   *Each internal work group or department.* Does the group meet the present and future needs of the organization? How well is the group presently performing, and how well should it perform in the future?

I *Individuals.* How well are people preparing for or are prepared for future advancement? (Each person can be assessed overall and a dot placed on a grid to represent status.)

I *Job categories.* How well-matched to job requirements are job incumbents? (WLP practitioners can then use one dot to represent the *overall* perceived status of the job category.)

I *External groups.* How well do the general public and key external groups understand the business, its products or services, and its operational needs?

The choice of how many grids to use depends solely on whether the emphasis is on meeting the needs of external groups, work groups, individuals, or job categories. WOTS-UP analysis provides an overview of the "big picture" of the organization's human skill strengths, weaknesses, threats, and opportunities. It is helpful because, much like its counterpart in strategic business planning, it supplies a logical and comprehensive framework for considering what strategy to choose and why.

Step 4: Consider possible solutions. No strategy is absolutely "right" or "wrong." The range of possible organizational strategies for Talent Development is broad.

1. Should the Talent Development effort *grow* by doing *more* of what is already being done? This strategy means adding to planned learning activities sponsored by the organization.

2. Should the Talent Development effort *retrench* by doing *less* of what is already being done? This strategy means cutting back on the number or type of planned learning activities sponsored by the organization.

3. Should the Talent Development effort *diversify* by *changing* the learners served? Needs addressed? Emphasis placed on each potential market of learners? Projects/services offered? Instructional methods used? Subjects offered? Content treated in each planned learning experience?

4. Should the Talent Development effort *integrate* with other efforts by increasing or decreasing the relationship between Talent Development to

other functions or activities within the organizations or groups outside the organization? This strategy means tying Talent Development to other HR functions (like recruitment) or other organizational functions (like marketing).

5. Should the Talent Development effort *turn around* otherwise-failing Talent Development activities by first retrenching and then pursuing another Talent Development strategy? For example, placing increased emphasis on education rather than on training might be a step in a turnaround strategy.

6. Should the Talent Development effort *combine* any or all of the preceding strategies by pursuing two or more at the same time? Each group of learners may be the focus of one type of Talent Development activity more than other groups or types of activities.

Each strategy is possible under *any* environmental conditions. The question is, *how appropriate is it?* This question leads to the next step.

Step 5: Choose organizational strategy for the development of talent. This step corresponds to the choice of a solution in the problem-finding process. It involves narrowing down possible solutions to one that is workable and practical, cost-effective and cost efficient, likely to be accepted by others, and likely to overcome weaknesses, build on existing strengths, avert future threats, or seize future opportunities. WLP practitioners and top management strategists rarely have total freedom to pursue what they believe is the "best" or "optimal" choice; rather, they must consider possible strategies for long-term learning efforts based on tests of acceptability.

The Grand Strategy Selection Matrix is one helpful tool in this process (Pearce and Robinson 1985). Used in strategic business planning, it focuses on two key issues: Should strategists devote attention to overcoming present weaknesses, or to building on present strengths? Or should strategists concentrate efforts inside the organization, or outside it? The matrix is shown in Exhibit 5–4.

Each alternative Grand Strategy can be translated into Talent Development terminology. See Exhibit 5–5.

Exhibit 5–4: A Grand Strategy Selection Matrix

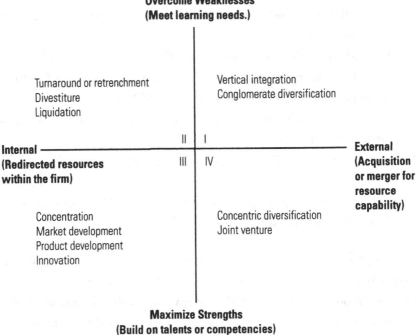

Overcome Weaknesses
(Meet learning needs.)

Turnaround or retrenchment
Divestiture
Liquidation

Vertical integration
Conglomerate diversification

II | I

Internal ——————————————————————— **External**

III | IV

(Redirected resources
within the firm)

(Acquisition
or merger for
resource
capability)

Concentration
Market development
Product development
Innovation

Concentric diversification
Joint venture

Maximize Strengths
(Build on talents or competencies)

Source: Pearce, J., and Robinson, R. (1985). *Strategic Management: Strategy Formulation and Implementation* (2nd ed.). Homewood, IL: Richard D. Irwin, p. 261.

After reviewing the definitions in Exhibit 5–5, look again at Exhibit 5–4. For WLP practitioners and managers, one choice of long-term strategy is to concentrate on overcoming present weaknesses (learning needs). That can be accomplished through effort directed inside or outside the organization. As shown in Cell I of the grid shown in Exhibit 5–4, two choices are possible if strategists want to overcome weaknesses externally: vertical integration or conglomerate diversification.

Vertical integration means tying the Talent Development effort more closely to

 | Internal "suppliers" of talent, such as the recruitment/selection function. Clearly, the kind of people hired will affect long-term and short-term learning needs.

Exhibit 5–5: Meanings of Different Grand Strategy Choices for Organizations and for Talent Development

Grand Strategy	Traditional Meaning in SBP	Meaning for Talent Development
Vertical Integration	Purchase businesses that provide a firm with important supplies.	The Talent Development effort is tied formally to "suppliers" or distributors of talent within the firm (e.g., the recruitment/ selection division of HR) or outside the firm (e.g., university programs).
Conglomerate Diversification	Purchase another business solely because it is a good investment, not because it is at all related to the business of the purchaser.	Expand into totally new areas of service that are not necessarily related at all to the firm's past Talent Development efforts.
Concentric Diversification	Purchase another business with markets, technology, or products related to the purchasing firm.	Use the Talent Development effort to acquire new markets or customers for the business.
Joint Venture	Two firms pool resources to compete in a given market.	Two or more Talent Development efforts are combined in an industry association.
Divestiture	Sell part of the business.	Contract out for major portions of services previously handled by an internal Talent Development group.
Liquidation	Sell off the assets of the business.	Sell off assets related to or used in developing/training employees.
Concentration	Continue to concentrate on the business in which the firm is presently operating.	Continue to meet developmental needs (deal with weaknesses) in ways traditional to the firm's past Talent Development effort.
Market Development	Target new customer groups different from those historically served by a firm, and adapt methods of distributing products and advertising in order to attract them as customers.	Expand planned learning experiences previously limited to one group (e.g., in-house executives) to other groups inside and/or outside the firm.

Exhibit 5–5: *(continued)*

Grand Strategy	Traditional Meaning in SBP	Meaning for Talent Development
Product Development	Change the type of product/service of the firm so as to expand the range of potential buyers.	"Make an old product new." Come up with a new look for the products/services of the Talent Development effort. Use new methods of delivery, different names, etc.
Innovation	Come up with an utterly new approach or novel idea, that is still compatible with the firm's philosophy of business, purpose, goals, and objectives.	The Talent Development effort is tied to stimulation of employee/managerial creativity. It produces new ideas rather than helps people master information derived from experience or that comply with company policies and standard operating procedures.

▪ External "suppliers" of talent, such as university programs that prepare people for jobs in fields critically needed by the organization. Clearly, education received by potential employees affects their learning needs once employed.

▪ Internal "distributors" of talent, such as major operating departments that hire large numbers of people into entry-level jobs. Clearly, what supervisors in these departments do with their newly hired workers affects the supply of labor that can be promoted or transferred to other work groups in the organization.

▪ External "distributors" of talent, such as organizations that frequently hire former company veterans who are moving on to "greener pastures." Assuming that the organization has conducted research on turnover and managers know where their employees are going, the Talent Development effort can be geared in part to improving ties with key company suppliers or distributors. (Some organizations deliberately train more new hires than needed because they know that many trainees will be snatched up by company suppliers and distributors, where they can exert influence favorable to the organization that trained them.)

Conglomerate diversification means expansion into totally new areas, regardless of their present benefit to the organization itself. The idea is to maximize profits. One approach is to make Talent Development a profit center—a relatively autonomous business enterprise. The manager of the department is free to market departmentally-designed materials, products, and services to groups inside and outside the organization. At the same time, line managers in the organization are free to contract for Talent Development services externally through universities, community colleges, or private vendors, or internally through the WLP department. The logic of the marketplace is brought to bear on the Talent Development effort. The WLP manager might find external markets more receptive and/or more profitable than internal ones. Indeed, the Talent Development effort might even be directed more to obtaining profits outside the organization than to meeting learning needs inside the organization.

In the second cell of the grid shown in Exhibit 5–4, strategists can choose to overcome weaknesses by redirecting resources within the organization. Faced with an unfavorable external environment, they might want to look inward and (1) cut back on Talent Development activities generally (retrenchment); (2) begin with a retrenchment strategy, followed by a redirection of activities (turnaround); (3) cut back on some internal Talent Development activities by contracting out for selected instruction that can simply be produced cheaper outside, perhaps with help from government funding (divestiture); or (4) sell off assets used in developing the organization's talent, such as machines or facilities used in training (liquidation).

There was a time when Talent Development efforts—particularly training—were the first to go when a company facing unfavorable environmental conditions decided to reduce spending. That is less true today than it was five years ago. Executives are recognizing that drastic cutbacks in Talent Development produce dramatically negative long-term side effects. These include (1) greater difficulty in orienting new hires once the company's environment improves; (2) greater awareness of competitors' moves ("If they don't cut their training staff, we won't either"); (3) greater awareness that the most appropriate time to work for productivity improvement through Talent Development is precisely when the odds against the organization are most unfavorable; and (4) recognition that employee morale suffers when layoffs occur, and Talent Development activities are often necessary to deal with that problem. The morale of white-collar workers whose expertise might be of greatest value to competitive success is especially vulnerable to drops in company productivity.

In the third cell of the grid shown in Exhibit 5–4, notice that strategists who concentrate their efforts on maximizing internal strengths can choose organizational strategies for Talent Development, such as these:

I   *Concentration*, in which Talent Development activities continue without interruption so as to sharpen the skills of workers who are already performing well.

I   *Market development*, in which Talent Development is geared to new learner groups inside or outside the organization whose needs have not been previously addressed (for example, more clerical instruction or a start-up effort for customer training).

I   *Product development*, in which Talent Development is expanded to offer new products, new services, or new delivery methods (for example, job aids, procedure manuals, OD consulting, and expansion into areas such as self-study videotape or computer-based training, in addition to classroom instruction).

I   *Innovation*, in which Talent Development is directed toward creating new ideas, stimulating strategic thinking, and providing new experience (rather than purveying old ideas).

A *concentration strategy* is probably what managers would most *like* to do. It is generally associated with swelling profits and staff, as well as increasing salaries. Generally, morale improves, too, during growth. After all, promotions, salary increases, and bonuses tend to occur more often when an organization is growing. However, care must be taken to avoid the so-called killer curve in which a period of growth is followed by one of stable sales and eventual decline because no marketing strategy was ever developed (Graham 2000).

By contrast, innovation is the toughest and riskiest of organizational strategies for Talent Development. The aim is to try to create new ideas or to speed up acceptance of state-of-the-art know-how, and perhaps even to create that know-how as a means of giving the organization a strong competitive advantage. For those who are brave enough to blaze this trail of new ideas, times can be hard. They face resistance to change and should try to harness the conflict implicit in change to generate new ideas. As the lifespan of a solution decreases, so too does the time available to allow people to participate in decision-making and consider the consequences of action. If old ways of looking at past experiences are followed, people will be even more misled. Yet a Talent Development strategy of innovation may become increasingly appropriate for all organizations as the role of Talent Development shifts from (1) problem-solving after the fact to problem-finding before the fact; (2) being a tool for socialization of employees, a rite of passage, to one for adaptation to—or even anticipation of—change; and (3) purveying methods based on past experiences, institutional memory, and culture to a means of creating new information and changing culture.

Look now at the fourth cell of the grid shown in Exhibit 5–4. A final choice of organizational strategy for the development of talent is to maximize strengths while focusing outside the organization. Appropriate strategies include concentric diversification or joint ventures. In concentric diversification, the Talent Development effort becomes a means for acquiring new markets or potential clientele. Suppose an organization wants to introduce a new line of products. What could be more logical than to go out and buy a Talent Development consulting firm already offering instruction to this consumer market? If a high-technology manufacturing company that is introducing a new line of personal computers purchases an organization specializing in classroom-based instruction on home computers, then the high-tech firm has acquired a necessary means to reach its new "customers." In joint ventures, Talent Development activities of several organizations are combined for common advantage. This happens occasionally when a group of small businesses, each with a need for Talent Development but each too small to afford a full-time WLP staff, pools resources to form an industry association that specializes in offering Talent Development activities for member firms. Both strategies direct resources outside rather than inside the organization, and both strategies add to existing talents rather than meet deficiencies.

Special Issues to Consider in Choosing Organizational Strategy

Several major issues should be considered when selecting organizational strategy for the development of talent. They include (1) past strategy, (2) environmental uncertainty, (3) dependence on key groups, (4) attitudes about risk, (5) in-house politics, (6) timing, (7) need for a special focus, (8) available skills, and (9) relationships to other plans.

Past Strategy. Start with past strategy. Strategists look at the past direction and the present direction of an organization in order to decide, in light of expected environmental change, whether a new direction or strategy is needed. The greater the perceived gap between actual and desired results in the past, the greater the necessity to choose a radically different strategy in the future.

The same notion can be applied to a Talent Development effort. In what ways has Talent Development been serving external groups, internal work groups, individuals, and job categories? How well has it been meeting past and present instructional needs stemming from

I External stakeholder/public expectations and relations with an organization?

I Organizational requirements?

I Individual career plans?

I Job requirements?

Are Talent Development experiences, like training courses, generally viewed as "hard work"—or are they viewed in other ways? How often are they treated as "rewards" for good performers? How often are they used solely to remove problem performers from the work setting?

Past Talent Development strategy is thus important because it establishes expectations about future activities. It is necessary to know what needs the Talent Development effort is meeting and not meeting before thinking about future strategy. Will continuation of organizational strategy for the development of talent contribute sufficiently to the attainment of future objectives for the effort? If so, major changes are not needed; if not, the Talent Development effort might require a major change in emphasis. When major change is needed,

WLP practitioners must think creatively, and might have to transform the Talent Development effort into something utterly different from what it has been in the past.

The Degree of Environmental Uncertainty. Organizations face different kinds of external environments. Some industries, such as the aerospace and computer industries, exist in highly turbulent environments. The more uncertain and dynamic the external environment, the greater the necessity for practitioners to devise flexible strategies in which contingencies have been planned in the event of radical environmental change. This principle is equally applicable to strategic business planning and organizational strategy for the development of talent.

The Degree of Dependence on Key Groups. If an organization is highly dependent on one or just a few external environmental conditions, then strategic choice hinges more on addressing those conditions. In short, the greater the dependence of successful strategic business plans on support from key groups inside and outside the organization, the greater the need to anticipate the reactions of these groups before choosing a new strategy.

Most WLP practitioners will concede that they likely serve all groups inside an organization, as well as major groups outside it. But the issue of dependence has to do with this question: Who controls the resources? In most organizations, WLP practitioners report to either a vice president for Human Resources or to a vice president of WLP who, in turn, reports to the chief executive. In these cases, either the HR chief or the CEO controls the resources. The Talent Development effort competes with other organizational activities for needed resources. It is thus important to base organizational strategy for the development of talent on expectations of those who control resources, or else persuade those people to form new expectations.

However, matters are somewhat different if the Talent Development effort extends beyond employees to include customers, suppliers, distributors, or others. If the WLP department is operating as an autonomous enterprise that "sells" products and services to outsiders, it gains greater flexibility of choice. The WLP manager is an entrepreneur serving two markets: the organization of which the WLP department is a part *and* external groups served by the department.

Attitudes about Risk. Just how much risk are WLP practitioners and line managers willing to take? The range of strategic options increases as managers become more inclined to take risks. Risk-taking managers explore opportunities more than their risk-averse counterparts do. This inclination to explore alternative solutions to any problem is particularly important in volatile industries in which technology changes rapidly, posing both threats and opportunity. Research has shown that attitudes about risk affect success in autonomous business units (Gupta and Govindarajam 1984).

The same principle applies to Talent Development. When WLP managers are willing to take risks in pursuit of outcomes matching the purpose of the Talent Development effort, they are likely to perform more effectively than their risk-averse counterparts.

In-House Politics. Choice of organizational strategy for the development of talent depends on the ability to influence others. *Power* is equated with the ability to influence; *politics,* related to power, has to do with distributing resources and dealing with special issues that fall outside formal roles and organizational policies.

Strategic business planning theorists have long conceded that politics plays an important part in all facets of strategy formulation, implementation, and evaluation (see, for instance, Bennett, Ketchen, and Schultz 1998). Managers engage in political activity to further their personal and parochial interests. Mutual concerns sometimes lead to the formation of managed coalitions. These coalitions exert influence on decision-making, outcomes of decisions, and methods of evaluating the success of outcomes. In a classic study, Mintzberg, Raisinghani, and Theoret (1976) found that managers frequently try to hide the influence of politics in strategic choice. These researchers also found that politics is a crucial factor in decision-making as much as 30 percent of the time. Other writers over time have traced the influence of politics on strategic choice (Cyert and March 1963; Fahey and Narayanan 1983; Macmillan 1978; Mintzberg 1979a, 1979b).

Clearly, the Talent Development effort can be the focus of considerable political activity when managers view Talent Development activities as central to the achievement of their goals. Managers may try to control identification of learning needs, the direction of the Talent Development effort, choice of organizational strategy for the development of talent, resources provided to Talent Development, and means of implementing and evaluating Talent Development strategy. In each case, powerful managers may try to turn the Talent Development effort to their own advantage, regardless of the opinions expressed by WLP practitioners or others in the organization. On the other hand, if Talent Development is not viewed as an activity that contributes to goal achievement, then political maneuvering about it will be minimal because nobody cares.

Obviously, politics exerts considerable influence on choice of organizational strategy for the development of talent. WLP practitioners have too often been outgunned by more-powerful and politically savvy managers when political maneuvering is an issue.

Timing. To underestimate the importance of timing in strategic choice would be foolish indeed, whether the focus is on strategic business plans, HR plans, or Talent Development plans. Crisis is a powerful stimulant that favors departures from past or present modes of operation. Abell (1978) suggested that managers should take advantage of "strategic windows" in which key competencies of their organization match market requirements for its products or services, and that view is just as relevant today as it was when Abell first expressed it. The strategic thinker anticipates when these windows will appear and how the organization's competencies should be matched to market or consumer requirements at given times. These "windows" exist for only brief time periods. Timing is thus crucial to success.

The same principle holds true for Talent Development. As top management strategists and learners experience problems, they search for solutions. If WLP practitioners anticipate problems before they arise, they improve their chances of gaining acceptance for Talent Development strategies designed to deal with future problems. Further, if the process of deciding on organizational strategy for the development of talent can be used to focus attention on possible future problems, then it serves an important purpose as a vehicle for environmental scanning.

The Need for a Special Focus. Organizational strategy for the development of talent is usually comprehensive in scope. It unifies planned learning intended to anticipate the needs of the organization, external stakeholders, the public, individuals, or job incumbents.

However, it is not always necessary to be so comprehensive in scope. WLP practitioners and line managers can choose to focus *solely* on the long-term learning needs of any *one* of the following:

1. *Organizational culture.* The emphasis is placed on organization development.
2. *External groups.* The emphasis is placed on nonemployee development.
3. *Internal groups.* The emphasis is placed on employee development.
4. *Individuals.* The emphasis is placed on employee education.
5. *Job categories.* The emphasis is placed on employee training.

Moreover, any *one* work unit, type of individual, or job category can be emphasized more than others.

When the *strategic thrust* (emphasis) is placed on training, organizational strategy for the development of talent focuses on meeting the learning needs of each major job category in the organization. Line managers and WLP practitioners in the organization decide on a holistic instructional plan for the organization that is based on job categories and their duties.

When the strategic thrust is on employee education, then a separate learning plan (individual development plan) must be negotiated with each employee. Instructional plans are individualized. The time frame is longer than for training. The aim is to help individuals prepare for new jobs and thus achieve their career goals.

When the strategic thrust is on employee development, a group-learning plan is prepared for each work unit. It is geared to the collective skill requirements of the organization. The time frame is longer than for education. The Talent Development effort becomes a tool for organizational learning.

When the strategic thrust is on nonemployee development, a learning plan is established for one or more external groups. The aim is to improve relations between the organization and that group or else meet the learning needs of a group or groups. The time frame is long, though specific training and educational activities undertaken to help realize the plan can have time frames of brief duration.

When the strategic thrust is on organization development, learning activities are planned around special issues. The focus is on cultural change at the group or organization level. The time frame is long.

Available Skills. In choosing organizational strategy for the development of talent, another issue to consider is this: Does the organization possess the talent necessary to implement the strategy or, failing that, can the organization obtain that talent externally? In short, are the necessary skills available?

Of course, the WLP department is the first place to look for these skills. Relative to organizational strategy for the development of talent, how well staffed is the department? Are specialists available? If not, are WLP staff members willing to work toward a new long-term learning strategy through new methods? If not, what accounts for their resistance to change? How valid are their reasons?

Another place to look for skills is outside the WLP department but inside the organization. Relative to the Talent Development strategy, are exemplary performers available in other departments? How likely is it that they can be or want to be involved in implementing a new Talent Development strategy? Will these people participate in planning and offering instruction? Will they transfer to the WLP department for extended time periods so that they can help? What incentives exist to encourage them to cooperate?

Finally, the environment outside the organization is another place to look for skills matched to Talent Development strategy. If skills are not available internally, how likely is it they can be found among potential new-hires for the WLP department or among published authorities in the area, or even among vendors and/or other contractors?

It is thus very important to identify precisely what talent will be needed to implement organizational strategy for the development of talent. Is it a question of needing leadership talent, technical expertise, consulting skill, or all of them? If skills are not available internally and are difficult to find externally—or if necessary resources to obtain these skills are lacking—then a proposed organizational strategy for the development of talent might not be feasible.

Relationships to Other Plans. People involved in choosing organizational strategy for the development of talent should consider its relationship to (1) corporate-level plans, (2) business-level plans, (3) human resource plans (HRPs),

(4) Talent Development functions, such as training for different categories of employees, and (5) individual career plans. At each level, issues of key concern differ somewhat. At the corporate level, managers concern themselves with maintaining a profitable portfolio of organizational assets. Key *corporate* issues and corresponding Talent Development issues can be summarized as shown in Exhibit 5–6. Key *business-level* issues and corresponding Talent Development issues can be summarized as shown in Exhibit 5–7.

Human resource plans encompass the full range of HR activities in the organization. These plans integrate recruitment, training, compensation/benefits, labor relations, employee assistance, and other HR functions in a unified effort to close the gap over time between the number/types of people needed to achieve strategic business objectives and also realize business/corporate plans and the number/types of people available at present. HRP encompasses all efforts to improve

Exhibit 5–6: Corporate Talent Development Issues

Corporate Issues	Related Talent Development Issues
▌ What businesses should the corporation be involved in? ▌ What goals and objectives are appropriate for the corporation? ▌ What distinctive business competencies are associated with success in each business in which the corporation is involved? ▌ What are the long-term prospects for the corporation and for each business? ▌ What Grand Strategy for the corporation will help it avert threats or seize opportunities in the future?	▌ What human skills, competencies, and knowledge are equated with success in each business and in all businesses? How can they be obtained through planned learning? ▌ How should planned learning contribute to the achievement of corporate goals and objectives? ▌ How much should planned learning contribute to the choice of corporate goals and objectives? ▌ What distinctive human skills are related to business competencies? How can they be acquired or improved through planned learning? ▌ What changes outside and inside the corporation affect learning needs over the long term, and what changes outside and inside each business affect learning needs over the long term? ▌ What long-term learning plan for the corporation will help maximize the skills necessary for organizational success and/or minimize performance problems that may impede organizational success?

Exhibit 5–7: Business Talent Development Issues

Business Unit Issues	*Related Talent Development Issues*
▮ What is the mission of the business unit relative to the corporation? ▮ How is it possible to compete successfully in the industry? ▮ Who are the customers? How does the business serve them? How should the business serve them?	▮ How can human knowledge and skills help realize the mission and related goals and objectives? ▮ What human skills are needed to compete in the industry? How much does the organization possess them? How can it acquire those skills through planned learning? ▮ What human skills are needed to serve consumers? Does the business possess those skills? ▮ What skills, if any, do consumers need to use the product or services of the business? Do they possess those skills? If not, how can those skills be improved?

present employee performance and develop future performance potential. In considering the relationship between HRP and Talent Development, practitioners should think about such issues as those shown in Exhibit 5–8.

HR practitioners have long been criticized for failing to integrate their activities, with the result that these activities have sometimes worked at cross-purposes. From the results of one extensive and classic study conducted in 1985, it appears that some functions in the HR field are working toward integrating their efforts with others. Nkomo (1986, 78) found that "recruitment/staffing, management succession and training and development were the major areas for which strategies and programs were developed as part of the human resource planning process." These HR program areas rated significantly better in this respect than other functions such as health and safety, labor relations, employee benefits, compensation, and affirmative action.

Finally, individual career plans should be considered in the process of selecting organizational strategy for the development of talent. This level is particularly difficult because individuals vary in career orientation.

WLP practitioners often bear important responsibilities in their organizations for establishing career policies and offering instruction to individuals on career

Exhibit 5–8: HRP Issues Related to Talent Development Issues

HRP Issues	Related Talent Development Issues
▌ What is and what should be the long-term role of HR plans in helping realize strategic business plans/objectives? ▌ What is and what should be relationships between such HR program areas as recruitment, selection, compensation, benefits, and labor relations?	▌ What is and what should be the role of the Talent Development effort relative to organizational goals and objectives? HR plans? ▌ What is and what should be the relationships between the Talent Development effort and other HR activities? ▌ What is and what should be the relationship between HRP and organization development, nonemployee development, employee development, employee education, and job training? ▌ How can the gap be narrowed between what people know/can do at present and what they should know or be able to do in the future?

planning. It is important to formulate an organizational strategy for the development of talent that is flexible enough to allow growth opportunities for individuals with career orientations different from the traditional upwardly bound path of increasing responsibility. The need for this flexibility is likely to increase as organizations (1) lay off employees in the wake of increasing automation and corporate downsizing efforts and (2) experience morale problems stemming from baby boomers who, due to sheer numbers, will probably not attain the levels of responsibility they desire.

Planning for Contingencies

Suppose a team of managers, employees, and WLP practitioners develops a unified organizational strategy for the development of talent. Then suppose that something unexpected happens:

1. Two months after the strategy is developed, a persistent rumor of a pending merger is publicly confirmed.

2. The organization's most important domestic manufacturing site votes in favor of union representation. (This union has strong views about Talent Development as a tool for keeping employee skills up-to-date.)
3. A giant in a related industry decides to enter markets presently dominated by this organization.

What should be done in these circumstances? Should a new organizational strategy for the development of talent be formulated from scratch? Should practitioners and others just sit tight and hope the Talent Development effort will not be affected by unexpected changes?

This problem underscores the inherent problem of relying on a programmed, rather than a contingency, strategy. A *programmed plan* is inflexible and has to be changed completely when a major change occurs in the environment or when important assumptions made during planning are proven to be false. *Contingency plans* allow managers to adjust what they are doing when changing conditions make adjustments essential. Generally, programmed strategies are appropriate only in very stable industries. In all other cases, contingency strategies should be used.

How is this idea applied to organizational strategy for the development of talent? WLP practitioners should ask exemplary performers in their organizations about events or trends that were not initially considered in formal planning or that could produce new learning needs. In each case, practitioners should prepare *contingency scenarios*—short narratives that describe what to do in case these events do occur or trends produce effects different from what is expected (see Willmore 1998). Try to avoid being caught off guard by competitors by using competitor-focused scenarios to predict how competitors will act or react to environmental trends (Fahey 1997).

Choosing Organizational Strategy for Talent Development: The Product

The term *curriculum* means "the plan of instruction for learning experiences or events." It is synonymous with organizational strategy for the development of talent, the product of strategic choice (McDowell 1996). Let's discuss this in detail.

History. Academic writers have devoted considerable attention to defining curriculum and tracing how the term has been used. Tanner and Tanner (1980, 36) found that "Curriculum has been variously defined as: (1) the cumulative tradition of organized knowledge, (2) modes of thought, (3) race experience, (4) guided experience, (5) a planned learning environment, (6) cognitive/affective content and process, (7) an instructional plan, (8) instructional ends or outcomes, and (9) a technological system of production." These definitions can be transformed into nine questions: (1) What has been the sum total of human learning to date? (2) How do we think? (3) What has the human race experienced? (4) How can learners be guided through experience? (5) How can the learners' environments be structured to facilitate learning? (6) What information, facts, and feelings are worth knowing, and how do learners come to know them? (7) How can learning be organized and prepared? (8) What results are sought from a learning experience? (9) What tools, methods, and techniques are needed to produce desired learning?

Lewis and Miel (1972) classified definitions of curriculum along similar lines. They found that the term has variously denoted (1) a course of study, (2) intended results of learning, (3) experiences of learners during instruction, (4) experiences actually provided to learners, and (5) opportunities provided for learning.

On the other hand, Geneva Gay (1980, 122–137) distinguishes between four different ways of thinking about curriculum. The first is the *academic,* which identifies what should be learned through intensive examination of "learners, society, subject matter disciplines, philosophy, and the psychology of learning." The second way of thinking about curriculum is the experiential, which "theorizes that personal feelings, attitudes, values, and experiences are critical curriculum content." The curriculum should be a product of inquiry carried out by those who participate in learning. The third way of thinking about curriculum is the *technical,* which "seeks to maximize educational program proficiency and performance through applying the same principles of scientific management and production operating in industry." Fourth and finally, a curriculum can be thought about pragmatically. In this sense, practitioners "perceive instructional planning as a particularistic, localized process that is specific to the sociopolitical milieu of the content in which it occurs." While these definitions overlap, the point is that WLP practitioners can choose to focus on learning as it is affected by the outside world *(the academic),* learner desires and experiences *(the experience),* efficiency and effectiveness in designing instruction *(the technical),* or the unique corporate culture in which the instructional planning process is carried out *(the pragmatic).*

Since publication of the first book on curriculum (Bobbitt, 1918), academic writers have devoted their attention to curriculum issues at primary and secondary school levels. Far less attention has been directed to the university curriculum, to in-service training for teachers at any level of public education, or to corporate training, education, or development efforts.

For the most part, however, curriculum means the same in Talent Development settings as it does in public school settings. The differences stem from

- *The kind of learners.* Educators deal primarily with children; WLP practitioners deal with adults.
- *The kind of subject matter.* Educators deal with fundamental skills (reading, writing, and arithmetic) and with broad, general information about the world in which we live; WLP practitioners, on the other hand, deal with the application of knowledge or disciplines to specific job tasks, career paths, and organizational setting.
- *The kind of setting.* Educators are representatives of society and the community. They select and impart knowledge, and teach youngsters how to think. WLP practitioners are usually representatives of management. Their aim is to build competencies, and teach workers how to work smarter (more effectively), as well as how to achieve more economical output for the time, labor, and resources expended (more efficiently).

For WLP practitioners and educators, a curriculum is "an organized set of formal educational and/or training intentions" (Pratt 1980, 4). It is a comprehensive plan for learning and instruction over time. The plan can cover a five-minute lesson or a series of courses and job rotations lasting several years (Rowntree 1982).

Curriculum Design. *Design* implies a deliberate effort to establish direction. *Curriculum design* is thus "a deliberate process of devising, planning and selecting the elements, techniques and procedures" of learning (Pratt 1980, 5). It is similar to *strategy formulation*, the process of identifying "major actions or patterns of action for attainment of objectives" (Paine and Naumes 1974, 7). However, strategy is formulated "ahead of time or emerges over time based on ad hoc decisions" (Paine and Naumes 1974, 7).

Curriculum Development. *Development* denotes gradual evolution and growth. Development implies implementing a plan. Hunkins (1980, 19) defined curriculum development as "procedures employed in translating general program and instructional objectives, guided by a basic conceptualization of the curriculum, into contents, experiences, and educational environments."

Curriculum is thus an instructional plan; *instruction* is the process of implementing the plan. *Curriculum design* involves coming up with long-term goals and objectives for the Talent Development effort; *curriculum development* means implementing activities to achieve those goals and objectives.

In a very important sense, curriculum issues have to do with strategy-making. "When you do curriculum planning in the broad educational sense," explains Patricia McLagan (in Zemke 1981, 33), "you ask questions about how a program need gets chosen, or why one particular program is built and other apparent needs are ignored. And that's the essence of strategy development in business: making rules for what you will and will not become involved in." For McLagan, the curriculum development process in Talent Development is synonymous with strategy formulation. It involves considering four key issues: (1) What is the company whose needs Talent Development is trying to serve? (2) What do managers in the organization think of people generally, and people-development specifically? (3) What are the present philosophy and assumptions about curriculum development in the organization? and (4) What is the purpose of the Talent Development effort in helping external groups, internal work groups, job incumbents, and individuals achieve their learning objectives? Just as strategic business plans provide long-term direction to organizational initiatives, a curriculum provides long-term direction to a Talent Development effort.

Consider the following conversation between an external consultant and a WLP manager:

Consultant: How do you decide what instruction to design and deliver in this organization?

WLP Manager: It is an informal process. It all starts at the plant level. Each training director or WLP manager in each of our plants conducts a needs assessment every year. Training directors vary in how they approach the task. Some sit in their offices and draw up plans without consulting anybody. Some wander through the plant and talk informally to managers and sometimes supervisors and employees about what training they would like to see in the coming year. Some make the process more formal by mailing questionnaires to managers, first-line supervisors, and employees. Others develop plans based on staff meetings and formal advisory boards composed of representatives from different levels. In short, they use about any method you can think of.

Consultant: You mean that there is no set list of courses—a training curriculum, if you prefer the term—that describes the instruction an employee should have, depending on his or her job category or title or length of time in the position?

WLP Manager: No, we have no such thing as that. We do distinguish between courses appropriate for managers, supervisors, certain professional groups such as engineers and computer professionals, and secretaries. By the way, that's an interesting use of the term *curriculum*. I always thought it referred to the plan of instruction for one course. Sort of like a syllabus.

Consultant: Your use of the term *curriculum* is, I venture to say, rather common. Some people use the term *program planning* in this way. They also use program planning to mean the scheduling of offerings by the WLP department. But I mean something completely different from short-term program planning.

WLP Manager: Really? What?

Consultant: I mean a long-term plan of instruction for the entire organization. You look at job categories, individual career plans, organizational or work group and nonemployee needs and then create learning experiences—not just classroom courses, by the way—to meet recurring needs.

WLP Manager: Sounds interesting. But I'm not sure it would work here. After the years I've been here, I'm not sure our managers know what they are doing from one minute to the next. They are *really* one-minute managers, because one minute is about as far into the future as they ever plan!

Consultant: I think you are selling them short. Granted, there are times when learning needs are nonrecurring. They are met by nonrecurring instruction, such as a one-time course offering. But other learning needs are predictable. They can be met by a long-term learning plan.

As can be seen from this discussion, there is some difference of opinion about the meaning of curriculum. The WLP manager in the dialogue describes the term in a way not significantly different from the practice in many businesses. On the other hand, the consultant uses the same term in a completely different way.

Approaches to Curriculum Planning

How does a WLP practitioner go about planning a curriculum? In what different ways can the practitioner approach the process? This section addresses these questions.

The Curriculum Planning Process. Curricula may differ by

1. *Focus.* What is to be the basis of the change effort?
2. *Scope.* How much change is desired?
3. *Time horizon.* How long is the change effort expected to take?
4. *Approach.* How can the curriculum be organized, and how should the instructional plan be carried out?

Let us look for a moment at the process of planning a training curriculum. We choose training because managers and employees often understand the need for training when they cannot readily see the need for longer-term efforts like employee education or development.

It is important to bear in mind that a training curriculum implies more than just a training program or a schedule of "courses" for a one-year period. "The challenge of curriculum design," writes Julia Galosy (1983, 48), "is to build a coherent, sequential plan which will provide structure and unity to the full gamut of . . . training programs." A curriculum is based on recurrent or expected job training needs over time.

According to Galosy (whose classic 1983 article on this topic should be required reading), curriculum planning of this type is a six-step process in which WLP practitioners

1. *Formulate goals.* What is the guiding philosophy of the curriculum? What general results are sought? For what purpose(s)?
2. *Generate groups.* How can employees be categorized into distinct groups?
3. *Determine needs.* What are the recurrent training needs of people in each job category?
4. *Differentiate needs.* What are learning needs, as opposed to nonlearning needs?
5. *Scope and sequence programs.* What instructional experiences will meet recurring needs of employees in each job category? How can instructional experiences be sequenced so that learners build from foundational knowledge to advanced knowledge and skills?
6. *Design the curriculum.* How are instructional programs organized?

These steps are important enough to warrant elaboration.

The first step, formulating goals, means sorting out the purpose of the instructional effort. As Galosy explains, "goals provide an underlying philosophy, a mission, and a values statement to guide design efforts." Coming up with goals can be as simple as articulating what results are sought from training. Goals reinforce existing company culture, strategy, and values. Alternatively, they can be directed to changing culture, strategy, and values.

The second step, generating groups, means "looking at all divisions and functions and superimposing a logical grouping" (Galosy 1983, 49). In previous chapters, we have already described the various markets and market segments to which the Talent Development effort can be directed. Decisions about what markets and market segments should be served stem from a sense of the purpose of the Talent Development effort.

The third step, determining needs, means more than simply identifying what learners should know or do to carry out their jobs. In a curriculum content, the intent is identification of all *critical* learning needs. Historically, what levels of performance exist in the organization? What opportunities exist to improve performance? What performance improvements are necessitated by the strategic business plan? Answers to these questions should produce "a finely tuned but comprehensive list of skills." This is the starting point for designing a curriculum, with training for each job category geared to performance requirements at each level. Remember, "you should approach curriculum design from a holistic viewpoint, not as individual programs" (Galosy 1983, 49).

The fourth step, differentiating training needs, takes up where the previous one ended. In short, what skills are needed for each market segment of learners? WLP practitioners and line managers match up skill requirements to learner markets. Galosy suggests using a matrix as an aid in this process. At each level, practitioners decide how the "subject" or "skill" needs to be treated and how previous treatments should influence future ones. For instance, first-line supervisors may need "decision-making" to be treated in one way to match their job requirements. Middle managers may also need exposure to the same subject, but the treatment has to be modified to match up to their job requirements and build on instruction they previously received as supervisors.

The fifth step, scoping and sequencing instructional programs, means deciding how much emphasis to place on specific subjects at each level, and how to sequence subjects so that learners are exposed to topics in a logical way.

How much emphasis to place on subjects is a strategic issue. It affects future capabilities of learners. Traditionally, WLP practitioners make decisions about how much to emphasize a subject by first determining the subject's importance for successful job performance. Important subjects are emphasized more and are reinforced several times across courses. How to sequence subjects depends on curriculum goals. Are they intended to *present distilled experience from the past?* (In that case, a logical sequence from simple to complex subjects is appropriate.) Are they intended to *pool the experiences of learners?* (In that case, a sequence based on how learners perceive the importance of different issues might be appropriate.) Are they intended to *create new experience and new knowledge?* (In that case, a sequence beginning with an upending event/situation, such as simulation of a never-before-encountered problem, might be appropriate.) For the most part, however, "it is difficult to find a basis for correct sequencing of the entire set of topics for a course or set of courses other than a kind of 'common-sense' logical ordering" (Gagné and Briggs 1979, 140).

The sixth and final step, curriculum design, produces a list of courses and other planned learning experiences that constitute the curriculum. "At this point, you are breaking down the matrix you built and recombining the ... dimensions into individual [instructional] programs" (Galosy 1983, 51). The result is a learning plan for each job class or job category in the organization. It can then be communicated to employees and line managers as a simple list of courses or as a course matrix. An example of a matrix is shown in Exhibit 5–9, and it is suitable for use in planning the curriculum of a department as part of a unified organizational strategy for the development of talent.

The steps in planning a training curriculum can be modified in planning organization development, nonemployee development, employee development, and employee education. Differences may exist in what groups are served, how needs are identified, how needs are addressed, what planned learning experiences are offered to what groups, and how those experiences are offered. Yet all these planned learning initiatives are unified through a common direction—an organizational strategy for the development of talent.

Alternative Approaches to Curriculum Planning. No doubt the previous section will lead many readers to believe there is only one right way to go about curriculum planning. That is not so. There are at least *four* major ways to go about it (Rothwell and Sredl 2000): (1) *the course-centered approach*, (2) *the experience-centered approach*, (3) *the goal-centered approach*, and (4) *the learner-centered approach*. This figure can be doubled from four to eight by distinguishing between curricula intended to *distill* past experience and knowledge from those intended to *create* new experience and knowledge.

The most familiar approach is the course-centered. "Historically and currently, the dominant concept of the curriculum is that of subjects and subject matter therein to be taught by teachers and learned by students" (Saylor, Alexander, and Lewis 1981, 4). WLP practitioners and managers often associate "courses" with "curriculum" because they base their expectations about Talent Development on their own experiences with grade schools, high schools, and colleges. In

Exhibit 5–9: Curriculum Matrix

Directions: For each job category you listed in the left column below, list the *title of a training course* that you feel would be appropriate at each stage of an individual's level of experience in it. "Entry" means "upon entry to the job category." "Intermediate" means "after 1–2 years." "Advanced" means "after the individual has been in the job category for 3–5 years." There are no "right" or "wrong" answers; rather, the aim of the activity is to begin to organize a training curriculum. Use additional paper as needed.

Department Name

Job Category	Entry	Intermediate	Advanced

Exhibit 5—9: *(continued)*

Job Category	Entry	Intermediate	Advanced

schools, "the term *curriculum* has been and still is widely used to refer to the set of subjects or courses offered...."

Designing a course-centered curriculum is not very complicated. The WLP practitioner only needs to ask subject matter specialists what should be included; arrange the content in a logical sequence; and install it. Subject-matter specialists can include top managers, line managers, experienced employees, published authorities, or members of a work group. Typically, the result will be a list of *course titles*. The content of any single course offering ("offering" means each time the course is given) depends on preferences of instructors and, to a lesser extent, on learner needs at the time the course is delivered.

Perhaps a simple example will clarify how this process works. Suppose a consultant is asked to develop a curriculum for employees of a large personnel department. All new employees enter as corporate recruiters or trainers. After completing a six-month probation in which they receive training, new employees are rotated to other parts of the department.

The consultant would begin the curriculum design process in the training and recruitment divisions. The consultant asks managers and perhaps experienced employees of each division what they think newcomers need to know about during their first six months. The consultant then compares their responses, identifies areas of agreement, labels each area of agreement with a course title, and arranges these titles in a logical sequence. The final step is to feed back the list of titles to the department manager for comments or suggestions. The ambitious consultant might even ask: (1) What topics should be treated in each "course"? (2) How soon after date of hire should newcomers attend each "course"? (3) What delivery method—for example, individual study or classroom-based—is desirable for each course? Why? A similar approach can be used to identify instructional needs *beyond entry* as employees prepare for rotations to new divisions within the department; enter new, temporary jobs in the new division; or settle into semi-permanent jobs presumably different from those to which they have previously been rotated. The same process is repeated in every *department* of the organization so that each department has its own curriculum.

The course-centered approach can be modified to anticipate the future rather than distill experiences from the past. To design a curriculum of this kind, the

WLP practitioner should first assess the goals of instruction. In short, what is the focus and purpose of the curriculum? Second, examine trends in the environment outside the organization. How are they likely to affect nonemployee groups, work groups, individuals, and job categories? Third, appraise present strengths and weaknesses inside the organization. What are the deficiencies and proficiencies of work groups, individuals, and job categories? Fourth, decide on a curriculum prioritized by critical issues having to do with expected future learning needs. Fifth and finally, install the curriculum. These steps are illustrated in Exhibit 5–10.

Exhibit 5–10: Steps in a Strategic Course-Centered Approach to Curriculum Planning

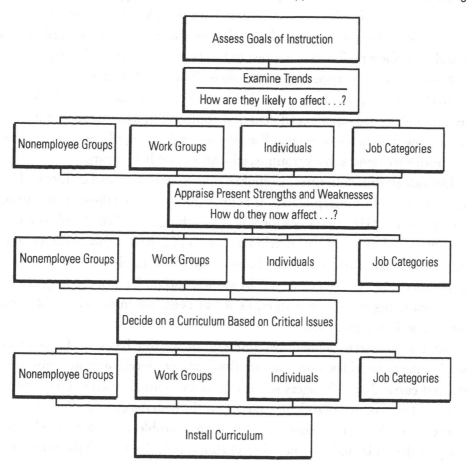

The future-oriented approach to course-centered curriculum design differs significantly from its traditional counterpart. In the future-oriented approach, courses are selected for the curriculum on the basis of *anticipated needs*. In contrast, the traditional approach selects courses from *needs identified through experience*.

Simplicity is the chief advantage of the course-centered approach. It should not take much time or effort to poll a few people about repetitive learning needs of new employees in one job category. Yet this process provides the basis for making simple instructional plans to meet common training needs on a regular basis.

A chief disadvantage of the course-centered approach is that it does not focus on outcomes. The curriculum is just a list of course titles, giving no indication of *what learners will be able to do* once they have completed a course. In fact, the content of each course may vary, depending on who the instructors and learners are and what their preferences happen to be at the time a course is offered.

A second way to approach curriculum design, different from the course-centered approach, is to base it on what learners experience during the learning process. This is the experienced-centered approach. It assumes that individuals vary in how they perceive events. People "see" things in different ways because their prior experiences, backgrounds, education, and beliefs vary.

Individuals thus "interpret" unspoken rules of organizational culture in different ways. When this interpretation is faulty, other people let them know through remarks such as "Hey, that's not the way we do things here," or "Don't you know we're supposed to. . . ." If an individual persists in behavior that violates cultural norms, he or she is ostracized by the work group or disciplined by a superior. Corporate culture is often conveyed by stories, and (in fact) storytelling can be a tool in changing corporate culture, as it has been, for instance, at 3M (Shaw, Brown, and Bromiley 1998).

Action Research, sometimes thought of as the basis of Organization Development, provides one way to think about developing an experience-centered curriculum. Managers sense a need for cultural change. They contract with an internal or external change agent to assist with the change effort. The consultant then (1) collects information about the "problem," including what it is, how prevalent it is, and how people feel about it; (2) feeds back the information to decision-makers and people who provided information about the problem; (3) helps participants in the change effort establish objectives for change; (4) gathers information as action is taken; and (5) periodically feeds back information to participants in the change effort, helping them establish new plans for change. These steps make up a cyclical change process, which replaces one-shot learning experiences with continuous learning.

The experience-centered approach is instrumental in initiating and bringing about change through learning

I   *In the organization.* The focus is usually on cultural change, helping intact work groups in the organization adopt new norms of behavior.

I   *With individuals.* The focus is on stimulating individual insight, helping each person discover new ideas or new approaches.

I   *Across job categories or within them.* The focus is on hierarchical relationships between supervisory and nonsupervisory employees, or between members of the same occupation within the firm.

The impetus for the learning effort is usually crisis. Destructive conflict between work groups is frequently a symptom that signals a need to reexamine goals, work methods, and results.

Curriculum theorists have long noted that potential disparities may exist, too, between what curriculum planners say they are doing and what, in fact, others perceive they are doing. It is thus possible to distinguish between the curriculum plan as it is (Saylor, Alexander, and Lewis 1981) and the curriculum plan

I   As documented in writing or discussed by curriculum planners (formal curriculum),

I   As perceived by instructors (perceived curriculum), and

I   As viewed by external observers or by learners attending instructional events (experienced curriculum).

The difference between formal curriculum and perceived curriculum "is symptomatic of separating means and ends in education. The ends . . . are responses to the question, 'What shall be taught?' while the means of education are responses to the question, 'How shall it be taught?' When means are separated from ends, the curriculum experienced may vary from the curriculum planned" (Saylor, Alexander, and Lewis 1981, 5). This difference between planned and experienced learning is similar to differences between *espoused theory and theory-in-use* (Argyris and Schön 1974 and 1978). *Espoused theory* is what decision-makers and others say should be; *theory-in-use* is how they actually behave. "Individuals may or may not be aware of the incompatibility of the two theories" (Argyris and Schön 1974, 7). By using the action research model, WLP practitioners and others in the organization reveal discrepancies between curriculum intentions and results.

To transform experience-centered curricula to a future orientation, WLP practitioners must mobilize support for change. To do that, they collect information from people inside and outside the organization about future threats and opportunities likely to affect external stakeholders, work groups, the organization, individuals, and job categories. This information is fed back to decision-makers to *create* impetus for change. Another way is to identify dissatisfied people in the organization and collect information from them to create a "picture of reality" that will shock decision-makers out of complacency, because it is radically at odds with what they believe. A third way is to bring together groups in conflict and let them confront each other (Beckhard 1967). These methods stimulate long-term planning for future-oriented change. Organized learning activities are tools for engineering change.

Comprehensiveness is a chief advantage of the experience-centered approach to curriculum design. It makes the Talent Development effort a tool for *critical* change, not solely *individual* change.

A chief disadvantage of this approach is the difficulty of measuring long-term change. When productivity increases or measures of employee morale show improvement, how can it be determined for certain that the cause is attributable to these change efforts? It is difficult to measure effects that stem from large-scale, long-term change initiatives. However, attempts have been made to do so—some rather successfully.

A third approach to curriculum design is goal-centered. Public education has been profoundly influenced by the notion of curriculum as results (outcomes) to be achieved through instruction. Through the writings of Robert Mager (1997a), the goal-centered approach has had perhaps an even greater influence on HRD, WLP, and other Talent Development efforts. The reason is that its bottom-line, results orientation appeals to WLP practitioners and line managers.

There are essentially two ways to design a goal-centered curriculum: base it on performance or base it on competencies.

The curriculum planner using the performance-based approach thinks of the Talent Development effort as a tool for satisfying learning deficiencies. The starting point for curriculum planning is *a problem* with individual performance that is wholly or partly attributable to lack of knowledge or skill (Gilbert 1967). The planner (1) identifies performance problems by job class, work unit, or individual, (2) identifies training, education, and development needs by separating them from other problems not attributable to lack of knowledge or skill, (3) assesses training, education, and development needs from the standpoint of the group, individual, and/or job, (4) synthesizes needs, (5) establishes instructional goals to correct the needs, (6) examines the willingness of key decision-makers to satisfy needs, and (7) installs the curriculum through instructional activities.

The starting point for planning a performance-based curriculum is an examination of recurring or critical problems in

I *The environment.* WLP practitioners look at problems between the organization and its suppliers, distributors, customers, and others.
I *The organization.* Using an organization chart, practitioners identify work groups and then examine each group, asking this question: What performance problems are common at this time in this group?
I *Individuals.* Practitioners categorize individuals into groups, such as "new entrant to the job," or "promotable tenured employee," and then consider common performance problems, if any, among employees in each group.
I *Job categories.* Practitioners classify employees by job categories. They then ask: "What performance problems are common in each category?"

This examination produces four separate but related lists of learning needs. Each list provides a foundation for preparing behavioral objectives describing what learners should be able to do upon completion of a planned learning experience. Objectives are grouped together logically as the foundation for planned learning experiences.

The chief advantage of the performance-based approach is its strong emphasis on results. It is especially appealing to decision-makers, whose interests it serves. Learning needs are linked directly to problems; instructional objectives are linked directly to solving problems. The chief disadvantage of the performance-based approach is that it relies on past problems as the basis for future learning. Problems must be experienced before they prompt action. This approach is sometimes defended on the grounds that adults are highly motivated to learn while grappling with a problem.

The trouble is that future conditions might turn out utterly unlike those experienced in the past or present. Anticipating the future and engaging in future-oriented curriculum planning requires a different approach, one that prepares learners *before* or *as* they encounter problems. Unfortunately, "it is hard to imagine an adult's deciding to engage in paradigm shifting, perspective transformation, or the replacing of one meaning system with another purely on his or her own volition. What will induce this exploration . . . is some kind of external event or imperative" (Brookfield 1986, 49–50). A present or impending crisis is often necessary to stimulate change through learning.

To transform the performance-based approach to a future orientation, the WLP practitioner should be a catalyst for change who creates occasions when "context shifting" can occur. "Context shifting" means giving learners and decision-makers opportunities to place themselves artificially at a future point in time, think about problems likely to be encountered, and then retrace their footsteps to the present in order to determine future learning needs. This is more than just "blue sky" forecasting: it puts people on the spot to function in conditions they themselves believe will occur in the future. The result is a new, firsthand awareness of future learning needs. "The assumption is," writes Brookfield (1986, 248), "that if you are successful in changing adults' perceptions of the world in which they live, you will not need to *teach* adults to acquire new skills and knowledge—they will be eager to discover these for themselves."

To do this, WLP practitioners can try to (1) help learners scan the environment to detect future trends or issues that may affect them in the future; (2) give learners opportunities to pinpoint, through simulations and other artificial exercises set in the future, problems that are likely to come up; (3) separate future training, education, and development needs from noninstructional needs stemming from other sources; (4) assess future needs by stepping back to the present but looking ahead to what performance will be needed at a future time; (5) establish instructional goals or objectives that, if satisfied, will meet future learning needs; (6) help learners and decision-makers identify instructional methods and resources for satisfying their learning needs; and (7) install the curriculum through instructional activities, but still plan for contingencies if future conditions do not turn out as expected.

The competency-based approach to curriculum planning differs in a few key respects from its performance-based counterpart. Unfortunately, *competency* is a term that has been used in several different ways. As a consequence, some confusion exists about what it means. Some writers do not consider competency to be different from *behavior*. Others define it as *performance* (results of behavior). Perhaps the best definition is Klemp's (1979):

A competency is a generic knowledge, skill, trait, self-schema, or motive of a person that is causally related to effective behavior referenced to external performance criteria, where

- *Knowledge* is a set of usable information organized around a specific content area.
- *Skill* is the ability to demonstrate a set of related behaviors or processes.
- *Trait* is a disposition or characteristic way of responding to an equivalent set of stimuli.
- *Self-schema* is a person's image of himself or herself and his or her evaluation of that image.
- *Motive* is a recurrent concern for a goal state or condition that drives, selects, and directs behavior of the individual (Boyatzis 1982, 42).

Competency, Boyatzis holds, is an *underlying characteristic,* one manifested in many ways.

To plan a competency-based curriculum, the WLP practitioner needs to

1. Design a competency model for each work unit, job category, or other group by

    ▪   Asking a panel of experienced practitioners to identify crucial outputs of the work unit, job category, or group.

    ▪   Asking a second panel of practitioners to synthesize major outputs.

    ▪   Reviewing past studies of work units, job classes, or other groups so as to develop a tentative list of competencies necessary to succeed.

    ▪   Preparing a list of tentative competencies, reviewed and approved by experienced members of each work unit, job category, or other groups.

    ▪   Assigning priorities to identified competencies.

    ▪   Developing, for each competency, "behavioral anchors"—narrative descriptions of behavior associated with a competency. These descriptions are arranged in a three- or four-step continuum, from basic to advanced levels of proficiency.

2. Analyze the current level of performance. In other words, what competencies are now evident in the work unit, job category, or other group? What competencies are not evident? How proficient are members of the work unit/job category/group in each competency area?

3. Specify desired levels of performance. In other words, what competencies are desirable in the future? What competencies are not desirable? How proficient should each work unit, job category, or other group be in the future?

4. Compare present to desired future competencies.

5. Prepare instructional objectives to narrow gaps between present and desired future competencies.

Unlike its performance-based counterpart, this approach to curriculum development attempts to transform the fictional into the real. To put it another way, competency "models"—descriptions of human characteristics underlying performance—can be future-oriented. In using the competency-based approach, curriculum planners start out with a model that (1) describes exemplary performance, but (2) exists nowhere in the organization, group, or job category at present. Instructional objectives are geared to creating "super performers," despite vagaries about environmental conditions in the future. The performance-based approach, however, begins with *either* minimum or desired job standards. Present performance is then compared to standards established in the past. When actual performance differs from standards and this difference results from lack of individual knowledge or skill, then instruction is one way to address the problem.

The difference is important. The performance-based approach tends to focus on *nonrecurring problems,* often brief shortfalls between desired standards and actual results. Since standards are developed in the past, present results are compared to past requirements. The competency-based approach focuses on *recurring problems* or *future expectations.* As a consequence, it helps people cope with future requirements.

Performance-based curriculum planners find it difficult to establish long-term instructional plans, because they use Talent Development as a "fix-it" tool. This satisfies managers who want immediate justification for instructional expenditures, but it does not help avert future performance problems before they occur. On the other hand, competency-based curriculum planners establish long-term instructional plans. Moreover, they *may* identify future-oriented rather than past-oriented competencies. This is, in fact, the chief advantage of the competency-based approach. However, not *all* competencies are necessarily future-oriented. If managers list competencies based on their estimations of past performance, then the curriculum will *not* be future-oriented. To ensure that a competency-based curriculum is future-oriented, WLP practitioners must base competencies on the results of environmental scanning efforts.

A competency-based curriculum is time-consuming and expensive to develop. It is not an undertaking that any novice can begin or end successfully. Even experts disagree about the meaning of "competency-based," so wide variations in instructional planning activities are possible.

The learner-centered approach is the fourth approach to curriculum design. It rests on the belief of adult educators such as Malcolm Knowles (perhaps its most vocal advocate in HRD or WLP circles) that adults differ from children in how they learn. Knowles is an articulate champion of the adult as a self-directed learner.

The learner-centered approach to curriculum design stresses the desire of individuals to participate in the process of identifying and meeting their own learning needs. As Greene (1977, 283) explains, "Curriculum, to me, ought to be a means of providing opportunities for the seizing of a range of meanings by persons open to the world." In short, learning helps individuals become more of what they are capable of becoming.

Malcolm Knowles fervently believed in *androgogy,* the art of teaching adults. It is founded on several key assumptions: First, adults need to see a reason for learning before they will be motivated to make the effort. In this respect, adults are unlike children. Second, adults are self-directing; they want to take charge of their learning and their lives (Knowles 1984). Many adult educators believe that their chief purpose is to help learners achieve a state of self-directedness (Evan 1982). Third, adults view learning through the filter of experience. As people mature, "they increasingly define themselves in terms of the experiences they have had." Fourth, adults are motivated to learn while grappling with immediate problems confronting them. Timing is thus crucial for learning. As Knowles points out, though, "It is not necessary to sit by passively and wait for readiness to develop naturally." There are ways to create readiness to learn, including (as Knowles points out) modeling of behavior, counseling, and simulation. Fifth, adults tend to be problem-centered in their orientation to learning. They "are motivated to devote energy to learn something to the extent that they perceive that it will help them perform tasks or deal with problems that they confront in their life situations" (Knowles 1984, 58–59). These ideas, central to the notion of learner-centered curriculum development, have been widely examined and criticized. Brookfield (1986) found research results that seem to be at odds with Knowles's assertions: (1) not all adults are self-directed learners, nor should they be, and (2) adults proceed in their learning more by accident than by deliberate planning (Brookfield 1980; Danis and Tremblay 1985).

To develop a learner-centered curriculum, the WLP practitioner

1. Identifies learners as members of work groups, as individuals with their own career aspirations, and as representatives of various job categories.
2. Helps learners explore present problems and surface new ideas worthy of exploration.
3. Guides learners to people, activities, situations, and other sources that will help them meet their learning needs or identify new issues worth exploring.

Alternative models of curriculum development appropriate to the learner-centered approach have been suggested by others.

In developing a curriculum using the learner-centered approach, the WLP practitioner categorizes learners according to their work group affiliation, individual life stage and career interests, or job concerns. The WLP practitioner then helps learners identify and explore problems they have experienced or expect to experience in the future within the organization, their careers, and their jobs. More than that, WLP practitioners assist learners so that they arrange experiences that help them become more aware of future problems worthy of exploration.

Finally, WLP practitioners serve as advisors and brokers who connect resources for learning with individuals desiring them. Practitioners scan the environment inside and outside an organization for people, events, and situations that can facilitate learning.

The learner-directed approach to curriculum design is well-suited to anticipatory thinking. Such techniques as inquiry-oriented instruction widely advocated by Jerome Bruner (1960) and John Dewey (1938) rely on questioning, "context shifting," simulations, and other techniques that produce knowledge. In this respect, the learner-directed approach lends itself to the creation of new ideas, rather than the distillation of experience.

Results of Curriculum Planning and Choice of Organizational Strategy for the Development of Talent

The result of curriculum planning and choice of organizational strategy for the development of talent is a comprehensive instructional plan for (1) groups outside the corporation or business, (2) work groups or departments inside the organization, (3) individuals aspiring to new jobs, and (4) job categories. Organizational strategy for the development of talent and the curriculum can thus be synonymous. This long-term instructional plan integrates and unifies organization development, nonemployee development, employee development, employee education, and training.

Activity 5–1: A Worksheet for Problem Framing

Directions: In the spaces below, describe the performance problem. Then consider each question, relative to that problem. Remember, you are focusing here on **employee performance problems** only.

1. **What is the problem?** *(Describe it. Be sure to clarify* What is *[current condition] and* What should be *[desired status or criteria].)*

2. **Is the problem repetitive or nonrepetitive?** *(Does it appear or can it appear at regular intervals? If so, explain the circumstances. If not, explain what you think caused this problem.)*

3. **Is the problem short-term or long-term?** *(Will this problem require some time to correct, or can it be corrected in a relatively brief time period?)*

4. **Is the problem critical, or not so critical?** *(How important is this problem? Explain why it is or is not important.)*

5. **Does the problem call for creative or noncreative solutions?** *(How well will tried-and-true methods work in correcting the problem? What could happen in the future that would render those solutions inappropriate?)*

6. **Will instructional or will noninstructional improvement efforts be most appropriate for dealing with the problem?** *(Is formal instruction the only way to solve the problem? What alternatives exist? What are the relative advantages and disadvantages of each one?)*

Activity 5–2: A Case Study on Organizational Strategy for the Development of Talent*

Directions: Read the case below and answer the questions that follow.

The Texarkana Office of Auditor General is a state agency employing 120 people. Its annual budget is $12 million. The agency conducts financial, compliance, management, and program results audits of all state agencies in Texarkana.

By state law, financial and compliance audits must be conducted at least once every four years. On the other hand, management and program results audits are only undertaken when the Texarkana Office of Auditor General is directed by the State Legislature to do them.

The structure of the agency is a simple one: There are only five divisions. As Exhibit 5–11 illustrates, four are related directly to audit work. A fifth division supports audit activities. Job classes are nearly as simple as the agency structure (see Exhibit 5–12). There are only 23 job titles in the agency.

Questions

1. How would you go about designing and developing a course-centered curriculum in this agency?

2. How would you go about designing and developing an experience-centered curriculum in this agency?

3. How would you go about designing and developing a goal-centered curriculum in this agency? (Answer this question for a performance-based *and* for a competency-based curriculum.)

4. How would you go about designing and developing a learner-centered curriculum in this agency?

5. How would you ensure that for each approach to curriculum design/development used, some provision is made to (a) build computer skills? (b) build expertise in personnel matters? and (c) help learners produce audit reports in "lay language"?

6. Assume that the agency's strategic plan covers a six-year time horizon. What time horizon should the curriculum cover?

7. What nonemployee development needs do you feel should be considered? How can agency top managers see to it that those needs are assessed and that instruction is planned accordingly?

* This case is fictitious.

Exhibit 5–11: Organizational Structure of the Texarkana Office of the Auditor General

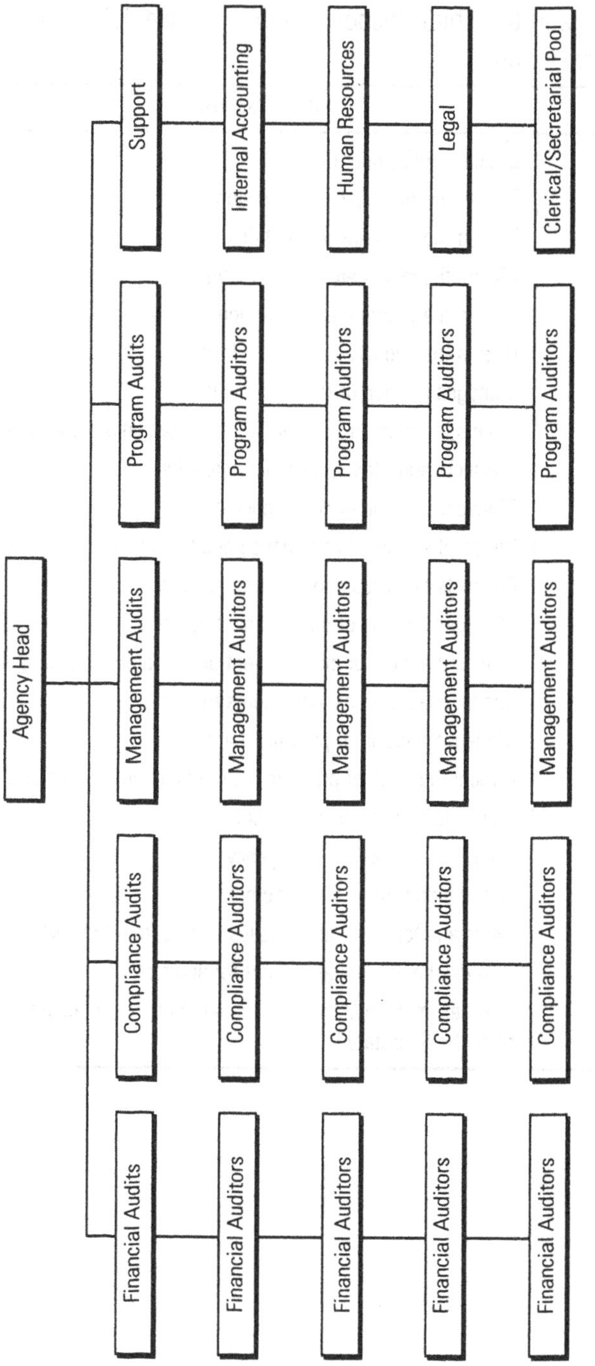

Exhibit 5–12: List of Job Titles and the Chief Responsibilities of Each Job in the Texarkana Office of the Auditor General

Job Title	Chief Responsibility
1. Agency Head	Directs agency operations
2. Director, Financial Audits	Directs the financial audit division
3. Director, Compliance Audits	Directs the compliance audit division
4. Director, Management Audits	Directs the management audit division
5. Director, Program Audits	Directs the program audit division
6. Director, Support Operations	Directs the support operations division
7. Financial Audit Manager	Manages a group of financial audits
8. Financial Audit Senior	Directs the work of financial audit juniors on a daily basis
9. Financial Audit Junior	Conducts audit tests; documents results
10. Compliance Audit Manager	Manages a group of compliance audits
11. Compliance Audit Senior	Directs the work of compliance audit juniors on a daily basis
12. Compliance Audit Junior	Conducts audit tests; documents results
13. Management Audit Manager	Manages a group of management audits
14. Management Audit Senior	Directs the work of management audit juniors on a daily basis
15. Management Audit Junior	Conducts audit tests; documents results
16. Program Audit Manager	Manages a group of program audits
17. Program Audit Senior	Directs the work of program audit juniors on a daily basis
18. Program Audit Junior	Conducts audit tests; documents results
19. Internal Accountant	"Keeps the books" of the agency
20. HR Officer	Recruits and trains agency employees
21. Legal Technician	Helps auditors with legal issues arising from their work
22. Secretary I	Provides basic clerical support for auditors
23. Secretary II	Provides more demanding clerical support for auditors than does the Secretary I

IMPLEMENTING ORGANIZATIONAL STRATEGY FOR THE DEVELOPMENT OF TALENT

Implementation is the process of turning plans into actions. Implementing organizational strategy is perhaps the single most important step in developing talent. Without careful forethought about what actions to take, when to take them, and who should take them, no strategy will ever be successful.

Implementation is sometimes cited as the weakest link in strategic business planning. Implementation, if it is to be successful, does take a long time, yet no plan will be useful until it is implemented (DeFeo and Janssen 2001; Hacker and Akinyele 1998). In one classic study, Ackerman (1975) studied two organizations and concluded that changes initiated by top managers required about six years to implement. Dramatic changes at odds with organizational culture can take even longer. Resistance to any new strategy is likely to be pronounced—especially when a proposed change differs radically from tradition. People resist such changes because they know that it will take time for people to learn how to act in new ways consistent with new business plans and it will come at some cost. People have different perceptions about what a change means and are likely to distrust others' motives, feel anxious about the change, and be confused about what to do and what will be expected of them. There will also be vested interests in maintaining the status quo. The length of time required for successful implementation and resistance to change itself are not problems limited solely to strategic business planning. Time and resistance can indeed affect the implementation of organizational strategy for the development of talent.

More than one authority has called for more research on strategy implementation (Guffey and Nienhaus 2002; Noble 1999), but the subject has historically been researched less than most other topics in strategic planning (Huff and Reger 1987; Noble 1999). This is particularly important because as much as 70 percent of all strategies fail during implementation (Corboy and O'Corrbui 1999). While the trend is to share strategic plans with employees in a bid to gain acceptance (Higgins and Diffenbach 1989), employee awareness of plans does not necessarily correlate precisely with acceptance or ownership (Guffey and Nienhaus 2002).

Steps in Implementing Organizational Strategy for the Development of Talent

Think of implementation as a series of steps in which WLP practitioners and line managers

1. Establish operational objectives for the Talent Development effort.
2. Review and revise Talent Development policies.
3. Examine leadership in the corporation or business.
4. Review the structure of the organization, the WLP department, and the learning experiences sponsored by the organization.
5. Review reward systems.
6. Budget for resources to implement strategy.
7. Communicate about organizational strategy for the development of talent.
8. Develop functional strategies for Talent Development.

Establishing Operational Objectives for the Talent Development Effort

Writers on the subjects of strategic business planning and Talent Development repeatedly emphasize the importance of objectives. Objectives provide guidance for the outcomes sought from any undertaking. Business planners often advocate a Management by Objectives (MBO) approach to implementation because it is results-oriented. It matches resources to priorities during annual budgeting. MBO also builds commitment through participation at lower levels in the corporate hierarchy, because objectives should be negotiated at every level. It clarifies priorities, evaluates individual performance, allocates rewards based on predefined criteria, and prepares individuals in ways directly tied to long-term, intermediate-term, and short-term requirements of the organization, work groups, and jobs.

When MBO is used in strategic business planning, top managers usually establish objectives for the entire organization and then for their respective areas of responsibility. Within each top manager's area of responsibility, objectives are allocated to different departments. Mid-level managers then negotiate objectives with superiors and subordinates. Objectives are established all the way down to front-line employees. In this way, everyone has an opportunity to negotiate objectives for their jobs. Periodically, managers at each level meet with subordinates to discuss their progress toward meeting objectives.

Typically, an MBO program is geared to meeting objectives. However, longer-term objectives can be established for five or more years. These objectives reflect action toward implementing a strategic business plan.

Despite the advantages of an MBO approach to implementation of strategy, it is by no means foolproof. Good objectives are time-consuming to write and negotiate, and they require skill to prepare and monitor. If they are thrust upon employees without give-and-take negotiation, they create hostility and frustration.

Instructional objectives are more limited than the organizational objectives prepared in MBO. They are widely advocated and used in HRD, WLP, and related fields. They link learning needs and the instruction designed to meet those needs. Instructional objectives were popularized in the 1960s.

A good instructional objective answers three fundamental questions: (1) What will the learner be able *to do* upon completion of a learning experience? (2) *Under what circumstances and/or with what tools or equipment* will the learner be able to perform? and (3) *How well* will the learner be able to perform? (Mager 1997). It is not always necessary to address the second question—because sometimes circumstances are understood—but the other two questions should always be addressed.

Not all objectives deal with the same issues. In fact, Benjamin Bloom and his colleagues (1956) distinguish between three learning "domains": (1) the *cognitive,* having to do with thinking and knowledge, (2) the *affective,* having to do with feeling and values, and (3) the *psychomotor,* having to do with physical skill. Each domain is arranged in hierarchical order from least complex to most complex. More-complete treatments of them can be found in classic books by Bloom (1956), Krathwohl, Bloom, and Masia (1964), and Simpson (1969).

Just as organizational objectives vary by time horizon, so too do instructional objectives. As Briggs pointed out in a classic treatment in 1970, they can be viewed as (1) *long-term objectives,* reflecting desired change that occurs throughout life; (2) *medium-term objectives,* reflecting desired change that occurs from formal learning; (3) *short-term objectives,* reflecting desired change that results from a single, discrete learning experience; (4) *unit objectives,* reflecting desired change that results from a section of a course or a group of related lessons; (5) *lesson objectives,* reflecting desired change that results from a single portion of a course section; and (6) *specific behavioral objectives,* reflecting desired change that results from going through one lesson. Other writers have also suggested that objectives can be viewed according to time horizon and type of change desired.

This idea has profound implications for implementing organizational strategy for the development of talent. Top managers, WLP practitioners, and others can establish different kinds of instructional objectives to specify desired changes to be achieved through different (but related) learning experiences. For instance, objectives should be established in a comprehensive organizational strategy for the development of talent to bring about change in

1. Which knowledge, skills, and issues are implicit in organizational procedures and in the interaction of groups/people within the organization. The intent is to influence the organization.

2. What the general public knows about the corporation and its products or services. The intent is to influence the broad external environment.

3. What key external stakeholders such as consumers/clients, suppliers, and distributors know about the corporation and its products/services. The intent here is to influence key stakeholders.
4. Which people are available to meet the collective skill needs of each work unit. The intent here is to influence the mix of available talents in each work unit.
5. Which people are available for what new jobs. The intent is to influence the direction of individuals' careers.
6. What knowledge and skills people can apply on their present jobs. The intent is to influence present job performance.

These objectives form a taxonomy in their own right. At the highest level is cultural change in the organization, which takes time and is the most difficult to achieve. Below that is change relative to the external environment, which corresponds to nonemployee development. At the center of the hierarchy is change in the work unit, which corresponds to employee development. At the lowest levels are objectives focused on changing individuals (employee education) and job performance (training). The lowest-level objectives take less time to achieve than higher-level objectives.

A further distinction between objectives can be made on the basis of *change direction*. Is the intent to narrow a gap between what is and what should be at present? Or is it to narrow the gap between what is and what should be in the future? In other words, is planned learning intended to solve past performance problems, or to anticipate future performance threats or opportunities? The choice of change direction depends entirely on the nature of organizational strategy for the development of talent. A strategy focusing on correcting past weakness usually requires little dramatic change. In contrast, a radically new organizational strategy for the development of talent calls for utterly new competencies to be cultivated over time.

Establishing objectives for each type of change is a key to formulating organizational strategy for the development of talent, and following those objectives is a key to successful implementation of that strategy.

There are several ways that objectives can be used in implementing organization strategy for Talent Development. One method is to prepare Talent Development objectives to correspond to each strategic business objective. After all, individual competencies are necessary to achieve strategic business objectives. As strategists formulate business objectives, they should also think about corresponding learning objectives.

Another method is to separate strategic business objective-setting from instructional objective-setting, but still preserve continuity by involving the same people in each process. Managers at each hierarchical level establish strategic business objectives and then, in a parallel process, establish corresponding objectives for training, education, employee development, organization development, and nonemployee development.

After objectives are established for the organization, corporate planners schedule periodic meetings to compare notes on progress and pinpoint problems associated with achieving them. The same approach can be used in monitoring progress on Talent Development objectives. WLP practitioners can schedule meetings with managers to report progress and identify problems. Alternatively, both planners and WLP practitioners can work together so that one meeting provides feedback on achievement of business objectives and Talent Development objectives. In this way, results of action are fed back to the managers who set objectives in a way reminiscent of the Action Research Model popularized by Organization Development practitioners. In Action Research, feedback and further problem-solving efforts follow objective-setting and action in a continuous, long-term cycle.

Creating, Reviewing, and Revising Talent Development Policies

Policies are formal pronouncements intended to guide behavior. They ensure that decisions made at lower levels conform with desires at higher levels, and that actions taken conform with strategic business plans and objectives. Most organizations have at least some formal policies that reflect their experience.

Written policies have distinct advantages when compared to unwritten ones. Policymakers seldom waste time writing about matters they do not consider important. In addition, the process of writing helps clarify issues among policymakers, flushing out areas of disagreement for discussion and resolution.

Clearly, policies should always be reviewed upon choice of a new strategy. After all, it does not make sense to expect people to behave one way if policies intended to guide behavior lead them to behave another way.

Many corporations have Talent Development policies on matters such as

I   Delivering speeches to associations, groups, or societies about the activities of an employer.
I   Preparing articles for publication about the employer.
I   Serving in professional societies or civic groups.
I   Reimbursement for college tuition, and fees for workshops, seminars, conferences, and professional accreditation.
I   Training, both off-the-job and on-the-job.

Policies state the employer's philosophy, and sometimes provide procedures for getting approval for training, education, or other improvement efforts.

Some large corporations also have policies on Talent Development. Policies of this kind describe how WLP practitioners should approach needs assessment and instructional design, delivery, and evaluation.

A third type of policy is more rare, but it is also important: Some corporations, government agencies, and not-for-profit enterprises establish formal policies about the Talent Development responsibilities of supervisors and employees. Policies of this kind clarify precisely what the supervisor should do and what employees should do in the Talent Development process. Some organizations establish a predetermined number of hours per year to be devoted to formal learning.

It is important to formulate a written Talent Development policy and review it for possible modification whenever there is a change in the purpose of the Talent Development effort or WLP department; the organizational strategy for the development of talent; the higher-level strategy of the organization or overall HR (personnel) practices.

Examining Leadership

Leadership refers to the ability to influence others. If there is one thing that can make or break successful implementation of any strategy, it may well be the lack of leadership. Successful implementation depends on appropriate leadership because strategy is, quite simply, a human manifestation requiring human guidance.

In examining leadership's importance in the implementation of organizational strategy for the development of talent, WLP practitioners should ask: (1) *Who* are the key decision-makers in the organization? (2) *What* do they value? (3) *What* do they think of Talent Development generally? (4) *What* do they think of Talent Development as a tool for improving relations with the general public, corporate suppliers, customers, and distributors, for developing both the organization as a whole and specific work groups, for helping realize corporate/business strategic plans, for preparing individuals for career mobility, for helping individuals realize their career plans, and for improving job performance? Organizations with strong value systems, ideologies, and cultures tend to attract and retain individuals and leaders who embody those same things. When the importance of Talent Development is not presently emphasized in the culture or supported by top managers, building support for it or for changes in organizational strategy for the development of talent will necessarily be difficult.

The most important leader to analyze is the chief executive, who is the chief organizational strategist. WLP practitioners should ask these questions of the CEO: (1) How worthwhile does the CEO believe a Talent Development effort is? (2) How much does the CEO believe a Talent Development effort can contribute to successful implementation of strategic business plans? and (3) How much real support does the CEO provide to Talent Development efforts? Does the CEO take an active interest in Talent Development and encourage others to do so? Undoubtedly, the greater the CEO's interest in Talent Development, the greater the likelihood it will attract attention from others. Moreover, when the CEO actively encourages a change in organizational strategy for the development of talent through public and private statements, the greater the likelihood is that the change will also attract attention from others.

Lower-level managers also exert influence on the success or failure of organizational strategy for the development of talent. The role of lower-level managers is to give support, provide resources, and reward HR efforts.

But what should WLP practitioners do when leaders of their organization do *not* see the relevance of Talent Development initiatives to their needs or those of the business? One answer, of course, is for practitioners to look for employment elsewhere. But for those too stubborn to give up without a fight, here are a few suggestions:

1. *Start small.* Tackle one highly visible problem successfully. Collect anecdotes stemming from success in dealing with the problem, and use every channel of information available to emphasize the value of Talent Development as demonstrated by this case.

2. *Build a following.* Start with the most powerful clientele that can be approached, and work on satisfying their needs and concerns. Expand gradually beyond that clientele.

3. *Insert information about Talent Development activities in company publications.* Build lower-level support if top management is hard to reach.

4. *Demonstrate how Talent Development activities can avert problems.* Use every occasion when problems come up to show how Talent Development activities could have prevented them and how present Talent Development activities can help rectify them.

Practitioners will have to work on building support for Talent Development over time, often over many years. This "strategy" can be successful if approached with persistence, diligence, and patience. But what about resistance to changing organizational strategy for the development of talent, assuming support already exists for Talent Development generally? A good starting point is diagnosis. *Why* are people resistant to change? Think about possible causes.

Reviewing Structure

Structure has long been viewed as important in strategic business planning. Chandler (1962), the first writer on strategy, hypothesized that decision-makers in any organization adjust structure once strategy is chosen. Later researchers have shown that matters are not as simple as Chandler's early hypothesis suggests. Indeed, as Galbraith and Nathanson (1979) have shown, structure can constrain strategic choice.

Structure refers to a way of organizing work to ensure control and facilitate purposeful behavior (Gibson, Ivancevich, and Donnelly 1997). It affects behavior in several ways: First, structure implies allocation of job tasks, duties, and responsibilities in the organization. Each task requires specific knowledge/skills from individuals and requires interactions with people in related jobs. Second, structure affects who reports to whom and thus how many and what types of people are grouped together. The numbers and types of people grouped together affect how much people communicate with each other, how close together they feel, and how creative they are. Third, structure affects the level of conflict present in the work group or organization. Conflict results when two work groups are interdependent or when they differ in goals or perceptions about what is important. There is little doubt that structure affects both organizational and individual performance. What is less clear is *how* structure affects performance.

Structure is obviously important in implementing organizational strategy for the development of talent. It can be viewed on three levels: (1) organizational, (2) departmental, and (3) instructional. Organizational structure means the pattern of reporting relationships and duties allocated to departments in the organization. Department structure is similar, referring to reporting relationships established within a work group and work duties allocated within the group. Instructional structure connotes relationships between learning experiences sponsored by the organization.

Any change in organizational structure can create new learning needs. It is entirely possible that a radical reorganization will make all prior instructional planning obsolete. There are several reasons why: First, a reallocation of tasks changes job duties and thus training that is appropriately focused on jobs or job categories. Second, as relationships between jobs change, employee education based on prior career paths is affected. Third, as old work groups are disbanded and new ones are formed, individuals find that they have to learn not just new tasks, but also how to interact with new people and how to deal with a new group purpose. Fourth and finally, as duties are shifted, work groups begin to serve external groups in new ways. The effect of a corporate reorganization on the Talent Development effort is much like throwing a stack of cards up in the air. Not all changes can be predicted, and not all changes will be desirable.

Less-radical reorganizations should be analyzed to determine what tasks, duties, and responsibilities will be affected and over what time period effects will be evident. Employees can be trained in anticipation of change so that they know what to do and when they are expected to do it. They can also be counseled about changes in their career prospects. Reorganizations of any kind open up new career paths even as old ones fade away. Clearly, if a work group is being changed, team building is in order from the outset. The important point to remember is that any change in organizational structure—including downsizing—creates new learning needs before, during, and after the change.

Radical reorganizations are traumatic for employees and fraught with potential dangers for managers. For this reason, they are rarely appropriate, even in failing firms. An alternative is to begin with the replacement of key personnel, such as the CEO and his or her immediate subordinates, and then follow that up with gradual retrenchment. Research by Bibeault (1982) revealed that a successful turnabout strategy requires, on average, about seven and a half years to implement. Rather than face this long-term prospect, some corporate managers prefer more-drastic alternatives, such as selling assets of a failing division (*liquidation*), spinning off a failing firm *(divestment)*, or selling a division to another firm (also called *divestment)*. Smaller divisions are more likely to be sold off so that the corporation can use the cash resulting from a sale to find a better return on investment elsewhere. Divestments are more often successful when managers in the division participate in the process than when the decision comes as a surprise to them.

It is worth noting that corporate Grand Strategy can have an impact on talent. Indeed, mergers, acquisitions, and takeovers can create massive infusions of talent to the acquiring organization. Likewise, a divestiture may result in a net talent loss. Other Grand Strategies may each bring unique impacts on Talent Development efforts.

Dramatic changes in organizational structure are rarely appropriate if the intent is to introduce a radically new product or service requiring methods utterly unlike those handled previously by the firm. Perhaps the best approach is to create a parallel organization or at least isolate sites where change is being introduced. Human resistance to change is so great that radical changes work best when a new unit is created, people are socialized in it, and the culture develops separate from that of the sponsoring organization.

Structural changes within the organization require a review of the WLP department's structure. For example, a shift from a centralized and functionally structured organization to a decentralized, regionalized organization may well create the need for reorganizing the WLP department. There are many alternatives:

1. Decentralize and regionalize Talent Development, too. (In effect, eliminate the corporate-level department.)
2. Create informal or formal liaisons in each region who communicate regularly with the centralized WLP department.
3. Separate the duties of a centralized WLP department from duties of "one-person operations" in each facility or from duties of small bands of itinerant WLP "marauders" who move from site to site in each region.
4. Create a field operations chief at the corporate level whose job involves traveling to different regions and reporting back to the corporate-level WLP department.
5. Create a separate but smaller WLP department within each division or region that interacts with one-person operations in the field on one hand and with the corporate WLP department on the other hand.

Matters can become even more complicated if the organization's change in strategy calls for the introduction of a new project or matrix structure. A *project structure* is characterized by temporary work teams assigned to one-time efforts such as product start-ups. *Matrix structures* are similar, except that project managers are equal to division chiefs in status and are not, as in a pure project structure, of lower status. Project structures are common in turbulent environments or in temporary job assignments requiring tight control from beginning to end. Professionals such as engineers, accountants/auditors, research scientists, and even physicians frequently work in project structures. A structure of this kind is also common in the start-up of a new venture—a new product, a new service, or a new plant or production facility.

A project environment differs radically from a functional or divisional one. Each project team works on an issue or assignment utterly unlike anything that is currently being worked on by others and, in some cases, utterly unlike what has been worked on before or will be worked on again. Scheduling Talent Development activities in the classroom is difficult because each team (ranging from two or three people to as many as several thousand in rare cases) is at a different stage of progress. Time out for the classroom disrupts work schedules within or between teams.

If a project structure is introduced, WLP practitioners may find they need to reexamine every facet of their work. If the organization is large enough, classroom efforts may continue, but they will not be enough. They will tend to attract team members when they are at a "low point" on a project, not necessarily when they need instruction. For this reason, it might be appropriate to create outreach efforts so that WLP practitioners call on project teams while they work. Alternatively, WLP practitioners might be assigned to project teams. Instructional delivery methods will have to be geared more to individualized learning such as programmed instruction, computer-based training, and on-the-job training so that team members receive instruction at the work site during slack periods. New hires should be trained *before* they are assigned to projects to avoid sacrificing training for pressing work assignments.

Finally, any change in organizational structure or in organizational strategy for the development of talent will also require a review of how learning experiences are sequenced (that is, how the curriculum is structured).

There are different, albeit appropriate, methods of sequencing training, education, and development. The method of sequencing depends on whether the curriculum is subject-centered, goal-centered, experience-centered, or learner-centered. On one level, the issue of sequencing seems simple enough: Learners should be introduced to subject matter or skills in common-sense order, going from the known to the unknown. Each instructional lesson should thus build on what precedes it, and should prepare learners for what follows it. This approach works well enough for most cognitive (knowledge) instruction. The WLP practitioner analyzes, for example, a work task and considers three questions: (1) What behaviors have to be performed? (2) How well does each behavior have to be performed? and (3) What does the learner already have to know or be able to do before exhibiting the behavior? Answering these questions will help construct a *learning hierarchy,* a depiction of what skills or knowledge should precede others. Hierarchies are useful in sequencing instruction. Learners are then tested prior to instruction to determine their entry-level skills.

The notion of the learning hierarchy is a powerful one, especially for manual and technical training at a detailed level. It is not as well or as easily applied for white-collar workers, large blocks of learning, or employee education or development. The learning hierarchy does not work for white-collar workers because analysis of their work requires other methods. Learning hierarchies do not work for large blocks of learning because the preparation of a learning hierarchy requires massive amounts of work. Learning hierarchies do not work for employee education or development because they take place over much longer time spans than training does.

When WLP practitioners are faced with sequencing large blocks of instruction over long time periods, they find that much of the literature in the field is no longer very helpful or relevant. It tends to be too detailed and designed around task-oriented instruction. It also tends to be biased toward a bottom-up approach to instructional design, in which the sequence of activities in each job task is analyzed as the basis for instruction. Of course, this approach is past-oriented because it assumes that the ways tasks have been performed will be appropriate for the future. However, people may find that new, utterly different tasks are not just necessary, but are required.

How, then, is it possible to sequence large blocks of instruction—say, a dozen "courses" or a five-year planned group of learning experiences? There are several ways (Rothwell and Kazanas 1998):

1. From simple to complex—begin with job "basics" and keep adding.
2. From particular to general—start with examples of job duties or activities, and then draw conclusions to reach generalizations.

3. From tangible to intangible—begin with concrete examples, and progress to abstractions.

4. From one activity to another, related activity, and so on—treat related tasks or duties in order.

5. From whole to part—start with an overall model of job performance, and then treat each part in isolation.

6. From a brief and incomplete treatment of one topic to a more complete treatment of another topic to a more in-depth treatment of the first, and so on—topics are selectively introduced in a cyclical pattern and reintroduced over time. (This is called a *spiral curriculum*.)

Each approach to sequencing is appropriate under particular circumstances.

The question is, will strategic change affect appropriate sequencing of instructional experiences over time? If there is a change in organizational strategy for the development of talent—the way employees and other learners are prepared over time—a change in the sequencing of instruction may also be necessary.

Reviewing Reward Systems

Behavioral scientists have long stressed the importance of *reward systems,* the ways and means by which managers allocate tangible and intangible rewards according to employee performance, longevity, or other factors. Clearly, reward systems are important because people do what they are rewarded for doing and slight what they are not rewarded for doing. Managers do not pay close enough attention to the consequences of reward systems in Talent Development efforts. Even before implementation of any change, the reward system should be analyzed to determine whether it will facilitate or impede. If it will impede change, then the reward system itself may have redesigned before implementing the strategy.

Types of Rewards. To diagnose reward systems, it is first necessary to understand what they are. Rewards fall into two broad categories: (1) *extrinsic,* stemming from actions of other people (examples of extrinsic rewards include salary increases, achievement awards, and promotions), and (2) *intrinsic,* stemming from work or activity itself (examples of intrinsic rewards include pride of accomplishment, increased self-esteem, satisfaction with a job well-done, and joy at seeing results of one's hard work).

Intrinsic rewards result from interaction between the individual and work. Important intrinsic factors include (1) meaningfulness, (2) responsibility, and (3) awareness of results (Hackman and Oldham 1975). *Meaningfulness* denotes how much individuals view their work as important. *Responsibility* is associated with how much individuals feel accountable for work results. *Awareness of results* refers to feedback that individuals receive on their performance. To produce satisfaction, a job must rate high on all three factors (Hackman and Oldham 1975). It should require varied activities, produce identifiable results, and influence others. These factors are linked to meaningfulness. The job should also lead to independence. This factor is linked to responsibility. Finally, the job should yield feedback on results. This factor is linked to awareness of results.

Extrinsic rewards should meet five criteria described in classic descriptions by Lawler (1977) and Burke (1982). The first is *significance*. Employees must value the likely rewards stemming from their efforts. The second is *flexibility*. Since individuals vary in what rewards they desire, a successful reward system must allow for individual differences. The third is *frequency*. The more often rewards are given and the sooner they follow behavior, the more effective they are likely to be. Of course, some rewards lose their value when awarded frequently. The fourth is *visibility*. Rewards are enhanced when other people know about them. The fifth is *expense*. Can the organization afford to give out the reward?

Learning and Rewards. People learn for different reasons. It is important to understand why people learn if they are to be motivated and rewarded for it.

In a classic study, Houle (1961) classified adult learners into three general categories: (1) *goal-oriented*—people who undertake learning to achieve clear results or solve a problem; (2) *activity-oriented*—people who seek social contact through learning; and (3) *learning-oriented*—people who think of learning as an end in itself.

Reviewing Rewards and Changes in Organizational Strategy for the Development of Talent. The two previous sections have described types of rewards and reasons for learning. Use them as a starting point to consider several questions:

1. How much does your organization presently reward learning in general? How does your organization specifically reward people for achieving desired results from training; for preparing for advancement and career mobility through employee education; for improving the work group, department, and organization through planned development; and for improving relationships between the organization and outside groups?

2. How much *should* your organization encourage learning in general? How much should the organization reward people in the future for achieving desired results of training; for preparing for advancement and career mobility through employee education; for improving the work group, department, and organization through planned development; or for improving relationships between the organization and outside groups?

3. What gaps exist between the conditions discussed in items 1 and 2?

4. What extrinsic and/or intrinsic rewards can help narrow the gap and thus help implement the organizational strategy for the development of talent?

5. What distinctions can be made in the allocation of these rewards based on different individual orientations to learning and styles of learning?

WLP practitioners should be aware that traditional compensation systems are not always best for implementing radical changes in organizational strategy for the development of talent. One promising alternative is *skill-based pay*, which compensates people for what they learn that is practical and useful for achieving results. Learning activities are planned by job category, by work group, and by career intentions. They are organized in "skill blocks," and employees are rewarded on the basis of speed and level of mastery. While there are disadvantages to skill-based pay (difficulties in linking productivity increases to learners, in using this incentive system for white-collar workers, and in dealing with people who master all "skill blocks" available to them), it is an idea worth pursuing when implementing radical changes in organizational strategy for the development of talent.

Getting Necessary Resources

The ultimate test of management commitment to any plan is the extent to which resources are allocated to it. Budgeting is thus an important tool in implementing any strategy. It is the process of converting objectives into resource requests necessary to achieve them. Budgeting typically takes place annually, though some expensive items such as buildings or high-cost equipment may have to be budgeted for over several years.

The aim in this discussion is not to provide a primer on how to prepare an annual budget for the WLP department. The point of this discussion is instead that an annual budget should stem from an organizational strategy for the development of talent and from long-term Talent Development objectives. For this reason, it is important to look beyond annual budget horizons and consider several questions. First, what is going to be the complete cost of achieving a strategic Talent Development objective over the full time horizon of the strategy—five years, for example? Second, what estimates can be made now of the company's financial position over that time period? Will it probably erode over that time span due to external conditions like new competitors or a weak market position? Will the Talent Development effort be affected heavily or not so heavily by cutbacks and growth? Why? Third and finally, would it make more sense to put higher priorities on some strategic objectives in early annual budgets in a five-year sequence so that cutbacks later will not be felt so much? If so, what should be emphasized early on, and what should be emphasized later?

Some WLP practitioners will object that questions like these are not very useful for them because they must live with budgets imposed from above. In some organizations that is true: higher-level managers handle budgeting. This is called a nonparticipative *budget process.* However, it is probably more the exception than the norm: most organizations allow at least some negotiation in the process.

Communicating about Strategy

Poor communication is a frequent cause for failure in many planning efforts. For this reason, it is essential to consider communication when implementing organizational strategy for the development of talent. In this context, *communication* means conveying information and building support.

Clearly, communicating about organizational strategy for the development of talent is easiest when the organization has a coherent and unified communication policy to inform employees and supervisors about such matters as ongoing activities of the corporation; corporate, business, and HR plans; and sensitive or controversial matters.

Without a unified organizational communication policy, there is a tendency for controversial issues to be skirted or questions about them to be handled inconsistently by different managers. With such a policy, WLP practitioners and line managers have clear guidance on how to communicate about Talent Development generally; how to address supervisory and employee concerns about changes in training, employee education, and employee development practices; and how to use various media to communicate about Talent Development. In organizational settings in which Talent Development is considered an important matter, communicating changes about it can easily affect subsequent employee acceptance or rejection.

A key goal of an organized communication effort is to overcome the many barriers to effective communication that exist in the organization. Multiple channels of communication are more likely than a single channel to reach the intended audience and to overcome barriers. Representative downward channels include placing advertisements or articles of interest on bulletin boards, sending direct mail to employees or supervisors at home, sending memos to employees or supervisors at work, placing articles or announcements in company newsletters and magazines, inserting information in personal handbooks, issuing special publications such as training catalogs or brochures, holding meetings, holding one-on-one discussions, and enclosing notices with paychecks. Upward channels of communication include receiving information from in-house suggestion systems, meetings, attitude surveys, one-on-one discussions with supervisors, and questions posed by employees through union representatives. Talent Development activities are also important components in the in-house communication process and are useful tools in communicating about business plans and employee performance.

Three specific communication methods can be used most effectively in implementing organization strategy for Talent Development: (1) meetings, (2) training sessions, and (3) advisory/oversight committees.

Meetings. One way to communicate about strategy is to hold meetings to discuss it.

Meetings have several purposes. First, they are vehicles for informing managers and supervisors about company strategy. Second, meetings garner support and motivate participants. Third, meetings provide guidance to managers at all levels in the hierarchy. Fourth, meetings allow participation in planning processes and provide an avenue for feedback to strategic managers about specific problems impeding progress at the operational level.

Talent Development can be included in the agenda as an issue for discussion during strategic business planning meetings. Managers and supervisors can then be asked what training, education, or development would contribute to the implementation of strategic business plans by building employee competencies essential to implement those plans. Talent Development priorities can be set and action plans can be established at that time so that the link between Talent Development activities and company plans is indisputable.

As an alternative, meetings on organizational strategy for the development of talent can be arranged to parallel meetings on strategic business plans. The advantage of this approach is that more time and effort will be devoted to Talent Development than when business plans and Talent Development are considered together. The disadvantage is that it may be difficult to keep participants on target in matching up business needs and the skills and training necessary to meet those needs when skills are treated separate from business plans.

Meetings devoted exclusively to the Talent Development effort may also be scheduled regularly with managers and supervisors at different levels and locations. They are useful for identifying future trends or issues affecting the

Talent Development effort *or* specific training, education, or development needs. Meetings also provide supervisors with opportunities to discuss relationships between instructional methods and organizational strategy for the development of talent. Supervisors can brainstorm on problems they encounter as they try to implement organizational strategy for the development of talent. A major advantage in holding meetings of this kind is that they raise consciousness at all hierarchical levels about the importance of business planning *and* Talent Development. Meetings also emphasize the value of a unified organizational strategy for the development of talent, allowing discussion about it and possible modification to it. When Talent Development activities are not accepted in the organizational culture, meetings can be a starting point for a long-term cultural change effort to make Talent Development part of the culture.

Training. Some strategic business plans fail because people do not possess the necessary skills to make them work or because managers themselves lack appropriate skills or experience. For this reason, some firms sponsor training soon after the choice of a new business strategy to build the competencies that people need to begin implementation.

Training may also facilitate the implementation of organizational strategy for the development of talent. Several kinds of training may be appropriate. Each serves a different purpose. *Orientation programs* focus on questions like these: What is organization strategy for Talent Development? How does it help operating managers? What are their responsibilities? *Implementation programs* focus on methods of implementing organizational strategy for the development of talent and on objectives for Organization Development, employee and nonemployee development, education, and training. *Simulation programs* identify what future conditions will be like inside and outside the organization, and assess learning needs based on artificially simulated experience of the future. *General training on planning* focuses on issues like the nature of strategic business planning. How is it used in the company? What are company plans at present? What is the role of Talent Development, among other functions, in the process of implementing business strategy?

Training may be developed in-house, jointly developed by company WLP staff and outside consultants, or developed solely by outside consultants. Steps in designing training of this kind are no different from those in any other type of instruction: (1) identify purpose, (2) assess needs, (3) establish objectives, (4) prepare tests (if appropriate), (5) develop instructional materials or modify those available from other sources, (6) pilot-test the training, (7) make final revisions to material, (8) offer the training on a large scale, and (9) evaluate results.

Advisory or Oversight Committees. Another fruitful way to build support for organizational strategy for the development of talent is to create a standing advisory committee on employee training, education, and development, or separate committees at different hierarchical levels or in different departments. School systems have long used "committees" in a similar way. In a sense, a school board is a committee, though it governs like a board of directors. Curriculum committees have been established at many schools. Similar committees are used to administer federal training programs for economically disadvantaged or technologically displaced workers. Curriculum committees are also widely used in higher education.

Similar committees have been suggested for Talent Development (Kruger 1983). They structure participation in setting Talent Development priorities. They make Talent Development activities more visible; underscore the responsiveness of WLP practitioners to needs at many levels; set priorities while allowing for many perspectives and viewpoints; settle jurisdictional issues; and coordinate activities when solutions are difficult to arrive at, when many specialties may be needed, and when broad, long-term support is desirable. Operating best in organizations with clearly defined department structures, advisory or oversight committees prove useful in interpreting needs assessment results, designing curricula at different levels and locations, and setting priorities. Members of these committees are likely to find committee work useful for their own development.

There are many ways to establish and run a Talent Development committee. It is not necessary for a committee to be specially commissioned, though that is typical. For example, it is possible to form a committee consisting of all top managers—the chief executive and his or her immediate reports. They meet to establish the long-term direction of the Talent Development effort so that organized learning is tied directly to strategic business plans. Alternatively, Talent

Development issues can be treated during top-level management planning meetings and retreats. Similar committees may be formed at other hierarchical levels in the organization to ensure that the Talent Development effort is responsive to needs at those levels.

In establishing a committee, WLP practitioners should take care to (1) clarify the committee's purpose and objectives from the outset (a written charter is helpful—see Exhibit 6-1); (2) select members with great care, consistent with the committee's purpose; (3) establish a way of maintaining some continuity on the committee while, at the same time, ensuring that there is a regular infusion of new members so that the group does not stagnate; and (4) find ways to feed back information for decisions to the committee and feed back results of prior decisions or recommendations of the committee. The most important point is to build member involvement while not burdening members with so many demands and so much information that they become unable or unwilling to participate in decision-making.

Committees on Talent Development should be kept relatively small—between five and nine members are best.

I   Members can be temporary or permanent.
I   They can consist of insiders, outsiders, or some combination.
I   They can be asked to make decisions, offer recommendations, or simply generate ideas.
I   Members can be representative of different groups, or limited to people at the same hierarchical level, people from the same location, or people in the same occupation.

Most committees are chaired by a member, not by a WLP practitioner. Chairpersons should be selected for their ability to (1) lead discussions, (2) create and preserve a psychologically comfortable climate conducive to group member interactions, (3) select members, (4) attend to administrative details, (5) prepare meeting agendas, and/or (6) schedule meetings. Members should be selected on the basis of their willingness to serve, as well as their competence and whether or not they can help the committee meet its goals. (Kruger 1983).

Exhibit 6-1: Talent Development Advisory Committee

Basic Purpose

The purpose of the Talent Development Advisory Committee is to establish priorities and guidelines for the selection, scheduling, development, and evaluation of all staff training, education, and development. It shall provide the Director of Talent Development with advice on selection and scheduling of formal and informal learning experiences, assist in reviewing and developing instructional content and form, recommend time frames for delivery of experiences, and evaluate the effectiveness of the Talent Development effort. As an ongoing *advisory* committee, its recommendations need to be approved by upper management before being formally adopted for the entire organization.

General Oversight of the Talent Development Effort

The Talent Development Advisory Committee will provide oversight of the Talent Development effort, developed by the Talent Development Director and others. The committee will evaluate the effectiveness of the Talent Development effort in meeting the organization's needs. It will recommend necessary revisions, in consultation with the Talent Development Director.

Selection of Experiences

The Talent Development Advisory Committee works with the Talent Development Director each year to select and schedule training and educational and developmental activities attuned to organizational needs.

Scheduling of Learning Experiences

The Advisory Committee works with the Talent Development Director to set up learning experiences to members of job categories, to individuals sharing common career aspirations, and to some work groups in which developmental needs have been planned. It can recommend time frames for the development and scheduling of planned learning activities.

Developing Specifications for Learning Experiences

The Advisory Committee advises the Talent Development Director in developing specifications for learning experiences based on staff needs. Such specifications will include: the purpose of the experience; objectives stated in terms of what employees will be able to do after completion; methods to be used in delivering the experience(s); and minimum acceptable qualifications for those chosen to lead training courses, serve as career mentors, or guide developmental efforts.

It is unwise to rush into establishing committees without first assessing how much support they will receive and, once the idea is accepted, without "training" members. Nothing can be so frustrating to committee members as to propose an idea and learn later that WLP practitioners were unable to accept their advice because it was not approved by higher-level management or because necessary resources were not available. It is also unreasonable to expect managers or employees to advise on Talent Development issues that they know little about. A good briefing on the Talent Development effort and the practices of the WLP department is a necessary first item in any kickoff meeting of a committee. Further, if committee members are to provide input on future-oriented learning needs, they will undoubtedly require instruction on strategic-thinking skills.

Advisory committees are important. In many respects, they can serve in the same capacity as strategic business planning committees. They can identify present strengths/weaknesses of an organization's long-term learning efforts, compare them to expected future demands, and set priorities for planned learning. These are not matters of minor consequence, nor should they be treated as such, because they can yield support to guide implementation of the organization's strategy for Talent Development in line with business and staffing plans.

Developing Functional Strategies for the Development of Talent

As traditionally discussed in strategic business planning, *a function strategy* is the short-term plan for a key functional area in an organization. Functions include production/operations, marketing, finance, and personnel. The purpose of a functional strategy is to translate the organization's Grand Strategy into specific strategies for areas of the organization.

We have written elsewhere about the importance of establishing functional strategies within HR (Rothwell and Kazanas 2002). It is essential to integrate overall HR Grand Strategy with organizational strategy so that personnel initiatives support business plans, and to integrate the strategy for each "activity area" within HR with that of the overall strategy of the HR function so that each activity area of personnel supports others (Alpander 1982). These "activity areas" include hiring/selection/recruitment, training, compensating, and dealing with organized labor. The purpose of HR Grand Strategy is an important one. The steps in formulating HR Grand Strategy resemble those in formulating strategic business plans, and appropriate HR goals depend on organizational goals.

Organizational strategy for the development of talent is an important component of HR Grand Strategy* because plans for building individual competencies for the future are closely related to plans for ensuring that the right people are in the right places at the right times and that they possess the right skills.

But within organizational strategy for the development of talent there can also be *functional strategies.* They differ in purpose because they focus on different kinds of change. They also focus on different learners. These functions are

1. *Organization development*—a long-term effort for changing the culture of an organization or group.
2. *Nonemployee development*—a long-term effort for improving relations between a business, the general public, or external stakeholders.
3. *Employee development*—a long-term effort for matching up the collective competencies of a work group and the responsibilities assigned to the group by the organization.
4. *Education*—an intermediate-term effort for helping individuals achieve their career objectives, keep abreast of changes in their occupations, and gain new insights about themselves.
5. *Training*—a short-term effort for helping job incumbents meet their responsibilities.

Each function is a component of a unified organizational strategy for the development of talent. Each contributes, in its own way, to the implementation of that organizational strategy for the development of talent. Yet each can be distinct from other functions and can be guided by separately prepared objectives, policies, and activities. Part IV of this text focuses on each function.

---

* We use the term *HR Grand Strategy* to mean plans for all HR activities.

Activity 6–1: Objective-Setting for Implementing Organizational Strategy for the Development of Talent

Directions: Use this activity to do some brainstorming. For each issue listed in Column 1, describe in Column 2 what long-term outcomes are to be achieved over a five-year time period. Then describe in Column 3 what specific, measurable outcomes are to be achieved through organized HRD activities in one year. It might be helpful to diagram, on separate sheets, the relationship between long-term objectives (in Column 2) and short-term objectives (in Column 3).

Column 1	*Column 2*	*Column 3*
Issue	What long-term outcomes are to be achieved over a five-year period?	What specific, measurable outcomes are to be achieved in a one-year period?
1. Changes in what the general public knows about the corporation and its products/services		
2. Changes in what key external stakeholders know about the corporation and its products/services		
3. Changes in the organization, its departments, or its work groups through learning		
4. Changes in individuals so that they are ready for movements between jobs		
5. Changes in what individuals know about their present jobs		

Activity 6–2: Evaluating the Comprehensiveness of an Organization's Talent Development Policy

Directions: In Column 1 below, you will find a number of issues that should be covered in an organization's Talent Development policy. In Column 2, check whether your firm's present policy addresses the issue. In Column 3, describe what changes in Talent Development policy are appropriate in light of any changes in the organizational strategy for the development of talent.

Column 1	*Column 2*		*Column 3*
Does your organization's Talent Development policy cover:	Response		What changes in the Talent Development policy are appropriate in light of the change in the Grand Strategy for Talent Development?
	Yes (✔)	No (✔)	
1. The purpose of the Talent Development effort as it relates to:	( )	( )	
A. The general public?	( )	( )	
B. Key external stakeholders?	( )	( )	
C. Work groups/departments?	( )	( )	
D. Individuals and their careers?	( )	( )	
E. Job categories?	( )	( )	
2. The relationship between the Talent Development effort and organizational purpose, goals, and objectives?	( )	( )	
3. Responsibilities of			
A. Managers at each level for Talent Development?	( )	( )	
B. Employees for Talent Development?	( )	( )	
4. Under what circumstances Talent Development policy should be changed?	( )	( )	
5. The needs to be met through the Talent Development effort?	( )	( )	

Activity 6–2: *(continued)*

Column 1	Column 2		Column 3
Does your organization's Talent Development policy cover:	Response		What changes in the Talent Development policy are appropriate in light of the change in the Grand Strategy for Talent Development?
	Yes (✔)	No (✔)	
6. How to finance the Talent Development effort?	( )	( )	
7. How to staff activities conducted for Talent Development?	( )	( )	
8. How top managers should be involved in the Talent Development effort?	( )	( )	
9. How managers and employees at lower levels should participate in planning for the Talent Development effort?	( )	( )	
10. Other matters? List other important issues:	( )	( )	

Activity 6–3: Leadership and Implementation of Organizational Strategy for the Development of Talent

Directions: As in the two previous activities, use this activity to do some brainstorming. In Column 1, consider: Who are the key leaders? In Column 2, consider: How receptive are these leaders to changing organizational strategy for the development of talent? In Column 3, consider: How can these leaders be persuaded of the value of a new organizational strategy for the development of talent? Write notes to answer these questions in the space below each question.

Who are the key leaders?	*How receptive are these leaders to changing organizational strategy for the development of talent?*	*How can these leaders be persuaded of the value of a new organizational strategy for the development of talent?*

Activity 6–4: Rewards of Implementation of Organizational Strategy for the Development of Talent

Directions: Use this activity to think about rewards and organizational strategy for the development of talent. Go through each of the following sections and answer the questions. Use additional paper if necessary.

I. Present Rewards

1. How much does your organization presently reward learning (generally) and each of the following (particularly)?

    A. Achieving desired results from training?

    B. Preparing for career mobility through planned employee education?

    C. Improving the work group through planned development?

    D. Improving relationships between the organization and external groups?

II. Future Rewards

2. In the future, how should your organization encourage:

    A. Achieving desired results from training?

    B. Preparing for career mobility through planned employee education?

    C. Improving the work group through planned development?

    D. Improving relationships between the organization and external groups?

III. Identifying Gaps

3. What gaps exist between the conditions discussed in items 1 and 2?

IV. Rewards

4. What extrinsic and/or intrinsic rewards can help implement the organizational strategy for the development of talent? Who should be rewarded? How?

Activity 6–5: Budgeting and Organizational Strategy for the Development of Talent

Directions: Answer the questions in each section. Use additional paper if necessary.

I. The Complete Cost

1. Have you considered the long-term costs of implementing the organizational strategy for Talent Development? If not, prepare a five-year budget for the Talent Development effort. Use additional paper as necessary.

II. External Conditions

2. What estimates can you make of the company's financial condition over a five-year time period?

A. Will this position erode? If so, why?

B. How will the Talent Development effort be affected by the company's financial position? Why do you think it will be affected (if at all)?

III. Priorities

3. What priorities should be assigned to each initiative described in the budget?

Activity 6–6: Communicating about Organizational Strategy for the Development of Talent

Directions: Answer the questions in each section. Use additional paper if necessary.

I. Present Communication

1. *How well are issues associated with the Talent Development effort being communicated to supervisors and employees in your organization?*

II. Future Communication

2. *How do you think issues associated with the development of talent should be communicated to supervisors and employees in your organization in the future?*

III. Important Issues

3. *What Talent Development issues are most important to communicate about in the future? To whom should this communication be directed?*

IV. Channels

4. Through what channels should information about Talent Development be communicated in the future? Why?

Activity 6–7: A Case Study on Implementing Organizational Strategy for the Development of Talent

Directions: Read the case below and answer the questions that follow.

The Worthington Corporation* is a fully diversified, multinational manufacturing firm that produces consumer electronics goods such as televisions, compact disc players, videotape machines, and cassette tape recorders. Worthington's largest manufacturing facilities are located in Taiwan and Korea. Marketing, research and development, and finance are handled through the firm's large corporate headquarters complex in Duluth, Minnesota.

Worthington established a corporate-level Talent Development Department at the Duluth headquarters only ten years ago. The firm has historically leaned toward decentralization. Prior to 1977, all Talent Development activities were handled on-site (at plants or at the corporate headquarters).

Worthington employs 35 professional Talent Development practitioners at corporate headquarters. Most of them hold doctoral degrees in Talent Development or instructional technology. Corporate headquarters offers management, executive, engineering, and other high-level training seminars in a new $6 million training complex. In addition, the corporate-level Talent Development department produces professional videotapes, computer-based training software, and other instructional resources for use in company plants abroad.

Though the corporate-level Talent Development department offers the highest-cost seminars on-site, each plant is staffed by at least one experienced Talent Development practitioner. Typically reporting to a plant's HR manager, each Talent Development practitioner at a company facility prepares an annual training and development plan for the facility. Coordination between line managers and Talent Development practitioners at all levels is essential to avoid expensive overlapping of training.

Worthington does not conduct comprehensive HR planning. No attempt is presently made to integrate company recruitment, Talent Development, compensation/benefits, or other HR activities.

Worthington does plan strategically at the corporate level. However, the chief focus of these plans is on future markets, company financial condition, and product lines. No attempt is made to draw conclusions about human skills needed or available to carry out these plans.

Worthington faces stiff competition from foreign firms, some of which enjoy substantially lower labor costs on goods produced. However, Worthington possesses a well-known corporate name worldwide. Company management plans to expand and automate manufacturing facilities, increase expenditures on marketing and research and development, and decrease labor costs. The corporate Talent Development Department will receive more resources and staffing—perhaps as much as 50 percent more resources—over the next few years. That is most unusual in a firm that is (generally) decreasing its staffing levels worldwide.

Assume that you are hired as an external consultant by Worthington's corporate-level Talent Development Department to help establish an organizational strategy for the development of talent.

Activity 6–7: (continued)

Directions: Read the case below and answer the questions that follow.

Questions

1. Prepare a list of questions about the purpose of the Talent Development effort to use in an initial interview with the corporate-level director of Talent Development. What should you want to know about the purpose?

2. What problems are created by the lack of a company strategic business plan and comprehensive HR plan? What can be done to overcome these problems, assuming that the corporation will not change its planning methods?

3. How can you develop a comprehensive list of Talent Development–oriented strengths/weaknesses and threats/opportunities facing Worthington? Discuss how you would prepare such a list.

4. Consider the range of organizational strategies for Talent Development available to Worthington. List what they are and discuss what each one means. What problems, if any, can you foresee in attempting to formulate and implement an organizational strategy for the development of talent in the Worthington Corporation? How do you suggest handling each problem?

* A fictitious company

FUNCTIONAL STRATEGIES FOR TALENT DEVELOPMENT

Most managers, HR practitioners, and HRD or WLP practitioners will be familiar with functional strategies for Talent Development if they have had to handle organization development (OD) interventions or administer employee development or employee education programs. These are called *functional strategies for Talent Development* because they are approaches or methods by which to implement organizational strategy for the development of talent. This part deals with these and other functional strategies for Talent Development.

Part IV consists of five chapters.

Chapter 7 on organization development defines OD, explains how it is distinguishable from other change methods, reviews how OD can relate to organizational learning, describes typical problems with OD interventions, and introduces strategic OD as a means by which to implement organizational strategy for the development of talent.

Chapter 8 focuses on nonemployee development—Talent Development efforts directed at stakeholder groups rather than at employees. This chapter defines nonemployee development, summarizes how to carry it out, and shows how it can play an important role in implementing organizational strategy for the development of talent.

Chapter 9 is about long-term efforts to develop employee talent, such as rotation programs, action learning, and informal learning projects. The chapter describes some of these methods and shows how they play a key role in implementing organizational strategy for the development of talent.

Chapter 10 focuses on employee education, which prepares individuals for vertical advancement (up the chain of command) or horizontal advancement (along a continuum of professional abilities). The chapter defines employee education, explains the part that it can play in organizational strategy, and offers advice about how to carry it out.

Chapter 11 focuses on employee training. The chapter explains what training means, what it is intended to do, and how it can be carried out. It also emphasizes the role it can play in organizational strategy for the development of talent.

CHAPTER 7

ORGANIZATION DEVELOPMENT

This chapter deals with preparing *groups* of people for the future by changing organizational culture or group norms. This process of change is called organization development (OD).

Definition of Organization Development

OD connotes more than its literal meaning of "fostering long-term growth of an organization and people within it." Instead, it means

> a process that applies behavioral science knowledge and practices to help organizations achieve greater effectiveness, including increased financial performance and improved quality of work life. OD . . . focuses on building the organization's ability to assess its current functioning and to achieve its goals. Moreover, OD is oriented to improving the total system—the organization and its parts in the context of the larger environment that affects them (Cummings and Worley 2001, 1).

OD means "a systemwide application of behavioral science knowledge to the planned development, improvement, and reinforcement of the strategies, structures, and processes that lead to organization effectiveness" (Cummings and Worley 2001, 1).

OD focuses on long-term change that is compatible with what top management wants. It does this in the context of work groups or work teams, and is often carried out by an external consultant as a catalyst for change, who uses specialized techniques drawn from such behavioral sciences as sociology, psychology, political science, archaeology, and cultural anthropology.

How is organization development distinguishable from other change methods?

There are three very general approaches to change in any organization (Chin and Benne 1969).

The first approach to change is through *persuasion*. The goal of persuasion is to convince people to change because there is some benefit to them by doing so. Since people act out of self-interest and are keenly interested in what's in it for them, they will change if they see a benefit from doing so.

The second approach to change is through *coercion*. The goal of coercion is to frighten people into changing. Out of sheer fear for the consequences of not changing, they will change.

The third approach is through *education*. The goal of education is to show people new ways of behaving and creative approaches to solving problems. People will change when they know how to do so.

OD is directed to bringing about long-term change through learning that is done in group settings. It is thus based on an educational approach to change. Unlike employee development, it is directed to changing *culture*—the elusive, often unarticulated and taken-for-granted standards and norms of appropriate behavior in an organizational or group setting.

What is the relationship between organization development and organizational learning?

The essence of strategic planning and thinking is the awareness of how future conditions can or should be factored into present decisions or past actions. Strategy-making helps avert problems or seize opportunities that might arise at a future time and that are consequences of external trends, events, or conditions over which managers in one organization have little control. In short, strategic planning is based on adapting to and even anticipating external environmental change.

Learning is one means, though not the only means, for individuals and groups to adapt to external change. While WLP practitioners typically devote much attention to such individually oriented change efforts as employee training and education, it is clear that organizations and work groups also "learn." Though neither organizations nor groups "learn" in precisely the same way as individuals, they are human institutions and are influenced by phenomena to which individuals are subject.

It is time that WLP practitioners begin to adopt a broader, more strategic view of their role: they are agents who facilitate learning for organizations and work groups, as well as for individuals. Viewed from this broader standpoint, OD can be interpreted to mean any planned learning activity intended to help groups adapt to future external environmental demands.

The Work Group. The work group consists of an employee, the employee's immediate supervisor, and other employees who work together. They share common work space and are placed in close enough physical proximity to interact socially. French and Bell (1984) call this the *family group*, the intact and relatively permanent team consisting of employees and their immediate supervisor.

Much attention has been devoted to individual performance in team settings and, more generally, to *group dynamics*. The latter term refers to the interactions of individuals in a group. Many influential thinkers in the behavioral sciences stress that group change is a means of facilitating individual and organizational change. For example, Lewin (1951) pointed out in a classic description that *work group norms*—the unspoken and often unexamined beliefs about how individuals should behave—pose barriers to change because if individual behavior is at odds with group norms, the individual will be pressured by group members to conform to accepted practices. When individuals do not conform, they are punished or ostracized by peers. Chris Argyris (1962) discussed the relationship between the individual and the organization, asserting that the hierarchical nature of most groups and organizations forces individuals into passive and dependent roles. In frustration, they leave the organization, seek freedom through acquisition of more power, withdraw mentally from the job, or form new groups such as unions to fight for their interests.

The nature of work groups varies substantially, depending on how tasks are carried out in the organization. In some settings, individuals work closely with others to achieve a common goal. For example, a product manufactured on an assembly line is handled by many people. Team work is not, however, restricted to blue-collar settings: it is very common among doctors, lawyers, and accountants. On the other hand, some work is solitary and highly individualized, such as that of the medical research scientist.

A second important issue has to do with organizational structure. Managers in most organizations have considerable freedom to determine how work will be divided among various groups and, indeed, what kinds of groups and how many of them will exist. Beyond that, jobs *within* each group vary widely and contribute to pressures favoring or impeding cooperation.

Groups share common characteristics (Gibson, Ivancevich, and Donnelly 1997). First, individuals are accorded *status* within a work group based on the authority associated with their positions and such individual characteristics as educational level, experience, age, and relationships with superiors. Second, groups vary in *cohesiveness,* a force pulling members together as a group and away from other groups. Third, all groups have *norms*. These are standards of conduct that are rarely articulated, but pervasive in their influence. They arise as groups are formed and are sustained through socialization, the process by which new members are inducted to a group. To remain a group member, an individual must behave in ways consistent with group norms. Fourth, all groups manifest three types of leadership behavior: behavior concerned with task accomplishment; behavior concerned with preserving good interpersonal relations between group members; and behavior not relevant to group needs (Benne and Sheats 1948). How leaders behave exerts considerable influence on group performance and morale (Fiedler 1972; Tannenbaum and Schmidt 1973). Fifth, members of any group adopt *roles*—patterns of behavior associated with their jobs and with group allegiance. Individuals receive messages from others about how they are expected to behave and, in turn, send messages about roles through words and deeds (Katz and Kahn 1978). Behavior inconsistent with the role expectations of others excites comment and, perhaps, sanctions by the work group or its leader. Individual performance in jobs affects group performance that, in turn, affects organizational performance (Gibson, Ivancevich, and Donnelly 1997).

Work groups, like individuals and organizations, progress through predictable life cycle stages in which some concerns dominate others. A group's stage of development is important because it affects productivity and the learning experiences to which the group is susceptible. Stated rather simplistically, the stages are (1) creation, (2) communication, (3) production, and (4) fixation (Gibson, Ivancevich, and Donnelly 1997). In the first stage, new members meet for the first time. They are not necessarily familiar with either the work task confronting them or with each other. In the second stage, group members interact to deal with the task confronting them. They often rebel against the task and against authority figures. They sort things out and learn how to deal with the task and with each other. In the third stage, group members resolve initial problems with what should be done and how group members should get along with each other. They devote their energies to the task/problem and cooperate with each other. In the final stage, group members become fixated on certain ways of doing things and ways of interacting. Norms regulate group member behavior, often to the point that fresh approaches are stifled. Indeed, members may be subject to *groupthink*, a general unwillingness to innovate when it means increasing intragroup conflict (Janis 1973).

The stages of group development are most keenly felt in organizations where there is a project or matrix structure in which heterogeneous teams are forced temporarily; where there is rapid turnover in leadership, or where there are start-up efforts of any kind. As Exhibit 7-1 illustrates, some change efforts are particularly appropriate in each stage of group development.

Organizational Learning. There are some key similarities and differences between individual and organizational learning. An individual has limited experience and finite knowledge, skills, and memories. On the other hand, an organization is characterized by (1) a broad store of experiences composed of aggregate individual experiences over time—not just present employees, but all past employees who have "left their mark"; (2) a much broader store of knowledge and skills than possessed by one person; and (3) an institutional memory made up of a "hard component" embodied in job descriptions, organizational structure,

Exhibit 7-1: Appropriate Group Development Efforts by Phase of Group

Group Phase	Brief Description of Group Phase	Group Development Effort
Creation	▪ Members meet for the first time. ▪ Productivity is predictably low because group members are uncertain of what to do and how to interact.	▪ The supervisor should focus attention on what is to be done and provide specific, concrete directions as much as possible.
Communication	▪ Members of the group learn how to interact.	▪ The supervisor and/or change agent should facilitate group interaction and help members of the group establish roles and work methods.
Production	▪ This phase of group development is characterized by the highest level of productivity.	▪ The supervisor and/or change agent should allow group members to participate to the extent they wish to do so, in decisions affecting them.
Fixation	▪ Group norms are fixed and may suffocate innovation.	▪ The supervisor and/or change agent should initiate teambuilding and team development efforts and foster constructive reviews of existing group interaction and work methods.

policies, and procedures, as well as a "soft component" embodied in stories, myths, and legends about what works and what does not. An organization is relatively permanent and possesses a history distinct from that of individuals. Work groups share this characteristic with organizations.

However, there are two similarities between individual and organizational learning. First, learning stems from a perception of need, a sense that something is not as it should be or that something will change in the future; and second, learning is influenced by past experience. For organizations and groups, needs pinpointed by managers provide a basis for action. Not all needs have to do with individual competencies, but many do. That is why organizational strategy for the development of talent that is focused on meeting learning needs and building competencies is so important in strategic business planning. However, experiences guide assessments of need and interpretations of what is worth knowing or doing. Like individuals, organizations change what they do based on experience.

Organizational or group *culture* is the embodiment of experience. It is the sum total of what has been learned. It influences how individuals behave and how they are socialized as they become members of the organization.

OD efforts are geared to changing culture and thus to facilitating organizational learning (Senge 1990). Since strategic business plans may require cultural change for successful implementation, OD efforts are capable of facilitating organizational and group change in line with strategic needs.

Methods Associated with Organization Development

Traditionally, OD has been based on *action research*. Different OD change efforts, called *interventions*, stem from action research and are chosen on the basis of need.

Space here does not allow for an exhaustive treatment of these subjects, but they are important for WLP practitioners to know about because implementation of a large-scale, integrated organizational strategy for the development of talent can be treated as an OD intervention. Another reason is that implementation of strategic business planning methods generally and one strategic plan specifically may require cultural change of the kind handled best by OD.

Action Research. Both an approach to change and an approach to organized learning, *action research* is a process comprising a specific, ongoing chain of events. It is an approach to problem-solving.

Action research stems from work of John Collier and Kurt Lewin. Collier learned from experience that cooperation is essential to success in any change effort. Lewin believed that research of value to practitioners is very important, a way of linking action and reflection or linking creative problem-solving to work activities.

Action research is a cyclical process. The first step is a perception that change is needed. This perception is often triggered by crisis. The second step is a realization that outside consultants, drawn from another part of the organization or from outside, are needed to facilitate the change effort. Outsiders are chosen because they are not bound by the chain of command in the same way as insiders.

From that point on, the steps in action research are clear enough:

1. *Define the problem.* What needs to be changed?
2. *Collect information.* What facts can be found about the problem? How do people feel about it?
3. *Provide feedback.* What information has the consultant collected about the problem? How can it be fed back to managers and employees to help them diagnose the problem and take corrective steps?
4. *Plan action collaboratively.* On what plan of action, based on feedback, can managers, employees, and the consultant agree?
5. *Take action.* What steps are taken to correct the problem previously diagnosed?
6. *Assess results.* What outcomes resulted from the action?
7. *Provide feedback.* What information has the consultant collected about the problem and about the results of steps taken to correct it?
8. *Plan action.* What further steps should be taken?

These steps continue indefinitely, as shown in Exhibit 7–2.

Exhibit 7–2: The Steps in the Action Research Model

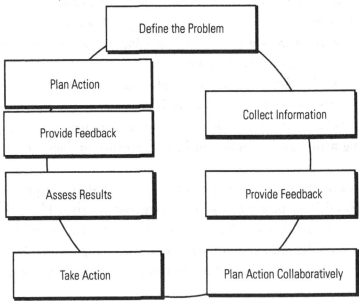

Action research is fundamentally an approach to experiential learning (Kolb 1984). The Lewinian action research model uses "immediate concrete experience as the basis for observation and reflection. These observations are assimilated into a 'theory' from which new implications for action can be deduced. These implications then serve as guides in acting to create new experiences" (Kolb 1984, 21). Group learning results from collective or individual experiences.

OD Interventions. An intervention is a change effort. Psychologists use *intervention* to mean a *therapeutic change effort*. Chris Argyris (1970, 15) provides the classic definition: "To intervene is to enter into an ongoing system of relationships, to come between or among persons, groups or objects for the purpose of helping them." OD interventions are undertaken to produce desired change in line with objectives for change established by members of the organization. By definition, an OD intervention is highly participative and collaborative.

Let's look at three ways to think of OD interventions. First, they can be classified on the basis of *what is to be changed.* According to one typology, the least complex OD interventions are directed to changing elements of the *formal organization* (the public, rational, and observable) such as structure, policies, employee appraisal, and management attitudes/skills. More complex interventions are directed to changing the *informal organization* (the private, affective, and unobservable), such as behavior within or between groups or between individuals.

Second, OD interventions can be classified by *who is to be changed.* Some interventions focus on individuals; some focus on groups of two or three people; some focus on interactions within teams or groups; some focus on relations between teams or groups; and some focus on an entire organization. Of course, even broader interventions are possible and can include industry-wide change, cross-industry change, and even global or planetary change (such as diplomatic efforts to address the problem of global warming).

Third, interventions can be classified by *what methods of change are emphasized.* Some interventions rely on feedback; some rely on changing norms; some rely on improving communication; some rely on working through differences using confrontation; and some rely on training or employee education.

Many OD interventions can support change and help meet objectives planned to bring it about. They include (1) the role analysis technique, (2) interpersonal peacemaking, (3) process consultation, (4) team building, (5) survey-guided development, (6) the organizational mirror, and (7) strategic planning interventions.

The *role analysis technique* (RAT) deals with group-performance problems in which members face unclear or conflicting role expectations from their colleagues. A role is, of course, the behavior associated with a job or position in a group or an organization.

Roles arise naturally in group settings as members learn how to approach work tasks and interact with each other. During the early stages of group development, the roles of all members are unclear. Productivity is predictably low until both task and group process issues are worked out. New group members confront a similar problem in that existing group roles have already been established, but newcomers do not know what they are. For example, an individual trained in accounting has a general idea of what to do, but is not necessarily aware of specific job requirements or the modes of interaction between people in one organization.

Individuals enter work settings with their own expectations about their roles and the roles of others. How they behave and what they say about their jobs send *role messages* to other people, who respond by providing *feedback* about those messages that may subsequently influence behavior (Katz and Kahn 1978). When the behavior of role incumbents clashes with the expectations of others, they are sure to hear about it. Some individuals will then modify their behavior to match the expectations of others; some will try to change the expectations of others; and some will ignore or misperceive role feedback at odds with their expectations. Generally, aggressive or self-satisfied individuals will not modify their role behavior to satisfy others (Katz and Kahn 1978).

To apply the role analysis technique, a role incumbent lists role expectations in a group setting. Then group members list what they expect from the incumbent. They negotiate the lists, arriving at consensus. The process is continued in round robin fashion until each role incumbent in the group has been discussed.

An alternative to face-to-face group discussion is a modified Delphi procedure in which individuals are surveyed about the roles of other group members and themselves. Of course, there are practical limitations to this method: It will not work for groups exceeding eight or nine people because large groups produce voluminous data, and those data are difficult to feed back.

If the role problem stems from a difference in perceptions between the individual and the supervisor, then it can be handled during the employee appraisal process. Using the job description, the supervisor and the individual separately prepare narratives about what the individual is to *do*. They then meet to compare notes and work out differences.

The value of the RAT in implementing organizational strategy for the development of talent should be apparent. A long-term change in strategic business plans may require the creation of new groups, changes in individual role behavior, and changes in role behaviors within existing groups. The RAT may thus be used to compare present with desired future roles as a tool for pinpointing individual and group learning needs.

Interpersonal peacemaking is a fancy name for a process of resolving *destructive* conflicts between two or more individuals. On occasion, it is also appropriately used in resolving destructive conflicts between two or more groups.

Note the emphasis on the word *destructive* in the previous paragraph. Not all conflict is necessarily destructive. Indeed, constructive conflict is an important ingredient in individual and organizational learning and innovation, but only if it occurs in a mutually supportive and nonthreatening environment.

Walton (1969) provided the classic description of interpersonal peacemaking. The change agent brings together two or more conflicting individuals or groups; focuses on the feelings of individuals or group members, encouraging them to explain the sources of their feelings; summarizes, underscores, and encourages feedback; and helps individuals establish common grounds for future understanding and interaction. By drawing attention to the importance of interpersonal relations and providing a structure by which to improve relations between conflicting groups or individuals, this intervention can be an important tool for OD practitioners.

In implementing organizational strategy for the development of talent, there may be a use for interpersonal peacemaking when relations between two individuals negatively affect organizational goal achievement—particularly two supervisors or managers. In some cases, a manager resists plans when a rival advocates them. In such cases, an interpersonal peacemaking intervention may be in order.

Process consultation is an OD intervention focusing on how people interact. *Process* refers to the *ways of interacting between two or more individuals or groups.* It is distinct from work methods, which are what people do to get the work out. Interactions between people clearly affect work methods, just as work methods influence interaction. In short, how people interact influences their productivity and their willingness to be open and honest.

Let's take meetings, for example. If interpersonal relations are poor, there is a good chance the meeting will not be productive. People sit around in silence, not wishing to provoke confrontation. One person may dominate the discussion, interrupting others or undercutting what they say. If a supervisor leads the discussion, he or she may dominate it and assume that silent listeners acquiesce.

In process consultation, change agents participate silently in group activities. They observe what is going on and how group members interact. A passive consultation strategy involves (1) providing feedback about what consultants observe during the group experience *after* it occurs; (2) helping group members focus their attention on their behaviors in dealing with others; and (3) helping participants establish their own plans for improvement. In short, consultants silently monitor activities, but focus group attention on process issues at the end.

An active process consultation strategy is somewhat different. Consultants participate fully in group activities, but focus their attention on group interaction during those activities. They may call a "time out" during a task and ask group members to express how they are feeling about themselves, their behavior, the task, the group, or something else that seems to be impeding progress.

Process consultation helps produce behavioral change through immediate and concrete feedback. Some process consultants may go further and model or demonstrate appropriate behavior for group members, coach participants, or ask group members to role play.

Process consultation can modify behavior when interpersonal relations are inconsistent with requirements for interdepartmental cooperation in line with strategic business plans. Process improvement techniques may prove useful in settings like strategic planning or Talent Development planning meetings, where group interaction tends to influence outcomes and decisions.

Team building, sometimes called *team development,* is the general name for many OD interventions. Geared to change at the work group level, it is perhaps the single most important OD intervention. The work group is crucially important in establishing norms of behavior that can facilitate change. *Team building* is undertaken to improve group performance and the interpersonal relations of group members.

Team building can only be used in group settings where members share at least one common goal and cooperative group behavior is essential to individual achievement. Moreover, there must be an up-front determination that a problem in group performance stems from group interaction, rather than from a lack of individual motivation or knowledge. As Dyer (1977, 35) explains in a classic treatment of team building, "A program should not begin unless there is clear evidence that a lack of effective teamwork is the fundamental problem. If the problem is a group issue, a technical difficulty, or an administrative foul-up, team building would not be an appropriate change strategy."

Generally, team building is appropriate for any newly formed group. With existing groups, it is also useful in clarifying member roles, establishing priorities, examining or improving patterns of member interaction, examining or improving group decision-making and problem-solving, allocating tasks, improving work operations, and planning learning experiences for people in the work group.

Assuming that a team development effort is needed and managers are willing to devote adequate time and resources to it, the first step is the choice of a change agent to facilitate the process. While every supervisor is in a sense a change agent, not all supervisors are ideally suited to lead team development efforts or, for that matter, any OD intervention. One reason is that they may not possess the necessary competencies (see Rothwell, Sullivan, and McLean 1995). Another reason is that they are associated with the existing organizational hierarchy of authority, group culture, and status quo. For both reasons, an external change agent (drawn as an internal consultant from another department or brought in from outside the organization) is probably appropriate in most cases.

After a consultant is chosen, the intervention begins with a meeting in which group members discuss the organization, hear from the consultant about team building in general, and formulate a dream of the group's future that they would like to make a reality. From there, they establish change objectives and, over a long time period, focus on solving problems and implementing solutions. These steps parallel those in the group life cycle.

Shorter-term interventions may be carried out to achieve a single purpose, such as setting goals or priorities, allocating work, examining and improving specific procedures or processes, and clarifying role relationships between team members. In these instances, one meeting may suffice to rectify a problem.

Team building is a powerful OD intervention. It can be used in several ways that are related to strategic business planning and organizational strategy for the development of talent.

Top managers should operate as a team. The chief executive and immediate subordinates constitute a work group. A team-building effort carried out with this group can have far-reaching consequences, including improved relations and a greater willingness to work together effectively. These changes can ripple throughout the organization and contribute to increased creativity, improved cooperation, and more-effective organizational planning.

Team-building efforts can have similar benefits at all levels of an organization if handled properly. Indeed, there is potential to use team building to generate new ideas of use as the future unfolds in the present, foster joint planning among group members for Talent Development activities, and provide a structure to help identify and work toward realizing new individual and group roles in line with strategic business plans. In these ways, team building may serve as a tool for formulating and implementing organizational strategy for the development of talent and strategic business plans.

Survey-guided development is useful in changing the culture of an entire organization or any component of it, but is not generally applicable to individual change efforts. Survey-guided development stems from the enduring work of Rensis Likert (1967). He found that employee attitude surveys are not useful by themselves to create an impetus for organizational or group change unless they are paired with feedback and joint planning efforts.

One of Likert's important contributions to OD was a technique called the *interlocking conference.* This technique is simple but powerful. The results of an attitude survey are fed back to members of the organization through special meetings. A change agent meets first with the chief executive and his or her immediate subordinates to summarize survey results, help participants in the meeting to pinpoint areas requiring action and prioritize those areas, and lead meeting participants to devise concrete action plans for organizational improvement. Following this initial meeting, subsequent meetings are held at successively lower levels, but always in work groups consisting of supervisors and their immediate subordinates. The meetings are "interlocking" in that all supervisors are members of two groups: one group consisting of their superior and peers, and a second group consisting of their subordinates. Through these meetings, plans made at higher levels are factored into plans at lower levels in a collaborative, long-term, and far-reaching improvement process.

While survey-guided development takes a long time, it does improve problem-solving because groups tend to do better than individuals in solving complex problems (Rosenberg 1983). It also increases participation of employees in decisions affecting them, and clarifies the direction of organizational efforts. These benefits are quite important for establishing and implementing strategic business plans and organizational strategy for the development of talent. Planning is an activity from which all can benefit.

The *organizational mirror* is another OD intervention, primarily useful for departments or work groups (Fordyce and Weil 1971). Information is collected and fed back to group members about how others in the organization perceive them. The organizational mirror can also reveal how group members perceive themselves. In short, it reflects group image so that group members can use that information as a starting point for corrective action.

Several approaches can be used in carrying out this intervention. People in the organization are contacted about their perceptions of one work group, or through written questionnaires, phone surveys, or selected interviews. Surveys can be scaled or open-ended.

One place to begin is with the group or department being examined. Group members are asked such general, open-ended questions as these:

I   What is the primary purpose of your group?

I   How does your group contribute to achieving organizational objectives?

I   In your opinion, what are the chief strengths of your group? What are its chief weaknesses?

I   What trends outside the organization will have the greatest impact on your group in three to five years?

I   What trends inside the organization but outside the work group will probably have greatest impact on your group in three to five years? Why do you think so?

I   What should your group do to take advantage of future opportunities stemming from trends outside the organization and to avert future threats stemming from trends outside the organization?

I   What should your group do to take advantage of future opportunities stemming from trends inside the organization but outside your work group and to avert threats stemming from trends inside the organization but outside your work group?

As an alternative, questions can focus on the quality of group decision-making, communication, problem-solving, and conflict resolution methods. Group members and those outside the group are separately surveyed. The results stimulate planning.

The organizational mirror gives group members a means to compare their view of the group to the way it is viewed by others. Major differences stimulate insights and interest in taking corrective action.

Sometimes differences in viewpoint stem from conflict. Any two groups in an organization can potentially be in conflict. As the level of conflict increases, group members close ranks and exhibit the characteristics of highly cohesive groups (Janis 1973): First, the *development of an ideology*. Group members moralize about what they do and how much better it is than the behaviors of others. Second, *stereotyping*. People in other groups are seen as a mass rather than as individuals. Third, *low tolerance for self-criticism or new ideas*. Members grow intolerant of internal group conflict, even that which is constructive, if they are engaged in conflict with external groups.

Conflicts stem from many causes. Generally, any one group will be in conflict with all others it is in contact with, a principle called *the law of interorganizational conflict*. Common sources of conflict stem from *interdependence* (the degree to which two groups must rely on each other) and from differences in *goals* (the results sought by each group).

While some conflict is desirable because it prompts innovation, much conflict is counterproductive to organizational performance and morale. Degrees of acceptable conflict differ across groups and organizations. When conflict becomes too great, you will see the symptoms of increased turnover, strident complaints, union grievances, and perhaps even sabotage.

The organizational mirror uses conflict as a starting point for change. The change agent's role in this process is an important one, because group members may become defensive, hostile, and unwilling to accept viewpoints that conflict with their own idealized images of the group. They must be led by others to accept responsibility for who they are and how they are viewed. A change agent begins this process by reporting the perceptions of others, both good and bad.

The organizational mirror can initiate and implement change in line with strategic business plans and organizational strategy for the development of talent. There are several ways to do so. First, OD practitioners can focus the mirror on strategy, top-management perceptions of a department, and department members' perceptions of themselves. In what ways do top managers believe a group has been contributing to the organization's mission? How has it not been contributing? What are the group's strengths and weaknesses? What are its prospects for the future? The same questions can be posed to group members separately and then the results can be compared. Second, OD practitioners can focus the mirror on group learning needs. Others in the organization are asked to describe the learning needs of different work groups. The answers are compared to the results of a separate but similar assessment of group members themselves. These results serve as a starting point for devising a group action plan, developed through joint planning with group members. Through these and other approaches, the organizational mirror stimulates change in line with strategic business plans, identifying and pinpointing long-term talent needs.

Strategic planning interventions are the last group of OD change efforts we shall discuss here. The introduction of strategic planning in an organization that has never before used it calls for specialized skills, knowledge, and information; interaction between members of the top management group; and a "culture" that supports key assumptions of strategic business planning. These conditions do not come about on their own. It is apparent from the number of organizations that have trouble implementing strategic business planning methods that too little attention is paid to these issues.

The action research model provides guidance for what to do in a start-up planning effort. The first step is to perceive that change is needed. The second step is to consider who should facilitate the change effort: should it be someone from inside the organization or someone from outside the organization? Additional issues are worth raising: Where can you go to find people who know about strategic planning and group interaction? Is the expertise already available in the organization, or will an outsider or a team of outsiders be necessary? Another issue: are funds available for this purpose? If not, then an insider such as a member of the WLP department or corporate planning staff might have to serve as group facilitator.

Assuming that top managers perceive a need for strategic business planning and locate someone who can help introduce it, subsequent steps in an intervention of this kind are based on the action research model. The consultant helps strategists define the problem and collect information. Using this method, top managers can develop a genuinely effective planning process that influences future organizational performance.

Of course, specific interventions may also be used in tandem with this general approach. The role analysis technique (RAT) can assist top managers, lower-level managers, and employees in defining their respective roles in establishing and implementing strategic business plans. Interpersonal peacemaking helps iron out personality conflicts, particularly between top managers, before they begin group planning efforts. Techniques from process consultation are useful during strategic planning meetings to improve the interaction, and thus the ideas, of team members. Team building interventions are appropriate before, during, and after strategy formulation sessions. Survey-guided development can surface important ideas from lower-level employees as a starting point for planning. An organizational mirror can contribute to improved relations between groups and can be used before, during, and after strategy formulation to improve implementation.

Problems Associated with Traditional Organization Development Interventions

There are problems with traditional OD efforts. To mention a few:

I Managers are sometimes unaware of OD's purpose.

I They do not always realize how much organizational culture and/or group norms can affect productivity.

I They have trouble seeing the contribution of OD to bottom-line considerations such as profitability, return on investment, return on equity, or market share.

I They feel the need for OD most intensely during a crisis; OD interventions are often undertaken as a reaction to problems, rather than in anticipation of them.

I They expect immediate, and sometimes dramatic, results from OD.

I They refuse to participate in OD efforts (they may see an intervention as a "quick fix strategy" geared to their subordinates only).

I They associate OD with a few controversial intervention methods, such as sensitivity training.

I They view OD efforts as ends-in-themselves, rather than as part of a more comprehensive, unified organizational strategy for the development of talent.

For these reasons, it might be necessary for WLP practitioners to demonstrate the value of OD by training others in their organizations about it.

Some WLP practitioners have found it best to start on a modest scale with a simple, relatively short-term OD intervention in response to some pressing operational problem at a relatively low level. From this modest beginning, practitioners can demonstrate the value of OD. After its value has been demonstrated, more elaborate interventions can gradually be undertaken.

Recent Themes in OD and How They Impact Strategic Talent Development

An examination of the writings on OD in recent years shows that several key themes have emerged as topics for repeated study and discussion. Those themes are worth knowing about. After all, each key theme is related to emerging topics in the strategic development of talent. As you read about these themes, think about their possible applications to SDT. WLP practitioners who focus on OD

I   Ponder how new scientific views about the nature of the universe (as revealing order amid chaos—so-called *chaos* or *complexity theory*) can be applied to diagnosing or addressing organizational issues and problems (Olson and Eoyang 2001; Titcomb 1998; Wah 1998).

I   Worry about the stress induced among individuals by change efforts (Heifetz and Laurie 1997; Pritchett and Pound 2000).

I   Reflect on the growing importance of values and spirituality in workplace settings (Briskin 1996; Cloke and Goldsmith 1997; Flynn 1997; Hultman 2001; Mitroff and Denton 1999).

I   Discover and try out techniques for assessing an organization's readiness for change (Hanpachern, Morgan, and Griego 1998; Harrison 1999; Moravec 1995; Trahant and Burke 1996).

I   Examine specific ways to overcome resistance to change (Harrison 1999; Hultman 1998; Maurer 1997).

I   Consider ways of managing employee cynicism about change efforts (Reichers, Wanous, and Austin 1997; Topchik 1998).

I   Apply innovative approaches to communicate during change efforts (Akin and Palmer 2000; Arthur 1999; Burton 2000; Frady 1997; Grensing-Pophal 2000; Raimy 1998).

I   Focus attention on the essential importance of building and maintaining trust during change efforts (Burke 1997; Caudron 1996; DiFonzo and Bordia 1998).

I   Examine the special challenges created by multiple, simultaneous change efforts (Rieley and Rieley 1999).

Having the potential for an even greater impact on OD is *appreciative inquiry* (AI), which is a paradigm shift from the traditional, problem-oriented approach to change. AI begins with an examination of what is going right (strategic strengths), rather than what is going wrong (problems or strategic weaknesses) (Cooperrider and Srivastva 1987; Raimy 1998; Watkins and Mohr 2001; Zemke 1999). Once a dream of an ideal future is created, members of an organization are challenged to formulate a plan by which to make that dream become a reality. The positive energy unleashed by AI is a refreshing change from the destructive effects of criticizing and placing blame, which are sometimes associated with the problem-solving approach to change that is hard-wired into the action research model.

Finally, WLP practitioners who seek the greatest impact think about whole-systems change, a process whereby a total corporate culture change is sought on an accelerated basis (Sullivan, Fairburn, and Rothwell 2002). One way to help encourage such a change is to hold a large-scale group event (LSGE). In a large-scale group event, the decision-makers and stakeholders are brought together to address common challenges (Showkeir 1999).

Consider: *How do you believe these recent themes in OD can have an influence on the strategic development of talent?*

Strategic Organization Development

Unlike traditional organizational development, strategic OD is (1) comprehensive, (2) future-oriented, and (3) integrated with other components of organizational strategy for the development of talent.

Conceptualizing Strategic OD. Think of strategic OD as consisting of a series of steps in which managers and employees:

1. Identify what group norms and organizational culture should exist to facilitate implementation of strategic business plans.
2. Assess future pressures favoring change.
3. Assess existing pressure impeding change.
4. Compare present and future pressures.
5. Carry out OD interventions to deal with future pressures favoring change and existing pressures impeding it.

Identify the Norms that Should Exist. The study of norms is really the study of culture. Culture can be difficult to define. Units of analysis are not always easy to pinpoint. Work groups within organizations differ in norms, creating subcultures. An appropriate methodology for researching corporate culture is difficult to find, because meanings are implicit and are not easily revealed through such common data collection methods as surveys, interviews, observations, and document reviews. The problem is further complicated in that group or organizational members may be unaware of prevailing norms, since they are (by definition) what is taken for granted.

If it is hard to identify *present* norms and culture, it is even harder to envision what they *should be in the future*. Think of this issue from another standpoint. When confronted with a problem, managers can pursue at least two possible courses of action: (1) They can examine it from the perspective of past beliefs, ideas, and theories or through interpretations of prior observations, or (2) they can question their basic assumptions, based on past beliefs or past observations, and thereby create a new understanding of the problem itself. The first course of action is related to what Argyris and Schön (1978, 18–24) call *single-loop learning* in which "members of the organization respond to changes in the internal and external environments . . . by detecting errors which they then correct so as to maintain the central features of organizational *theory-in-use*." In this context, *theory-in-use* refers to interpretations of observations—what observers see when they watch managers. It is distinct from *espoused theory*—what managers talk about. The second course of action is akin to what Argyris and Schön call *double-loop learning*, "those sorts of organizational inquiry which resolve incompatible organizational norms by setting new priorities and weighings of norms, or by restructuring the norms themselves together with associated strategies and assumptions."

It is difficult to stimulate double-loop learning and thus identify new norms that should exist in the future (Argyris 1982). Several specific methods can be used. One method is *visioning*. Members of a work group are asked to imagine what the future will be like, and then step back into the present. Transition teams are developed to help bring into reality the future that is envisioned. A shared image leads group members to their own normative change.

A second method is *changing the purpose of the organization or group*. This change is followed by others in such areas as work methods, politics, and culture (Tichy 1983). A third method is *creating new, alternative organizations or work groups* rather than trying to change the existing system (Levy and Merry 1986). The development of new norms is a long-term, torturous, and expensive process. Hence, the greater the difference between present and desired future norms, the greater the length of time needed for change and the greater the potential for failure.

Assess Future Pressures Favoring Change. Pressures favoring change stem from many sources (Levy and Merry 1986): (1) *external crisis,* such as recessions, technological innovations, changes in laws or regulations, or competitive maneuvers by other organizations; (2) *internal crisis,* such as reorganization, management reshuffling, or the exodus of a key member of top management; (3) *external opportunities,* such as new markets or new and unexpected financial resources; and (4) *internal opportunities,* such as task forces, problem-solving groups, and freestanding committees. In most cases, the impetus for organizational change comes from a single visionary manager (Levy and Merry 1986) that some people call a *change champion,* because he or she takes up a cause and fights for it. This manager is brought into the organization from outside and is thus relatively immune from the dampening effects of socialization and existing culture. However, it is also possible to tap progressive groups in an organization and use their energy to create the impetus for change.

To assess future pressures favoring change, WLP practitioners and line managers should examine factors influencing the organization as a whole and each department or work group. Strategic business planning methods are adequate for the first of these.

To examine each work group or department, however, WLP practitioners and managers need some means of classifying them. There are, of course, several ways to classify work groups: (1) by reporting relationships, (2) by location, (3) by tasks or types of activities, and (4) by the length of time the group members must stay together to work on a common goal. An organization chart is one place to start. It should depict employees reporting to each supervisor. In small, centralized organizations, all work groups may be classified solely by the reporting relationship. But if the organization is large and decentralized, it may also be necessary to identify groups by location. Employees might share the same supervisor, yet are scattered geographically. If the work group is heterogeneous—that is, made up of employees involved in different lines of work—an alternative classification scheme can be developed that focuses on activity. Finally, some groups are relatively permanent, such as those on assembly lines; other groups, such as start-up teams and project groups, are not. As a result, it is necessary to consider the duration of the work group's existence as a basis for developing a classification scheme.

A classification scheme is important because it provides a more specific framework for analysis than the entire organization, and it draws attention to unique norms and conditions affecting individual performance. To assess future pressures favoring change, members of each work group can be surveyed regarding their relative level of satisfaction with present conditions. When dissatisfied groups and individuals are identified and their ideas are fed to higher-level management, the potential for widespread change is increased.

Assess Existing Pressures that Impede Change. Any organization is essentially a dynamic field in which some forces favor change and others impede it (Lewin 1951). There are many reasons why members of an organization might resist group change consistent with strategic business plans. Failures in OD stem from such things as low commitment of top managers to change, as well as poor rapport between the change agent and members of the organization.

Compare Pressures Favoring and Impeding Change. The basic assumption underlying Lewin's force field analysis is that a comparison of forces favoring change and forces impeding change can pinpoint areas in which to take action. Organizational change occurs when forces favoring change are strengthened, or forces impeding change are weakened. Generally, Lewin favored weakening the forces that impede change because the alternative tends to increase resistance.

Carry Out OD Interventions. The final step in strategic OD is to carry out OD interventions so as to narrow the gaps between what exists at present and what should exist in the future. In short, OD facilitates the implementation of strategic change through efforts designed to strengthen forces favoring progressive, long-term change or weaken forces impeding such change, or through efforts that strengthen forces favoring change *and* weaken those impeding it.

OD thus becomes a tool for changing cultural norms in line with future needs. When Talent Development activities geared to changing individuals are paired with OD activities geared to cultural change, the combined and synergistic effects can produce individuals who possess the competencies essential to perform in ways that help realize strategic business plans and work groups characterized by greater openness so that what individuals learn will more readily be accepted by the groups in which they work. The result should thus be greater progress toward implementing strategic business plans and gradual, evolutionary change in corporate or work group culture.

Activity 7–1: A Worksheet for Identifying Forces Favoring Change in an Organization

Directions: Use this activity to brainstorm about forces favoring change in line with strategic needs in an organization. Answer the questions in the sections that follow. There are no right or wrong responses. Use additional paper if necessary.

External Forces

1. What forces outside the organization are driving it toward change? Describe them. (Some examples: increased competition, technological advancement.)

2. Are some work groups, departments, or divisions of the firm facing a greater degree of external pressure toward change than others? If so, describe which groups are so affected and why.

Internal Forces

3. What forces within the organization, if any, are creating pressure for change? (Some examples: new top managers, strong groups within the firm.)

4. Are some work groups, departments, or divisions within the firm facing a greater degree of internal pressure toward change than others? If so, describe the groups affected and why they are under pressure.

Assessment of Strength

5. What forces inside and outside the firm are exerting the most pressure favoring change? List them. Start with the strongest forces first.

	External	Internal
1.		
2.		
3.		

Activity 7–2: A Worksheet for Identifying Forces Impeding Change in an Organization

Directions: Use this activity to brainstorm about forces favoring change in an organization. Answer the following questions. There are no right or wrong responses. Use additional paper if necessary.

External Forces

1.   What forces outside the organization (if any) are keeping it from changing? Describe them. (Some examples: substantial market share, commanding leadership in the industry.)

2.   Are any work groups, departments, or divisions of the firm facing a greater degree of pressure to impede change than others? If so, describe which groups are so affected and why you believe this is happening.

Internal Forces

3.   What forces inside the organization, if any, are keeping change from occurring? (An example: top management philosophy/attitudes.)

4.   Are any work groups, departments, or divisions inside the firm facing a greater degree of internal pressure to impede change than others? If so, describe the groups affected and why they are affected.

Assessment of Strength

5.   What forces inside and outside the firm are exerting the most pressure *against* change? List them. Start with the strongest forces first.

	External	*Internal*
1.		
2.		
3.		

Activity 7–3: A Worksheet for Comparing Forces Impeding and Favoring Change

Directions: Use this activity to compare forces impeding and favoring long-term change in line with strategic business plans. Answer the following questions. There are no right or wrong responses. Use additional paper if necessary.

Strategic Plans

1. Describe the long-term direction of the firm. What specific changes are sought?

Forces Favoring and Impeding Change

2. What forces are favoring and impeding changes that are in line with strategic business plans? List them. Start with the strongest forces first.

Forces Favoring Change	*Forces Impeding Change*
1.	
2.	
3.	

Roles of OD

3. How can a long-term Organizational Development intervention be planned to weaken forces impeding change? (What other actions might also be taken? How can OD help in taking those actions? Consider: structural reorganization; changes in leadership; changes in rewards; and changes in policies.)

CHAPTER 8

NONEMPLOYEE DEVELOPMENT

Talent Development has traditionally focused on meeting learning needs inside an organization. It is easy to see, then, why such efforts have often been confused with employee training. However, it is not necessary to limit Talent Development efforts to employees alone. As a matter of fact, there are good reasons for designing and delivering "instruction" to those *outside* the organization. Yet the literature of the field offers surprisingly little advice about preparing instruction to meet the present learning needs of other people, let alone anticipated needs. No doubt one reason is that many WLP practitioners are often organizationally positioned in HR departments, where the natural emphasis is on employees rather than on external groups. It is therefore likely that 40 percent of all e-learning is directed at the strategically important external audience.

However, a strategic orientation to Talent Development implies that WLP practitioners as well as managers and employees bear a responsibility to look outside as well as inside their organizations for learning needs. A strategic orientation emphasizes the external environment. Present performance weaknesses and future opportunities for performance improvement are not found solely inside an organization. They exist outside, too. Consumers who do not know how to use a product will not buy it (Kaeter 1994), and training or other developmental opportunities directed to customers can provide an organization with a competitive advantage (Garrett 1999). Stockholders who do not know about the firm in which they have invested will not be inclined to invest more. Suppliers who remain unaware of an organization's unique production or service delivery needs will have a tough time meeting them (Kay 1999). Retailers unfamiliar with an organization's products will not be inclined to stock them for long, and will not be knowledgeable enough to do a credible job of selling and servicing them for consumers if they do. Legislators who pass laws or government officials who create regulations will not be able to make informed decisions if they are unaware of unique conditions faced by business.

In all these cases, people outside an organization experience learning needs. The Talent Development effort can be used to meet present needs and anticipate those arising in the future. Managers and strategists can thus step beyond efforts to adapt the organization to changes taking place externally. Indeed, they can change the environment itself through organized, externally directed Talent Development activities. We call activities of this kind *nonemployee development* to emphasize that the orientation is different from employee-oriented learning activities. This chapter focuses on nonemployee development, describing each step in a model.

Steps in Nonemployee Development

Think of nonemployee development as consisting of a series of steps in which WLP practitioners and operating managers:

1. Classify members of the public and external stakeholders by their general interests or concerns.
2. Analyze existing relationships between the business and each group identified in the external environment whose learning needs managers wish to address.
3. Determine what these relationships are at present and what they should be in the future.
4. Pinpoint
   a. Discrepancies between what is and what should be with each group at present.

b. Opportunities for narrowing anticipated gaps between what is and what should be in the future.

5. Separate Talent Development needs from other needs, such as the need to change the work environment to make it more conducive to individual performance.

6. Decide what changes should occur in relationships between the corporation and external groups.

7. Design Talent Development activities that are consistent with desired changes.

8. Select instructional content and delivery methods.

9. Follow up, over time, to meet new instructional needs or maintain efforts intended to meet the continuing needs of external groups.

Creating Classification Schemes

People outside an organization vary in what they need to know and what they are interested in knowing about. In analyzing learning needs, managers and WLP practitioners thus find it helpful to classify external groups by needs or interests. This process is akin to what market specialists call *segmentation*. It means dividing up a group into subgroups and creating special strategies for marketing to each niche based on the unique needs of members in the subgroups.

The General Public. Any individual, group, organization, or community that affects an organization is part of its general public. The nature of a corporation's general public depends on its *scope of operations* and *its purpose*. The scope of a small business is limited. Its public and consumers may be restricted to one town or city. The scope of a large corporation is not limited and may be affected at the local level. Will an employer expand and hire more people? Or close down and throw people out of work? Is the employer acting in a socially responsible manner, taking care to avoid unnecessary environmental pollution and discrimination in employment?

External Stakeholders. External stakeholders are those individuals or groups with whom members of the organization interact directly, or those who influence the organization's functioning. They include suppliers, distributors,

competitors, investors, consumers, and employees' families as not just an enter
prise but also as a tool for implementing public policy and effecting social change.

The manager who ignores public concerns will pay the price. Past business
abuses, real or imaginary, lead to the enactment of laws and regulations that
impose burdensome requirements on businesses and other organizations, perhaps exacting an even higher price. Ignoring the concerns of stakeholders is
equally problematic.

To deal with the general public, managers should have a framework. Most
writings about interactions between the organization and the environment adopt
a sociological perspective. The organization is viewed in relation to institutions
and, to a lesser extent, special interest groups. There will be different levels of
institutional-environmental interaction, depending on the geographical scope of
business operations (see Exhibit 8–1).

As Exhibit 8–1 illustrates, top managers tend to deal with broad groups from
the general public; lower-level managers deal more often with narrower groups,
such as one community. There will be exceptions: The opening of a large, new
plant in a community, for example, might stimulate interaction between the corporate level and local governments. Most interactions between business and the
public take place at the local level, but a major occurrence at a local facility such
as a disaster can prompt national and even international attention. For the most
part, however, the highest corporate levels tend to deal with the federal government, special interest groups, and large numbers of people through the mass
media. Managers of local company facilities more often interact with (1) city,
township, and county governments, (2) local pressure groups, and (3) groups of
local people, often through methods other than mass media.

While corporate and national issues are important, the public image of business is more often apparent and crucial at the community level than at the national
level. It is in the community where the otherwise faceless monolithic bureaucracy
of a large corporation takes on the face of a neighbor, friend, or fellow citizen
employed by the company. (And it is for exactly that reason that some companies
have taken the step of training their employees about their role as individual mar-
keters of the organization. You never know who your next door neighbor might
happen to be.)

Exhibit 8-1: Relationships between the Organization's Hierarchy of Authority, Geographical Scope, and the Primary Groups with Which Managers Come in Contact

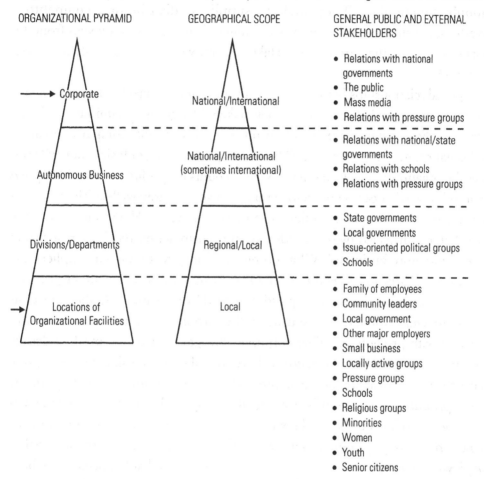

ORGANIZATIONAL PYRAMID

→ Corporate

Autonomous Business

Divisions/Departments

→ Locations of Organizational Facilities

GEOGRAPHICAL SCOPE

National/International

National/International (sometimes international)

Regional/Local

Local

GENERAL PUBLIC AND EXTERNAL STAKEHOLDERS

- Relations with national governments
- The public
- Mass media
- Relations with pressure groups

- Relations with national/state governments
- Relations with schools
- Relations with pressure groups

- State governments
- Local governments
- Issue-oriented political groups
- Schools

- Family of employees
- Community leaders
- Local government
- Other major employers
- Small business
- Locally active groups
- Pressure groups
- Schools
- Religious groups
- Minorities
- Women
- Youth
- Senior citizens

Needs of communities differ substantially by type and degree. Communities range from large metropolitan cities to suburbs, medium-sized cities, and small towns. In each setting, people interact in different ways. The key to community relations and development is to figure out how people interact and find ways to interact successfully with them.

Regardless of the community, some issues are of common interest at the local level.

External stakeholders are the people or groups with whom members of the organization interact directly, or the people or groups who influence the organization's functioning. They include suppliers, distributors, competitors, investors, consumers, and employees' families. (We exclude employees from this discussion, since they are internal stakeholders; we will focus on them in later chapters).

Special relationships between an organization and its stakeholders call for special communication between them. Each stakeholder group has unique needs and interests. For instance, *investors* want to know about company financial performance. Are investments safe? Is the company making or losing money? How does the organization make money? What accounts for profits or losses? *Suppliers* want to know what can be done to get more business. How well-satisfied is a corporate customer with the supplier's products or services? How well are the supplies that are furnished by one vendor meeting customer needs? Is there a chance of securing more businsses? What problems, if any, exist between suppliers and customers? *Distributors (retailers) or sales agents* want to know about products they sell so that they can answer questions posed by consumers. At the same time, distributors may wonder: How satisfied is the corporate supplier with product display and with promotion? What corporate changes are likely in product design, warranties, and marketing? *Consumers* have special needs in using the firm's products or services, maintaining those products, or even deciding prior to purchase whose products or services will best meet their needs. They may also want to know about new products to be marketed by the organization in the future, improvements in existing products, and any other information of potential value. *Employees' families* are silent partners in the business. What happens in the business affects their well-being and that of the family member employed by the organization. They are rightfully curious about these events.

Much has been written about identifying different consumer categories within which an organization does business. Less has been written about how to look at the organization's interaction with suppliers, distributors, investors, or employees' family members, however.

There are several ways to structure this "audit" of stakeholders: (1) by product or service type and those interested in them, (2) by geographical areas and the consumers located within these areas, and (3) by types of stakeholders, such as institutional versus individual.

Analyzing Relationships between and among the Corporation, Its Public, and Its Stakeholders

What is the current relationship between a corporation and members of the general public, and between a corporation and external stakeholders? In other words, how well is the corporation presently meeting the needs of the individuals, groups, and organizations with which it transacts business? What about the needs of those it does not transact business with who can influence business operations in some way? Answering these questions involves analyzing existing relationships between the corporation and its general public and/or external stakeholders.

Many WLP practitioners consider this step to be part of learning needs assessment. Any data collection method commonly applied to needs assessment can be used to find out about the learning needs of external groups. Professionals in fields outside WLP advocate similar starting points for their efforts. In public relations, as in most spheres of human endeavor, it is important to begin with fact-finding. What problems exist in relationships between the public and an organization? Using systematic research rather than intuition to answer this question distinguishes public relations from publicity. In marketing, professionals research types of buyers, buying decisions made by consumers, and factors influencing consumer buying behavior. This information is a starting point for making decisions about future marketing strategies. In organizational communications, broad analysis of current status precedes efforts to pinpoint specific problems, solutions, and actions worth taking in the future. In community and economic development, diagnosis is an early step in which practitioners collect information on a community's ideas, values, beliefs, and norms.

These similarities of approach are really not all that surprising: data gathering and analysis are fundamental to rational problem-solving. Managers begin problem-solving by identifying or clarifying a problem, and then collecting information about it. Managers experience a "felt" need before they know what the problem is. They want to find out why something is going wrong or is not going as well as expected or desired. *Felt need* is a vague irritation with the present status of things.

However, WLP and Talent Development should not be confused with public relations, marketing, organizational communications, or community and economic development. Talent Development activities are geared to identifying and solving problems that stem from lack of knowledge or skill. They help groups external to an organization learn how to interact better with the firm, and they sensitize employees to the needs and issues affecting external groups.

It is unwise to rely solely on the perceptions of business executives about corporate relationships with the public and external stakeholders. Likewise, it is unwise to rely solely on a plant manager's perceptions about the relationship between a local facility and the surrounding community. In both cases, information collected from inside an organization is suspect. High-level executives are socially insulated. They are difficult to reach by members of the public or even by key suppliers or distributors. As a consequence, they often remain unaware of prevailing consumer or public beliefs until too late—often until a major crisis occurs. Relying on their perceptions of public opinion will be like staring at an airbrushed photograph: all blemishes have been removed.

How, then, can accurate information be collected? There are several ways. The organization's managers should

1. Establish a formal method to monitor the public and stakeholders at every level:
    a. Monitor international, national, and local mass media such as television, radio, and newspapers for stories about the company, industry, or issues associated with them or that will affect them.
    b. Monitor issues and concerns at the community level—that is, at every major business site. Establish community "focus groups" or advisory councils composed of representatives from different socioeconomic classes to deal with relationships between the business and community.
    c. Solicit input, good or bad, from the company's Web site.

2. Hire consultants to conduct in-depth studies of external groups periodically. While expensive, these studies furnish useful information for subsequent business, marketing, and talent-related planning.

3. Establish *formal* methods of obtaining feedback from consumers, suppliers, distributors, and investors about what they think of the company, its products/services, and its methods of doing business. What improvements do they suggest and why?

Here are several ways to collect data:

I Consult national opinion polls.

I Use community polls at major company facilities.

I Include surveys with company products, annual reports, bills sent to consumers/distributors, payments sent to suppliers, and Web site reaction forms.

I Make follow-up phone calls to suppliers or distributors to find out how interactions between the two companies can be made more efficient or effective.

I Make follow-up calls to randomly selected consumers to find out how satisfied they are with new products or with the services they receive.

I Hold open meetings, seminars, and conferences for consumers, suppliers, distributors, investors, and/or members of the community.

I Hold a corporate "open house" for the public: Invite citizens and family members of employees in to see how products are made.

I Schedule tours of company facilities and hold follow-up discussions.

As an alternative to these methods of data collection, managers or third-party consultants can undertake a comprehensive *social audit,* which reviews an organization's general contributions to society and/or communities in which company facilities are located. There is no standardized approach: Some audits are mere catalogs of company social programs and some are detailed examinations of corporate social responsibility and actions stemming from it, conducted by external consultants or special in-house management committees. Information collected from these and similar efforts can help identify a company's *present* strengths and weaknesses in dealings with the public and external stakeholders.

Analyzing Present and Future Criteria

What are strategists' current objectives regarding desired relationships with the public and with external stakeholders? How should those objectives be changed in the future, in light of changing external trends? The first question focuses on present criteria; the second, on future criteria. These issues have to do with what company executives or WLP practitioners would like to see at a future time, not necessarily with what actually exists at present.

In many treatments of problem-solving, criteria are assumed. Yet just about everyone acknowledges that problems and opportunities do not exist in isolation. Rather, managers must recognize a difference of some kind between what is (condition) and what should be (criteria). When actual conditions are not as good as desired ones, a discrepancy exists that should prompt corrective action.

It is worthwhile in its own right for managers to think about these kinds of questions:

I   What are corporate social responsibilities?
I   What is the role of business in society?
I   What may account for public dissatisfaction with business and with an industry of which an organization is part?
I   What should be the "public image" of a corporation at the national/international level, regional and state level, and community level?
I   What objectives are worth establishing in corporate relationships with the public and with stakeholders?
I   How can achievement toward these objectives be measured?

By thinking about these questions, managers clarify how they want to interact with external groups, individuals, and organizations. Answers to these questions are particularly important for such externally oriented functions as marketing and public relations. They are also important for the organization's Talent Development effort, which is one tool for correcting present problems or heading off future problems attributable to the public or stakeholder knowledge about a business, its operation, and its products or services.

However, conditions in the world do not remain static. Americans have learned how to mobilize organized opposition to government and business actions. Examples of organized opposition are easy to find among consumer advocates, environmentalists, civil rights activists, and opponents of abortion or proponents of a woman's right to choose. Whole industries face such opposition as managers at nuclear reactor sites, logging camps, and petroleum firms know too well. Pressure groups have learned how to capture and even manipulate mass media attention, use courts and other government agencies to block business activities, and influence law-making through funding and campaign support during elections.

The question is: *What social concerns will dominate in the future?* Clearly, the corporation that anticipates and acts on these concerns ahead of time will enjoy a substantial advantage over competitors and may benefit through increased public credibility. Answers to this question will generate valuable new ideas about future business objectives. In this sense, objectives are geared to closing a gap between what is (present condition) and what should be at a future time (future criteria). These objectives may reveal initiatives for corporate programs; indeed, Talent Development activities should be part of dealings with people outside the corporation.

How are such social concerns or trends detected? Sociopolitical forecasting is one approach. There are several ways to devise such forecasts. *Social monitoring* is one way not previously treated. It involves examination of what is happening in such bellwether states as New York, Massachusetts, and California. Trends apparent in these locales usually appear later in other parts of the United States. Issues arise when business abuses such as major accounting scandals are widely publicized. They elicit public outrage and calls for reform, subsequently making their way into public policy through laws, court rulings, and regulations.

Do some research. Identify pressing issues in New York, Massachusetts, and California. Analyze the content of leading newspapers and pending legislation in those states. Then summarize these trends and establish corporate-level and community-level objectives on these issues.

Pinpointing Discrepancies

What differences exist between the actual and the desired relationship of the corporation, the general public, and external stakeholders? Answers to this question help pinpoint present discrepancies that may require immediate action. What differences, on the other hand, exist between the actual and the desired future relationship of the corporation, the general public, and external stakeholders? Answers to these questions help pinpoint issues requiring long-term action. Use Activities 8-7 and 8-8 at the end of this chapter to structure your thinking on present strengths and weaknesses and future threats and opportunities.

Separating Instructional from Noninstructional Needs

Why are there discrepancies in relationships between the corporation and its general public and between the corporation and its key external stakeholders? In other words, from what causes do differences between *what is* and *what should be* stem? (A *discrepancy* is, of course, any difference between *what is* and *what should be.*)

Discrepancies stem from many causes. Only some lend themselves to correction through learning efforts geared to managers/employees inside the corporation or people outside it. Instruction is not appropriate if you are dealing with problems stemming from

1. Lack of *motivation*. Managers/employees feel no need to improve external relations with the public or with stakeholders such as customers, suppliers, distributors, or owners/stockholders. Those outside the firm feel no need to find out more about the firm or its products and services.
2. Lack of *feedback*. Managers/employees hear little from members of the public or from stakeholders.
3. Lack of *structure for organizing feedback*. Front-line employees receive consistent or pervasive feedback from consumers, suppliers, distributors, and/or people in the community, but have no way to channel this

information up the chain of command to be used in subsequent top-level decisions.

4. Lack of *consequence*. Managers/employees do not see the effects of their actions. This problem is particularly acute at the highest corporate levels. For example, the decision to close a plant in a small community might make good business sense, but it can also have a devastating effect on a small, local economy and produce public embitterment with one firm for a long time.

If managers, particularly top managers, see no need to improve relations with the public, then it is not very likely that one-shot efforts will contribute much to effective external relations. Likewise, if members of the public and stakeholder groups see little need for improving relations with the corporation, then it is not too likely that one-minute television commercials or full-page newspaper ads will keep the public informed, because citizens feel no need to listen.

For corporate managers and WLP practitioners interested in improving external relations, there are several places to begin analyzing deficiencies:

▮ By *community*. What concerns dominate in each community in which the firm has a presence? How well is the organization perceived to be meeting its responsibility as a good corporate citizen in dealing with those community concerns?

▮ By *product or service line*. What are the chief concerns of product users or service recipients? How well is the organization dealing with these concerns?

▮ By *market segment*. Different types of consumers have different needs that are met by a product or service. How well is the organization meeting each different need?

▮ By *type of interaction with the corporation*. Political activists and concerned citizens who do no business with the firm have very different needs from consumers, suppliers, distributors, or shareholders. What are the needs of each group? How well is the organization meeting them?

In each case, it is important to consider what people in each group *need to know* and *want to know*. What are their interests? How has the organization been responding to them in the past? What changes is the organization contemplating in the future? By focusing on these questions, managers can pinpoint areas in which Talent Development efforts can help meet the learning needs of nonemployee groups.

Of course, it is difficult to answer these questions if managers have no information available. For this reason, they should select some systematic means to assess the needs of various external groups. A few methods for doing so are briefly summarized in Exhibit 8–2.

Exhibit 8–2: Systematic Methods for Assessing the Needs of Various Groups

To assess needs of:	Use such methods as:
A Community	▪ Written/phone surveys ▪ Call-in shows on local TV/radio stations ▪ Surveys published in newspapers ▪ "Focus group" composed of community leaders/representatives ▪ Door-to-door interviews
Product/Service Users	▪ Surveys enclosed with products/advertisements ▪ Direct-mail appeals ▪ Phone follow-ups on filed warranties ▪ Names collected during promotion campaigns ▪ Random interviews ▪ Random phone surveys
A Market Segment	▪ Same methods as for product/service users above, but restricted to special market segments
Special Groups ▪ Public	▪ Same methods as for community (above) ▪ Same methods as for product/service users (above)
▪ Suppliers	▪ Surveys/interviews/logs of problems in dealing with each major supplier kept by purchasing staff
▪ Distributors	▪ Surveys/interviews/logs of problems in dealing with major distributors kept by marketing staff
Pressure Groups	▪ Monitoring local news ▪ Monitoring national news ▪ Management task forces

The act of assessing needs may raise the consciousness of each external group about the corporation and its products or services. It can also demonstrate how much the corporation's managers and employees care about the needs of those with whom they transact business at present and in the future. In short, the process of needs assessment can itself serve as a useful tool in building good external relations and meeting some informational needs about the organization. Of course, some organizations have also found that meeting the needs of customers or other groups for information can also be a money-making opportunity in its own right.

Deciding What Changes Should Occur

What is to be changed? By how much? These questions are the focus of this step in nonemployee development.

Change efforts can be directed

I   *Outside the organization.* The aim is to improve what those external to the corporation know about it and its products or services.
I   *Inside the organization.* The aim is to improve what managers or employees know about the needs of the community, product or service users, market segments, or specialized groups so that these needs can be better served in the future.

Instruction directed outside the corporation can range from long-term to short-term change efforts. It is possible to view the influence of the Talent Development effort on a grid in which one axis represents the time horizon and another axis represents the type of change desired. WLP activities directed inside the organization can be viewed in much the same way.

There is no right or wrong direction. Rather, the questions are these: What changes are desirable? Why are they desirable? By addressing these questions, corporate decision-makers can set priorities and appropriate time horizons.

It may be difficult for managers and employees to envision alternatives to existing relationships between the corporation and external groups. In these instances, management meetings, training seminars, and brainstorming sessions can help formulate innovative approaches to promoting better external relations and meeting the present or possible future learning needs of the public and external stakeholders.

Designing Instruction Consistent with Desired Changes

While approaches to designing instruction may differ, instructional design generally consists of these steps:

1. Identify a past performance problem or avert possible future performance problems before they arise.
2. Clarify actual conditions. (What *is?*)
3. Clarify desired conditions. (What *should be?*)
4. Compare actual to desired conditions in order to pinpoint instructional needs (discrepancies between what is and what should be that stem from lack of knowledge or skill).
5. Establish learning objectives designed to close the gap between actual and desired conditions.
6. Create tests, linked to instructional objectives, to measure achievement of objectives.
7. Design tailor-made instructional materials or select content from existing sources (in compliance with copyright laws) that will help learners meet objectives.
8. Select delivery methods appropriate for the content and learners.
9. Prepare and deliver instruction.
10. Evaluate results.

We have already discussed the first few steps of instructional design as they might be applied to individuals, groups, or even entire organizations outside the corporation.

Formal testing has limited applicability to most instruction designed for individuals, groups, and organizations outside a firm. It can be used, of course, when

(1) consumers participate in organized training, seminars, and workshops in product use (tests can be administered, for example, to newly trained computer operators or to secretaries trained on a word processing package); (2) distributors participate in organized training on a product they will sell or service (indeed, service personnel, for example, can be given paper-and-pencil tests, or can be asked to diagnose the cause of a machine breakdown and then repair the machine); and (3) disadvantaged workers, sponsored by various governmental training programs, can be tested for their abilities at the end of an apprenticeship effort or a welfare-to-work program.

In most cases, however, externally directed instruction will not lend itself easily to formal testing. In community development and other long-term change efforts, the only way to "test" may be to conduct a full-scale social audit before, during, and after a change effort to assess the value added to the community or to society by the Talent Development efforts sponsored by an organization.

Selecting Content and Delivery Methods

What information will help targeted learners meet instructional objectives? What methods of delivering that information will be most efficient and effective? These questions focus on the step of instructing the public and/or key external stakeholders.

It is difficult to deal in the abstract with issues of instructional content and delivery for different groups of learners and different instructional objectives. For example, members of the community may have needs quite different from those of consumers, suppliers, or distributors. The nature of a corporation's business and the intentions of its managers may also have much to do with what instruction should be offered, what content should be chosen, and what methods should be used to deliver it.

A simple illustration may help clarify what we mean here. When you have a chance, investigate the community service offerings of a local hospital (the bigger the hospital, the more likely it is to have such courses). These can be very instructive for WLP practitioners in business, industry, or government. Hospitals typically go beyond employee training/education and even patient (consumer) training, adopting a holistic view of their community presence. They are quite likely to offer a range of workshops, some oriented toward preventive health care (for example, "Keeping Fit," "Eating Right," or "How to Stop Smoking"), and some oriented toward the specialized needs of the community (for example, "Parent Training," "Becoming a New Father," "Becoming a Big Sister," or "Dealing with a Family Member Who Is an Alcoholic").

Community colleges also run such workshops, typically for no credit, minimal fees, and with instructors drawn from the community rather than from the college. These courses are offered for fun, not for a degree, and range from practical subjects (for example, "Fixing Your Car," "Building Your Own House," and "Finding a Job: A Course for Displaced Homemakers") to leisurely pursuits (for example, "Aerobics," "Growing Plants," and "Making Home Movies").

Some managers might point out that few hospitals or community colleges are for-profit, so they have considerable flexibility in what they can do. The point is that there is no reason why businesses can't offer similar community service seminars, unless this conflicts with management values.

As a matter of fact, there might be sound business reasons for doing so. Consider the advantages of public seminars:

1. Public seminars increase the visibility and credibility of an organization in the community, perhaps spurring interest in—and purchases of—its products.
2. Public seminars can easily become money-making ventures in their own right, perhaps subsidizing employee training and education.
3. Public seminars can serve as a means to teach consumers about company products or services before they need to buy them.

In many cases, the best minds are found in businesses. Who is better than a successful investor at teaching people about investments? Who is better than a successful contractor at discussing home remodeling? Who is better than an owner of a computer store at teaching people about computers? In short, Talent

Development can become a distinct marketing advantage and even a service worthy of being marketed in its own right.

On one end of a continuum, some externally oriented instruction is geared solely to improving a community's quality of life. Business leaders can lead seminars and participate in efforts to improve the management of schools, public agencies, religious groups, charitable organizations, and civic groups. They may also be prominent in community development efforts to attract industry, promote tourism, and lead popular social reform movements to improve the plight of minorities, women, and the economically disadvantaged.

On the other end of a continuum, organizations can choose to devote their energies to activities with more-obvious bottom-line relevance. In such cases, they can devote their energies to seminars pertinent to actual or prospective consumers. The nature of such seminars will differ by the type of business and the type of consumers it serves, but business leaders might want to structure instruction around product adoption and use, product repair, and specialized product needs or concerns of distinct market segments. Some representative course titles might include: "Using and Maintaining Your Home Computer," "Making Simple Repairs to Your Computer," and "Choosing a Computer System Appropriate for Farmers" (or other groups). An entire curriculum consisting of related courses can be designed to meet consumer needs.

The choice of what instruction to offer depends on present or anticipated problems. Consider:

1. Is there anything consumers absolutely must know before they can use the product or service? Is it worth offering instruction on this prerequisite knowledge?
2. What are the most common problems confronting a first-time product or service user?
3. What future changes in product design might pose problems for consumers?

Similar questions can be posed about suppliers and distributors. They should be answered when selecting instructional content.

Choice of delivery methods depends on who is to be reached, what instruction is to be delivered, and what level of behavioral change is desired. For example, the methods used in dealing with members of the community may have to be oriented to mass media or personal contact, unless the organization's managers are willing to be more innovative in approach. Public seminars can be offered to most groups. "Exotic" delivery methods can be used with groups such as suppliers or distributors with which the organization does business: teleconferencing, video-assisted or video-based instruction, audio-assisted or audiocassette-based instruction, computer-assisted or computer-based instruction, Web-based or CD-ROM–based instruction, and so on.

Following up on Instructional Needs

How well are the instructional offerings of an organization helping to narrow the gap between what is and what should be concerning corporate relations with the general public and external stakeholders? These questions center on the ninth step in the process of instructing external groups. They involve following up on needs *after* instruction to assess whether and how much instructional objectives were achieved.

This step is relatively simple if the focus of instruction is on a change effort with a discrete beginning and ending. Public seminars are examples. WLP practitioners can test knowledge at the end of seminars to determine how well participants mastered the material, and follow up with participants several months after they attend a seminar to determine how effectively instruction changed their behaviors or attitudes.

Other long-term change efforts, on the other hand, will be more difficult to assess. How is it possible, for instance, to determine whether corporate-sponsored community development efforts are successful? If the goal is as broad as improving quality of life, success may also be hard to measure. Perhaps the best method is to identify attributes associated with instructional objectives at the outset of the process—that is, during the establishment of instructional objectives—and then measure achievement toward these attributes. At the community level, company managers may link their objectives to existing community development plans. When they contribute to realization of those plans, their own goals will be successful.

The Relationship between Organizational Strategy for the Development of Talent and the Talent Development Effort Planned for Groups outside the Organization

Offering instruction to external groups is important because it (1) heightens awareness of managers and employees about the needs of the general public and external stakeholders, (2) creates pressure, via external groups, for change within the corporation, (3) removes barriers to efficient and effective interactions between the corporation, the general public, and external stakeholders, and (4) provides information to consumers about the corporation's products or services.

How can nonemployee development contribute to the implementation of strategic business plans? How can nonemployee development contribute to organizational strategy for the development of talent? There are no absolutely right or wrong answers to either question. In fact, the best answers depend on the organization and on the environment in which it resides. For this reason, consider the questions as they apply to your organization. Use Activities 8–15 and 8–16 at the end of this chapter for this purpose.

Activity 8–1: Pinpointing Key Institutions and Issues at the Community Level

Directions: Use this activity to structure your thinking about key institutions and key issues in each community in which your firm does significant business (for example, the firm operates a plant at the site). If you are unable to complete the activity without more information, then identify what information you need and collect it before beginning the activity. (The realization that you need information is important in its own right.) Use additional paper if necessary.

I. Community Presence

1.   At what locations does your firm do such significant business that conditions at the community level could have an impact on operations? Identify major sites of your firms.

II. Institutions

2.   In each location you pinpointed in response to Question 1, identify the major institutions that exert significant influence on life in the community (for example, employers, family, government, schools, religious organizations).

III. Importance of Institutions

3.   In each community, which institutions listed in response to Question 2 seem to be *most* important? *Least* important?

IV. Key Issues at the Community Level

4.   In each community, what issues seem to be of greatest concern (for example, the economy in a depressed farm community; government issues; economic development; flight of the able-bodied to other locations, etc.)?

V. Importance of Issues

5.   In each community, prioritize the most-important issues. Start with the most important.

Activity 8–2: Pinpointing External Stakeholders

Directions: Use this activity to structure your thinking about the relative importance of external stakeholder groups. Use additional paper if necessary.

I. Key External Stakeholders

1. List the most important external stakeholders of your corporation (for example, shareholders/owners, consumers, important suppliers, important distributors).

II. Importance of Each Stakeholder Group

2. Not all managers value different groups and their opinions equally. List, in order of priority, the corporation's stakeholder groups. (Think about groups discussed frequently by top executives. That should serve as an indication of which groups are considered most important.) List the most important ones first.

III. Issues by Stakeholder Group

3. What appear to be the major issues of concern to each stakeholder group you identified in response to Question 1?

IV. Importance of Issues by Stakeholder Group

4. List in order of importance (1= greatest importance) the issues of greatest concern to each stakeholder group. Begin with the most-important group (as identified in Question 2).

Activity 8–3: The Relationship between the Corporation, General Public, and External Stakeholders

Directions: Use this activity to brainstorm about relationships between the corporation and outside groups. There are no right or wrong answers. Use additional paper if necessary.

I. The Corporation and the General Public

1. Generally, what is the relationship between the corporation and the general public? More specifically, in what ways is the corporation presently viewed positively by the public? How do you know? In what ways is the corporation viewed negatively? How do you know?

2. What problems, if any, are created for the corporation because of a lack of public knowledge about it?

II. The Corporation and External Stakeholders

3. Generally, what is the relationship between the corporation and such external stakeholders as consumers, major suppliers, major distributors, shareholders/owners, and so on? More specifically, in what ways do you think the corporation is viewed positively by members of each group? Negatively? How do you know?

4. What problems, if any, are created for the corporation by lack of knowledge about it among
    a. Consumers?
    b. Major suppliers?
    c. Shareholders/owners?
    d. Other important groups outside the corporation?

Activity 8–4: Collecting Information

Directions: Use this activity to think about ways of collecting information from outside groups about the corporation. Use additional paper if necessary.

I. The General Public

1. How can the corporation's managers systematically collect information about the general public? Consider such possible sources as communities in which the firm does significant amounts of business, social activists, professional groups/associations, etc.

II. Key External Stakeholders

2. How can the corporation's managers systematically collect information about shareholders/owners, consumers, major suppliers, and major distributors? (Consider each group separately.)

Activity 8–5: Clarifying the Role of the Corporation in Society

Directions: Use this activity to structure your thinking. Answer each question. Use additional paper if necessary.

I. Corporate Social Responsibility

1. What are the responsibilities of a corporation to the society of which it is part?

2. Why do you think the general public might be dissatisfied with business in general?

II. The Role of Business in Society

3. Why do you think the general public might be dissatisfied with the industry of which your firm is a part?

III. Public Image of the Corporation

4. What do you think the "public image" of your corporation should be at the national level? The international level?

5. What should be the public image of your corporation at the regional or state level? Are there good reasons to work for a different image at this level than at the national or local levels?

6. What should be the public image of your corporation at the community level? Are there good reasons to work for a different image at this level than at the national or state/regional levels? Should a different image be cultivated at some location, but not at others?

IV. Objectives

7. What objectives should be established to improve corporate relations with the general public through planned learning activities?

8. What objectives should be established to improve corporate relations with external stakeholders through planned learning activities? (Prepare separate objectives for consumers, major suppliers, major distributors, owners/shareholders, and other groups.)

V. Evaluation

9. How can the achievement of objectives be measured?

Activity 8–6: A Worksheet for Social Monitoring

Directions: Collect information about conditions/issues over the past two years in such bellwether states as California, New York, and Massachusetts. (Use newspapers, magazines, government reports, pending legislation, and discussions with anyone residing in these locales.) Then answer the following questions. Of course, there are no right or wrong responses. Use additional paper if necessary.

I. Trends

1. What social trends are noticeable in California, New York, and Massachusetts? Explain why you think so. How can planned learning activities help prepare employees for changes likely to occur as these trends are felt?

II. Objectives

2. What corporate objectives should be established in anticipation of the trends listed in Question 1?

Activity 8–7: Pinpointing Weaknesses and Threats in Relationships between the Corporation and External Groups

Directions: Use this activity to brainstorm about present weaknesses and future threats to relationships between the corporation and external groups. Use additional paper if necessary. Answer each question in the space provided.

I. What is?

1. What is the present relationship between the corporation and the general public? (*Describe it.*)

2. What are the present relationships between the corporation and such external stakeholders as consumers, shareholders, major suppliers, and distributors? (*Describe the relationships.*)

II. What should be?

3. What should be the relationship between the corporation and the general public? (*Describe it.*)

4. What should be the relationships between the corporation and such external stakeholders as consumers, shareholders, major suppliers, and distributors? (*Describe the relationships.*)

III. What are the weaknesses and threats?

5. Describe present weaknesses and future threats to relationships between the corporation and the general public.

6. Describe present weaknesses and future threats to relationships between the corporation and such external stakeholders as consumers, suppliers, distributors, or shareholders.

Activity 8–8: Pinpointing Strengths and Opportunities in Relationships between the Corporation and External Groups

Directions: Use this activity to brainstorm about present strengths and future opportunities in relationships between the corporation and external groups. Use additional paper if necessary.

I. What is?

1. What is the present relationship between the corporation and the general public? (*Describe it.*)

2. What are the present strengths in relationships between the corporation and such external stakeholders as consumers, shareholders, major suppliers, and distributors? (*Describe the strengths.*)

II. What should be in the future?

3. What should be the relationship in the future between the corporation and the general public? (*Describe it.*)

4. What should be the future relationship between the corporation and such external stakeholders as consumers, shareholders, major suppliers, and distributors? (*Describe opportunities for improvement.*)

III. What are the strengths and opportunities?

5. Describe present strengths in relationships between the corporation and general public. Describe future opportunities to improve those relationships.

6. Describe present strengths in relationships between the corporation and such external stakeholders as consumers, shareholders, major suppliers, and major distributors. Then describe future opportunities to improve those relationships.

Activity 8–9: Types of Change Sought through a Talent Development Effort

Directions: Use this activity to organize your thoughts about what changes in relationships between the corporation and external groups should be the result of Talent Development efforts. Answer the questions that follow. Use additional paper if necessary.

I. Types of Changes

1. What changes in relationships between the corporation and the general public are being sought through instructional efforts? (*Describe.*)

2. What changes in relationships between the corporation and external stakeholders are being sought through instructional efforts? (*Describe.*)

II. Rationale

3. Why are these changes appropriate?

4. Why are instructional efforts appropriate for helping bring about these changes?

Activity 8–10: Providing Instruction to External Groups through Innovative Approaches

Directions: Read the brief introduction to creative problem-solving that follows. Then answer the questions in the boxes. Use additional paper if necessary.

An Introduction to Creative Problem-Solving

The essence of creativity is the process of bringing one body of knowledge into a totally different, and seemingly unrelated, line of inquiry (for example, bringing ideas, techniques, or methods from, say, physics to bear on a problem-solving activity in history, business, or economics). In short, creativity involves combining two unrelated ideas to produce a new idea.

The process of creative problem-solving is reasonably predictable. It begins with *basic training*—that is, someone familiar with the field of inquiry. People who have no knowledge of a subject will be unable to provide contributions to it. The second step in the process is a *felt need*, a vague irritation with the way things are. The creative person feels that something is not as it should be. The third step is *deliberation*, the process of rolling over a problem in the mind, perhaps for years. The fourth and final step is *affirmation*, the belief that some otherwise-unrelated subject area provides ideas that shed light on the problem at hand. The individual then elaborates on his or her ideas—or those of other people.

I. Present Methods

1. What methods, if any, are presently being used to identify and meet the instructional needs of the general public?

2. What methods, if any, are presently being used to identify and meet the instructional needs of external stakeholders?

II. Creative Methods

3. Apply the following list of actions to the methods described in your answers to Questions 1 and 2. Explain how each action can be used to change the methods listed.

    A. Substitute methods

    B. Rearrange methods

    C. Combine with methods used in public relations, marketing, personnel, or other functions

    D. Reverse methods

Activity 8–11: Establishing Instructional Objectives for External Groups

Directions: Use this activity to help you clarify and formulate instructional objectives for groups outside a corporation. Answer the following questions. Use additional paper if necessary.

I. Conditions

1.   What should members of the general public know about the corporation and its products/services upon completion of the instructional effort?

2.   What should each group of key external stakeholders know about the corporation and/or its products/services upon completion of the instructional effort?

II. Time Frame

3.   Describe the time horizon for bringing about the change cited in Question 1.

4.   Describe the time horizon for bringing about the change cited in Question 2.

III. Criteria

5.   How will successful progress be measured for Question 1?

6.   How will successful progress be measured for Question 2?

Activity 8–12: Deciding What Instruction to Offer to External Groups

Directions: Use this activity to brainstorm about what instruction to offer to external groups. Answer each question in the space provided.

1. Is there anything this consumer must know before being able to use the corporation's products or services?

2. Is it worthwhile to offer instruction to consumers, particularly those who are first-time product users?

3. What are the most common problems of first-time product users?

4. What future changes in product design (or service offerings) might lead to problems in consumer use of company products or services?

5. How can instruction improve the future ability of consumers to use the products/services?

Activity 8–13: Deciding How to Deliver Instruction to External Groups

Directions: Use this activity to brainstorm about the best ways to reach appropriate learners. Answer the questions in the space provided.

1. In what ways does your corporation presently interact with potential learners outside the organization?

2. How can instructional delivery methods be geared to the means by which your corporation presently interacts with potential learners?

3. What other delivery methods can be used to reach potential learners? What are the relative advantages and disadvantages of each method?

Activity 8–14: Deciding on Evaluative Methods

Directions: Use this activity to brainstorm on the means to evaluate instruction offered to external groups. Answer the questions in the space provided.

1. How can progress in achieving instructional objectives relative to communities be measured?

2. How can progress in achieving instructional objectives relative to product or service users be measured?

3. How can progress in achieving instructional objectives relative to consumers be measured?

4. How can progress in achieving instructional objectives relative to major suppliers be measured? Major distributors?

Activity 8–15: Integrating Corporate Grand Strategy and Instruction for External Groups

Directions: Use this activity to brainstorm how instruction for external groups can support corporate Grand Strategy or suggest new strategies for the organization. Answer the questions in the space provided.

1. How can Talent Development activities, geared to the general public, support implementation of corporate Grand Strategy?

2. How can Talent Development activities, geared to external stakeholders, support implementation of corporate Grand Strategy?

3. What new Grand Strategies are suggested by any past Talent Development activities geared to external groups?

Activity 8–16: Integrating Organizational Strategy for the Development of Talent and Instruction for External Groups

Directions: Use this activity to brainstorm about the relationship between organizational strategy for Talent Development and externally oriented instruction efforts. Answer the questions in the space provided.

1. What is the role of instruction directed to the general public in implementing organizational strategy for Talent Development?

2. What is the role of instruction directed to external stakeholders in implementing organizational strategy for Talent Development?

3. What should be the future role of instruction geared to the general public in implementing organizational strategy for Talent Development?

4. What should be the future role of instruction geared to key external stakeholders in implementing organizational strategy for Talent Development?

CHAPTER 9

EMPLOYEE DEVELOPMENT

Employee development is an extension of externally oriented instruction because it helps employees of an organization adapt to change and build their competencies. As the organization's competitive environment changes, employees are affected. Employee development prepares people for these external changes. Employees and managers of any firm are *internal* stakeholders in organizational survival and success, as recent interest in so-called open book management indicates. Thus they have vested interests in organizational performance. Among these interests, employees are particularly concerned about present job security and future advancement.

This chapter defines employee development (ED), explains how to identify ED needs, and summarizes special methods associated with ED. Finally, problems with traditional ED are explained, and a new strategic approach to ED is also described.

Definition of Employee Development

Employee development cultivates employees in line with organizational, departmental, and/or work group needs. As Nadler (1979, 88) explained in a classic and still relevant definition, "Employee development is concerned with preparing employees so that they can move with the organization as it develops, changes and grows." It thus makes individuals agents for organizational and group change and organizational learning.

Differing from employee education and training in key respects, ED is not always directly tied to observable, behavioral change. It cultivates individuals so that their organization and work group collectively possess the competencies essential to meet present responsibilities and prepare for future ones. Employee development "... is concerned with the future of the organization and the individual in directions which are not [always] clearly definable" (Nadler 1979, 88). For this reason, ED is hard to justify solely for immediate return on investment.

Employee development efforts are widespread, but are seldom well-planned. Most managers can think of a few occasions when they sent an employee off to a professional conference, assigned work to an employee, or otherwise tried to "broaden" an individual or improve the mix of competencies available in the work group. ED encompasses these efforts. Since ED is often combined with work assignments—temporary rotation to other jobs is a frequently mentioned method of development—it is hard to distinguish from work itself. As a result, not enough information is available about successful and not-so-successful employee development methods.

Nor is enough emphasis placed on employee development. It is easily lost in the shuffle of daily work activities for several reasons: First, too little effort is made to identify long-term competency needs and think through means of building them. Second, too much time is spent trying to demonstrate immediate, short-term payoffs from Talent Development activities to hard-eyed skeptics, with the result that long-term developmental efforts are sometimes neglected. Third and finally, too many managers do not understand the purposes of Talent Development activities. While they may give lip service to employee development, they are unsure of what it is and are sometimes reluctant to commit time, money, or other resources to it when they are.

Identifying ED Needs

A planned ED program means that WLP practitioners and operating managers should

1. Identify each work group in the organization.

2. Clarify the group's actual purpose, activities, and responsibilities.
3. Plan changes to group purpose, activities, and responsibilities so that they match the desired purpose, activities, and responsibilities of the work group.
4. Determine how many and what kind of people are presently available in the work group.
5. Plan how many and what kind of people are needed to change group purpose, activities, and responsibilities in line with desired group purpose, activities, and responsibilities.
6. Compare desired human resources to available supplies.
7. Establish long-term action plans for each work group in order to narrow gaps between desired and available HR supplies through planned ED.

This model resembles HR planning. That resemblance is no accident: Employee development should be one tool for implementing HR plans. Unfortunately, it rarely is because ED is seldom planned.

It is also important to emphasize that not all employee development is a result of organizational efforts. Individuals can take steps to build their own competencies through self-initiated learning projects such as those reported in a classic work by Tough (1979) and more recently in efforts to describe workplace learner competencies (Rothwell 2002).

In many organizations today, decision-makers identify developmental activities that can build the competencies tied to successful work performance (Dubois and Rothwell 2000). Individuals need only take initiative as competent workplace learners to learn in real-time and on their jobs.

Step 1: Identify each work group. A work group consists of all employees reporting to one supervisor. These groups should be easy to identify with an organization chart.

Step 2: Clarify the group's purpose, activities, and responsibilities. Why does the group exist? What does it do? Which other groups, inside and outside the business, interact with it and depend on it for materials? By answering these questions, supervisors clarify the present purpose, activities, and responsibilities of their work groups.

Step 3: Plan changes in group purpose, activities, and responsibilities. Any change in an organization or its leadership implies that at least some activities of the work group should also change. From the standpoint of executives and managers, why should the work group exist? What should it do? Why? What other groups depend on it, and in what ways? By answering these questions, supervisors clarify the desired purpose, activities, responsibilities, and expected results of their work groups. (Managers can apply the same approach to determine what others in the organization expect of a department. Executives can similarly apply the approach for several departments.)

Step 4: Determine how many and what kind of people are available. How well is the work group performing? How well is it serving the purposes other people want it to serve? What kind of people (and how many) are presently available in the group? By answering these questions, supervisors examine the strengths and weaknesses of their work groups. They match production (output) levels to numbers of people available; they match quality of work to the competencies available.

Four methods are traditionally used in assessing HR supplies. The first method is a *comprehensive HR information system*, which takes stock of the competencies available among an organization's workforce. Typically computerized, it contains information about such things as employee education, experience, skills, competencies, performance appraisals, and career interests. It can be tailored to the unique needs of one organization, or it can be purchased from outside vendors to meet general needs. The second method is an *HR audit*, which is usually carried out to assess how well the HR department is functioning. The third method is *succession planning*, which identifies replacements for key executives and is used at lower levels as a foundation for a systematic development plan for the organization. The fourth method is a combination of the other three methods.

Each method can be modified to assess available HR supplies—the actual numbers and competencies of employees—in a work group. Supervisors create a skill inventory by listing the major tasks of the work group and then rating each employee work group relative to it. Supervisors carry out HR audits to identify special performance problems (deficiencies) and talents (proficiencies) of the work group. Supervisors plan for succession by identifying a "back-up" for each worker, except those carrying out the simplest duties. Each method helps identify available HR supplies in the work group.

Step 5: Plan how many and what kind of people are needed. What changes should be made to the work group so that it will perform in ways consistent with what other people desire? What kind and how many people are needed to serve a desired purpose for the group, carry out desired activities, and meet desired responsibilities? These questions focus on identifying desired HR supplies, as well as the needed number and competencies of the work group.

To determine desired HR supplies, supervisors should discuss with other people what changes should be made to the activities of the work group. Supervisors must first address what should be the activities and results of the work group before they can address what number and what type of people are needed to carry out the activities and achieve desired results. One way to go about this process is to create a flowchart of activities that must be carried out by the work group in order to achieve desired results. Each step on the flowchart requires special skills or competencies, some of which may not be available presently in the work group.

Step 6: Compare desired to available HR supplies. How many and what kind of people are presently available in the work group? How many and what kind of people are needed in the work group to meet desired group responsibilities? By answering these questions, supervisors identify gaps between available and desirable staffing. This comparison should be made regularly to pinpoint differences between HR supplies and demands or between competency requirements and competency availabilities.

One way to answer these questions is by comparison. Supervisors list actual group activities and then list those that other people want their group to carry out at present. They then list all employees in the group and rate each employee on the ability to perform each activity, and then rate each activity on the number of people needed for it. Discrepancies are revealed through this method. Of course, that same task can be accomplished through a 360-degree assessment.

Another way to answer these questions is to estimate. Supervisors determine what the work group should be doing and what people will be needed to do it. They can then compare that to their present output and staffing to identify discrepancies between how many and what kind of people are needed. Instead of making estimates by activity, they simply make a general estimate.

Step 7: Establish action plans. Employee development is one way to narrow gaps between what the group is actually doing and what others want it to be doing. It is appropriate when three conditions are met. First, supervisors must prefer investing in the organization's employees rather than hiring externally or using alternative ways to get the work done. Second, high levels of trust must exist between employer and employees. Supervisors must not fear that developing individuals will increase turnover as high potential employees are snatched up by competitors. Third, supervisors must believe that neither external contractors nor recruitment from outside will be as effective as employee development in building the competencies needed in work groups. When these conditions exist, ED is appropriate to cultivate talent in work groups.

An ED program encourages the preparation of individuals for meeting the collective requirements of a work group or department. Supervisors in each work group establish measurable objectives, or at least articulate goals, so that the numbers and the competencies of employees match up to what the work group should be doing at present. In each work group, individuals are then developed *in a planned way* through one or more methods. Of course, individuals may also take their own self-directed actions, as competent workplace learners are likely to do (Rothwell 2002).

Specialized Methods for Employee Development

Objectives for employee development can be achieved through such methods as (1) long-term, informal mentoring programs, (2) long-term, formal mentoring programs, (3) long-term, formalized transfer or exchange programs across organizations, divisions, departments, work units, or jobs, (4) short-term rotation programs, (5) special job assignments, (6) action learning projects, (7) field trips, (8) professional conferences, (9) behavior modeling, and (10) think tank experiences.

Long-Term, Informal Mentoring Programs. Mentoring remains a popular buzzword in the WLP field, and much research has been focused on it (Hegstad 1999). A *mentor* is a more experienced and often higher-placed individual who establishes a special relationship with others referred to as *protégés* or *mentees*. It is possible to establish such relationships between two people of equal organizational status in which one is more experienced than the other.

The classic mentoring relationship develops informally through the initiative of the protégé, not through planned pairings of individuals. It satisfies a protégé's need for specialized guidance by an individual who becomes a role model for them. It also satisfies a mentor's need to pass on a legacy of knowledge and to experience the intrinsic satisfaction of helping others realize their potential.

Some authorities contend that truly effective mentoring relationships cannot be engineered. All true development, they contend, is really self-development. There is some truth to this notion, because successful people are motivated from within rather than from without. They are truly competent workplace learners who take responsibility for and have cultivated ability to learn (Rothwell 2002).

WLP professionals do not always take an active part in matching up people at lower levels with prospective mentors at higher levels, but they can exert moral persuasion on decision-makers so that they see the benefits of mentoring to their organizations. They can also raise the consciousness of employees and managers alike about the advantages to be gained through mentor-mentee relationships, and offer training on mentoring skills. Through these and other approaches, WLP practitioners create a climate that encourages creation of helping relationships between aspiring employees and their more experienced counterparts. These relationships can be the starting point for employee development.

Long-Term, Formal Mentoring Programs. One way to develop employees is to establish a formalized mentoring program for all employees. Such programs have been used in management development. They have also been the focus of work around school-to-work programs in education, and in that context have generated several excellent and inexpensive resources (see Bidwell 1997a and 1997b; Morrow and Fredin 1999). But when an employee development philosophy prevails so that the goal is to create a "learning organization," the same logic is applied throughout the organization—not just for the benefit of high potential executives.

A formal mentoring program is established by the direct pairing of individuals. WLP practitioners identify experienced people who can act as mentors and provide training to them on how to coach their mentees, protect them, offer them challenging work assignments, provide them with advice and feedback, and make them visible to higher-placed people who can positively affect their development and career progress. WLP practitioners also identify inexperienced people who need mentoring, and meet with them to explain what mentoring is and why it is important. The final step is the direct matching of mentors and mentees. To be successful, a formal mentoring program should be based on the belief that preparing future leaders and technical workers is important to the business.

Mentoring programs are beneficial for improving succession planning, reducing the induction period of the newly hired or promoted, reducing turnover, and increasing communication. However, their success depends on overcoming barriers that may be created by senior management, tradition, and organizational culture.

The WLP practitioner plays the role of linking pin in a formal mentoring program, coordinating interactions between learners and mentors. The practitioner takes special care to assess individual needs and help learners meet them. Learning is highly individualized. To be part of an organized ED program, such learning should be guided by the collective needs of the work group in which the individual is positioned.

Long-Term, Formalized Transfer Programs. Another way to foster employee development is by long-term, formal transfer programs in which individuals are rotated for long periods to other organizations, departments, divisions, work groups, or jobs. Such transfers may last several months or years. Some firms participate in exchange programs in which they trade employees with other firms.

Exchange programs build bridges between a corporation and institutions exerting broad influence, such as schools, colleges, government agencies, major suppliers, distributors, or institutional customers. Exchange programs increase communication between a corporation and its stakeholders, serving a threefold purpose in developing individuals, strengthening ties with external groups, and building individual competencies that are valuable to the work group.

Some organizations actively promote exchange programs with universities. For example, "Executive in Residence" programs enable universities to draw on the expertise of real executives, thereby enriching student exposure to "real-world" thinking and problems. At the same time, the corporation is able to develop the executive through exposure to new ideas, approaches, and challenges. Of course, the executive also represents the corporation to students. Depending on the executive's success as a role model and resource, he or she can attract talent to the corporation, thereby promoting recruitment, and influence faculty and perhaps even future academic offerings so that the university serves effectively to prepare students for the future.

Transfer programs can also be established for a company's sales agents or product dealers, or the employees of key suppliers, distributors, and institutional customers so that they can learn firsthand about a firm with which they are conducting business. Quite apart from the increased efficiency and effectiveness that may result from the presence of a firsthand liaison, the experience broadens individuals in liaison roles. Alternatively, employees of the business may be sent to spend time at a supplier, distributor, or institutional customer. Employees return with firsthand knowledge of problems encountered by the firm's key supplier, distributor, manufacturer, or other group. More than a few firms, for example, recruit their sales trainers from the ranks of successful salespeople (Rothwell, Donahue, and Park 2003). They enjoy instant credibility with trainees—and learn more about the operations of the company while on transfer from the field.

Transfer programs may also be established internally between divisions, departments, or work groups. Much like externally oriented exchange programs, they increase communication between two groups. The individual transferred to another unit serves thereafter as a linking pin and liaison. Individuals also build their competencies through exposure to a different part of the organization, which in turn provides a source of information for the individual's work group.

Job transfers often stem from pressing organizational needs, such as lack of talent in one location but a surplus of talent in another. But no individual should be transferred without taking into account the needs of the whole person. Managers who rose through the corporate ranks by moving from one work site to another should not necessarily expect unquestioning acceptance of geographical transfers from all new workers who might need to refuse transfers if they are too disruptive to their spouse's careers, eldercare, children's education, homeowner obligations, or personal preferences for reasonable life balance. For this reason, a contemplated transfer should always be preceded by a frank discussion between employee and supervisor.

This discussion should deal with such issues as these:

▪ The *intended benefits of the transfer.* What will the company and the individual's work group gain from the transfer? How will the employee gain from it? What objectives, both instructional and noninstructional, will be established? In short, what outcomes are expected?

▪ *Possible barriers.* What problems will a move pose for an employee, his or her spouse (or significant other), his or her children, elderly parents or relatives, etc., for whom the employee is responsible?

▪ The *degree of company support.* What, if anything, can the company do to ease the burdens of a geographical transfer when it is necessary? Some organizations offer extensive help in relocation; others do not.

▪ The *consequences of decisions made about a transfer.* What will happen if an employee refuses the transfer? If he or she agrees? Will it influence future advancement? Will concern about these issues prompt the employee to look for employment elsewhere?

The handling of a transfer is quite important, providing an opportunity for the employee and an organizational superior to discuss the individual's long-term development and the organization's needs.

Long-term rotation programs are commonly used to prepare managers for increased responsibilities. They are rarely formalized, but they should be in order to clarify the purpose and desired outcomes for individuals and for their sponsoring work groups. To develop special competencies, managers may be assigned to (1) start-up efforts (new ventures); (2) problem departments (turnabout efforts); (3) line positions (if the manager will become a staff manager); (4) staff positions (if the manager will become a line manager); (5) overseas jobs (if there is a need to develop cross-cultural or international sensitivity); and (6) other long-term assignments. Each builds important competencies that prepare the individual for future advancement. In the meantime, the individual carries new competencies back to the original work group that can enrich its talent pool.

Short-Term Rotation Programs. Job rotation, the short-term movement between jobs, first received attention in assembly-line work. It was used to reduce worker ennui and expand an individual's repertoire of tasks. Short-term rotations can range from a few minutes to a few months. Many organizations have used short-term rotations for management employees. In today's turbocharged corporate environment, they seem to be more appropriate than long-term rotations.

One approach is to use short-term rotations during company orientation. Individuals are rotated from department to department, sampling the work and learning firsthand about the organization's activities, people, and culture. At the end of the orientation period, individuals are either permanently assigned to one unit or are asked to choose the department or work group in which they want to work on a long-term basis.

It is not a good idea to rotate people without a plan. Instead, WLP professionals must approach rotation as a form of instruction. That means they should

❘ *Establish long-term learning objectives for the rotation experience.* What should learners know at the end of the rotation? What should they be able to do?

❘ *Establish human support and continuity.* How can newcomers be made to feel welcome? Amid rotations, how can individuals establish long-term interpersonal ties for the future?

❘ *Establish objectives for each phase of rotation.* What should employees, temporarily transferred, know about the department when they leave it?

❘ *Structure the experiences.* A line manager or WLP practitioner should meet with learners before a rotation to focus attention on the purpose of the impending experience. Has the experience been structured in some way? Are there planned activities in which learners are expected to take part? If so, what are they? Why are they being provided? (WLP practitioners should assist line managers in developing outlines or lesson plans to structure rotation programs so that each phase is planned and produces results for which learners can be held accountable.)

▌ *Reinforce the experience.* Individuals vary in their styles of learning. Several different ways should be used to present information and structure experience during a rotation.

▌ *Provide for debriefing.* Just as meetings before rotation help learners understand the purpose of rotation experiences in which they participate, meetings afterward tie together and reinforce experiences.

In an orientation, for example, learners participate in training, which is then followed by rotation to the work setting. Before the rotation, learners are told how the work relates to the training that preceded it. During rotation, the supervisor emphasizes the task on which the training was focused. After rotation, learners are asked to interpret what happened. They also receive concrete feedback about their performance during the rotation experience.

Perhaps a description of such a program will help clarify what it is and how it works. In one large company, a downsizing effort unexpectedly robbed the organization of experienced middle managers, many of whom had accepted attractive early-retirement offers. Stepped up recruitment produced a flood of management trainees. The company was not prepared for them because it never had a planned Talent Development program or a centralized WLP department.

In the situation we are referring to, the company hired an experienced WLP practitioner from outside. She immediately formed a management-development advisory committee (MDAC), consisting of experienced supervisors and managers from different levels of the hierarchy and from different departments. Though new to the firm herself, she organized a planned job-rotation program for management trainees in short order.

Her approach was simple enough. She asked members of the MDAC to identify key experiences to which management trainees should be exposed during their first six months of employment. She then asked committee members for the names of people in the company who could discuss each topic and supervise each experience. She then developed a simple questionnaire and surveyed the "experts" about issues that should be discussed with trainees during short, informal, one-on-one discussions. She compared responses (at least two people were designated as experts for each topic) and identified common issues. The survey results provided a foundation for on-the-job lesson plans to ensure that each newcomer would consistently receive certain basic information, regardless of who discussed it. Specific, planned rotation experiences were designed to follow each discussion.

Job rotation programs do not have to mean a stint in every department. Nor do they have to be elaborate, time-consuming, or expensive: They can be restricted to movement between groups in one department, or jobs in one specific work group. Nor do they have to be limited to orientation: They can be tied to job posting programs or used by themselves to foster cross-training within a work group so that everyone has at least some familiarity with the jobs and tasks of their peers.

Special Job Assignments. *Special assignments* can mean (1) researching a problem or issue; (2) developing a solution or recommendations for dealing with a special problem or issue; or (3) assuming responsibility for a project. Assignments like these resemble what Tough (1979) calls *independent learning projects.* Tough reports that one key difference is that independent learners identify their own projects and resources for learning, while a special job assignment is structured and planned by an organizational superior or by a company talent-review committee.

For example, suppose that a department is experiencing excessive downtime, high scrap rates, or some other performance problem. Rather than look into the matter, the department manager calls in an employee and says something like this: "We've been experiencing a problem with . . . (*manager provides description*). Would you look into the matter for me, find out the nature of the problem, and bring me a list of one or more recommended solutions within . . . (*some specific time period*)? Write up the results in a memo that is short and succinct. State the problem(s), proposed solution(s), reasons for selecting the solution(s), costs associated with the solution(s), and any problems that might stem from the consequences of implementing the solution(s)."

An assignment like this gives an employee an opportunity to build his or her competencies and exercise responsibility. Astute superiors plan many occasions like this over time to develop their employees. If superiors do their jobs as developers well enough, employees are eventually prepared to accept higher levels of responsibility, and the collective competencies of the work group are expanded.

Some superiors prefer to let such broadening assignments emerge from daily work activity. Others plan these assignments in advance as part of an annually negotiated Management by Objectives agreement, a short-term personal performance contract (PPC), or an individual development plan (IDP) with each employee. Some managers deliberately prepare a plan of informal experiences or job assignments for each employee to ensure the systematic, planned development of *all* employees in the work group. (The latter approach is a true employee-development program when it is explicitly matched to work group purpose, objectives, and duties.)

Action Learning Projects. Action learning projects have been gaining popularity (see Rothwell 1999a). While not always called by the name *action learning*, they are really a specialized approach to special job assignments. Invented in the early 1970s (Revans 1971), action learning was originally an approach to executive development. The idea is to team up executives to solve a work problem so that they can share experiences across the hard-wired silos of the organization's reporting structure, and thereby gain exposure to other silos without rotating valuable performers for prolonged periods. The approach has been adapted more recently to virtual teams working across international boundaries and through cyberspace, and to classroom environments in which students work together to solve problems posed by a trainer.

While many variations to action learning exist, the basic approach is to find a company problem. Then a team is formed of individuals who share two characteristics in common: they need development and cross-functional exposure, and they can bring special skills to the team to help tackle solving the problem. Team members are briefed on the problem and are then given the freedom to experiment to find solutions. The challenge is to keep the team members working together cohesively; for that, a WLP practitioner is often called in to serve as a team facilitator.

Action learning can be a powerful approach to building individual competence and organizational bench strength without needing to surrender exemplary performers for prolonged training or rotation experiences. Managers like it because they can get a real-world problem solved at the same time that they are building individual competence for the future. The flexibility of the approach also has much appeal, and individuals can be assigned to action-learning project teams that work full-time or part-time, or even virtually.

Field Trips. Any journey undertaken as a learning experience is a field trip. Elementary school pupils take trips to zoos, amusement parks, and historical sites. In college, students take trips related to their academic majors: business students tour corporate offices and factories; history students visit historical landmarks; drama students visit theaters; and WLP students visit WLP departments. In a training program on machine operation, an instructor might use a field trip to show trainees a real machine in operation.

In recent years, field trips have become a popular method of fact-finding; they are widely used in best-practice benchmarking. American executives go abroad to learn firsthand about management practices, production methods, and cultural matters in Japan, Taiwan, Korea, China, the Philippines, Australia, Russia, and other countries. U.S. economic development and government officials do likewise. In turn, the United States hosts itinerant emissaries from abroad, many interested in learning about such specific American industries as health care, higher education, agriculture, manufacturing, or government.

Developmental field trips need not be restricted to senior executives. Indeed, they can be used by any supervisor to give employees brief exposure to other sites in the organization, stimulate new insights and creativity, and motivate them to learn more.

Much like special job assignments, field trips can stem from immediate problems in the work setting or can be planned well in advance, perhaps as part of an annually negotiated individual development program. If a field trip is planned on short notice, the supervisor simply asks employees to visit a specific location and report back with ideas, observations, and (perhaps) solutions to identifiable problems. On the other hand, if the trip is planned long in advance, the supervisor has time to leisurely reflect on this question: *What should employees know when they return?* The superior prepares a list of competencies and behaviors related to the needs of the work group, and systematically plans specific field trips in which employees can observe a competency being demonstrated (and perhaps practice it as well). Trips are planned for their value in furnishing guided learning activities as part of an organized employee development program. They can also give employees exposure to best-practice inside or outside the company, and they can thereby contribute to process improvement efforts.

To use a field trip for maximum advantage, the supervisor should meet with employees beforehand and pose broad questions to be answered upon their return. (That same approach, incidentally, is used in planning benchmarking trips to observe best practices.) Employees may also be asked to keep a diary or log during the experience to record insights, feelings, and ideas. The act of writing down thoughts clarifies them, as well as preserves them for future reference. Supervisors use field trips to focus employee attention, stimulate thinking, direct individual experience, build bench strength, and expand the competency mix available to the work group.

Professional Conferences. Many professional societies, industry groups, and vendors offer professional conferences each year. They range from trade shows that display state-of-the-art services, equipment, and issues in a field or industry to short workshops on innovative approaches. The annual conference of the American Society for Training and Development exemplifies a typical large conference. There are different "tracks" of speakers delivering talks concurrently in different rooms. A large exhibit hall provides participants with opportunities to review new products and hear about new services. Social networking activities are planned so that participants can meet people sharing similar interests, and special events such as film screening and computerized learning exhibits are abundantly offered for the curious.

Sending employees to professional or industry conferences is a developmental activity intended to (1) update skills and knowledge, (2) evoke new insights and fresh ideas, and (3) provide for social networking opportunities so that attendees can hear about practices in other organizations. Conferences resemble field trips: They are typically located at some distance from the work site, and often the outcomes are difficult to plan in advance. As with field trips, supervisors and WLP practitioners help conference participants take maximum advantage of the learning opportunity by providing them with an advance list of questions to be answered upon their return. Employees may be asked to keep a diary or log of experiences. Other methods for maximizing the value of the experience include (1) having participants brief their colleagues orally on conference highlights; (2) circulating literature or handouts collected at the conference; and (3) asking participants to write up a report on the conference for circulation to co-workers. Sending individuals to a conference to meet the present or future needs of a work group is a valuable employee-development tool.

Many employers and vendors have also been experimenting with various forms of distance education to achieve the same results as traditional conferences. Examples include so-called *webinars* in which participants remain seated in front of computers at their desks (in their places of employment), but they simultaneously visit a common Web site and participate in a conference call. Webinars bring together diverse participants from geographically scattered locations. While not as powerful or memorable as on-site conferences or seminars, they are far less expensive and they avoid the hazards of travel. No doubt people will continue to experiment with such approaches. Desktop consulting in real time will also increase because the videocameras are now available for personal computers.

Behavior Modeling. Just like it sounds, *behavior modeling* involves a two-step process of (1) demonstrating appropriate behavior and then (2) asking learners to demonstrate it. Behavior modeling has been widely advocated for building some competencies in classroom settings. Trainees observe behaviors enacted on videotape or by an instructor. This approach works particularly well in training supervisors how to give orders, interview prospective employees, carry out disciplinary counseling, and conduct employee appraisal interviews.

Behavior modeling can also be a more subtle, long-term development method. By rotating employees to work with exemplary supervisors or performers, they learn through observation how to think and behave like the *role models* with whom they are paired. As in many developmental efforts intended to build complex interpersonal competencies, specific outcomes from a learning experience may be difficult to plan. Learners are encouraged to pay special attention to the exemplary performers to whom they are rotated.

Behavior modeling is grounded solidly on the social learning theory of Bandura (1971, 1977; Bandura and Walters 1963). Bandura believed that people learn through observation of others and by imitating them. The effects of observation can be powerful. For example, if one employee successfully manipulates a supervisor or gets away with breaking the rules, other employees observe and then imitate the same behavior. The key, then, is to be selective in exposing employees to appropriate role models over a long time period and in reinforcing—through praise and other rewards—the employee's imitation of desirable behavior that is aligned with company strategic objectives.

Think-Tank Experiences. A *think tank* is an organization or group formed for the purpose of devoting special attention to a specific problem or group of related problems. Think tanks were originally stand-alone institutions. The most famous was established by the Rand Corporation to study military problems. Since the creation of the first think tank, many others have been set up to focus on a wide range of issues.

Think-tank experiences are characterized by the following key conditions (Delbecq 1967):

I Open communication between group members
I Willingness and even eagerness to participate in problem-finding and problem-solving
I Clear separation between generating ideas and evaluating ideas
I Relaxed relationships in the group
I Courtesy between group members
I Support for creativity
I A nonauthoritarian point of view
I Appreciation for humor, playfulness, and exploration of seemingly bizarre notions
I A desire for consensus, but a willingness among group members to accept majority rule

These conditions should characterize a single problem-solving or problem-finding effort or else characterize the climate of a creative, participative work group, team, department, or division.

Examples of think-tank employee-development experiences include (1) retreats for management or employees, (2) task forces, (3) free-standing employee committees, (4) staff meetings, (5) impromptu problem-solving groups, and (6) confrontation meetings. Developmental think-tank experiences like these serve to broaden the existing competency mix available to the work group.

Management or employee retreats are usually held off-site, somewhere other than the work setting. A *management retreat* gives executives or managers an opportunity to reflect, as a group, on past company performance and on prospects for the future. Retreats are frequently used as settings for formulating or reviewing the strategic business plan. An *employee retreat* serves a similar purpose. Members of a work group step back from the pressures of immediate work demands, and reflect on past problems or future opportunities for improving group performance. It is a growth experience for individuals, allowing them to exercise creativity, contribute to increased productivity, improve relations with co-workers, and build individual competencies. It is a tool for employee development because it equips participants with new ideas about what they do and how they interact as a group.

A *task force* is a committee formed to deal with a special issue or problem. Very often a task force represents different hierarchical levels and work groups. Usually temporary in nature, it exists just long enough to investigate a specific problem. Task force experiences give employees opportunities to exercise creativity and gain new insights about organizational operations. Supervisors control which employees get these development opportunities because they set up the task force. Task forces serve the needs of employee development when they are linked to the problems or issues confronting the individual's work group, and when they produce new knowledge that somehow benefits the work group.

Free-standing employee committees are similar to task forces, but they are enduring rather than temporary. Individual members rotate on and off, but the committee remains. One example is a committee for Talent Development that is formed to provide advice to WLP practitioners about company training, education, and development efforts. Other committees can be permanent: new product committees; budget committees; sales promotion committees; and committees composed of representatives from the community, industry, or sales force. Serving on a committee develops individuals because it gives them a chance to exercise creativity.

Staff meetings are a tradition in many organizations. Their primary purpose is to organize and schedule work or provide updates on progress. They also give supervisors an opportunity to communicate with all members of a work group at once. They become developmental experiences if group members are encouraged to air suggestions, raise problems, or cooperate on solutions.

Impromptu problem-solving groups are less formal than task forces, free-standing committees, or even staff meetings. When a problem comes up, the supervisor calls in a few handpicked individuals for a short brainstorming session. Members are chosen for what they know about the problem and what contributions they can make in solving it. By allowing for individual participation in decision-making, these groups foster individual growth and serve a developmental purpose.

Confrontation meetings stimulate creativity. First described by Beckhard (1967), meetings of this kind bring together two groups with conflicting views on an issue. Group members state their ideas and then argue them out to promote greater understanding.

These think-tank experiences contribute to employee development by giving individuals opportunities to hear about new ideas, experience new insights, and improve interpersonal skills. As individuals are enriched, they provide new talents and skills to be tapped by their work units. The developmental value of these experiences can be increased (1) if they are guided by some kind of systematic improvement plan for the work unit and individuals in it, (2) if they are preceded by a discussion between employee and superior to clarify what an employee should learn during the experience and why it is worth learning, (3) if individuals are encouraged to keep a log or diary during the experience so that they may record observations and insights, and (4) if these experiences are followed up with a debriefing in which the employee and the organizational superior discuss what was learned, why it is important, and how it is related to individual and work unit improvements.

Other Development Experiences. The developmental methods described in this part of the chapter are not the only ones that can be used. In fact, many other methods can help build individual competencies and group or organizational talent. Once the competencies are known for a job category, department, or occupation, it is possible to identify a range of strategies by which to build those competencies (Dubois and Rothwell 2000). Indeed, Lombardo and Eichinger (1989) have identified 88 ways to develop people. Various printed or online guides such as Learning Navigator and other resources are available to assist in identifying appropriate developmental strategies to build individual competencies (see, for instance, Gebelein et al. 2000; Kravetz 1995; Strategies 1999). People can even be trained to be more effective in taking charge of their own learning and development (Peterson and Hicks 1995; Rothwell 1996).

Problems with Traditional Employee-Development Programs

Traditional employee-development programs suffer from several problems. First, they are rarely planned. The process (if something so informal can be called that) works in most organizations the same way one top HR executive described it:

"Our supervisors watch their subordinates and those reporting to other supervisors. When a promising person comes along, a supervisor will think *Now there's a person I can use someday*. Supervisors talk over the matter among themselves and arrange for an exchange. Then they talk to a union steward. One day, the employee is told to 'report to so-and-so today and come back when you are told to.' "

No attempt is made to think through the collective skill needs of each work unit. Individuals are not told the reasons for developmental experiences in which they are asked to participate. Lack of planning results from an inability of supervisors to project the collective competencies needed by their work groups. Individuals are kept in the dark about the reasons for developmental experiences because, as one executive explains it, managers are afraid of the possible consequences. Why? As the executive explained:

"If we told the person why he or she was chosen to participate, we might find ourselves saddled with someone with a swelled head. The person would think a promotion and pay raise was looming just over the horizon. We might find ourselves facing blackmail at raise time or else constant questions about when a promotion or transfer would take place. To avoid all that, we prefer to keep employees ignorant of our plans for them. We don't always *have* plans, in any case."

Developmental experiences are rendered less effective than they might otherwise be as a consequence of trying to avoid problems that might not even come up. To employees, these experiences may be unsettling and frustrating. *Does the boss want to get rid of me?* they secretly wonder. Under these conditions, developmental experiences will not be maximally effective because the need for secrecy will rule out frank talks about what the individual should try to learn during the experience, why it is worth learning, and what competencies the employee should try to build during a developmental experience. Nor will it be possible to debrief employees after such experiences, because debriefings will sometimes raise unrealistic employee expectations about the future.

A second problem is that employee development is too often viewed as a reward for individual behavior, rather than as a vehicle for building present or future competencies needed by a work group or an organization. WLP practitioners should closely examine requests for professional conferences or other developmental activities that do not, on the surface, appear to mesh with the long-term strategic objectives of a unit or the organization.

A third problem with employee-development programs is that they tend to perpetuate past traditions only. It is easy to see how that happens: Employees are rotated to performers who have proved themselves in the past, rather than rotated to performers whose progressive views mesh with strategic business plans; employees are given broadening job assignments that perpetuate traditions rather than raise questions about them; and employees are sent off to conferences to bring back information about state-of-the-art innovations, rather than think about how to apply those innovations to the tasks facing the work group.

There are, of course, instances when such past-oriented approaches to employee development are appropriate:

I   When the work unit's environment is relatively stable

I   When the organization does not face competition

I   When the organization's strategic business plan calls for slow, stable growth without radical changes

▮ When the future HR demands of a work group do not differ significantly from existing HR supplies

On the other hand, a future-oriented approach is necessary when

▮ The work group's external environment is volatile
▮ Competitive advantage is sought by the firm and is essential to long-term organizational survival and success
▮ The strategic business plan calls for long-term, radical change—particularly change in some work groups or departments more than others
▮ Future HR demands at the work group level differ significantly from existing HR supplies

In today's competitive environment, most organizations probably fall into the second category.

Strategic Employee Development

Strategic employee development (SED) adopts an approach different from its traditional counterpart. Unlike traditional employee development, it should be explicitly linked to a long-term organizational strategy for the development of talent, which in turn supports the plans of the organization and HR generally. It should be distinctly future-oriented, based on a comprehensive, long-term view of organizational and work group needs, planned explicitly and deliberately for *each* work group and *each* department, and treated as part of strategic business planning efforts.

Conceptualizing Strategic Employee Development. Much like traditional employee development, strategic employee development begins with questions about long-term HR needs and demands. Think of it as a series of questions:

1. What competencies will be needed by the organization to implement strategic business plans?
2. What competencies will be needed *by each department or work group* to carry out new duties or meet new responsibilities stemming from strategic business plans?

3. What competencies exist at present in the organization and in each department or work group?

4. What discrepancies exist between competencies needed in the future and those already present in the organization and in each department or work group?

5. What long-term employee development methods can be planned to rectify the discrepancies identified in Question 4?

The focus is on identifying and meeting the *future* collective competencies required of each work group and department. While external recruitment and/or external contracting can potentially help meet these needs, development is another means of meeting needs. In this context, *competency* means "ability to perform." Strategic planners generally accept the notion that organizations have *core competencies*, proven abilities to perform successfully in certain areas of the business and/or with certain product lines.

Specialized Employee-Development Methods for Meeting Long-Term Organizational Needs

Each employee-development method described in the previous part of the chapter can be treated from a future-oriented rather than a past-oriented perspective. These methods include (1) long-term, informal mentoring programs, (2) long-term, formal mentoring programs, (3) long-term, formalized transfer or exchange programs across organizations, divisions, departments, work units, or jobs, (4) short-term rotation programs, (5) special job assignments, (6) action learning projects, (7) field trips, (8) professional conferences, (9) behavior modeling, and (10) think-tank experiences. When these methods are used to prepare people for meeting the future responsibilities of their work groups, they are tools for strategic employee development. Let's discuss long-term planning of related developmental experiences, and selecting, planning, and following up each experience.

Long-Term Planning of Related Experiences. Unlike the relatively unplanned approach characteristic of traditional employee-development efforts, strategic employee development requires planning for general change objectives for the organization and its departments or work groups. In short: (1) What competencies should be found in the organization in five years? (2) What competencies should be found in each department or work group, in say, five years? WLP practitioners and/or supervisors can choose many different methods to evoke individual insights and build competencies in line with strategic needs at the group level.

Select Experiences. Selectivity is the key to using developmental experiences strategically. Consider: (1) What experiences will elicit individual insights and develop the competencies needed by the work unit in the future? (2) What people and/or other resources can be identified that will provide those experiences? The idea is to pinpoint progressive people, events, or situations that can serve developmental ends.

Plan Each Developmental Experience. What supervisors do to prepare employees for developmental experiences affects outcomes dramatically. If supervisors say nothing, employees are left to draw whatever interpretations seem appropriate. Of course, these interpretations may not be appropriate.

In traditional employee-development efforts, the supervisor can guide individual experience by providing a list of questions in advance. As a consequence, a structure is imposed on otherwise inchoate aspects of reality. Open-ended questions prompt learners to make discoveries on their own.

Questions of this kind can be keyed to the past, present, or future. If past-oriented, they lead learners to focus on successful practices as proven by experience. For example, learners can be directed to ask such questions as (1) What methods have proven especially successful in the past? and (2) Why are these methods so successful? In contrast, present-oriented questions focus on current methods, problems, and issues. They help learners familiarize themselves with the state-of-the-art.

Future-oriented questions direct learner attention to anticipating possible future problems and issues. If these questions are asked of supervisors in other parts of one organization or in other organizations, they may stimulate supervisory creativity and planning as well.

Follow up Each Experience. It is just as important to follow up after each developmental experience as it is to build employee expectations beforehand. Supervisors and/or WLP practitioners should use a debriefing to

I   Hear from the employee about information gathered during the developmental experience.

I   Impose order on employee insights by careful questioning designed to maximize insights gained through the experience.

I   Expand on and enlarge key points and issues.

Questioning is a key skill because it guides learners by eliciting new insights and discoveries. It can prompt and direct creativity.

Strategic employee development is anticipatory, designed to avert problems or seize improvement opportunities before they come up. Each developmental experience should be planned for its value in anticipating the collective competencies needed by the work group. In this way, individuals are guided to learn in order to improve the aggregate talents of the organization and its work groups.

Activity 9–1: Developing a Formal Mentoring Program in Your Organization: A Brainstorming Exercise

Directions: Use this activity to brainstorm about matters essential to establishing a mentoring program in your organization. Answer the questions that follow. There are no right or wrong responses. Use additional paper if necessary.

Part I: Purpose

1. What is the primary purpose to be served by a mentoring program? Is it (1) to ensure a supply of talent needed to meet long-term organizational requirements? (2) To improve morale? (3) To involve managers and supervisors at all levels in long-term preparation of their employees in a formal way? (4) To meet some other need? (Specify.)

Part II: Objectives

2. What method or methods can be used to demonstrate results from this program? In other words, how can achievement be measured?

Part III: Conditions Favoring the Program

3. What existing conditions in the organization favor establishment of a formal mentoring program? (Consider: philosophy of management; recent problems created by lack of necessary human resources; stability of tenure among managers or supervisors at all levels.) How can these conditions be turned to advantage?

Part IV: Conditions Not Favoring the Program

4. What existing conditions in the organization do not favor establishment of a formal mentoring program? (Consider: major emphasis on short-term results; no rewards or recognition associated with long-term grooming of employees; recent scandals about management/supervisory relationships with employees.) How can these conditions be corrected?

Part V: Design and Delivery

5. Describe formal elements of the mentoring program that will be needed. Consider such matters as (1) how mentors/protégés will be matched up; (2) how long these formal relationships are intended to last; (3) on what basis these relationships can be dissolved; (4) third-party conflict resolution between mentors-protégés; (5) necessary restrictions (if any) on which people are eligible as mentors and as protégés; (6) a description of the mentoring program (that is, a policy); (7) roles of the mentor and the protégé (that is, what are they expected to do?); (8) how developmental experiences are to be selected/negotiated; (9) how expected developmental experiences are to be documented (that is, written down or otherwise clarified); (10) what, if anything, mentors should do during developmental experiences; and (11) how results of developmental experiences are to be used (that is, required debriefings).

Activity 9–2: Designing a Short-Term Rotation Program for New Employees

Directions: Answer the following questions in the space provided.

Part I: Purpose

1. Clarify the purpose of the rotation program. What is its primary reason for being? What results do you or other managers hope to see from this effort?

Part II: Constraints

2. Clarify existing constraints. Consider such matters as (1) amount of time that can be counted on for new employees (How long are they available? Can this time frame be counted on for sure?), (2) degree of support (How much do managers throughout the firm agree with the purpose of this effort? Understand it?), (3) degree of cooperation (Can everyone be counted on to participate?), and (4) other constraints that you can think of that need to be planned for or considered at the start.

Part III: Objectives

3. What long-term results are sought from this program for each work group and for the organization? How can the relative success of this program be demonstrated over time? (Although you may wish to establish measurement outcomes, you do not have to restrict them to end-of-program outcomes, because a program may provide better indications of long-term results.)

Activity 9–2: *(continued)*

Part IV: Program Design

---

4. Describe the rotation program, including (1) what departments, work groups, or job sites new employees should be exposed to; (2) how long each of these experiences should last; (3) to whom the employee should be assigned at each site; (4) what special experiences the employee should participate in while at each site; (5) in what order the departments, groups, or sites should be rotated; (6) what special outcomes or results are sought by exposing the employee to these sites; (7) what preparation the employee should receive prior to a new rotation; (8) what special coaching the employee should receive while at each site; and (9) what follow-up or debriefing the employee should receive at the end of each rotation.

Part V: Linkages

---

5. How will this rotation program link up to classroom-based training efforts and on-the-job training following rotation? Are some linkages between the program and other types of training/education especially desirable? If so, describe what the linkages should be and why they are important.

Activity 9–2: *(continued)*

Part VI: Linkages
---

6. Should some differences in the rotation program exist for employees entering some but not all job classes/positions? Is so, describe what additional or specialized experiences should exist for various groups of employees (for example, clerical/secretarial, technical, professional, managerial).

Part VII: Follow-Up
---

7. How will the value of the rotation program be demonstrated? Describe how follow-up after the rotations will be planned in order to collect information about its (1) value to newcomers; (2) effects, if any, on subsequent job performance/employee morale or job satisfaction; (3) strengths of the rotation program itself; and (4) weaknesses of the rotation program.

Activity 9–3: Critical Incidents

Directions: For each critical incident described in the left column, describe in the right column how a supervisor can use the occasion as a development experience for an employee. There are no right or wrong responses.

Critical Incident	How can the incident be used for employee development?
1. The employee makes a major mistake.	
2. An employee asks about the job duties of another employee.	
3. The work group faces a problem that it has never experienced before.	
4. The supervisor has to be away from work for several hours.	
5. The supervisor confronts a major problem.	
6. The supervisor wants to delegate work.	
7. The employee faces a problem in his or her job that he or she has never experienced before.	
8. The employee asks the supervisor for help.	
9. Several new employees enter the work group and need to be "shown the ropes."	
10. A new machine is being introduced to the work site.	

Activity 9–4: Assessing the Developmental Climate

Directions: Use this activity to assess the general developmental climate of a work group, department, or division. For each characteristic listed in the left column, rate your sense of its presence in the middle column. Then, in the right column, describe what should be done to improve the characteristic in the group. Use additional paper if necessary.

Characteristic	To what extent is the characteristic apparent? Not at all — To a great extent	What can be done to improve the degree to which the characteristic is evident?
	1 2 3 4 5 6 7	
1. Open communication exists between all members of the group.	1 2 3 4 5 6 7	
2. Group members are willing to participate in finding problems before they come up.	1 2 3 4 5 6 7	
3. Group members are willing to participate in finding problems after they come up.	1 2 3 4 5 6 7	
4. Group members are willing to participate in solving problems after they come up.	1 2 3 4 5 6 7	
5. Group members clearly separate the processes of generating and evaluating ideas.	1 2 3 4 5 6 7	
6. The group climate is relaxed.	1 2 3 4 5 6 7	
7. Group members are courteous to each other.	1 2 3 4 5 6 7	
8. Group members support creative ideas.	1 2 3 4 5 6 7	
9. The group maintains a nonauthoritarian point of view.	1 2 3 4 5 6 7	
10. Group members are playful in their attitudes when they are coming up with new ideas.	1 2 3 4 5 6 7	
11. Group members are open to "crazy ideas."	1 2 3 4 5 6 7	
12. Group members strive for consensus.	1 2 3 4 5 6 7	

Activity 9–5: Identifying Problems, Issues, or Challenges Confronting the Work Group

Directions: Use this activity to structure your thinking about problems, issues, or challenges confronting a work group that could benefit from think-tank experiences. Answer the following questions. Use additional paper if necessary.

Part I: Present Problems

---

1. What problems, issues, or challenges are confronting the work group, department, or division *at present?* List major ones.

Part II: Future Challenges

---

2. What problems, issues, or challenges will probably confront the work group, department, or division *in the future?* List major ones.

Part III: Priorities

---

3. Prioritize the problems listed in responses to Questions 1 and 2. List the most-important problems first.

Present Problems	Probable Future Problems

Part IV: Identifying Experiences

---

4. Which of the priorities, listed in response to Question 3, best lend themselves to think-tank experiences. Explain why you think they lend themselves to such experiences and what kind of think-tank experiences they lend themselves to.

Part V: Action Plan

---

5. Prepare an action plan for a series of planned think-tank experiences over time for each work group. Tell what should be done, by whom, when, and what outcomes are desired.

Activity 9–6: A Worksheet for Identifying/Summarizing Present and Desired Future Competencies of an Organization

Directions: Use this worksheet to structure and organize your thinking. Describe in the first part the key competencies of an organization at present. In what ways is the organization strong relative to other firms in the industry? What is it able to do better than any other? Tell why you think it possesses these competencies. Then in Part II, describe the organization's future plans. Finally, in Part III, describe what competencies will be needed to realize these plans.

Part I: Present Competencies

1.

Part II: Future Plans

2.

Part III: Needed Future Competencies

3.

Activity 9–7: A Worksheet for Identifying/Summarizing Work Group/Department Competencies in Your Organization

Directions: In the left column, list each major department of a firm. Under each department, list the units that make it up. (Example: Personnel department, HRD unit, Compensation unit, Benefits unit, Recruitment unit, etc.) Then, in the right column, explain the key competencies of each department/work unit. In short, what makes the unit/department special? How does it contribute, if it does, to key strengths/competencies of the organization as a whole? Simply describe. Use additional paper if necessary.

Departments/Work Units	Key Competencies

Activity 9–8: A Worksheet for Identifying Appropriate Employee-Development Efforts in an Organization

Directions: Answer the questions that follow.

I: Discrepancies

1. What discrepancies exist between the present competencies of the firm and those competencies needed/desired in the future? Describe them.

2. What discrepancies exist between the present and desired future competencies of each department and each work group in the firm? Describe them.

Department/Work group	Discrepancies between present/desired future competencies

II: Employee Development Efforts

3. What employee-development efforts are appropriate in each work group or department to narrow gaps between present and desired future competencies? Describe them.

Department/Work group	Appropriate Employee-Development efforts

Activity 9–9: Pinpointing Resources to Meet Strategic Employee-Development Needs

Directions: For each work group or department in the organization, summarize appropriate employee-development needs in line with long-term strategic business planning requirements, and then identify people or other resources inside or outside the organization that can help satisfy those requirements and meet those needs. (If none, write "None.") Use additional paper if necessary.

Department/Work group	Employee-Development needs	Resources

Activity 9–10: A Case Study on Employee Development

Directions: Read the case below and answer the questions that follow.

Larkin Memorial Hospital* is a full-service regional medical facility in a medium-sized city.

Larkin Memorial Hospital recently hired a management consulting firm to conduct an attitude survey of hospital employees. Among the results of that survey: Larkin should establish a comprehensive Talent Development effort, with particular emphasis placed on supervisory and management training, education, and development.

Larkin has long offered Staff Development activities to such professionals as nurses, medical technicians, and physicians. However, it has not offered in-house courses on supervision. The hospital administrator once summed up the reason for this: Let them go out to the local university if they want to learn about that. Clearly, employees did not agree with that sentiment, so hospital administrators grudgingly decided to hire a full-time Management Development Coordinator.

Larkin, like some Midwestern hospitals, has had difficulty recruiting professionals, particularly nurses. Those hired are typically assigned to special units such as Intensive Care, the Emergency Room, and others. Each unit is led by a head nurse, who is on duty eight hours a day during a 40-hour work week. The remainder of the time, a charge nurse is responsible for the unit. Charge nurses are selected from experienced staff in the unit. They rotate—different people take turns in this capacity. Charge nurses receive no training, informal or formal, to carry out their duties.

The Management Development coordinator hired at Larkin will be asked to set up a comprehensive Talent Development program for nurses at the hospital. It will combine classroom-based training, organized employee education, and employee development.

Questions

1. What problems, if any, do you suppose are created by the present "charge nurse" system at Larkin?
2. How can this system be used to advantage, such as for development? What should be done to convert it from its present form to a valuable developmental experience?

---

* A fictitious name for a real organization.

CHAPTER 10

EMPLOYEE EDUCATION

Imagine for a moment that you are a supervisor on a highly automated assembly line. Eleven people work on it—a mechanic, a supplier, four machine operators, three packaging operators, one laborer, and you. Your responsibility is to keep the line in operation. The mechanic makes repairs and the supplier transports raw materials to the line and finished goods from the line, and makes light repairs to machines. Machine operators operate equipment; packaging operators watch trouble spots on the line; and the laborer serves as janitor. The plant is not unionized.

One day you arrive at work to find that the mechanic, line supplier, and one machine operator have all called in sick. You waste little time contacting the production manager, but you are told, "Tough luck—you'll have to work with the crew you have." "But they don't know each other's jobs," you explain. What do you do?

If this problem strikes a responsive chord, then you should appreciate the value of employee education. This chapter defines employee education, emphasizing its relationship to career planning activities of individuals and career planning programs sponsored by organizations.

What Is Employee Education?

Employee education focuses on changing individuals to help them prepare for career advancement *vertically* (up the chain of command) or *horizontally* (across a continuum of professional competence). In this respect, it is unlike employee development, which focuses on changing the collective competencies of a work group or an organization. It is also unlike training, which focuses on meeting immediate job requirements. Employee education is a tool for *anticipatory socialization,* the process by which an individual acquires information about and experience in a job or role before entering it.

Traditionally, employee education prepares people for future work. However, it is not truly future-oriented, because most educational efforts perpetuate notions based on the experiences of others and on conventional wisdom about "right and wrong ways of doing things around here." Education passes on cultural norms from one generation of job incumbents to the next. It is for this reason that radical changes—that is, major departures from past group and organizational traditions—frequently require leaders to be brought in from outside.

The Relationship between Employee Education and a Career Program

To be effective, traditional and thus culturally bound employee education must be based on a comprehensive career program. While it is possible to "groom" individuals for new jobs without considering career issues, such short-term planning is often counterproductive if individuals are given no opportunity to participate in decisions affecting their future. Why? Consider the fact that there is ample evidence that employees and managers alike perceive career advancement opportunities to be severely limited in their organizations.

The Two Components of Career Programs. Career programs that make employee education genuinely effective have two components: *organizational* and *individual* programs (Rothwell and Sredl 2000). What individuals do in planning their careers should be matched by different (but corresponding) organizational efforts. Employee education stems from career programs in which individuals plan what they want to do and who they want to become. At the same time, managers should plan how many people and what kinds of competencies they will need over time. Employee education is one vehicle for helping individuals realize their career aspirations.

Key Terms. Terms can often be a source of confusion. For that reason, it is worthwhile to define some important terms. The term *career* refers to all the jobs held by people in the course of their lives. *Career planning* is the process of identifying career goals and establishing the means of making them a reality. *Career development* connotes activities undertaken by an individual to realize career aspirations. *Career management* is the process of charting out and describing relationships between jobs in an organization. *Career education* consists of learning experiences that enrich an individual's understanding of career issues. *Career counseling* is the process of helping individuals sort out career issues and make career decisions.

Career Planning: Some Considerations

Employee education is rarely adequate by itself to ensure promotion or other career moves. Individuals must, for example, maintain at least adequate (and quite often above-average) job performance in their present jobs to be considered for vertical (up the chain of command) or horizontal (across a continuum of professional competence) advancement. Additional elements are also important:

- *Visibility*. How well-known is an employee to superiors and to supervisors in units to which the employee would like to move? Does an employee's name come up if somebody says, "Who is ready to be promoted?"
- *Willingness to move*. Is the employee willing to leave the present work group to further his or her career? If the answer is no, the employee's potential for growth is often restricted.
- *Mentors*. How successfully has an individual identified and established mentoring relationships with people who can further his or her career?
- *Luck*. How lucky has the individual been? Has he or she been in the right place at the right time? While luck should not be relied on, it can be an important element in career progress.

By way of background prior to a more-detailed treatment of employee education, let's discuss career planning in organizations and individual career planning.

Career Planning in Organizations

A good place to begin when thinking about career planning from the organization's perspective is with the distinction between internal and external labor markets. According to labor economists, the *external labor market* consists of people *outside* the firm or industry. The *internal labor market* consists of people *inside* the firm or industry. Managers inside an organization enjoy much flexibility in setting wage scales, structuring work into jobs, and creating jobs. While such decisions are affected by external labor demands, managers exercise considerable control over who they choose to promote, prepare for other jobs, or compensate for work performed.

A related issue is the *dual labor market theory*. Economists have long emphasized the existence of primary and secondary markets outside organizations. The goal of programs created by the Manpower Development and Training Act of 1962, the Comprehensive Employment and Training Act of 1973, the Job Training Partnership Act of 1983, and the Workforce Investment Act of 1998 has been to lift disadvantaged individuals from the secondary to the primary labor market through government-sponsored training efforts and government-subsidized employer incentives.

Primary and secondary labor markets may also exist *inside* organizations. Some people enter jobs after careful screening. To qualify, these people must possess specialized academic training or relevant work experience. Workers of this kind are in line to receive more training, education, and development. This part of the organization's labor force is the *primary labor market.* In contrast, people hired into the organization after less rigorous screening to carry out jobs not requiring advance preparation make up the *secondary labor market.* The latter group has traditionally comprised inordinately large numbers of women and minorities.

Formalized career planning can serve any number of different purposes, some more emphatically than others. These purposes include (1) developing employees who are ready for short-term or permanent movement to different jobs; (2) reducing absenteeism and turnover; (3) cultivating realization of individual potential; (4) motivating employees to establish their own career objectives and act on them; (5) increasing management awareness of available talent within the organization; (6) helping satisfy employee needs for advancement, recognition, and achievement; (7) contributing to organizational preparation for long-term trends that might pose threats to or opportunities for strategic success; and (8) meeting Affirmative Action goals. Without management support for any or all these purposes, however, no career program is likely to be successful.

Steps in Establishing a Formal, Organizational Career Planning Program

To establish a formal, organizational career planning program, WLP practitioners and line managers in the organization should

1. Develop a climate conducive to career planning.
2. Establish a career policy in line with strategic business plans, HR plans, individual career plans, and organizational strategy for the development of talent.
3. Analyze the work, including jobs and career paths/ladders, and the competencies needed at present and in the future.
4. Analyze the workforce, including data on groups and individuals, to determine the supply of available talent.
5. Identify future talent gaps for work and the workforce.

Step 1: Develop a climate conducive to career planning. Managers play important parts in career planning. First of all, top managers set the tone. How much are they committed to a formal career planning program in the organization? If the answer is "not much" or "they'll only pay lip service to it," then the career program faces a problem from the start. In all likelihood, a career planning program cannot succeed if it lacks complete top management support and is not linked to, and supported by, other planning initiatives. Quite simply, top managers must see some business need to be met before they will back it. In many cases, it is up to WLP practitioners and line managers to make the case for a formal career planning program.

A good place to start is with career planning for managers. If a career planning program begins as a means to deal with the problem of management succession planning, it may well garner real support from top managers. In time, career planning efforts can be expanded to include all employees.

Top managers are not the only ones whose support is crucial to the successful implementation of a career planning program. Support from immediate supervisors is essential. There are several reasons why. First, immediate superiors exert tremendous influence over subordinates. Effective superiors advise employees about handling job tasks and dealing with organizational politics. Supervisors influence employee career progress by how they shape individual work habits and how they oversee work assignments and developmental or educational opportunities to which individuals are exposed.

An employee's peers also influence the success of career planning programs. Without trust in management and faith in organizational practices, they can sabotage the implementation of such programs and influence to what extent people are willing to participate in career planning.

Step 2: Establish career policy. A *career policy* is an official pronouncement by an organization's management that articulates the organization's stance on career issues. It puts the organization on the record regarding company responsibilities for career matters. Specific issues should be covered in such a policy. They include

I   *Purpose of the program.* What is the major purpose of the program? Are there limitations on its scope?

I   *Responsibilities of the individual.* What is the role of the individual in the program? What should the individual do?

I   *Responsibilities of the organization.* What are the responsibilities of the organization and its managers? What should they do?

I   *Methods of administering the program.* Who does what? Are one or more special committees appropriate for administering the program? If so, what committees? What are they to do? Why?

I   *Methods of carrying out the program.* What features of a career planning program are to be used by an individual?

I *Provisions (if any) for special groups or needs.* How much does management want to gear specialized career programs to meet the unique problems experienced by women, minorities, people with disabilities, those who are functionally illiterate, or other groups?

I *Relationship between career planning and strategic business plans.* How does career planning contribute to the realization of strategic business plans and company purpose? How clearly, and how convincingly, is that linkage made?

I *Relationship between career planning and HR plans.* What relationships exist between career plans and other HR efforts? How does a career program contribute to the realization of HR plans?

I *Relationship between career planning and the Talent Development effort.* What should be the relationship between career planning policy and Talent Development? Between career planning and employee development, education, and training?

Career planning policy provides direction to career planning efforts. Without unified direction, employees in one work group or department will probably receive treatment entirely different from those in other departments. Some managers, particularly in downsized organizations, may even "hoard" good people and thus thwart individual career advancement in order to make their own jobs easier by avoiding the need to train replacements. This practice stifles individual growth and is not beneficial to the long-term talent needs of the organization. A formal career policy provides a foundation for consistent and equitable practices across the organization.

Once adopted, a career policy should be relatively enduring. Remember that an individual's career can span an entire lifetime, from kindergarten through retirement. An individual can hold many different jobs in a career spanning a thirty- or forty-year period, even in one organization. Changes in career policy that are appropriate when there are changes in business plans or organizational strategy for the development of talent should not be undertaken lightly. The reason is that changes in career policy can well be interpreted by employees as affecting their chances for advancement or career mobility. The general idea is to align career planning processes and outcomes to be consistent with strategic business plans. However, *radical* changes may well give a signal to individuals that career opportunities are not as good as they once were. Turnover is one predictable result, as employees preparing themselves in line with one set of career expectations suddenly find that those expectations no longer apply and move to another place where their prospects appear brighter.

Employee Education and Strategic Business Plans. Employee education, like other Talent Development efforts, can help (1) build the competencies that managers need to formulate strategic business plans in problem-solving groups or meetings and (2) implement strategic business plans when used to prepare employees for future challenges.

Many large corporations formulate their strategic plans and follow up periodically on performance linked to those plans in meetings and retreats. To a great extent, group performance in these settings depends on the willingness and ability of members to interact. Climate is influenced by leader and situation; the willingness and ability of members to interact are influenced by the interpersonal skills of the members themselves. Leaders can be trained to run more-effective and creative meetings, and members can be educated to improve their interaction. In these ways, then, employee education can be instrumental in formulating strategic business plans.

By the same token, educational efforts can help implement plans. Remember that education can help the competencies that people need in the future. Often education is regarded as a way to prepare for promotion, but that is not its sole use. It can also help prepare people for other movements inside or outside the organization.

But for implementing strategy, educational efforts for promotion are crucial. The reason is that leadership at all levels must be consistent with business strategy. Particularly at the highest levels, it is important to make sure that managers have the appropriate abilities to make strategy work. Individuals might find it difficult to change, but they can at lower levels be groomed for promotion in calculated ways to ensure that they possess the competencies consistent with future organizational needs. In this way, employee education can help implement strategic business plans.

Employee Education and HR Plans. Employee education helps narrow gaps between present HR supplies and future HR demands. Employees can be tapped and educated to meet pending or existing HR needs. Employee education also prepares people for movement to specific jobs or job categories over time.

Employee Education and Career Plans. Career planning is the responsibility of the individual. However, it is also the responsibility of managers and WLP practitioners to make certain that the foundation is laid for meaningful planning by describing relationships between jobs in an organization. Employee education is a means to prepare individuals for movement along a career path.

Employee Education and Organizational Strategy for the Development of Talent. Recall that organizational strategy for the development of talent is the direction for all planned learning activities in the organization over time. While organizational strategy for the development of talent need not be driven solely by business or HR plans, it should at least be compatible with them. Employee education is an intermediate-term change effort. The primary thrust of employee education is not in determining what should be offered in the way of planned learning, an issue considered in strategy formulation; rather, the thrust is in the appropriate deployment of resources/activities to support efforts in line with organizational and individual needs.

In the framework of an integrated organizational strategy for the development of talent, employee education focuses on individual learning objectives. It helps meet individual career objectives and organizational objectives on an intermediate-term basis that can extend up to three years. Of course, employee educational efforts should be integrated with Talent Development initiatives such as employee development and training so that the cumulative effect of the Talent Development effort is greater than the sum of its individual parts.

Step 3: Analyze the work. The starting point for implementing a career planning program has traditionally been work analysis and career path analysis.

Work analysis gathers information about what jobs exist in the organization and what duties people are expected to carry out. Work analysis addresses two specific questions: (1) What are the activities/outcomes of each job? and (2) What knowledge, skills, and attitudes are needed by a job incumbent to carry out those activities or achieve those outcomes?

Work analysis is a logical starting point for career planning. It is necessary to know what people are presently doing and what knowledge, skills, and attitudes they presently possess before helping them think about the future. In any case, a present job is the point of convergence between the individual and the organization. It thus represents a place to start in planning.

There are many approaches to work analysis, some more detailed than others. Work analysis is synonymous with job, activity, or task analysis, and no single approach will be satisfactory for all situations.

It is not our intention to describe all work analysis methods here. That exceeds the scope of this section. It is, in any case, treated by us elsewhere (Rothwell and Kazanas 2002).

The traditional focus of work analysis is the present job. It is most appropriately used in planning *training,* a topic treated in the next chapter. However, work analysis must be carried out before it is possible to identify a *career path,* which is a description of the possible sequence of jobs or assignments that individuals may hold. Preparing for movement along the career path is the appropriate focus of employee education and a necessary requirement in formal career planning/programs.

Competency identification and modeling, now widely accepted, have gradually supplanted work analysis as a foundation for career planning. Decision-makers have encouraged that shift to realize the productivity improvement benefits. After all, one approach to competency identification is to focus on the differences between the exemplary performer and the fully experienced performer. When individuals at one point are compared to the competencies demonstrated by exemplary performers, they are being prepared to function as best-in-class (rather than as average) workers.

Career Path Analysis. A *career path* describes the sequence of jobs that individuals may hold. There are two types of career paths: *formal,* made explicit by the organization, and *informal,* made explicit by examining historical movements of employees. *Career path analysis* is literally the process of analyzing career paths. There are two different but related types: (1) *prescriptive,* detailing logical relationships between jobs and logically related competencies necessary to qualify for movement from one job to the next, and (2) *descriptive,* detailing historical employment experiences of individuals who have moved through the ranks over time.

If we lived in a perfect and stable world, there would never be a difference between formal and informal career paths. But the world is not perfect. Career progression does not depend solely on qualifications or fairness. Ample evidence proves that more-elusive elements play a part, and they include in-house politics, personal favoritism, visibility, timing, luck, family influence, ethnic background, and race. It is not too surprising, then, that neither managers nor employees are certain of performance requirements on the present job, let alone requirements for advancement.

Establishing *formal* career paths is not difficult, at least in theory. They can be based on several things:

I   *Work activities*—what people do to meet job requirements
I   *Work behaviors*—observable actions taken to carry out work activities
I   *Work perceptions*—what people believe

To base career paths on work activities, managers must have access to current information about job duties:

1. Managers must collect data about activities involved in each job, how important these activities are, and how much time is devoted to them.
2. Managers then infer from job information which competencies are necessary for incumbents to perform each activity.
3. Managers need to group jobs together in "families" or "clusters," based on common competencies.
4. Managers then pinpoint logical patterns of movement between jobs, based on similarities in the competencies required.
5. Managers then assemble results of all such analyses for the entire organization.

It is not necessary to undertake a time-consuming study of jobs to assemble career paths of this type; rather, job titles can simply be listed in logical progression. It is even possible, using this approach, to identify so-called *dual career ladders,* in which individuals can choose between increasing technical competence or increasing responsibility for supervising other people. The latter is associated with vertical movement on the chain of command; the former is associated with horizontal movement to higher levels of skill proficiency in the present job.

To base career paths on work behaviors rather than activities, managers go beyond job titles or job descriptions. They focus instead on relationships between actual behaviors or work outcomes/results in different jobs. This analysis is more time-consuming, but it is potentially more useful than activity analysis.

There are two different, though related, ways to carry out career path analysis based on behavior. One is called the discrepancy method; the other is the competency-based method.

The *discrepancy method* assumes that the highest-level jobs are terminal ones, at least from the standpoint of the internal labor market. (Of course, it is possible to make a career move to another organization, but that possibility is not emphasized.) Instead, top-level jobs are viewed as terminal steps in possible career paths. Managers then

1. Analyze each highest-level job in terms of the competencies equated with successful or exemplary performance.
2. Examine jobs immediately below these highest-level ones.
3. Compare each high-level job to those immediately below it to identify differences between competencies/behaviors required for successful performance at each level.
4. Compare differences between jobs at each hierarchical level.
5. Continue the process from the top to the bottom of the organization's hierarchy of authority.
6. Identify instructional needs (differences between jobs) that have to be satisfied by individuals desiring to move vertically, horizontally, or diagonally to other jobs.

The *competency-based method* is more challenging. For each activity carried out in each job, the analyst (1) identifies tangible outputs or outcomes traditionally associated with it; (2) describes several behaviors associated with successful performance; (3) pinpoints critical behaviors linked to successful performance; and (4) develops clusters of related jobs, regardless of titles or placements within departments. This method is based on key results sought.

To base career paths on work perceptions and experiences, managers rely on common interpretations of many people. Managers

1. Ask experienced people to describe their past jobs and assignments, as well as other matters that people feel have contributed to their career progress.
2. Ask these people to advise lower-level employees about what future jobs to prepare for, what future assignments to seek, and what educational opportunities to take advantage of.
3. Identify any similarities between these stories.

Through these steps, WLP practitioners can answer such questions as these: Are there common historical patterns in career paths? What are they? Are they still applicable at present? If so, why? If not, why not? Will they be applicable in the future? If so, why? If not, why not?

Step 4: Analyze the workforce. The counterpoint of work analysis is workforce analysis, the process of taking stock of the numbers and kinds of people employed by the organization at present and expected to be needed in the future. The workforce can be analyzed by focusing on individuals, positions, or occupational groups, or by departments, divisions, or work groups. Each focus is useful in its own ways.

Workforce Analysis by Individual. There can be a considerable difference between two individuals functioning in the same job.

Most organizations hire many people for their entry-level jobs. Each person occupies one position, but there may be any number of positions sharing the same job title and the same general job description. To cite a simple example: both the production manager's secretary and the training director's secretary share the same title. Technically, they function at the same level and in common jobs. Yet each position really has different duties.

At the same time, no two individuals fill the same job or position in precisely the same ways. Each person has his or her own role expectations, strengths and weaknesses, and unique aspirations for the future. As a consequence, distinct differences may exist in how two individuals carry out the same job.

One way to analyze individuals is by their backgrounds. For example, they may be asked to describe their education, prior experience outside the organization, prior experience inside the organization, training programs completed, specialized knowledge of foreign languages, and familiarity with computer languages.

Another way to analyze individuals is to review their performance appraisal ratings. How well have they been rated by superiors? Are historical patterns discernible? Have they done better in some capacities than in others? What are their unique individual competencies? What do they get repeated requests to do? What questions do others repeatedly ask of them?

A third way to analyze individuals is by *aspiration* (what they want to be) or *expectation* (what they believe they will be). This information reveals important clues about motivation. It can be cross-checked with work history. Have they undertaken increasingly challenging assignments when given the option to do so? How well did they do in meeting those challenges?

Workforce Analysis by Position. What people occupy jobs in the organization at present? What kind of people *should* be occupying those jobs in the future? These questions are addressed by workforce analysis when it is conducted position-by-position.

Perhaps the most common example of this type of analysis is replacement planning, the simplest form of succession planning. *Replacement planning*, a form of disaster planning, has traditionally been restricted to the upper echelons of the management hierarchy. Suppose the chief executive suddenly dies of a heart attack. Who takes over? Succession plans answer this question, providing for orderly transition until a permanent replacement can be found.

Nothing prevents succession plans from being extended all the way down the organization, and (indeed) the trend is to do that. Succession planning also helps identify long-term staffing issues or problems warranting attention. In one organization, for example, HR discovered that the firm's entire top management team would likely retire over a ten-year period. Of course, information of that kind is useful in preparing for predictable losses in personnel talent, dramatizing the need for employee development *and* employee education adequate to avert future problems.

Of course, workforce analysis by position does not need to be limited solely to replacement planning. In some job categories, it is important to plan for a mix of competencies. In fact, people from a variety of different backgrounds might be deliberately sought in order to create constructive conflict and prevent the conformist thinking that arises in groups where all members share identical academic training and similar work experience.

To analyze the workforce by position, group together everyone with the same job titles. Then, by individual, list pertinent facts. These facts may be about academic training/degrees by field, prior experience, length of services, and other factors deemed relevant. This list is a snapshot of the workforce as it currently exists. The next step involves making value judgments. Which individuals *should* be in those positions? Why?

Workforce Analysis by Occupational Group. An *occupational group* is a related cluster of jobs. For example, everyone in an organization may be classified into such groups as management/administrative, technical, professional, clerical/secretarial, skilled, and unskilled labor. Each group comprises two or more job titles sharing common characteristics. People occupying those groups are then examined much as they are by position.

Workforce Analysis by Department, Division, or Work Group. A final and more or less obvious method of workforce analysis is by structural unit—department-by-department, work group-by-work group.

There are two ways to do this: (1) by position or job title or (2) by competency. It is simple enough to list all job titles in a department. In many cases, that can be done in a few minutes. It requires nothing more than an organization chart.

It is not such a simple matter to inventory competency. There may be no problem at all in listing such traditional indicators as education, a chronology of individuals' jobs inside and outside the organization, hobbies and avocations, and knowledge of foreign languages. Yet these are not really indicators of what people can do, what track records of work achievements people have demonstrated, what problems others look to people to solve, what others regard as the individual's special talents, and other such factors. And yet these may be far more important for the long-term talent management of the organization than traditional facts about "highest degree earned."

To gather competency information at a detailed level, the supervisor and individuals must prepare a way to classify individuals' relative performance, and then develop some inventory of who can do what and how well they can do it. While no standardized approach exists to do that, software does exist to track, for example, who is asked what questions by e-mail, which might indicate what other people think an individual's strengths are.

Another approach is to conduct an analysis of the work group's total scope of work activities. An approach like **Developing a Curriculum** (DACUM) can be helpful for that purpose (see Norton 1997). Although DACUM is traditionally used to conduct occupational analysis, it can be applied to the work processes of a group or team (Rothwell 1995). Team members are assembled and are asked to describe what they do. This structured brainstorming activity is then used to help group or team members build a chart that shows, in detail, every step of the work processed by the group. Individuals can then be rated for their ability to carry out each step. That can become the basis for identifying competencies tied to the work, and it can also be a means by which to focus discussions around how to measure the quality of the work, how to identify the expected outputs of the work, and how to assess individual competencies related to the work.

Step 5: Identify future needs for work and the workforce. No task, work activity, job, or even career path remains the same forever. Nor do individuals remain the same. Under the influence of environmental changes, organizations change what they do. Similarly, changes eventually occur in tasks, activities, jobs, and even career paths. As individuals change what they do, their skills also change. Indeed, one appealing fact about competencies is that they are relatively enduring, since tied to individuals, and can thus extend beyond the quickly changing job environment of many organizations today (Dubois and Rothwell 2000).

A simple example may help clarify this point. Suppose a large, prominent manufacturer of baby food analyzes the environment and discovers that birth rates in the United States of America are declining. Demand for baby food will probably level off, as will sales. Top managers must then decide what to do. One choice, of course, is to do nothing. Management simply acknowledges that the market itself is stagnating or even declining. Perhaps they may choose to increase their commanding lead in market share by cutting into the business of their competitors. Other choices are possible: (1) increasing efficiency and thus profitability by preserving the same level of output but reducing inputs (for example, reducing worker numbers), (2) developing new markets by expanding into international markets where birth rates *are* increasing, (3) diversifying into new, more promising product or service lines, or (4) integrating with suppliers of critical raw materials or distributors through purchases, mergers, or takeovers.

Each strategy has unique advantages and disadvantages. The point is that some choices, such as increasing efficiency, may lead to actions within the organization that change how work is done and what competencies individuals must possess to do that work successfully. Choices such as international expansion imply that competencies probably not existing within the organization at present will have to be identified. That can be done, of course, by hiring individuals who possess that experience or by purchasing, merging with, taking over, or joint venturing with one or more organizations with employees who do possess those competencies. In the latter case, the organization will experience an infusion of new talent from a new setting.

To identify future needs for work and the workforce, managers and/or WLP practitioners should scan the future to determine how work will probably be done and what competencies will probably be needed to do it (Rothwell and Kazanas 2002). There are four steps in this process:

1. Clarify the present status of the organization, work, workforce, and relationships (career paths) between jobs.
2. Identify what environmental changes will affect the organization, work, workforce, and relationships between jobs.
3. Envision what the future will probably look like or what managers want it to look like.
4. Step back into the present in order to plan for the future.

We have already treated the first step, to clarify present status. Traditionally, that is as far as most writers on this subject take it.

Subsequent steps have already been treated at greater length elsewhere. Scanning the environment was discussed in Chapter 4 of this text; identifying future work, the workforce, and career paths was treated in Rothwell and Kazanas (2002). Once these steps are completed, it is possible to shift perspective back to the present and plan for the future. Employee education is one means by which to prepare individuals for the future, both in terms of their own career movement and in terms of the changes wrought by dynamic external conditions.

Career Planning: Individual Issues

Career planning is a joint responsibility of the organization and the individual. Managers, as agents of the organization, should clarify career paths, provide a climate conducive to career planning, encourage time spent in cultivating individuals, and make resources available so that people can achieve their career objectives. On the other hand, individuals should take advantage of opportunities provided to them and accept responsibility for managing their careers.

Purposes of Career Planning. From the individual's standpoint, formalized career planning

I   Establishes direction for occupational pursuits

I   Establishes time frames and objectives against which to measure individual career progress

I   Motivates the individual to act and assume responsibility for his or her career

I   Dramatizes emerging conflicts between an individual's career objectives and personal objectives

I   Emphasizes the value of training, education, and employee developmental efforts as tools for helping individuals achieve their career objectives

Some people also value career planning for its usefulness in discovering their *career anchors,* defined by Schein (1978, 127) in his classic work as "patterns of self-perceived talents, motives and values [which] serve to guide, constrain, stabilize, and integrate a person's career," such as the need for security, autonomy, creativity, or technical competence, or the need for power, status, and advancement.

A Model for Individual Career Planning. Many self-help books are available on individual career planning. To carry out planning, individuals should

1. Clarify their personal values and identities.

2. Make some decisions about the kind of people they would like to become in the future and the kind of jobs in which they would like to work.

3. Assess present personal strengths and weaknesses.
4. Scan the future environment and pinpoint threats and opportunities affecting career progress.
5. Establish a long-term career strategy.

This model resembles strategic business planning, and it is intended to.

Clarifying Personal Values and Identity. Career planning efforts start with the clarification of personal values and identity. Too often people make no effort to do this until they encounter a personal crisis or expect one in the near future. In this respect, personal values clarification is much like organizational change, which is also often stimulated by crisis.

Individuals can clarify their values and identity on their own or with special counseling. Many instruments exist that can aid in this process, helping provide feedback to individuals about their own interests and values.

Making Decisions. It is not enough just to clarify present identity and values. Individuals should also envision what kind of person they would like to become and the career or job in which they would like to work. Much like organizational planning, this process works best when people envision their idealized selves or idealized jobs and then gradually work toward the realization of this ideal.

Assessing Personal Strengths and Weaknesses. Assessing personal strengths and weaknesses is sometimes confused with clarifying personal values. It is not the same thing, because assessment of needs has to be made in comparison with something else. Once individuals are aware of their occupational interests, they are ready to consider how well their present competencies match up to what is necessary for entry into and advancement in a specific occupation. The characteristics that tend to improve their chances for entry to a field or advancement in a career are *strengths;* conversely, whatever characteristics tend to detract from their chances for entry or advancement are *weaknesses.*

Scanning the Future Environment. Conditions do not remain the same forever. They change. Just as strategists scan the environment to identify trends that might pose threats to or opportunities for accomplishment of stated organizational objectives, so should individuals scan environments inside and outside their employing organization and occupation. Key trends to consider include the economy, technology, the labor market in the occupation, social trends, and noticeable geographical movement of practitioners and businesses. How will these things affect achievement of career objectives?

Establishing a Long-Term Career Strategy. Business strategists compare organizational strengths/weaknesses to environmental threats/opportunities as a basis for establishing long-term plans. Individuals should also compare their present career strengths/weaknesses to future environmental threats/opportunities as a basis for career strategy.

Employee education is a tool to

I Build on present strengths
I Rectify present weaknesses
I Take advantage of future opportunities
I Minimize the effects of future environmental threats
I Narrow gaps between actual/present and desired/future competencies

Of course, a key difference between organizational and individual career planning is that individuals routinely can and do consider available opportunities outside one organization or occupation. In contrast, not many organizations provide advice about movements to other firms, unless it is in the context of an outplacement program.

Employee Education

Assuming that managers have laid out career paths in an organization and established other key components of a career planning system and that individuals have planned for their careers, they are ready to plan employee education.

But how are employee education efforts planned from the organization's standpoint and from an individual's standpoint? How is employee education delivered? How are educational efforts tied to organizational strategy for the development of talent? This next section addresses these questions.

Planning Educational Efforts: The Organizational Component

There are three ways to plan educational efforts: (1) by occupational group, (2) by special groups or needs, and (3) by stage of individual socialization or career.

By Occupational Group. When managers make career paths explicit, they lay the foundation for planned education by occupational groups.

Perhaps the most common method of doing so is to use the *pyramid model.* Individuals start their careers in an organization at the lowest rung of the occupational ladder and gradually move upward. Since pyramids narrow from bottom to top, there are always fewer high-level jobs and more low-level jobs. Movement up the pyramid involves pairing technical knowledge (most important upon entry) with interpersonal and conceptual skills. The highest level positions in any organizational pyramid are always management ones, which require well-developed conceptual and interpersonal skills.

Another way to think of occupational groupings makes use of the spiral concept popularized in a classic work by Bruner (1960). Each dot in a curriculum spiral configuration represents a learning objective; each dot in an employment spiral configuration represents a task. The spiral concept integrates education and occupational requirements over time.

However, the spiral concept preserves the pyramid notion. It is primarily organized around functional specialties, and there is less opportunity for horizontal mobility than there appears to be, because movement is assumed to be upward.

The assumption that career progress should always be upwardly bound and tied to increasing management responsibility creates problems for employers. For one thing, not everyone is interested in management careers. For another, demographic trends, organizational practices, and a host of other conditions are leading to slowdowns (or actual stoppages) in upward mobility for many people.

For these reasons, it is increasingly appropriate to rely on another method of describing career paths as a basis for planning education by occupational group—the *dual-career pathing method.* This assumes that individuals enter an organization with a technical specialty, but can choose to grow into either mana-gerial or technical positions at higher levels. Rather than *one* career path, *two* exist side-by-side. Employee education is planned accordingly, so choices can be made at each step.

By Special Groups or Needs. Substantial attention has been focused in recent years on the long-term needs of special groups within corporations, specific needs stemming from legislation and regulation, social issues affecting the workplace, and a trend toward educating the "whole person." It is clear, for instance, that women, minorities, and people with disabilities continue to face special career problems. Members of these groups are often denied the support and mentoring provided to men and non-minorities.

Legal and regulatory requirements should be considered in employee educa-tional planning. Employees should be prepared for career movement in part through exposure to laws, rules, and regulations influencing performance in positions to which they aspire. As people progress, they *must* have a grasp of the legal issues that will affect them when they enter the new job.

It should not be difficult to plan such instruction. WLP practitioners and managers need only

1. Identify legal and regulatory matters constraining company actions.
2. Pinpoint requirements contributing to legal/regulatory compliance at each job level in the organization.
3. Identify issues about which employees at each level and in each occupa-tional group should receive instruction.
4. Assess how well instruction is presently contributing to legal/regulatory compliance.
5. Plan instruction at each level in anticipation of career moves to other levels.

There may, of course, be company policies and procedures that also influence job performance. One example is labor agreements. Employees being groomed for promotion to first-line supervision may need education on labor contract admin-istration so that they will perform in ways attuned to current company policy and contractual obligations. They may also need information about specific provisions of existing labor agreements.

Special social issues also require employee education. Some issues may not be tied to specific future jobs, but may nevertheless be important. Some examples are instructional programs on employee drug abuse, alcoholism, personal crisis counseling, and AIDS. There might be employee assistance programs to provide in-depth counseling to employees who are experiencing these problems, but supervisors and peers might be able to (1) spot symptoms early on and (2) refer individuals to appropriate sources of help. At a minimum, employees should be educated about company policies on these matters. Supervisors require additional education so that they will know how to spot problems, open up dialogue with troubled individuals, handle work-related implications of these problems, and make referrals to professional help when necessary.

Programs of the kind just mentioned go a long way toward educating the "whole person." Some observers believe that trends in the WLP field are headed away from strict job-specific and even career-specific instruction. It does not make much sense to segregate an individual's personal (off-the-job) and occupational/organizational (on-the-job) interests, needs, and concerns into neat, but artificial, compartments. Each person spends about 2,000 hours a year on the job and 6,700 hours a year off the job. (Cell phones and e-mail have narrowed the artificial barriers between worklife and homelife, or have closed them entirely.) A person's life at work affects their life at home, and vice versa. Stress at work affects family, drug use, and sick time; stress at home affects job performance and relationships with co-workers.

By Stage of Individual Socialization or Career. Another way to plan employee education is to factor in an individual's stage in socialization and/or career. Effects of socialization are most pronounced when there are significant differences between expectations raised prior to job entry and actual experiences occurring afterward. This phenomenon is called *reality shock*. It occurs during transition from outsider (job applicant) to insider (entry-level job incumbent).

However, there is no need to speak of socialization solely in terms of organizational entry. Nor is reality shock limited to the first job: it can occur upon promotion or transfer whenever actual experiences prove significantly different from expectations. One reason for employee education is to manage expectations.

Another way to plan employee education is by individual career stage. Seminal work by Erik Erickson (1959) and other theorists have shown that individuals progress through predictable career stages. Most authorities agree that each stage is characterized by a central crisis that must be resolved before an individual can progress to the next stage. In addition, each stage, because it is characterized by a central crisis, presents some issues of particular concern. Individuals are especially motivated to learn when education is a tool for coping with this central conflict.

Planning Educational Efforts: The Individual Component

Not every educational experience offered by an organization is appropriate for everyone. The idea of preparing people for future work implies that individual needs differ, not only because the work is not the same, but also because each person brings his or her own unique strengths and weaknesses to a job. There are at least three ways by which to plan individually oriented educational efforts: (1) by employee appraisal, (2) by individual learning contract, and (3) by organizational offering.

By Employee Appraisal. Most organizations have some kind of formal employee performance appraisal to review patterns in individual performance on the present job, assess present strengths and weaknesses, and negotiate areas warranting future improvement. Appraisal results are used to (1) provide a basis for wage/salary increases, (2) identify instructional needs for short-term training and intermediate-term employee education, and (3) provide information for decisions about promotions, termination, transfers, and other employment moves.

Unfortunately, not all appraisal systems are equally good for all purposes. Employees often expect criticism when they enter an appraisal interview. The appraisal process may have negative or little impact on performance. Some authorities believe that appraisals should *not* be used for dealing with career planning or employee education because there are significant problems administering such systems.

Despite these problems, it is possible to use a Management by Objectives (MBO) approach to negotiate short-term training plans for improvement in a present job (a year at a time), but also to negotiate intermediate-term educational/career plans in preparation for the future (for one- to three-year time spans). External environmental conditions might change over that time period, so managers should avoid making promises they aren't sure they can keep. Having a negotiated and individualized educational plan helps establish benchmarks and time frames by which to prepare individuals for the future. Since MBO plans are negotiated, individuals participate in the planning process. As a result, they are more committed to the realization of the plan.

By Individual Learning Contract. An *individual learning contract* is a learning agreement. For many reasons, it just might be the best approach for helping individuals plan their own learning. As Knowles (1986, 38) explains in a classic description, a contract "may have as its purpose the accomplishment of the objectives of particular units or projects of a course or of a whole course, of a staff-developmental program, of a clinical experience or internship, of a total degree program, or of a personal development project." A contract can be self-initiated and self-monitored, or it can be negotiated between an individual and a supervisor, an instructor, a trainer, or even a committee.

Most learning contracts specify

I *Objectives.* What are the desired outcomes of learning?
I *Resources.* What materials and people will be needed to achieve desired objectives?
I *Methods.* How will the individual go about achieving objectives?
I *Time frame.* What time period will be necessary to achieve objectives?
I *Evaluation.* How will the relative success of the learning experience be measured? In short, how well were learning objectives achieved? (Knowles 1986)

Contracts may also justify a learning project or series of projects by showing the relationship between the proposed project(s) and (1) organizational plans/objectives, (2) individual career plans/objectives, (3) HR plans, (4) department, division, or work group plans/objectives, and/or (5) the individual's present job content and job performance. In short, the learning contract approach is very flexible.

Many organizations have adapted the learning contract approach, referring to it as "individual development planning." IDPs, as they are known, are negotiated between the organizational superior and the individual (see Dubois and Rothwell 2000; Rothwell 1999b). One-year time horizons are common for IDPs.

By Organizational Offering. Some people have trouble doing any planning. They take no action until they see an instructional offering that strikes their fancy. They handle career planning in the same way—with no organized effort at all. When a promotion or other career opportunity opens up, they scurry around madly at the last minute, trying to pick up whatever they can find that improves their chances for promotion or transfer.

There will always be those who are passive and/or lazy learners. They exist in every organization. About the only way to motivate them is to offer as much instruction as possible, as often as possible, and as conveniently packaged and presented as possible. These learners will participate in experiences that happen to coincide with their own problems and career interests. However, the trend is toward having self-directed learners who are more competent in learning how to learn (Rothwell 2002). They know that it is their responsibility to keep themselves up-to-date.

Kinds of Employee Educational Programs

What kinds of programs can be offered to meet employee educational needs? Adult basic education, career education, continuing education, and occupational education.

Adult Basic Education. The United States has a chronic literacy problem. This is particularly ironic, considering the fact that advancing technology calls for highly literate workers for an increasingly information-oriented society. Without basic skills, illiterate workers are placed at a great disadvantage when they enter the workforce or receive advanced training or education: Their potential for career advancement is severely restricted. They also suffer in more-personal ways because they often have low self-respect, low levels of aspiration, and general feelings of inadequacy.

What can be done about this problem? Adult basic education is one solution. It includes instructional activities intended to produce people who can read, write, and use simple arithmetic. Organizations can

I   Offer basic education in-house.

I   Offer basic education through outside groups (for example, local school programs).

I   Combine both internal and external sources to furnish basic education.

I   Give people time off with or without pay to attend off-site basic education programs full-time.

I   Encourage attendance at "night school," and reimburse employees for some or all of the cost.

Career Education. To help meet organizational and individual needs, many organizations offer special career education programs designed to help individuals better understand career issues. They can also serve organizational ends by motivating people to prepare for career movements within the organization and by directing management attention to career matters generally.

The most-common component of a career education program is organized instruction on career planning. The desired outcomes of such instruction vary widely. Group workshops are offered to help individuals plan their own careers without guidance of any kind from the organization's management; conversely, workshops are highly specific to the sponsoring organization, providing concrete guidance for employees establishing career plans. Some organizations simply make available off-the-shelf training packages for individualized use. Others design their own individualized, highly organization-specific workbooks. In recent years, some organizations have established career centers to encourage people to learn more about careers in the organization and online career counseling efforts to help geographically scattered people get access to trained career counselors.

There is no right or wrong approach in any absolute sense. It all depends on how much career education is valued by managers and employees of the organization. Ask yourself: Is career education, in the sense of formal instruction, a worthwhile endeavor for your organization? If so, why? If not, why? If it is worth offering, what end results should be sought from it? How should it be offered? When? For whom?

Continuing Education. Not many years ago, most people assumed that their lives consisted of two distinct phases: schooling and working. That point of view no longer makes any sense. The rate of change is so great that the skills of most people are in serious danger of obsolescence. In short, people need to think of *lifelong learning.* Continuing education, as its name implies, is well-suited to supporting such learning.

The problem of skill obsolescence is particularly acute in information-dependent professions like medicine, law, accounting, engineering, and even management. Without awareness of current methods, doctors will watch patients die unnecessarily; lawyers will lose cases to more up-to-date practitioners; accountants will get their clients in trouble; engineers will miss out on applications of new technology; and managers will find themselves placed at a significant disadvantage with more savvy competitors.

The stakes are higher than they seem. The trouble is that it is difficult to control the quality and measure the outcomes of continuing education. Often, relationships between education and productivity improvements are hard to demonstrate.

But for planning purposes, consider the following: What professions are sensitive to change? Are certain issues in the industry of special importance for some members of the organization to know about? How important are continuing education efforts relative (1) to each other or (2) to other possible instructional initiatives?

Occupational Education. As its name implies, occupational education is geared to meeting the special needs of specific job groups, families, or clusters. It implies *instruction intended to facilitate movement within or between job or occupational categories.* Employees in each category have their own distinct learning needs in their present jobs (a training issue) and in preparing for movement to new, future jobs (an educational issue).

What education is presently being offered to members of each occupational category in your organization? What education should be offered to them in the future? For what purposes?

Of special note is the emergence of interest in occupational certification in many fields (Hale 2000). *Certification* implies that an individual has met rigorous standards of competence. While many fields have long enjoyed certification, the success of certification programs in the information technology world has sparked attention across many other emerging fields.

Methods of Delivering Employee Educational Programs

How can employee educational programs be delivered? There are several ways. They include the following:

I In-house, through formal group instruction
I In-house, through informal group instruction
I In-house-sponsored, externally developed instruction
I External instruction, sponsored by senior-level universities
I External instruction, sponsored by community colleges
I External instruction, sponsored by vendors
I External degree programs
I Other delivery methods

Each delivery method has its own advantages and disadvantages. The appropriate choice depends on the cost versus the benefits and on the most likely means of achieving desired outcomes. Each is a way of preparing people to meet the demands of the future.

In-House, Formal Group Instruction. Similar to organized training, in-house, formal group instruction is defined as a group of people assembled for a structured, organized purpose designed and delivered by staff of the organization at the organization's work site, to prepare participants for promotion or other career movement. It is this emphasis on future career change that distinguishes in-house education from training.

Chief advantages of in-house programs include

I Cost efficiency gained through group, rather than individual, instruction
I Consistency of treatment for those on similar career paths

▪   Possibility of increased personal contacts and improved social interaction between people with similar career aspirations within the organization

There are two disadvantages: In-house trainers might not be as good as external trainers, and the costs of designing and delivering instruction might be greater than when external trainers are hired on a short-term basis.

It is worth emphasizing that in-house group instruction refers to *where* education is carried out, not *how* it is carried out. In short, participants in such instruction have membership in an organization in common with one another and can meet as a group. But it is possible to conduct such instruction in the classroom, online, or through a blend of multiple delivery methods. While many practitioners and decision-makers remain enthralled with online methods alone, others have discovered the great power and the complex issues involved in blending delivery methods (Rowley, Bunker, and Cole 2002).

In-House, Informal Group Instruction. This delivery method is similar to but is not precisely the same as formal group instruction. WLP practitioners and line managers identify people in line for promotion, transfer, or other work changes. These people are encouraged to form a study group and, in cooperation with each other and their superiors, draw up a learning plan to guide career preparation. They meet on or off company property; they can request guest speakers; and they can meet during the day or evening. Such groups often endure even after members are promoted or transferred.

This method places responsibility for learning on the learners. They are free as a *community of practice* to set their own learning objectives and meet them (Wenger 1999). The group setting provides learners with the support of other people like themselves from whom they can learn and with whom they can interact. However, this method depends heavily on the participation of members. Not all group members will participate, particularly when they regard others as competitors.

In-House-Sponsored, Externally Developed Instruction. This method is almost the same as in-house, formal group instruction, with the exception that educational materials are developed and delivered by outsiders. These outsiders can be faculty members from local universities or community colleges, e-learning vendors, or other sources of education. They can also be experienced consultants specializing in training for particular audiences, such as new or prospective supervisors, managers, or technical specialists.

In some organizations, consultants have been called in to offer instruction for such reasons as the following:

I   In-house WLP practitioners lack credibility with line managers, who always assume anybody from the outside is an "expert."

I   Decision-makers sometimes find an experienced instructor who requires less time to develop a planned learning event than in-house trainers will.

I   The consultant's quoted rates compare favorably to the costs of in-house presenters when a cost-benefit analysis is used.

I   In-house WLP staff members are scarce. They are already overburdened with duties, so temporary external consultants are used when extra WLP staff members are needed for short-term projects.

External Instruction Sponsored by Universities. Many senior-level universities offer extensive continuing education and special workshops. Some seminars are offered to the public regularly; others are tailor-made to meet the specific needs of one organization. Topics range from pure self-improvement to basic training on a range of topics.

For WLP practitioners who set out to meet a specific organizational need by this method, the best advice is to find out the names of the directors of continuing education at local universities. (Many can be found quickly on the Web.) Get on mailing lists and, when workshop brochures arrive, post them on bulletin boards or contact specific individuals who should attend. Better yet, organize a summary of many brochures and circulate it to those who have learning needs. Research the school, its offerings, and the specific programs before sending the information out to people. Ask for detailed course outlines. Check the reactions of employees who attend.

External Instruction Sponsored by Community Colleges. Local community colleges are also a source of instruction. Many have designated units to assist business. Government funding for training or retraining is sometimes available. Community colleges should be handled in much the same way as senior-level institutions. Start by finding out names. Then determine what needs they can help meet and how well they can help meet them.

External Instruction Sponsored by Vendors. There are thousands of WLP consultants and vendors in the United States. They range from one-person outfits to large, well-known firms. As with universities, the practitioner who wishes to find a good vendor faces a major challenge. Some common methods of locating vendors include word-of-mouth referrals, directories, and reviews of people who have published on the topic.

It might help to develop your own consultant inventory. That way, you have a base of proven people on which to draw for needs as they arise.

What about seminars and workshops offered by vendors? Handle them as you would university offerings. Look carefully at brochures announcing seminars to see if they match up to the needs of your organization or specific people. Look for course purpose, objectives, instructional strategies, content, instructor qualifications, cost, and location. If this information is not listed (for example, if the course outline is vague), contact the vendor directly. Try to find several sources of instruction on the same subject. Compare them. Ask for names of past students, call them, and inquire about the course.

External Degree Programs. The so-called external degree program is a means by which employed adults earn college credit or even college degrees, ranging from the two-year associate's degree to doctoral degrees. Costs, residency requirements, quality, and topics (majors) vary widely. In many respects they resemble correspondence programs, though there may be additional requirements. For WLP practitioners looking for ways to educate employees, external degree programs are one option. They should be evaluated in the same ways as external vendors and correspondence schools.

It is worth noting that traditional and nontraditional academic institutions offer educational programs on the Web. Indeed, there has been an explosion of interest in such programs. Institutional offerings of these *distance education programs*, defined as "a collection of innovative approaches to the delivery of instruction to learners who are remote from their teacher" (see Pam Dixon's work posted at http://wellspring.isinj.com/faq_dl.html),* continue to experience phenomenal growth. Pam Dixon estimates that some five to seven million people currently participate in some form of planned distance learning program. Estimates vary as to how many such programs exist, and the estimates range from 93 accredited programs to 700 programs.

How well have these programs been working? According to Dixon,

> "Preliminary findings from a number of studies have been quite positive: The U.S. Office of Technology Assessment, which is sponsored by the U.S. Congress, has found in several reports that distance learners do as well or better in their courses and on achievement tests than traditional students. Dr. William Souder taught the same graduate-level course simultaneously at two traditional campuses, Georgia Tech and the University of Alabama, and one online school, National Technical University, and found that distance students not only learned more but also gained social skills and a network of student peers. And annual comparisons done by the University of Phoenix have consistently found that distance students perform as well or better in their classes, and interact with the instructor and each other more, than their campus-based peers. There have been similar findings in numerous small, less-formal studies."

Other Delivery Methods. There are countless other ways by which to deliver employee education. In fact, delivery methods are limited only by the imagination of learners and WLP practitioners. Consider a few other delivery options, in addition to those already discussed:

I *Off-the-shelf training packages sold by book publishers, vendors, and others.* They can greatly reduce the time needed for course development, though they have to be treated in compliance with existing copyright laws.

I *Computer-based and computer-assisted instruction.* These sources offer great flexibility and individualized instruction. Some are nothing more than electronic page-turners; others are sophisticated video productions

---

* *Please note: These links existed at the time this book was written. However, not all Web links are durable. It is possible that these links are no longer available.*

that can be displayed by CD-ROM or DVD-ROM on the computer; and still others are interactive courses. (A good rule of thumb is that the more interactivity, the better.)

I   *Books.* College texts are particularly useful as self-study packages.

I   *Articles published in professional and academic journals.* These can be circulated to people in the organization to contribute toward their continuing education.

I   *Informal speakers' bureaus.* Identify knowledgeable people in the organization or community and ask them to meet with those who have specific needs. The setting need not be formal. Consider "brown-bag lunch discussions," for instance.

Tuition Reimbursement Programs. Though not a delivery method, a tuition reimbursement program is an important inducement for employee education. Often associated with college courses attended on the employee's own time, tuition reimbursement might be possible for virtually any external education, including pursuit of a GED certificate, attendance at public seminars or conferences, or degree or non-degree college course work.

Individuals participate in external instruction for many reasons. Among the most-common reasons are to advance in a career, build competencies, socialize with other people, and learn how to be a better citizen. Employers sponsor such programs to meet specific HR needs, comply with negotiated labor agreements, and improve employee job satisfaction and morale.

It is a good idea to develop a written company policy on tuition reimbursement and procedures for obtaining it. The policy should stipulate the purpose of the program and cover employee eligibility, types of courses (or other experiences) that qualify for reimbursement, extent of support (100-percent or only partial), the intended relationship (if any) between the program and job-related performance improvement, and the intended relationship between external and internal Talent Development activities.

Internally sponsored educational efforts should be closely tied to organizational culture, policies, and expectations. Externally sponsored educational efforts are more appropriate for giving employees the chance to gain new insights and hear about practices in other organizations. Procedures should clarify how to obtain reimbursement in terms of voucher preparation, minimum grade (such as C) necessary for reimbursement, documents that must be furnished as proof of course completion, travel policy, and approvals that may be necessary.

Tying Employee Education to Organizational Strategy for the Development of Talent

While employee education is geared toward individual improvement and preparation for advancement, it should be integrated with a larger, integrated organizational strategy for developing talent.

WLP practitioners, line managers, and even learners themselves should consider such questions as these at regular intervals:

I What is the purpose of employee education programs?

I How are these programs contributing to the realization of organizational strategy for the development of talent, HR strategy, individual career plans, and strategic business plans?

I How consistent are these programs with other learning initiatives? What causes any inconsistencies? How can inconsistencies be corrected?

I How do outcomes of employee educational efforts affect employee development and training for specific jobs? How should they be related?

I What employee education policy should be established? How should it be made an integral part of Talent Development policy?

By addressing these questions and acting on them, WLP practitioners can tie employee education to a strategic plan for developing talent.

Activity 10–1: Continuing Education

Directions: Use this activity to structure your thinking about continuing education. Answer the questions that follow in the space provided.

Special Needs

1. What professions/occupations in the organization are especially sensitive to change? List them.

Issues

2. Are certain issues in the industry of special importance for employees to know about? If so, list them.

Importance

3. How important are these efforts relative to each other? Are there other initiatives to which the organization could devote time and effort?

Activity 10–2: Occupational Education

Directions: Use this activity to structure your thinking about occupational education. Answer the questions that follow in the space provided.

Occupational Group	What education is presently being offered to members of this category by the organization?	What education should be offered to members of this category in the future?	Why should education be offered to members of this category in the future?
1. Executives			
2. Senior managers			
3. Middle managers			
4. Supervisors			
5. Professionals			

Activity 10–2: *(continued)*

Occupational Group	What education is presently being offered to members of this category by the organization?	What education should be offered to members of this category in the future?	Why should education be offered to members of this category in the future?
6. Executives			
7. Senior managers			
8. Middle managers			
9. Supervisors			
10. Professionals			

Activity 10–3: Tying Employee Education to Organizational Strategy for the Development of Talent

Directions: Use this activity to structure your thinking about how to tie employee education to organizational strategy for Talent Development. Answer the questions that follow in the space provided.

Purpose

1.   What is the purpose(s) of employee education?

Linkages

2.   How are employee education programs contributing to realization of

a. Organizational strategy for Talent Development?

b. HR strategy?

c. Individual career plans?

d. Strategic business plans?

3.   How consistent are employee education programs with

a. Formal training?

b. Developmental efforts of all kinds?

Activity 10–3: *(continued)*

Occupational Groups

What educational efforts should be offered to members of each of the following occupational groups to contribute to implementation of organizational strategy for the development of talent?

Executives	
Senior managers	
Middle managers	
Supervisors	
Professionals	
Technical employees	
Sales employees	
Office/Clerical workers	
Skilled workers	
Unskilled workers	

CHAPTER 11

EMPLOYEE TRAINING

Employee training is perhaps the activity most frequently associated with Talent Development. The evidence, however, suggests that efforts are not always linked to supporting the realization of the organization's strategic objectives, at least in the case of management training. A study in the United Kingdom, for instance, revealed that management training is rarely tied to strategy (Staunton and Giles 2001).

Training should produce immediate changes in job performance so that supervisors and trainees themselves can see the difference between job performance before training and job performance after training. Its effects should thus be more immediate than those for employee development or education.

This chapter defines traditional training and explains its relationship to job performance. It describes each step in a model for designing and delivering training and outlines the difference between traditional training and strategic training. A model to guide strategic training is described in the first few pages of the chapter.

What Is Employee Training?

Training is a short-term, individually focused change effort that is intended to improve job performance. It narrows the gaps between what individuals know or do and what they should know or do in order to be successful. The traditional approach to training is not the same as employee education, which prepares individuals for future jobs, and employee development, which contributes to organizational learning by cultivating the collective competencies of individuals in group settings.

What Is Job Performance?

Definition. In a classic definition, Bailey (1982,4) defined performance as "the *result* of a pattern of actions carried out to satisfy an objective according to some standard." It is not the same as *behavior*, which means observable action. Appropriate job behavior may or may not result in good job performance. Performance is equated with *results;* behavior is equated only with the *actions taken to achieve results.*

Job performance consists of three interrelated elements (Bailey 1982): (1) the *individual* (who?), (2) the *activity* (what?), and (3) the *context* (where?). Individual performance is influenced by *ability* (what are the individual's capacities to perform?) and *motivation* (how much does the person feel inclined to perform?) (Cummings and Schwab 1973). To improve job performance, change must occur in the individual, in the activity, in the context, or in some combination of the three.

What Is the Relationship between Training and Job Performance?

Training can improve job performance by (1) improving individual abilities, (2) stimulating motivation, (3) matching individual ability to activity requirements, and/or (4) matching the individual to contextual requirements. However, training cannot change job activities or work content. It changes individuals by building the competencies essential to performing the work.

How Is Training Related to Planning?

Training contributes to the realization of organizational strategy for the development of talent, HR plans, and strategic business plans.

Training and Organizational Strategy for the Development of Talent. To formulate organizational strategy for the development of talent, managers and employees must have a firm grasp of present strengths and weaknesses in job performance. The reason is that planning should begin with information about present conditions. Training needs assessment provides detailed information about present conditions.

Training and HR Planning. One way to narrow a gap between present labor supply and future labor demand is to improve the present productivity of job incumbents. In this sense, then, training helps implement HR plans by improving the productivity of people already employed in the firm. In short, training makes better use of existing employee talent.

Training and Strategic Business Planning. Training contributes to the realization of strategic business plans in two ways. First, it furnishes people involved in formulating plans with skills necessary to do it. Second, it provides new knowledge and skills to employees at each organizational level so that they can go about their jobs in ways leading to the realization of long-term plans.

A Model for Designing and Delivering Training

The Model. There are almost as many ways to conceptualize training design and delivery as there are authors on the subject. Variations exist because authors do not agree on the same philosophy of instruction or learning. For the purpose of this discussion, the traditional performance-based model of training design is a good starting point. It is commonly accepted in the WLP field.

To apply this model, the WLP practitioner must

1. Identify opportune occasions to apply it.
2. Assess learner needs.
3. Clarify key characteristics of learners that affect how they should be trained.
4. Analyze work and instructional settings and take them into account as training needs are identified.

5. Carry out detailed work analysis in order to determine what individuals do in their jobs.

6. Prepare training objectives designed to narrow gaps between what trainees *actually* know or do and what they *should* know or do.

7. Create tests and other ways of measuring performance.

8. Arrange training objectives in an appropriate sequence.

9. Identify appropriate instructional delivery methods.

10. Prepare and select appropriate content to match objectives.

Following these design steps, training is delivered and evaluated.

Identifying Occasions to Use the Approach. Training is one solution to a performance problem. When individuals cannot perform due to lack of knowledge or of a skill, they have a training need. On the other hand, when they are able to perform and *choose* not to do so, they have a non-training need that requires corrective action other than training.

Of course, problems in the real world rarely appear in a straightforward way. More often they are complicated and appear in random order. Managers and WLP practitioners must analyze problems so that corrective action addresses causes rather than symptoms. A WLP practitioner who confronts a job performance problem should ask several questions about it.

First, *what **should** employees be doing?* Have work standards been established and communicated? Employees can hardly be expected to perform when minimally acceptable work methods or outcomes have not been clarified. Nor can they perform appropriately when they have not been informed about those requirements.

Second, *what are employees **actually** doing?* How are employees presently carrying out their jobs? What results are they getting? It is hard to identify a problem when present status is unknown. Are some employees performing better than others? If so, why?

Third, *what differences exist between what employees **should** be doing and what they **are** doing?* Can WLP practitioners pinpoint particular "trouble spots" in work methods or in results achieved? Are these trouble spots common among groups of people, or only for individuals?

In a classic discussion, Laird distinguished between *macro* and *micro training needs*. The latter "exists for just one person, or for a very small population"; the former exists "in a large group of employees—frequently in the entire population with the same job classification." New employees, upon entry to the firm, possess macro needs; problem employees, who have trouble performing some facet of their jobs but are already experienced, possess micro needs. However, not *all* problems stem from training needs (Laird 1985, 49).

Fourth, *how **important** are discrepancies between what employees should be doing and what they are doing?* There is little point to wasting time correcting unimportant discrepancies. In fact, it is frustrating to employees to have their work "nitpicked." An effective manager knows when to intercede and when not to. If job performance discrepancies cost more than it costs to solve them, however, they are important enough to warrant corrective action. Training is one such action.

*Fifth, assuming that discrepancies are important and cannot be tolerated, what **causes** them?* Do employees know how to perform appropriately? Do they possess the necessary skills to do so? Or do performance problems result from other causes?

Sixth, *what should be done about **non-training needs**?* If a performance problem stems from a cause other than lack of individual knowledge or skill, WLP practitioners need to determine that cause. They can begin by looking at

I   *Allocation of work duties.* Are duties inappropriately allocated across departments or jobs? To solve problems stemming from poor or inappropriate allocation of work duties, job or work group redesign—not training—should be used.

I   *Policies.* Are company policies interfering with job requirements or with realities of the work place? If so, review policies and change them as necessary. Then train people to perform in ways consistent with the new policies.

I   *Rewards.* Are rewards, supposedly based on one set of behaviors or outcomes, really based on others? Examine incentives for and against people performing as desired. Change the incentives, if necessary. Training will not solve a problem stemming from incentives or rewards that are at odds with desired performance (Kerr 1975).

I   *Leadership.* How much do supervisors agree with goals and objectives established at higher levels? Team-building and key changes in leadership should be used to deal with leadership problems. Training should not be used when leadership issues or politics are the root causes of a performance problem.

I   *Feedback.* How well, how often, and how clearly do individuals receive feedback about their performance? From whom do they receive it? The frequency of feedback should be increased, or its quality should be improved, to correct problems stemming from poor feedback. If performance problems stem from lack of feedback, employee training will not solve them.

I   *Group norms.* How well do desired work methods and outcomes match up to traditions among co-workers? Organization development interventions, not training, should be directed to problems stemming from problems with group norms.

I   *Practice.* Are individuals asked to perform a task often enough to gain proficiency? If not, they should be given planned opportunities to practice on the job. Training should be used to provide practice only as a last resort, because it is too expensive to remove workers from the job just to give them practice.

I   *Motivation.* Do individuals believe their performance will lead to achieving the rewards or outcomes they desire? Do they value those rewards or outcomes? If not, training will not induce them to behave in desired ways, because incentives are lacking.

I   *Ability.* Is the individual mentally or physically able to perform as desired? If a job performance problem exists for one person even after corrective action, consider job transfer or termination. If it exists for everyone, consider automating the work or redesigning the job.

For more-detailed information about ways to solve performance problems caused by issues that do not lend themselves to training solutions, see Rothwell, Hohne, and King (2000).

Seventh, *what should be done about training needs?* Many people continue to associate "training" with off-the-job, classroom-based instruction, even as increasing amounts of information-based training is moved from classroom to various e-learning formats. Even many WLP professionals associate training with off-the-job, classroom-based instruction, perhaps because they associate it with traditional schooling.

Classroom training is an expensive solution. It is costly to develop and deliver. WLP staff members are tied up for long time periods; instructional materials cost tidy sums to develop; line employees must offer assistance during instructional design and are away from work during instructional delivery. In most cases, employees are not producing, but are being paid while receiving instruction.

For these reasons, WLP practitioners should consider alternatives to classroom training before designing it. There are a few specific issues to consider: (1) *The problem(s) to be solved.* Do they lend themselves to solutions other than classroom training? (2) *Time frame(s).* How much time is there to develop and deliver formal training to solve the problem? If sufficient time is not available, what alternatives exist? (3) *Expertise.* Is the requisite knowledge available in the organization to design and deliver training to solve the performance problem? If not, can it be located externally? (4) *Resources.* What resources are available for dealing with the performance problem? Are they adequate to fund training design and delivery? (5) *Importance.* Just how important is the problem to the organization? (6) *Scope of the problem.* How many individuals are affected? One? A group? Everyone in the department, division, or organization? (7) *Need for consistency.* Is there a special need for imposing consistency on the application of policies and/or procedures? Classroom training is appropriate only when the performance problems lend themselves to no other solutions, time frames are adequate, expertise is available, resources are adequate, the problem is important, many people are affected, and the need for consistency is great.

Here are a few alternatives to classroom training:

▎ *Job aids.* Can instructions be simplified and handed out for on-the-job use? If so, a job aid is appropriate. A *job aid* is any tool or set of instructions that can be used on the job.

I *Decision aids.* Similar to a job aid, a *decision aid* provides situation-specific instruction on what to do when certain circumstances exist. It answers this question: What should be done if all the following conditions hold true? Obviously, decision aids are appropriate only for relatively common problems. Checklists are decision aids (Joinson 1982).

I *Individualized instruction.* Can training needs be met through individualized instruction offered by computer, by written text, or by film or videotape?

I *On-the-job training (OJT).* Can the training needs of people be met through instruction delivered by peers or supervisors on the job? If so, well-designed OJT is appropriate (Rothwell and Kazanas 1994).

To consider the range of media by which to deliver training, consult Marx (1999).

If WLP practitioners still believe classroom instruction is warranted after reviewing alternative approaches, then they should continue with subsequent steps in the performance-based model of instructional design and delivery.

Assessing Learner Needs.

When it is apparent that a performance problem exists, is caused by the lack of appropriate knowledge and/or skill, and lends itself to a training solution, then WLP practitioners should focus on the problem in a more detailed manner. Many find that instructional systems design is an appropriate guide for developing rigorous instruction (Rothwell and Kazanas 1998). However, as with everything, there are always those who find fault, and that is no less true with instructional systems design as with anything else (see Gordon and Zemke 2000; Zemke and Rossett 2002).

As a first step, WLP practitioners should assess learner needs (Gupta, 1998). As traditionally defined, a *learning need* is synonymous with a discrepancy between *what employees should know or do* and *what they actually know or do. A training need* is more specific: it is a job performance discrepancy resulting from lack of knowledge or skill on the present job.

This step in designing training is crucial. If needs are improperly identified, no amount of instruction will meet them (Rothwell and Sredl 2000). As a consequence, all subsequent steps in the design process will prove fruitless.

Think of learner needs assessment as a flexible process. First, WLP practitioners decide how to carry out needs assessment. They ask themselves these questions:

I *What are the goals/objectives or desired outcomes of the assessment process?* What results are sought from it?

I *Whose needs are being assessed?* Is assessment focused on one job category, or on all of them?

I *How will information be collected?* What approaches to data collection are appropriate, given constraints on time, resources, and conditions in the organization?

I *What specific guidelines should be established in advance about data collection methods?* In other words, should special care be taken when using surveys, interview guides, work observations, or other methods of data collection? If so, why?

I *What analytical techniques should be used to interpret the results of needs assessment, once data have been collected?*

After these questions have been answered, WLP practitioners carry out the needs assessment, implementing the plan established in the prior step. They should take care to avoid getting sidetracked on issues unrelated to needs that have initially been pinpointed for examination. Only rarely should a needs assessment plan be altered during the assessment process. Departure from the needs assessment plan is appropriate only when new information comes to light that changes the assumptions on which the initial assessment plan was based.

Third, clarify the precise nature of performance problems that are to be solved by training. Following completion of needs assessment, WLP practitioners should clarify just what problems they plan to address through training. When they also uncover information about non-training (management) needs, they should relay it to executives so that additional corrective action can also be taken in areas unrelated to knowledge or skills.

The choice of how to approach a needs assessment depends on the skills of WLP practitioners and the assumptions made about training by line managers, employees, and top executives. Cost is often touted as the single most important issue, but it is not always as important as it is made out to be. What often matters most is what practitioners or line managers prefer, and how committed they are to solving a problem.

What little we know about common business practice in training needs assessment methods in the United States suggests that formal approaches are rarely used in even the largest corporations. Instead, informal approaches such as brief talks, meetings with line supervisors, interviews, and observation are more common. They are less time-consuming than formal studies, and WLP practitioners are often under pressure to act quickly in a way that makes detailed front-end analysis difficult. In addition, informal approaches do not raise expectations for improvement among many people in the same way that highly visible surveys tend to do. That is often an advantage. Unmet expectations create frustration among line managers and employees and eventually damage the WLP department's credibility.

Clarifying Key Characteristics of Learners

Who are the learners? What are their characteristics? How will those characteristics affect training? These questions should be considered after needs assessment, but before preparation of instructional objectives.

In most cases, WLP practitioners start out with a general idea of who will receive the training. In some cases, the task of identifying important characteristics of learners is easier than in others. For example, newly hired employees with no prior work experience share some common characteristics: (1) they do not know the organizational culture, (2) they have a limited store of personal experiences on which to draw, (3) they know relatively little about specific jobs, though they may have had formal education in the general field, and (4) quite often they are in the same general age group and stage of personal development.

More-experienced workers often have many things in common with members of their work group: the same attitudes, familiarity with group tasks, and similar socialization experiences. It is also likely that they have been influenced in their job performance by the expectations of the same superior, and perhaps are classified in roughly the same age group and career stage.

For WLP practitioners, information of this kind is valuable for gearing training to solve common problems, address common interests, and deal with individual concerns of a target trainee group.

Three questions about learner characteristics are important to consider prior to specifying training objectives. First, what learner characteristics will generally affect training on a particular activity, task, or job duty? Second, which learner characteristics will affect training on job activities, tasks, or duties for a specific group of people at a specific time? Finally, how can these characteristics be planned for? Long-term, general characteristics of learners are influenced by organizational selection, recruitment, and promotion practices; short-term, specific characteristics of one group are influenced by special problems or issues on the job that affect performance and that may also affect interests and expectations. Exhibit 11–1 illustrates this concept.

Exhibit 11–1: Key Issues to Consider about Learner Characteristics

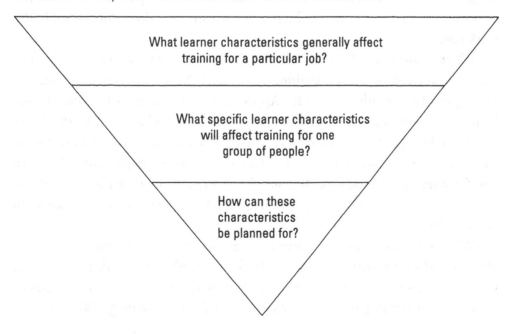

How do WLP practitioners deal with individual differences? Several strategies are possible. One is to identify prerequisites for all training and screen out those participants who do not meet the selection criteria. To minimize the influence of individual differences, restrict access to training: People who do not meet selection criteria for training because they do not possess prerequisite knowledge or skills are given remedial instruction to prepare them for it.

An alternative is to identify different ability levels of employees who are to attend training and establish different training for each level. This approach is similar to "ability grouping" in secondary schools. Trainees are divided into three categories, and training programs are geared to the needs of learners in each category.

Analyzing the Setting

Training should not be planned in a vacuum. It makes sense to analyze up front the settings in which (1) training will subsequently be applied and (2) training is to occur. Not surprisingly, training conducted in a setting resembling the work site is more likely to influence subsequent, post-instructional job performance than training conducted in a setting that does not resemble the work site.

What conditions face an employee in the work setting? Consider: (1) *Physical condition:* Are conditions adequate? Safe? (2) *Tools/resources:* Are they up-to-date? Easily accessible? Appropriate to the work? (3) *Group norms:* What work methods are acceptable to co-workers? What work methods are unacceptable? (4) *Supervisory expectations*: What do supervisors expect from trainees? (5) *Employee expectations:* What do employees expect from the work and from training? Much like learner characteristics, work-setting conditions affect the subsequent willingness of and job opportunities for people to apply training.

What conditions face a trainee in the instructional setting? Consider: (1) *Physical conditions:* How much do they resemble the work setting? Can they be made similar? (2) *Tools/equipment:* How closely do the tools and equipment used in training resemble those used in the work setting? (3) *Resources:*

Is there adequate time, money, and staff to carry out training effectively? (4) *Philosophy/beliefs:* Are employees exposed to a radically different philosophy in training than they are exposed to on the job?

Carrying Out Detailed Work Analysis

When the need for training is justifiable and when learner characteristics and work/instructional settings have been analyzed, WLP practitioners are ready to carry out a detailed work analysis to determine: (1) job duties, activities, and tasks; (2) their importance; (3) the order in which they should be enacted; (4) the frequency of their performance; and (5) background knowledge, skills, and attitudes necessary to carry out those duties, activities, or tasks. The purpose of work analysis is to clarify the *most appropriate* way to do the work. "Appropriate" is the operative word. It can mean: (1) the way an *experienced* worker performs the task, activity, duty, or job; (2) the way the *best (exemplary) worker* actually performs the task, activity, duty, or job; or (3) the way the task, activity, duty, or job should be *ideally* performed.

Regardless of how "appropriate" is interpreted, the usual starting point for work analysis is the task level. A *task* is a discrete activity with a definite beginning and ending. Many tasks, grouped together, make up a position occupied by one person in an organization. A *job* is the generic name for many positions with the same title. An *occupation* comprises similar jobs in different organizations.

Task analysis is a detailed examination of every discrete component of a job or position. There are many ways to go about doing it (Jonassen, Hannum, and Tessmer 1989). But the basic steps are simple enough: (1) break down the job into component tasks, (2) describe how each task is carried out, (3) identify which tasks are most important, difficult to learn, and most difficult to carry out, (4) sequence the tasks as they are performed on the job, and (5) determine what the worker must know or be able to do to carry out each task. Task analysis is appropriate for blue-collar jobs and manual trades in which work behaviors are easily observed. Alternative approaches are usually more appropriate for white-collar occupations.

Preparing Training Objectives

Objectives are obtained from work analysis and needs assessment. From work analysis, WLP practitioners obtain information about *what must be done to achieve desired performance;* from needs assessment, practitioners find out *what people are actually doing and where discrepancies exist.*

Instructional objectives clarify outcomes to be achieved by the end of a training experience. *Terminal objectives* are outcomes sought by the end of a planned learning event; *enabling objectives* are outcomes sought during the learning event to help the learner achieve terminal objectives. In short, terminal objectives express the desired outcomes of a course or other planned learning experience; enabling objectives express the desired outcomes at different points during a course. Enabling objectives are thus rationally related to and supportive of their terminal counterparts.

Instructional objectives are blueprints for training design. Trainees who achieve objectives demonstrate they can perform a job's activities or tasks. As Exhibit 11-2 illustrates, objectives should be linked directly to job activities. Achievement of objectives should demonstrate ability to perform tasks or activities.

There are different levels of objectives. In training, a terminal objective is specific. It describes what the learner can do, what tools or other requirements are necessary for the performance, and ways to measure the quality of performance. In employee education, a terminal objective is not as specific as in training. It clarifies what the learner can do and under what conditions, but not necessarily how well the learner can perform. It is too general to provide a criterion for performance. In employee development, a terminal objective is expressed for a work group—not, as in training or education, for individuals. The objective may specify what the group can do, under what conditions, and how well. Terminal training objectives are enabling objectives for employee education, as individuals prepare for performance at higher levels of technical competence or responsibility. Likewise, terminal objectives of training and employee education are enabling objectives for employee development (see Exhibit 11-3).

Exhibit 11–2: The Relationship between Work Tasks and Instructional Objectives

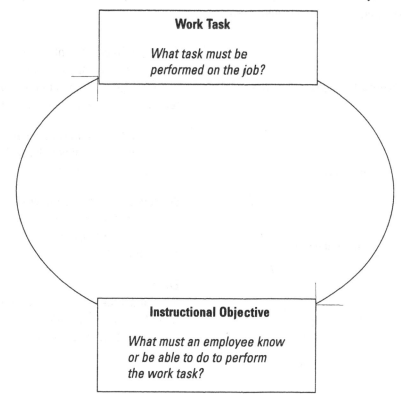

Several resources are available to help novice WLP practitioners write training objectives. The basic format is not difficult to master. A typical objective takes the following form (Mager 1972):

Upon completion of this [course, unit, or lesson], the trainee will be able to

▪ *Do what?*
▪ *How well?*
▪ *Using what tools or other resources? Under what conditions?*

Creating Tests

In performance-based training, test items are derived from objectives. They are prepared after objectives are created but before decisions are made about delivery

Exhibit 11–3: The Relationship between Instructional Objectives in Training, Employee Education, and Employee Development

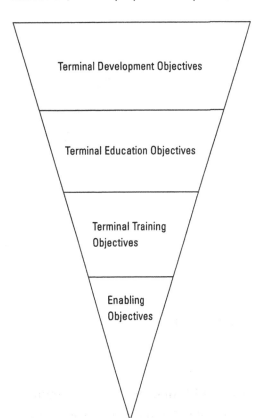

Terminal Development Objectives

Terminal Education Objectives

Terminal Training Objectives

Enabling Objectives

Employee Development Objectives
What must the employee know/be able to do in a group setting to contribute to realizing group goals and objectives?

Employee Education Objectives
What must the employee know/be able to do to prepare for a future job?

Employee Training Objectives
What must the employee know/be able to do to perform his or her present job competently?

Enabling Objectives
What must the employee know/be able to do to perform specific tasks of his or her present job competently?

methods and instructional content. Tests are the basis for decisions about delivery and content; test items are built-in benchmarks to measure trainee achievement during and after instruction.

The relationship between job task, instructional objective, and test item is thus quite close. The task is what the person is to do on the job; the objective is an instructional outcome linked to the task; and a test item measures how well the objective has been achieved or is being achieved.

There are several kinds of tests: (1) *oral,* administered by voice, (2) *written,* administered by written text, and (3) *performance,* administered by having a trainee demonstrate a task or an activity required on the job.

Oral and written tests take different forms: multiple choice, fill-in-the-blank, true-false, essay, and matching. The point worth emphasizing is that each form is more appropriate for measuring some objectives than others.

Arranging Objectives in Sequence

Sequencing objectives means arranging them so that they will provide a foundation for designing and delivering instruction. There are several approaches to sequencing. Objectives may be arranged

1. *From simple to complex.* Begin with simple ideas and progress to increasingly complicated ones. "Simple ideas" have few parts or distinctions; "complex ideas" have many parts, distinctions, or exceptions to rules.
2. *From known to unknown.* Base sequencing on prerequisites. Each idea, concept, or objective is a building block for later ones. The WLP practitioner begins with what learners know and progressively moves into unknown areas.
3. *From whole to part.* Begin with a simplified model of all steps or tasks in a job, introduce trainees to it, and then proceed to explore each part. With this sequencing method, trainees can place each part of the training experience in the context of the whole course or job.
4. *From past to present to future.* Begin historically, and focus on time. This method is appropriate when instruction is geared to contrasting past, present, or future methods.
5. *From simple to complex treatments of alternating subjects.* This is the spiral approach to organizing instruction. Several topics or issues are treated at a simple level. Later, they are treated again at a more complex level. Thus, "content topics are systematically reintroduced at periodic intervals. Two purposes are served by such a scheme. First, the previously learned knowledge of the topic is given a review, which tends to improve its retention. And second, the topic may be progressively elaborated when it is reintroduced, leading to broadened understanding and transfer of learning" (Gagné and Briggs 1979, 141).

6. *In other ways.* These five sequencing methods are by no means the only ones. There are others, including (1) *the pyramid,* in which some objectives are covered with all learners but other objectives are only covered with some learners, (2) *the doughnut,* in which a common core of instructional objectives is surrounded by specialized ones for some employee groups, and (3) *the network,* in which some objectives are related to others in a grand scheme (Knowles 1980, Romiszowski 1981).

Philosophy of Sequencing. The basic principle of sequencing is that prerequisite knowledge should always be treated first. Adults resist having learning sequences imposed on them, especially when they believe a different sequence is more appropriate to suit their needs or to cope with immediate job problems.

Identifying Appropriate Delivery Methods

Choice of delivery methods follows sequencing of objectives. At this point, WLP practitioners make decisions about *what media to use* (classroom, videotape, individualized text, etc.). But what are some delivery methods? What media should be used for delivery?

Huczynski (1983) lists and describes 350 delivery methods. Some are appropriate for lengthy instructional experiences; most are useful only for a portion of a course. But some of the more commonly used delivery methods are described in the sections below. Trainers should always consider the range of methods by which instruction may be delivered (Marx 1999).

Lecture. Despite the increasing availability of computer-based and video-based instruction, lecture remains the most popular and frequently used training delivery method. A *lecture* is a speech delivered in a classroom setting. Lectures can also be delivered by videotape or by teleconference to large groups at scattered locations.

Pure lecture is one-way communication: the instructor speaks and trainees listen. The burden rests with the instructor. Trainees are passive recipients of information. The average speed of thought is over 400 words per minute, but the average speed of talking is around 100 words per minute. Trainees have a tough time keeping their attention fixed on the lecturer. They grow bored quickly.

Fortunately, WLP practitioners need not restrict themselves to pure lecture. They can include visual aids to reinforce and dramatize what they say. They can also solicit questions and comments from their audience. Other techniques are also used to liven up lectures. Here are a few tips:

I Talk as fast as you please. Trainees can easily keep up.

I Vary the pitch and volume of your voice.

I Ask questions. In fact, try for one question every three minutes.

I Call people by name. That's an attention-getter.

I Be active. The more energetic and enthusiastic the presenter, the more lively the learners are likely to be.

I Use fill-in-the-blank. Give trainees handouts with key words missing. As you talk, tell them what words to insert in the blanks. Use the same approach with visual aids. Put them up on a blackboard or an overhead projector. Complete them as you talk.

I Pair the lecture with other methods such as exercises, case studies, and role plays so that trainees can participate and have to apply what they learn.

I Use lecture to do more than present information. Stimulate ideas and new lines of thought. Take advantage of small-group problem-solving methods (King, King, and Rothwell 2000).

In all likelihood, the lecture is here to stay. It will probably always exist in some form.

Independent Reading. Independent reading can be tied to other related learning experiences or can stand alone.

Independent readings can be assigned before, during, or after classroom training or tutorials. Reading is appropriate for (1) providing necessary background information that is too time-consuming to cover in a lecture, (2) adding information to a topic treated briefly in a lecture, or (3) giving the learner resources for future, self-directed learning.

It does not make sense to assign too many advance readings. The authors know of training situations in which learners were given hundreds of pages to read before class. Trainees ignored most of it. If that much background is needed, then a course should precede the training.

A better approach is to limit advance reading to less than 20 pages. Give readers instruction about what to focus on while they read. Any approach that motivates learners to read the material is good. If necessary, build in objectives and administer a follow-up test so that trainees treat advance reading as part of the course.

Reading can also stand alone. It may substitute for a lecture or a training course. Stand-alone reading is associated with off-the-shelf individualized training packages, assigned readings out of college texts or technical manuals, and programmed instruction.

Off-the-shelf packages purchased from publishers or professional societies vary greatly in quality. Some are short; some are hundreds of pages long. They are useful if reviewed and tailored to the organization by WLP practitioners and line managers before they are given to inexperienced trainees. Instructions should accompany them in order to clarify what the reader should pay special attention to and why the material is important. In most cases, readers should be asked to complete exercises included in the package. A face-to-face follow-up should be planned after completion so that learners can go over their answers to exercises with a subject matter expert who can check them and reemphasize important points from the training material.

Assigned readings should be treated like advance reading assignments: They should clarify what the learner should pay attention to and should build in learner accountability with tests, exercises, or guided activities.

Reading assignments are advantageous because they reduce training time and guide learners quickly through background material. They are especially useful in small organizations or in those with a small WLP staff or slow movement into or out of some job classes. They are disadvantageous because they may require substantial tailoring to work effectively in unique organizational settings.

Panels. A *panel* is a group of people, usually experts on a specific subject, who have assembled to discuss a topic. Panels may be highly structured and focused on one or more topics; they may be unstructured and cover many topics. In a *structured format*, each speaker on the panel (usually one of six or fewer) has a strict time allotment. In a *focused format*, each speaker addresses a different facet of a topic.

Panel discussions often resemble short lectures. Audience participation is discouraged. Question-and-answer sessions are structured after each speaker or after all of them. Few panel discussions encourage active interaction between panelists and audience.

To design a panel, simply decide on the learning objectives in advance. Then select speakers who can help achieve them. The choice of moderator is most important, because the moderator controls time used by speakers, encourages questions between audience and panelists, and guides panel members as they discuss a subject.

Panels are appropriate when participants bring open minds to the learning experience. They are also useful for exploring problems or issues for which pat answers are not available. Variations of the expert panel include learner panels made up of trainees, manager panels made up of trainees' supervisors, and open forums geared to freewheeling exploration of a problem or issue.

Buzz groups. A *buzz group* is a small group assembled to work on a problem and report solutions back to a larger group. They are frequently used in classroom training. They may also be used in simple problem-solving.

To arrange a buzz-group experience, the WLP practitioner: (1) selects group members or provides a means to do so, such as by counting off or drawing numbers out of a hat; (2) clarifies the task confronting the group and the results expected from the group; (3) makes clear any constraints (for example, "I'll give you 15 minutes" or "Don't look at your notes"); and (4) provides special instructions or materials. Group members may be asked to do almost anything: work on a case study or role play together; discuss an issue, problem, or common concern; define a term; classify information; or answer questions. Buzz groups stimulate creativity on a relatively structured problem or issue, particularly one just discussed in training. They are not appropriate when individual, independent mastery of subject matter is the aim of instruction. After all, it is hard to tell how much each person contributed to a group solution.

Exercises. This is a broad category of methods. Anything requiring learners to practice knowledge or skill is an exercise. Perhaps the simplest is a list of questions that learners answer individually or in groups. Other exercises include case studies, critical incidents, and role plays.

Case Study. Case studies are narrative descriptions of problem situations. Though often printed, they can be described orally by an instructor. Typically, the description is at least adequate to identify a problem and issues affecting it.

Case studies should have a real-life feel. They should excite interest and stimulate discussion. They are quite flexible. A case study can introduce a learning event, thereby serving to disorient trainees and dramatize their need for instruction. A case study is more often used in the middle or at the end of a longer discussion to illustrate a point, underscore the importance of a problem, or apply a principle.

There are six steps in preparing a case study:

1. Decide what outcomes are desired from the case study experience, as well as the general ideas that are to be illustrated.
2. Create a fictitious situation or identify a real one that serves the instructional purpose of the case.
3. Add details related to or symptomatic of the problem.
4. Create a cast of characters.
5. Write up the case.
6. Consider placing questions at the end in order to focus learner attention on key points raised by the case.

The chief disadvantage of the case study is that learners are not actually involved in the problem. For this reason, they sometimes give unrealistic answers. For more on case studies, see Boyd (1980), Ford (1970), and Pigors (1987). They have also been reinvented for application by self-directed learners (Rothwell 1999c).

The Incident Process. Sometimes called the "critical incident method," the *incident process* is a greatly condensed version of a case study. Trainees are given a one- or two-sentence problem situation and are asked to describe what action to take. Alternatively, the trainer may describe the problem situation and allow learners to pose questions for more information.

To write critical incidents, WLP practitioners follow the same basic steps as in preparing case studies. Alternatively, they may collect information about common problem situations confronting job incumbents and then provide critical incidents during training based on these problems. As a result, learners are exposed to the proper handling of real-life problems. A major advantage of the incident process is that it allows the instructor to cover much ground in a relatively short time. A major disadvantage is that trainees sometimes have trouble responding to incidents without more details.

The Role Play. *Role play* is a range of methods in which trainees put themselves in dramatic situations and act out scenes like actors in a play. A psychiatrist named Moreno is credited with the first use of role play in 1911. It was synthesized with case study and adapted for use in training by Norman R. F. Maier at the University of Michigan (Wohlking and Weiner 1981).

There are essentially two kinds of role play: structured and spontaneous. *Structured role play* helps individuals become more productive in some aspect of their work. *Spontaneous role play* helps individuals understand how they interact with others (Wohlking and Weiner 1981).

Structured role play is based on a case study. Participants receive instructions about a situation, the roles they are to play, and some goal to achieve during the role play. Preparing a structured role play involves most of the steps taken in preparing a case study: (1) decide what outcomes are desired, (2) create or identify a situation, (3) add details, and (4) create a cast of characters. From this point, the writer creates a separate role to be played by each "actor" in a "live" case.

Spontaneous role plays are based on momentary experiences. For example, an instructor asks participants to trade organizational roles, explain how they feel, put themselves in the place of another person, act out the part, imitate the behavior of one person in the group, or speak only one word at a time to voice their spontaneous feelings.

Preparation of spontaneous role play is informal. It relies entirely on spur-of-the-moment arrangements made by instructors. They prepare participants by polling the group for common problems, concerns, and issues. A brief description of role play is then provided. Instructors may even "model" a role play in front of the group, either by themselves or with handpicked confederates. In contrast, structured role plays are usually preceded by lecture, discussion, case analysis, exercises, films, videotapes, or other "warm-up" experiences. They are then followed by a description of role play. Like any experiential exercise, role play should be followed by a discussion of key points and participant insights to reinforce learning. The chief disadvantage of role play is that participants may experience difficulty in making the situation feel realistic and may resent being put on the spot to act a part or reveal their feelings in a group. If handled well, however, a role play can be very effective in stimulating insight or demonstrating a skill.

Role plays need not always be prepared by trainers. They can also be spontaneously developed by competent, take-charge learners (Rothwell 1999d).

Behavior Modeling. *Behavior modeling* is founded on social learning theory, whose proponents believe most learning occurs by observing and imitating what other people do (Bandura 1977). To prepare a training experience using behavioral modeling, the WLP practitioner (1) clarifies what results are sought, (2) analyzes behaviors of particularly effective and ineffective performers, (3) describes these behaviors, (4) acts out the behaviors to see if they are, in fact, related to appropriate and inappropriate performance, (5) develops methods to illustrate models of appropriate and inappropriate behavior (for example, on films or videotapes), (6) asks learners to practice or imitate the good performance model they observed, (7) provides feedback about how well learners exhibited desired performance, and (8) asks learners to repeat the process until they adequately demonstrate desired performance. Modeling is especially effective in supervisory training. In the latter case, instructors often choose to concentrate on interpersonal behaviors—how to get along with and lead others.

Demonstration. *Demonstration* resembles modeling. Trainers show learners how to perform tasks or operate equipment. In many respects it is perhaps the most common approach to on-the-job training (OJT), defined as planned and structured, albeit informal, instruction delivered by a supervisor to a worker at the job site.

To prepare a demonstration, the supervisor or WLP practitioner begins by (1) determining what outcomes are desired, (2) assembling necessary tools or materials, and (3) preparing a simple outline so that the process/work activity can be broken down into steps and then demonstrated. Subsequent steps are the same as those in Job Instruction Training (JIT), made famous by C. R. Allen in the 1920s. The actions of supervisor or WLP practitioner are to

1. Prepare the worker to receive instruction by putting the person at ease, determining what the employee knows already, motivating the individual to learn the task by explaining why it is important, and placing the individual in the correct position near equipment.
2. Present the process (that is, give the demonstration) by telling the worker what to do, showing the worker what to do, illustrating all steps, questioning the worker on key points, and emphasizing important points.
3. Allow the worker to demonstrate performance by asking the worker to tell what is done, having the worker demonstrate the process or steps one-by-one, asking the worker questions, and correcting any errors.
4. Follow up by making the worker subsequently responsible for performing the task/process, telling the worker who to see for more help if needed, checking up on performance frequently at first but less as time goes on, and encouraging questions (McCord 1976).

While other approaches to demonstration and on-the-job training (OJT) have been discussed, Allen's basic four-step model has withstood the test of time for 70 years.

Simulations/Games. A *simulation* resembles a lengthy role play in which many people participate. A game is a ritualized simulation, often modeled after key aspects of a work setting, in which teams compete while following pre-established rules.

Simulations take much time to prepare, test, and administer. They are appropriately used to (1) explore the elements of a large system, like an organization, because the nature of simulation allows process or system dynamics to be brought into the training situation, (2) test a course of action in situations when information is unreliable or hard-to-come-by, (3) stimulate conversation on otherwise controversial matters, (4) enliven boring material, (5) provide instruction in a context similar to that on the job, assuming the simulation replicates key features of the job environment, (6) provide an anchor for subsequent discussion of theory and concepts (or alternatively, a means to test theories and concepts previously discussed), and (7) substitute for real experiences, providing learners with opportunities to learn by experience without the attendant costs and detrimental side effects of making mistakes in real settings (Coppard 1976).

To prepare a simulation, WLP practitioners should probably begin by researching the thousands of simulations already available. It is easier to modify an existing simulation than to start from scratch.

For more intrepid practitioners who prefer to design their own simulations, the basic steps in the process appear to be deceptively simple:

1. Establish objectives. What are the intended outcomes?
2. Describe the setting. Is it to be a work site, a work group, a department, an organization, a community, or some other entity?
3. Develop a story line. Who are the key actors and actresses in the setting? What are they doing? Why?
4. Develop role descriptions. What does each actor/actress do in the setting?
5. Create the foundation for the simulation. (a) Clarify how actors/actresses are to interact. (b) Establish rules of the "game" or "simulation." (Do any procedures have to be clarified? Does a structure have to be imposed on group interaction?) (c) Create a means for decisions to have consequences. (Will players or teams be awarded points or be given feedback on how well or poorly they are performing?)
6. Test the simulation or game.
7. Revise it to fix any problems revealed through testing.

These steps are, of course, somewhat oversimplified.

The chief disadvantages of simulations have to do with time and cost. It takes much time to develop a good simulation, especially one complicated enough to portray a complex process or setting. Nor is this likely to be cheap. Yet these factors may be outweighed by the value of representing processes for training purposes.

What delivery method should be used to present instruction? The answer to this question has to do with media selection. It is one of two fundamental issues in instructional design. The other has to do with preparation or selection of content.

Over the years, instructional delivery methods have become increasingly sophisticated. Trainers have long realized that individuals vary in learning styles, and it is clear that some media are more appropriate than others for specific learning situations, trainees, and objectives. There is still much to be learned on these matters. The state of the art is not that advanced.

Many attempts have been made to develop *media models*—decision aids to help WLP practitioners select appropriate and cost-effective means of delivering instruction. Among key issues to consider in selecting media are these: (1) *Mandates:* Has somebody mandated what delivery method to use? (2) *Purposes:* What are the intended outcomes? Is the primary purpose to inform, instruct, entertain, or persuade? (3) *Constraints:* How much time, money, staff, effort, and equipment are available for designing instruction and for delivering it? (4) *Cost benefits:* Are some methods more cost beneficial than others? (5) *Flexibility:* Is there a great need to build in the possibility for easy revision at a later time? For example, group instruction is appropriate when management requests it; when more than one person has a need for instruction; when adequate people, time, and money are available; and when the need for flexibility is high. Individual instruction, on the other hand, is perhaps most appropriate when only one person has a need or when there is a good instructional reason to allow for individual differences.

Preparing or Selecting Content

There are three ways to develop content from instructional objectives: (1) WLP practitioners can prepare instructional content themselves; (2) they can select content from published or unpublished material and modify it for the uses at hand; or (3) they can prepare part of the content on their own and select the remainder from material prepared previously or available commercially. This choice is a make-or-buy decision, and costs are usually the deciding factor.

How are objectives transformed into lessons, units, courses, or other formats? What alternatives to this approach exist? This section addresses these questions.

The process of transforming objectives into instruction begins after sequencing them appropriately and selecting media. There are three major steps: (1) creating a syllabus; (2) grouping objectives together into courses, units, and lessons; and (3) preparing or selecting content at each level.

A *syllabus* is a list of objectives. Objectives are sequenced in a way deemed minimally essential so that learners have adequate preparation to perform tasks or undertake learning objectives requiring background knowledge. In many cases, sequence may be based on actual steps taken in performing a job task. Using the syllabus, WLP practitioners group together related objectives to create training curricula, courses, units, and lessons.

All *courses* needed to teach employees to perform their jobs to minimal competency levels constitute a *training curriculum* (Rothwell and Sredl 2000). A training curriculum is an organized and sequenced plan for training by job class. Without regard to specific titles, job classes are grouped together according to common characteristics. These groupings cut across the organization horizontally (see Exhibit 11-4). Each group has some relatively predictable needs. A separate training curriculum is designed for each job grouping, though all training curricula are interrelated (Rothwell and Sredl 2000). As a result, an employee preparing for promotion can begin basic training for the next higher job grouping.

A *course* is an organized learning experience with a discrete beginning and ending. Though typically associated with classroom training, courses do not have to be formal. In fact, they can be delivered on the job or in a college classroom off-site. Each training course focuses on a major task, activity, or responsibility associated with the job group.

Each course, in turn, comprises instructional *units* and *lessons*. A *unit* is a "chunk" of instruction. Its scope is smaller than a course, consisting of at least two units, and larger than a lesson, of which at least two are required to make up a unit. Each concept is, in turn, the basis of a *lesson plan*—a more detailed description of instructional activities than a unit.

Exhibit 11-5 illustrates relationships between a job curriculum, a course, a unit, and a lesson plan. Note that this relationship is one of increasing specificity, with job curriculum most general and lesson most specific.

Exhibit 11–4: Job Groupings for Training Curricula

Executives
Senior managers
Middle managers
First-line supervisors
Sales personnel
Professionals
Administrative employees
Clerical employees
Skilled production workers
Unskilled production workers
Customer Service representatives
Others

Each lesson focuses on *one* instructional objective. Frequently, that objective enables the learner to prepare for achieving a terminal or end-of-course objective. It is thus rationally related to a terminal objective, but is narrower in scope.

Many books and articles are available to provide guidance to trainers in preparing lessons and units. Units are usually scoped out in broad terms, describing (1) the relationship of the unit to terminal course objectives, (2) the enabling objectives of the unit itself, (3) the lessons making up the unit, and (4) the exercises or tests to reinforce principles.

Exhibit 11–5: Relationships between Organizational Strategy for the Development of Talent and Training Curriculum, Job Curriculum, Course Plans, Lesson Plans, and Instructional Activities

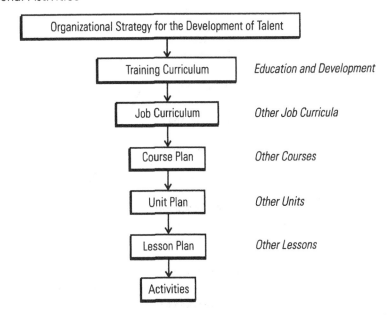

Lesson plans are more specific. They lay out in concrete terms what information to present, who should present it, and how to measure learner achievement. This format is not meant to be representative of the *only* right way to lay out a lesson; rather, it is one way to do so.

Lessons, units, and syllabi are combined in an *instructor's guide* for each training course. It is part of an *instructional package* for a course that contains the trainee guide, instructor's guide, course tests, and instructions on using the entire package (Rothwell and Kazanas 1998). The trainee guide can be prepared before or after the instructor's guide. It contains a course outline, notes, exercises, copies of visual aids, and such additional resources as supplementary reading or a bibliography of pertinent books and articles.

Of course, the advent of Web-based and other distance education instruction has changed the appearance of much instruction, but not the essential content. In Web-based courses, for example, all or most components of an instructional package may be available to the learners themselves.

Thus far, it seems that developing content from objectives is primarily a top-down process, beginning with course or curriculum development, and culminating in unit plans and then lesson plans. However, the process can work the other way, from the bottom up. WLP practitioners can begin with lesson planning, proceed to grouping related lessons into units, and in turn to grouping related units into courses (Rothwell and Sredl 2000). The danger of this approach is that it can result in poor overall planning.

In some corporations, WLP practitioners do not prepare formal lesson plans from behavioral objectives. The steps in the performance-based training design model are used in some instructional planning (in technical training, for example), but are not used in management and executive-level training.

There are three major alternatives to developing instruction from objectives: (1) skeletal outlining, (2) detailed outlining, and (3) guided questioning or discovery learning (Rothwell and Sredl 2000).

Skeletal outlining assumes that presenters are already versed in the subject matter. They need only a brief outline to list topics to be discussed in a training session. Otherwise, instructors ad lib. WLP practitioners provide a skeletal topic outline, but also a list of instructional objectives to clarify what results are sought from the training.

A detailed outline is more complete, but it is not as thorough as lesson plans or instructional scripts. Basing the outline on a thorough needs assessment and work analysis, WLP practitioners furnish subject-matter experts-presenters with outlines of topics and subtopics, recommendations about how much time to spend on each topic, and tests or exercises to measure and reinforce learning.

The source of the guided questioning approach is the Socratic method, made famous in the *Dialogues* of Plato. There are two ways to use this method: The first is *deductively,* in which instructors begin with a broad, general principle and guide trainees to specific conclusions. The second is *inductively,* in which instructors begin with specific details and guide trainees through skillful questioning to reach broad, general, but tentative conclusions.

In the first instance, the instructor will most likely guide trainees to "discover" what they already know and share it with other learners. The WLP practitioner has to analyze, in advance, every task and develop questions that will lead trainees to predetermined conclusions.

In the second instance, instructors are "co-inquirers," along with the learners. There are no "right" or "wrong" responses; rather, questions are designed to stimulate insights and create new information. The starting point is a series of participant problems, issues, or concerns. Instructors solicit a list of work-related problems from participants. They then (1) write the problems or issues on a blackboard, flipchart, or overhead so that all participants can see them; (2) group them into logical categories; (3) summarize each category with an open-ended question (that is, a question beginning with *who, what, when, where, how, could,* or *for what reason*); and (4) use the questions to begin a process of inquiry in which group members mutually explore issues and seek new knowledge together. That is the procedure as described in a still-classic treatment by Knowles (1980). Once decisions have been made about instructional content, the training design process is complete. The training is then tested prior to widespread delivery, modified based on the test results, and offered to targeted trainees.

Problems with the Traditional Model of Training

The model of training design and delivery described in the previous part of this chapter assumes that job performance is *always* improved by (1) analyzing how a job is presently being performed, (2) assessing how well individuals are carrying out the job, and (3) designing instruction to encourage individuals to conform to present ways of performing the job. The assumption is that individuals *must* perform in ways consistent with traditional practices and historical job requirements. In many cases, of course, that is true.

On the other hand, there are cases when training should help anticipate future job requirements utterly unlike those that have existed in the past. Instead of narrowing gaps between actual and desired job performance at present, the focus should be on gaps between (1) present, actual performance, and (2) future, desired performance. Exhibit 11–6 illustrates this concept.

The distinction really has to do with whether training should initiate first- or second-order change (Archer, Kelly, and Bisch 1984). *First-order change* is maintenance-oriented. Individuals learn existing work methods and steep themselves in organizational culture. Individuals adapt their behavior to organizational requirements. *Second-order change* seeks the discovery of new information, new approaches, and new ideas. When training is used in this way, it becomes a venue for research and development by providing people with an outlet for creative thinking and idea generation.

Exhibit 11–6: Differences in Focus between Traditional and Strategic Training

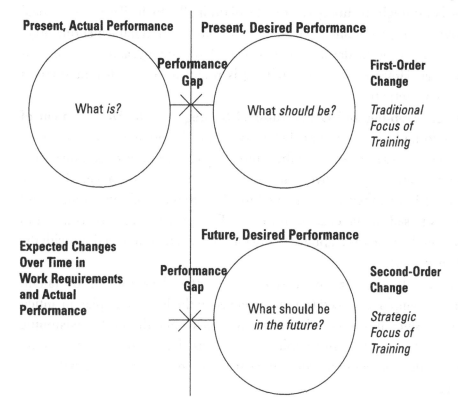

Present, Actual Performance | **Present, Desired Performance**

Performance Gap

What *is?*

What *should be?*

First-Order Change

Traditional Focus of Training

Expected Changes Over Time in Work Requirements and Actual Performance

Future, Desired Performance

Performance Gap

What should be in the future?

Second-Order Change

Strategic Focus of Training

Strategic Training

Strategic training prepares employees for changes in job or competency requirements wrought by external environmental conditions or by organizational policies, procedures, plans, or work methods. It is based on predictions of future job requirements stemming from strategic necessity. Strategic training requires WLP practitioners and managers to envision what future job performance should be under future conditions and prepare people for those conditions. In this sense, then, training is a method of changing the *organizational paradigm*—the culture or overall "rules" governing behavior in the firm. It is a vehicle for realizing a vision of what individual performance should be under relatively uncertain future conditions. Hence, strategic training is a tool for organizational and individual transformation, renewal, and creativity. Its focus is on working smarter, not working harder.

How is strategic training related to planning? Much like its traditional counterpart, strategic training contributes to formulating and implementing organizational strategy for the development of talent, HR planning, and strategic business planning. However, strategic training is useful in ways different from its traditional counterpart.

Strategic Training and Organizational Strategy for the Development of Talent. To formulate organizational strategy for the development of talent, managers and employees must envision the future. What are working conditions going to be in one year, two years, five years, and as business plans change? If people anticipate the future, they are positioned to take advantage of opportunities and avert threats posed by the changes it brings. This principle applies as much to individuals in their jobs as it applies to organizations in their interactions with the external environment.

To formulate organizational strategy for the development of talent, managers and employees need training to envision the future and plan in anticipation of it. Since future conditions are not fixed, like the past, envisioning them is a highly creative and subjective process. Future training needs are identified in the context of a vision of what future job requirements will be or should be.

Implementing organizational strategy for the development of talent is also highly creative and subjective. Since the future may not unfold as expected, WLP practitioners must plan for contingencies to cope with otherwise unexpected problems. To plan for contingencies, both WLP practitioners and operating managers may need instruction in the principles of contingency planning and in the use of scenario planning and response (Godet 2001; Willmore 1998).

Strategic Training and HR Planning. To narrow the gap between present labor supply and future demand, managers can do more than just make better use of available supply. They can also (1) change the allocation of work, which may affect the numbers and skills of people needed in the future; (2) automate; or (3) change the kind of people recruited into the firm. There are other strategies, too: reduce turnover and absenteeism; change the distribution of full-time and part-time employees; and introduce innovative practices such as job sharing or flexible work hours.

Any of these strategies will, of course, influence job training needs. In fact, WLP practitioners and managers may need to predict the likely future effects of each change in order to anticipate future training needs. Strategic training is necessary to avert future shortfalls in the supplies of skilled people. Examining past requirements or projecting past needs into the future are equally inadequate for this purpose.

Implementation of HR plans calls for action on several fronts at once: recruitment of skills from outside the organization; contracting for skills on a short-term basis; and training employees for skills they will need in order to implement strategic business plans.

Strategic Training and Strategic Business Planning. Strategic training contributes to strategic business planning in two ways. First it furnishes new, perhaps better, methods of doing work. Second, it prepares employees at each organizational level to carry out their jobs in ways that are consistent with future job requirements. The process of formulating strategic training may reveal issues appropriate for consideration in formulating business strategy. The process of implementing strategic training may also produce new information of value in subsequent organizational strategy-making.

When should strategic training be used instead of traditional training?

Use strategic training to (1) train people for anticipating new job requirements stemming from changes in organizational plans, work methods, policies, procedures, or structure; (2) come up with new, innovative, ways to perform jobs or work tasks; (3) create new information or ideas; or (4) evaluate future job conditions and provide individuals with artificial experience in performing under those conditions. For this training to transfer back to the job, it has to be linked to other change strategies as part of a long-term organizational improvement effort. Innovative methods are rarely accepted easily or painlessly.

A Model for Strategic Training

The Model. The model of strategic training we propose is similar to the traditional performance-based model of instructional design and delivery. However, it differs from the traditional model in key respects. To apply the model, the WLP practitioner must

1. Identify opportune occasions to use it, based on *problem-finding* rather than *problem-solving*.
2. Assess learner needs based on predictions of future conditions.
3. Clarify key characteristics expected of future learners.
4. Analyze the future setting in which training will be delivered and applied.
5. Carry out future-oriented work analysis.
6. Prepare strategic instructional objectives in order to narrow gaps between what learners know and do at present and what learners should know and do in the future if they are to perform their jobs in ways consistent with strategic business plans.
7. Create strategically oriented tests and other performance measures.
8. Arrange objectives in sequence.
9. Select and use appropriate delivery methods.

10. Prepare and select content for strategic training.
11. Deliver the training.

Step 1: Identify occasions to use the approach. The WLP practitioner who expects future changes to influence employee job performance should ask several key questions.

First, *what should employees be doing in the future?* Strategic business plans imply behavior and skills at every level of the organization's chain of command. If a plan calls for stable growth, employees may not need training. Past work methods may be appropriate.

On the other hand, dramatic changes in business strategy or external environmental conditions require utterly new duties and activities at every level of the firm. For example, the introduction of word processing in an office requires operators to learn how to use the equipment, people interacting with operators to learn how to deal with them under new conditions, and supervisors to learn new skills. The same is true, albeit on a larger scale, when strategic business plans are changed.

Second, *what are employees actually doing?* This question elicits information about present performance, knowledge, and skills of employees.

Third, *what differences exist between what employees should be doing in the future and what they are actually doing?* Are performance problems likely to arise in the future? Are these problems likely to affect entire job classes or only individuals? What differences exist between knowledge, skills, and abilities needed to perform a job competently at present and those that will be required in the future to perform the same job competently? Changes in future job requirements can either be mandated or evolutionary. If mandated, managers tell people how they should perform; if evolutionary, change is introduced gradually.

Fourth, *how important are these differences?* Can training priorities be established to avert problems expected in the future? If problems are important enough to prevent successful implementation of strategic business plans, for instance, then they are worth dealing with in advance through training or other methods.

Fifth, *what will be the cause of these differences?* Scan short-term conditions affecting job performance. Try to identify changes likely to result from

- New products being introduced by the firm, or new services being offered by it
- New policies of the organization
- New procedures or work methods
- New supervisors with expectations different from past supervisors
- New technology introduced in the work setting
- Trends in work flow (Will it increase, decrease, remain the same, or change in type or in form?)
- New methods of allocating work (Will changes be made to organizational, departmental, divisional, or work group structure?)
- New methods of measuring job performance (How will people be evaluated? What will be evaluated?)
- New methods of rewarding performance (How will people be rewarded for what they do?)

Changes like those listed provide the impetus for training to head off future problems.

Sixth, *what should be done about non-training needs expected in the future?* Future performance problems may stem from causes other than knowledge or skill deficiencies. No amount of training, for example, will solve problems resulting from improper allocation of work, inappropriate policies, reward systems that do not provide incentives in line with business strategy, lack of leadership, failures to provide individuals with feedback about their performance, group norms that are resistant to changes in line with strategic business plans, lack of motivation to prepare for the future, or lack of ability. Admittedly, it may be difficult to anticipate and head off future problems stemming from all these causes, but it is worth the effort to try.

And seventh, *what should be done about strategic training needs?* Classroom-based instructional experiences are admittedly expensive, and they are not only means by which information can be gathered about future problems and solutions, or by which training can be delivered in anticipation of future needs.

Alternatives to traditional training can sometimes be substituted for strategic training. They include

I *Job aids.* Can future problems be averted by simple instructions to employees about what to do if a problem arises in the future? Job aids can be prepared and handed out in advance.

I *Coaching.* Can future problems be averted by coaching employees individually about trends in the work or changes in their jobs that they need to prepare for?

I *Work simplification.* Can future problems be averted by siphoning off special problems to management or employee committees, task forces, or other groups established to deal with them before they come up?

I *Creative problem-finding techniques.* Can innovative approaches to finding and averting future problems be used? These approaches include the Delphi procedure and Nominal Group Technique. Of course, these approaches may also be used to identify strategic training needs and to deliver creative, strategically oriented "training" sessions.

However, if special benefits are associated with group training (such as the desirability of social interaction or the significant advantages to creative problem-solving that can be realized in group settings), then they may outweigh the high cost in lost production time of group training. In addition, these settings may be used to simulate future conditions so that learners experience them and can thus be motivated to prepare for them in advance.

Step 2: Assess strategic training needs. Historically, training and organizational planning have not mixed well. One reason is that much training is focused on first-order change, helping individuals become socialized to organizational settings. Of course, the future does not always resemble the past. Experience is not always an appropriate guide for grappling with changing future conditions.

Traditional training needs assessment identifies past or present discrepancies between *what employees actually know or do* and *what they should know or do*. Instruction is then designed to narrow this gap between *what is and what should be*. On the other hand, strategic needs assessment identifies possible future discrepancies between what employees know or do at present and what they should know or do in the future. Instruction is then designed to anticipate future discrepancies between *what is at present* and *what should be in the future.*

The real difference, then, between traditional and strategic needs assessment has to do with *criteria.* Present criteria are what managers and other employees expect by way of job performance from a job incumbent at this time. If job standards have been established, they are the criteria by which to assess present performance. Future criteria are what managers expect after job requirements and standards have been affected by changing conditions inside and outside the firm. To predict future criteria, WLP practitioners and others should determine what major changes will affect the organization, and how those changes should affect job standards or job performance requirements.

The process of predicting future criteria is tentative and highly subjective. It is based on environmental scanning for each job class. During this process, it is relatively easy to link up strategic business planning to training needs. WLP practitioners need only ensure that performance implications of strategic business plans are considered while planning the training for each job class in the firm.

What data collection approaches are appropriately used for strategic training needs assessment? Many of the same used in traditional training needs assessment can be used: (1) management requests, (2) record and report reviews, (3) informal group discussions, (4) questionnaires, and (5) observations/interviews. The key difference between traditional and strategic training needs assessment approaches really has to do with what questions are asked, not so much with what data are collected.

Management requests are usually past-oriented. By the time supervisors perceive a training need, performance problems have surfaced already. One way to handle this problem is to create an organizational training advisory committee for the purpose of identifying possible future performance/training problems before they come up. The WLP practitioner gathers information from various levels in the firm, presents the results to members of the committee, and listens to their opinions about which problems are likely to have the greatest future impact.

Training needs are then identified *before* they are perceived in bottom-line, dollars-and-cents losses.

Systematic reviews of reports and records provide a source of information for this purpose. So, too, do informal meetings at various levels in the firm. The important point to bear in mind is this: The focus of data collection efforts should remain on future trends at the job level, their potential importance relative to strategic business plans, and how these trends can be dealt with before they cause problems. In addition to surveys, interviews, observation, and record reviews, many other data collection approaches associated with future research may help identify possible future performance problems. They include the Delphi procedure, nominal group technique, scenario development and analysis, cross-impact analysis, and many more. The same techniques used to assess strategic training needs may also be used to deliver strategic training.

Step 3: Clarify key characteristics of future learners. Who will receive strategic training? What characteristics will they have in common? This section addresses these questions.

Two primary groups of people who will be affected by strategic training are (1) *present job incumbents,* which are known as the *horizontal market* of trainees because they occupy a job class at present; (2) *future job incumbents,* referred to as the *vertical market* of trainees because they do not occupy a job class yet, but might enter it before, during, or after future changes affect the job class (Rothwell and Sredl 2000).

Incumbents of the horizontal market are gradually prepared for changes in job requirements. However, only some remain in the job category by the time changes are felt. Others are promoted, retired, transferred, terminated, or otherwise leave the organization. In contrast, incumbents of the vertical market require *employee education* because they have not yet entered the job, but will do so eventually.

Employees presently working in a job may well be affected by changes in job duties and performance requirements resulting from changes in business strategy or external environmental conditions. But if the emphasis is on the future, some employees are gone (moved out of the job class) by the time changes are felt. Other employees will be moving into the job class.

It is thus necessary to predict who the learners will be. There is little reason to devote substantial time and money to preparing employees for future changes in jobs when they will not experience those changes. In addition, it may be possible to reduce the need for strategic training if hiring and promoting procedures are coordinated with it so as to include consideration of future job requirements. In short, WLP practitioners reduce the need to train people in anticipation of future job changes if they select for hiring or promotion people already possessing the requisite competencies needed for the future.

Planning for future learners is related to HR planning, not instructional planning. Since strategic training calls for a relatively short time horizon (anticipatory training is best carried out shortly before a change is about to occur so that learners do not forget needed skills), the issue is less pertinent to training for present job incumbents than for preparing future ones through employee education. Yet it should be considered for planning training nevertheless (see Rothwell and Kazanas 2002).

What learner or trainee characteristics will influence appropriate instructional design for strategic training? Consider:

▌ *Ability.* Do trainees have the ability to learn in anticipation of need?
▌ *Motivation.* How motivated are learners to prepare for future changes on the job? Are they likely to accept or reject training? Why or why not?
▌ *Necessary base of skills.* How much necessary background knowledge and skills do learners possess? For example, it will be pointless to try to train people for technological changes when they lack basic skills in reading, writing, or arithmetic.
▌ *Strategic thinking skill.* To what extent do learners possess the ability to peer into the future and work to anticipate it? This skill is learned. In some job classes, individuals might never need such a skill, especially when their work allows little latitude for individual discretion. What can be done to prepare people to think ahead when their jobs do allow for discretion?

Are other learner characteristics worth taking into account when planning strategic training?

Step 4: Analyze the future setting. In traditional instructional design, WLP practitioners analyze work and instructional settings in advance. The closer the match between them, the better: When training is delivered under conditions resembling the work environment, it is more likely to be transferred to that setting. In strategic training, the WLP practitioner has to visualize the future job or work environment and create an instructional environment to simulate it. The idea is to use the instructional setting to simulate future (but not yet existing) job conditions so that learners gain experience without incurring the costly consequences of doing so in a real setting. Mistakes and confusion in training, while not desirable, are at least less costly or significant than on the job.

What conditions will exist on the job in the near future? Consider: (1) *Tools.* Will new tools or technology be introduced? What kind? (2) *Physical conditions.* What will the job environment be like? (3) *Work methods.* What methods will be used? (4) *Policies/procedures.* What organizational policies and procedures will influence the job? and (5) *Group norms.* What will co-workers say and do? How might their beliefs influence job conditions in the future? Obviously, the future work setting will affect employee job performance. Can it be simulated for instructional purposes?

Step 5: Carry out future-oriented work analysis. Since training is geared to improving job performance, it makes sense to analyze job or task requirements. For this reason, work analysis is an essential component of any instructional design process. Once the WLP practitioner knows what a job incumbent is expected to do, training can be designed to help learners master the knowledge or skills associated with successful job performance. In designing strategic training, the WLP practitioner goes beyond the analysis of present work to determine what a job incumbent should be doing if performance is to be consistent with strategic business plans at a future time. We call this process strategic work analysis.

Perhaps the simplest method of strategic work analysis is based on job descriptions and job specifications. Of course, a *job description* simply summarizes major duties and responsibilities of a job. A *specification* lists minimum education and experience necessary to learn the job. Traditional work analysis yields a description of what job incumbents should be doing and what education and experience is necessary to do it. By way of contrast, strategic work analysis describes what job incumbents should be doing in the future and what education and experience will be necessary for them to do it. Discrepancies between traditional and strategic work analysis, as evident in job descriptions and specifications, constitute a gap that subsequent, strategically oriented training is designed to close.

Step 6: Prepare strategic instructional objectives. Instructional objectives express what learners will be able to do upon completion of a learning experience. They are traditionally intended to close a performance gap between what employees know or do and what they should know or do.

Strategic instructional objectives are no different. Like their traditional counterparts, they are designed to close a performance gap. However, the gap is different. Instead of expressing a discrepancy between what is and what should be at present, a strategic instructional objective is based on a discrepancy between what is at present and *what should be in the future.* When a strategic objective is met, a *planning gap* is closed.

In all other respects, strategic instructional objectives resemble their traditional counterparts. *Terminal objectives* express outcomes to be achieved by an entire course or other discrete learning experience; *enabling objectives* express outcomes to be achieved during a learning experience in order to measure progress toward terminal objectives.

Step 7: Create Strategically Oriented Tests. There is little difference in the way traditional and strategic test items are created. For each strategic objective, the WLP practitioner prepares at least one test item to measure achievement. Each item links measurement to instructional outcomes and to *future* work tasks/ activities. Strategically oriented tests are administered in writing, orally, or by demonstration.

Step 8: Arrange objectives in sequence. The arrangement of objectives in strategic training depends on the purpose of "instruction." There are two major purposes. *Non-directive training* produces new information. It fosters the sharing of insights, ideas, and innovative techniques among learners. *Directive training* is designed and delivered in anticipation of a future need that is soon going to be felt on the job. These purposes are not mutually exclusive; rather, they form a continuum. A training event can combine the two.

If the purpose is directive, instructional objectives are sequenced exactly as they are in traditional training. The WLP practitioner makes sure that instruction follows a sequence from what the learner already knows to what he or she does not know. In other words, prerequisite information must be provided first. Quite often this order is chronological: from what people now do to what they should do in the future.

On the other hand, if the purpose is purely nondirective, sequencing should depend on learner interests and concerns.

Additional issues may be suggested by the group leader. The learners, in cooperation with the group leaders, then sequence the topics or objectives in the order they wish to treat them. The sequence may thus be based on perceived importance rather than on logical groupings.

Step 9: Select and use appropriate delivery methods. The selection and use of appropriate delivery methods depend on the purpose of strategic training. When the purpose is purely directive, specific outcomes are desired. The choice of delivery methods is based on the same issues that are important in traditional training: cost, time, skills of WLP staff, and available materials. If the purpose is purely nondirective, specific outcomes are not necessarily fixed. The learning event is a discovery session where new ideas are created and new learning needs are identified.

For either purpose, however, many delivery methods can be used to provide information, reinforce learning, evoke new insights or new ideas, and simulate future job conditions or problems. Some of these methods have been discussed earlier in the chapter and are capable of being modified to help anticipate future needs as well as meet present ones. Nor are these the only ones. Each of the 350 delivery methods described by Huczynski (1983) can be reoriented to a strategic use.

Brainstorming is perhaps the simplest way to unleash group creativity to deal with problem-finding and solving. During the first stage of brainstorming, a problem is stated and discussed. In the second stage, the problem is restated and possible solutions are considered. In the third stage, one re-statement of the problem is selected to stimulate discussion of solutions. In the fourth stage, participants warm up by generating ideas in rapid fire for no more than five minutes. In the fifth stage, the process continues, but in a more serious vein, and the group leader writes down ideas for group members to see. In the sixth and final stage, the wildest idea is taken from the previous stage and used to stimulate more-serious ones.

Brainstorming continues to be applied in many settings in order to generate new ideas and approaches. Of course, it can be used to identify (1) training needs in each job class that result from strategic business plans, (2) new work methods and innovative approaches, and (3) potential performance problems.

Brainwriting is a modification of brainstorming. Two variations are common (Van Gundy 1981): (1) the brainwriting pool and (2) battelle-bildmappen-brainwriting (BBB). In the *brainwriting pool approach*, a problem is read to a small group (six is a good number). After group members brainstorm on the problem aloud, they are given several photographs or drawings unrelated to it. They then write down ideas suggested to them by the pictures. Solutions are read to the group and used to stimulate more ideas. In *batelle-bildmappen brainwriting*, a problem is read to a group and individuals are asked to scribble ideas on pieces of paper. After several ideas are listed on each piece of paper, they are placed in a pool at the center of the group. Individuals remove different sheets, record new ideas on them, and place them back in the pool. This process continues for 30 or 40 minutes.

Brainwriting, like brainstorming, can also be used in strategic training. It serves as a means to identify future training needs likely to stem from business plans or environmental changes. Similarly, it can unleash group creativity relative to future problems likely to confront job incumbents or methods for solving those problems.

Crawford Slip Writing is a variation of brainwriting that can be modified for strategic training. Charles Clark (1978) described the approach, in detail: It goes like this:

I   Give each participant a pad of paper (3" × 5") with at least 25 sheets and proceed to read a question to the group, such as (a) What problems are likely to confront you on the job in the next year? (b) What knowledge/skills do you feel you will need over the next year in order to solve problems you expect to come up on your job? (c) How can the organization deal with a major strategic issue?

❘ Ask group members to write one idea on each of their slips of paper.
❘ Tell group members to stop writing after five or ten minutes.
❘ Collect the slips of paper.
❘ Appoint a task force to evaluate the ideas, and sort the various slips of paper into categories, based on importance or practical use.
❘ Use the ideas to identify future training needs or content for future-oriented instruction.

The value of the approach should be apparent.

The Phillips 66 Technique is a way to stimulate ideas and identify future job-related problems, training needs, or issues for subsequent exploration.

To apply the approach to strategic training, the WLP practitioner follows these steps:

❘ Divide a large group into smaller groups of no more than six people each.
❘ Encourage group members to get acquainted.
❘ Ask each group to select a leader and a secretary.
❘ Read a carefully worded statement or question to the groups about a problem or issue to be considered by them.
❘ Ask each group to come up with one brief statement about one of the following: an issue of strategic importance to the organization; an issue of strategic importance to a division department or work group within the organization; a trend inside or outside the organization that will change job duties, tasks, or work methods; a future training need; or a solution to a future problem.
❘ Give the groups a time limit of 5 to 15 minutes to come up with a short single answer (or question).
❘ Ask a representative from each group to report at the end of the agreed-on time limit.

The Phillips 66 technique can thus help generate new ideas, identify future training needs, suggest new approaches to handling work, and recommend specific content to meet future training needs.

The *Delphi Procedure* is a method for reaching expert consensus. It can be used to scan the environment to identify possible changes and their effects, and to identify training needs, new work methods and approaches, and issues worth exploring.

The *Nominal Group Technique* can be used to identify likely future problems, training needs, and issues worth exploring. It takes its name from silent idea-generation used with a group of people whose relationship as a group is only "nominal."

Force field analysis is the creation of Kurt Lewin (1947). The WLP practitioner asks participants in a small group to identify any of the following:

1. A major trend in the external environment that is likely to affect job performance in the future
2. A major trend in the internal environment (inside the organization) that is likely to affect job performance in the future
3. The effect(s) of a major trend in the external or internal environment
4. Training needs resulting from major trends or their effects
5. Adequate training content, such as training to help people:
    I   Anticipate and meet future needs.
    I   Identify forces that *inhibit* a trend, its effects, training needs, or efforts to anticipate and meet those needs or *facilitate* a trend, its effects, training needs, or efforts to anticipate and meet those needs.
    I   Plan action steps to weaken forces inhibiting change, strengthen forces facilitating change, strengthen forces inhibiting change, weaken forces facilitating change, or some combination of the above.

Force field analysis is most useful as a needs assessment method, though it can also be used as the basis for experiential learning exercises to pinpoint possible future job performance problems and the training needed to deal with them.

Cross impact analysis examines relationships or consequences of events. A matrix is developed to summarize possible events and their relationships. To apply this technique to strategic training, WLP practitioners (1) identify possible events that might occur, (2) estimate probabilities of each event, (3) estimate possible linkages between events, and (4) come up with action plans to deal with likely events (Stover and Gordon 1978).

Probabilities are initially established by experts. Of course, when it comes to possible future events affecting job duties, incumbents may well be the best "experts." Predictions stemming from such analysis identify future training needs and instructional content adequate to anticipate those needs.

Scenario analysis is a quintessential tool in strategic business planning. The term *scenario* comes from drama, where it refers to a plot outline. In concrete terms, that is precisely what a scenario is—an outline, story, or flowchart of events. It is a plausible description of the future. To apply scenarios to strategic training, the WLP practitioners can use (1) a "training" session to develop one or more scenarios of conditions affecting incumbents of a job class, organization, division, department, or work group; (2) scenarios to stimulate thinking about future training needs or simulate future conditions so that learners can draw conclusions about their own training needs; or (3) scenarios to reinforce principles brought up in strategic training.

Developing a scenario sounds easy, but it is not. The instructional designer, manager, or group participant confronted with the task must do five things: (1) *Identify boundaries and scope.* Will the scenario encompass the organization, a division, department, work group, job class, community, or some other "unit"? (2) *Clarify time horizon.* For training, use periods of a year or two. Longer time frames are appropriate for strategic planning and employee education, but not for short-term training. (3) *Identify key elements.* What trends, problems, or issues are likely to exert influence and be important to future job performance, are highly unlikely to exert influence and are unimportant to job performance, or are somewhere in between? (4) *Adopt assumptions.* What will be the likely future effects of a problem, issue, or trend? (5) *Use "hard" or "soft" methods to generate the scenario.* Soft methods are intuitive; hard methods are strictly logical.

Multiple scenario analysis uses between two and four scenarios. Each is a plausible but different view of the future. By planning for alternatives, trainees gain different perspectives about future trends/problems/environmental conditions, possible effects of them, and training needs.

Morphological analysis divides and subdivides ideas into parameters or parts. It lends itself to the examination of trends, issues, and events. To apply the approach to strategic training, WLP practitioners and/or trainees (1) identify a problem, trend, or likely environmental change; (2) identify several dimensions of the problem, trend, or change; (3) generate a list of characteristics for each dimension; (4) create a two- or three-dimensional matrix; (5) list dimensions and characteristics on the matrix; and (6) use the matrix to identify solutions and effects (Van Gundy 1981). Morphological analysis, like other approaches described in this section of the chapter, helps trainees generate new ideas to deal with future problems before they come up, identify future training needs, and develop content for strategic training.

Checklists help generate new ideas by comparing items on a preexisting checklist to a given problem or a situation. This technique of problem-solving has often been applied to marketing as a way to identify new products or new consumer markets for development. For example, in one classic treatment, osborn (1953) suggests that managers ask the following questions when considering the development of a new product from an old one:

▪ What other product is similar? (Is adaptation possible?)

▪ How can a product be changed? (Is modification possible?)

▪ How can additions be made to the product? (Is magnification of existing features a possible alternative?)

▪ How can features be taken away from the product? (Is "minification" an alternative?)

▪ What can be used instead of this product or portions of it? (Is substitution of features possible?)

▪ What alterations in the product can be made? (Is rearrangement a viable alternative?)

I How can the needs that the product is designed to meet be turned around? (Is reversal possible?)

I What features of two or more existing products can be assembled into one new product? (Is combination possible?)

The same approach can be applied to work tasks, work methods, performance problems, future training needs, or even future training content.

Microsimulations are short, relatively informal practice sessions carried out under anticipated future work conditions. They are slightly more lengthy than role plays, which they resemble, and use such "props" as new equipment to support the simulation. Trainees perform under these artificial conditions. Their experience is artificial but does furnish a means to (1) motivate trainees to learn about new equipment by proving the need to do so, (2) train them in new skills not yet needed in the work setting, (3) let learners practice in a setting where mistakes will not prove to be too expensive, and (4) develop instructional content for future training.

Lateral thinking was developed by Edward DeBono (1970). It is meant to be distinct from traditional, logical thinking. Lateral thinking seeks new perspectives and ideas and avoids value judgments about "right" or "wrong." It welcomes unusual, chance intrusion of unrelated information and welcomes attempts to find the unique or different, rather than the obvious. Lateral thinking progresses illogically through patterns of free association.

Three major activities are used in lateral thinking: (1) *awareness*, used to change definitions and clear up current thinking, (2) *alternatives*, used to stimulate new ways of looking at problems or issues, and (3) *provocative methods*, used to develop new ideas (Van Gundy 1981). In the awareness stage, five different areas are looked at; in the alternatives stages, any one of seven techniques can be used; in the provocative methods stage, any one of seven techniques can be used.

The *devil's advocate* method assumes that conflict sharpens thinking about problems, issues, or solutions. Too often managers try to suppress conflict because they view it negatively as a destructive rather than potentially constructive phenomenon. Indeed, there is a tendency to reduce conflict on interpersonal matters (personality conflicts), rather than recognize that conflict can stem from different goals, perspectives, and role requirements.

The devil's advocate approach has been used in strategic business planning, and it can be applied in strategic training. Trainees work up a solution to a problem or identify an issue that they believe will increasingly pose a job performance problem in the future. They present it to their instructor or a panel of peers, and the instructor or panel deliberately adopts the role of critic, attacking ideas presented in the solution. Trainees defend their ideas under the assumption that good ideas will survive stiff challenge. This process trains employees in how to anticipate and plan for these challenges.

One variation of the devil's advocate approach is to place a special handicap on challengers: Every time they attack an idea, they must present a reasonable alternative to it. If they attack a solution on the basis of practicality, then they must present a more practical alternative. If they attack a solution on the basis of cost, then they must present a cheaper but equally effective alternative. An advantage of this variation is that it forces progressive thinking.

The *group debate method* examines an issue or problem from different points of view. Trainees are divided into at least two groups. They are then presented with an issue or problem. For example, they might be asked to begin with any one of the following questions: (1) What trends inside or outside the organization do you believe will influence your ability to do your job in the next year? (2) What problems do you expect to come up in your job in the next year? Why do you think they will come up? (3) What knowledge or skills will you need over the next year or two to anticipate work-related problems before they come up, and to deal with those problems before they arise? Each group answers the question. If their answers differ significantly, group members divide up into two panels and debate their ideas and solutions. Through opposition, they eventually arrive at a synthesis or consensus about (a) problems likely to come up, (b) actions needed to anticipate them, (c) training needs associated with likely future problems, and (d) instructional content for future training that is designed to provide employees with knowledge or skills before they are needed.

The delivery methods described in this section can be used in settings other than training: strategic business planning retreats; meetings of training advisory committees; and problem-identification or problem-solving meetings of work groups, departments, or divisions. When properly applied, these methods can help people anticipate problems, rather than react to crises.

Step 10: Prepare and select content for strategic training. If strategic training is directive, then instructional content is prepared in-house or selected from externally prepared training materials in precisely the same way that traditional instruction is prepared. Instructional objectives are elaborated into courses, units, and lessons. Great emphasis is placed on experiential methods to simulate future job conditions and prepare individuals for performing in them.

On the other hand, nondirective training produces new information, stimulates new insights, motivates trainees to prepare for the future, provides a means to simulate future conditions, and gives trainees a chance to gain experience before it is needed. Nondirective training is dependent on the skills of the group facilitator, who stimulates group thinking. Content stems from the "training" session and is a function of group interaction and methods used to elicit new ideas.

Step 11: Deliver the training. In directive training, whether traditional or strategic, effective delivery is synonymous with good public speaking. The instructor bears the chief burden, and must use good "platform skills." Much of what has been written on this subject boils down to a few key principles: (1) speak clearly, (2) use good eye contact, (3) vary tone and modulation of voice, (4) watch the audience and respond to nonverbal cues, (5) use questions to increase audience participation, and (6) reinforce ideas and enliven the presentation with visual aids.

In nondirective strategic training, most of the burden for delivery rests with participants, rather than with the instructor. The group leader is a facilitator—one who stimulates thinking—rather than pure subject-expert or instructor.

Good questioning skills are important for instructors, but are essential for successful group facilitators. Questions control discussions, stimulate thinking, and identify problems and solutions.

There are two types of questions. Closed-ended questions elicit "yes" or "no" responses. They begin with words such as "do" or "is." For example: "Do you believe that is correct?" or "Is that true?" Open-ended questions are difficult to answer with one word. They begin with words such as "who," "what," "when," "where," "why," "how," "how much," and "would." For example: "What are some reasons?" and "When would it be appropriate to do that?" Closed-ended questions control discussion because a "yes" or "no" response closes off further discussion. That is not always true, of course, because some trainees may object to a simple response. But it is generally true. Open-ended questions, on the other hand, stimulate further discussion. They invite talk, provoking problem-finding and problem-solving efforts. They can be used to prompt data gathering (such as defining, fact-finding, providing or eliciting examples, or prompting judgments), as well as data processing (noting relationships, comparing or contrasting ideas, etc.) and abstracting (drawing conclusions, coming up with generalizations, and predicting what will or may happen) (Hennings 1975).

Activity 11–1: A Structured Form for Analyzing Human Performance Problems

Directions: Use this form to structure your thinking about any problem having to do with people or events in a firm. Answer the following questions.

I. The Problem

1. Describe the problem. Explain, as clearly as you can, what it is, when it first manifested itself, how it manifested itself, who is involved with it, where (part of the firm or location) it is most noticeable, and why it or its consequences are important.

II. The Cause

2. To what extent does the performance problem stem from lack of *individual knowledge or skill?* To what extent does the problem stem from some other cause? Describe the principal cause(s) of the problem.

3. To what extent is the problem caused by *a poor allocation of work duties?* If that is a major cause of the problem, what changes in work duty allocation can solve the problem?

4. To what extent is the problem caused by *inappropriate policies?* If a policy (or policies) contributes to a problem, what changes in policy can help solve the problem?

Activity 11–1: *(continued)*

5. To what extent is the problem caused by *reward systems* that are not consistent with desired employee performance? What changes in reward systems can contribute to solving the problem(s)?

6. To what extent is the problem caused by *leaders at lower levels who do not agree with goals/objectives* established at higher levels? What can be done to solve problems stemming from leadership?

7. To what extent is the problem caused by *lack of feedback* to employees about their performance? How do they hear about their mistakes? What can be done to improve feedback to employees about their work performance?

8. To what extent is the problem caused by *group norms*? Do employees, as a group, seem to support changes? What can be done to improve performance when problems stem from group norms?

9. To what extent are *individuals able to practice their skills and apply their knowledge* on a regular basis? To what extent do performance problems stem from lack of practice? What can be done to increase opportunities for practice?

10. To what extent do performance problems stem from lack of individual motivation? Do employees know what results they need to achieve? Do they associate getting results with consequences important to them? What can be done to correct problems stemming from lack of motivation?

11. To what extent do performance problems stem from lack of individual ability? Are individuals capable of performing correctly? If not, what can be done to correct the problem?

12. To what extent do performance problems stem from causes other than those listed in this activity? List some possibilities and consider them.

Activity 11–2: Alternatives to Classroom-Based Training

Directions: Use this activity to structure your thinking. Consider: Does the training you contemplate lend itself to alternatives other than formal, classroom-based experiences? Answer the questions that follow.

I. Description

1. What training needs are you intending to meet? Describe them.

II. Alternatives

2. Would any or all of the needs described in Question 1 lend themselves to instruction other than classroom-based training? Consider each of the following ways of providing training:

   Job aids

   Decision aids

   Individualized instruction

   On-the-job training

   Other methods (*describe*)

III. Costs

3. Prepare an estimate of how much it will cost to deliver training using each delivery method listed in Question 2. (Be sure to consider the cost of time spent away from work, including costs of lost production and salary expenses.)

IV. Special Consideration

4. Are there special considerations that might outweigh cost? List the relative advantages and disadvantages of each method in Question 2. Then compare them to the advantages and disadvantages of classroom-based training.

V. Conclusions

5. What delivery method(s) should be used to meet training needs?

Activity 11–3: Carrying out a Needs Assessment

Directions: Use this activity to structure your thinking about important issues in carrying out the needs assessment. Answer the questions that follow.

I. Goals/Objectives

1. What are the goals and objectives of the training needs assessment process? What general results are you hoping to achieve? What specific outcomes are desired? Are there secondary goals, such as building interest in a change effort, raising expectations for performance improvement, or improving employee morale?

II. Target Group

2. Whose needs are being assessed? Define the target group.

III. Data Collection

3. How will information about the training needs of the target group be collected? Are some approaches to data collection better than others?

IV. Special Guidelines

4. What special guidelines should be established, in advance, regarding the use of data collection methods?

V. Analysis

5. What analytical techniques should be used to interpret the results of needs assessment efforts? Why should those techniques be used rather than others?

Activity 11–4: An Activity on Learner Characteristics

Directions: When planning for training, consider learner characteristics. Use this activity to do some brainstorming on this issue. Answer the questions that follow.

I. Training Need

1. Describe the need that the training will be designed to meet.

II. General Characteristics

2. What learner characteristics generally affect training for a particular job?

3. How can these general characteristics be planned for?

III. Specific Characteristics

4. What characteristics of learners will be especially pertinent to training at a given time? Consider: Topical issues affecting the job, the work group, the department, the division, or the organization.

5. How can these characteristics be planned for during training design?

Activity 11–5: The Work Setting and the Instructional Setting

Directions: It is important during the planning of training to consider the work setting in which the training is to be subsequently applied. Generally, the more the instructional setting resembles the work setting, the greater the likelihood that training will transfer successfully back to the job. Use this activity to consider the key features of the work setting, the instructional setting, and ways to make the instructional setting resemble the work setting. Answer the following questions.

I. Work Setting

1. Describe important features of the setting in which the individual will apply their training. Be sure to cover physical conditions, tools/resources, group norms, supervisory expectations, and employee expectations. (*If you can't yet describe these features, research them and complete the question later.*)

II. Instructional Setting

2. Describe important features of the setting in which training is to be delivered. Be sure to cover physical conditions, tools/equipment, resources, and philosophy/beliefs.

III. Ways to make the instructional setting like the work setting

3. How can the instructional setting be made to resemble the work setting?

Activity 11–6: Designing a Traditional Training Curriculum

Directions: Using your own employer, list job titles in Column 2 that correspond to the general categories in Column 1. Then, for each job grouping, note the most important duties in Column 3. For each major duty listed in Column 3, list a corresponding instructional objective or series of objectives in Column 4. Finally, for each objective listed in Column 4, list a course title for training in Column 5. If necessary, use additional sheets.

Column 1 Job Groups	Column 2 Jobs	Column 3 Key Duties	Column 4 Instructional Objectives	Column 5 Training Courses or Experiences
1. Executives				
2. Senior managers				
3. Middle managers				
4. Supervisors				
5. Professionals				
6. Sales workers				
7. Clerical workers				
8. Skilled workers				
9. Unskilled workers				

Activity 11–7: A Checklist for Creative Reconsideration of Work Activities/Job Tasks

Directions: Answer both parts of each question that follows for a work activity or job task of your choice.

I. Description of Present Status

1. Describe a job task or a work activity. What is it? How is it carried out? When is it performed? Why is it important? Who performs it or is involved with it? List steps in the task, or flowchart the stages of the task.

II. Reconsideration of Status

How can the job task or work activity be changed?	Describe the change.	What are the advantages/disadvantages of the change over present methods?
2. What other tasks/work activities are *similar*? (Is it possible to handle this like a different one?)		
3. How can the tasks/work activities be *changed*? (Is modification possible?)		
4. How can *additions* be made to the task or work activity? (Is magnification of existing features a possible alternative?)		
5. How can features be *taken away* from the task or activity? (Is simplification of features possible?)		
6. What other tasks/activities can be *used instead* of this task/activity or portions of it?		
7. What *alternations* to the task/activity can be made? (Is rearrangement of steps a possible alternative?)		
8. Is it possible to *reverse* steps in the task/work activity?		
9. What features of two or more existing tasks or work activities can be *combined* to create one new overall task/activity?		

Activity 11–8: A Case Study on Employee Training

Directions: Read the case below and answer the questions that follow.

The Washington General Insurance Company* is an industry leader. The Training Department at Washington just completed a needs assessment for a training course on Customer Relations. Company trainers surveyed managers, supervisors, and wage-earning employees about this issue. The trainers then followed up the survey with intensive interviews of randomly selected supervisors and hourly employees.

Among the findings:

1. Customers (policyholders *and* sales agents) are often bounced around from one department to another when they call in with questions. The reason: Nobody is sure who handles some issues.

2. Telephone etiquette of wage-earning employees leaves much to be desired. Customers often complain that they are made to feel like they are bothering the person who is supposed to be helping them.

3. Letters from customers are not always answered promptly. In some cases, over two months elapse between the time a letter is received at the home office and it is answered.

4. Supervisors feel that if a customer relations "problem" exists, its cause has less to do with training needs than with staffing.

5. Older employees believe that younger employees are simply "less polite."

Company managers are concerned that employees need training on customer relations. The Washington's training staff is therefore planning to offer a one-day seminar on the topic for all employees. It will cover telephone etiquette, letter writing, and other matters.

In the meantime, a task force of company executives is investigating the possible creation of a special Customer Service center. All incoming calls and letters will be directed to the center, which will be staffed with specially-trained employees drawn from work units in the company. They will handle all problems until resolved to the customers' satisfaction.

Questions

1. How might creation of a special Customer Service center affect appropriate present training of employees on customer relations?

2. How might creation of a special Customer Service center affect appropriate future training of employees on customer relations?

3. Should training staff members at the Washington General Insurance Company handle the issue of customer relations training from a traditional standpoint or a strategic standpoint? Why do you think so?

*A fictitious company.

EVALUATING TALENT DEVELOPMENT

Part V concludes the book. It consists of only one chapter, which focuses on the all-important process of evaluating Talent Development. Decision-makers almost always ask what they will get from the Talent Development effort. Chapter 12 addresses this question, explaining how evaluation should permeate all aspects of the Talent Development process.

CHAPTER 12

EVALUATING TALENT DEVELOPMENT

Evaluating the Talent Development effort means collecting and using information to make effective decisions about the choice, implementation, and follow-up of all development, education, and training efforts of an organization. It is part of a comprehensive appraisal of an organization and is the culmination of evaluative activities having to do with choice, modification, or follow-up of each planned learning experience. This chapter defines the evaluation of a Talent Development effort, summarizes its importance, describes ways to think about it, and provides information about evaluating training, education, development, and the entire Talent Development effort. Recent thinking focuses such evaluative efforts around a so-called *balanced scorecard* (Kaplan and Norton 1996). In this context, evaluation becomes equated with score-keeping (Dalton 2002).

What Is Evaluation?

Evaluation means simply placing value. To a great extent, evaluation of Talent Development is in the eyes of the beholder. What does the beholder value? How well do Talent Development activities match up to those values? These questions are of central importance in evaluating anything.

In a classic definition of *value*, Rokeach (1973) defined it as "an enduring belief that a specific mode of conduct [*read behavior*] or end-state of existence [*read outcome*] is personally or socially

preferable to an opposite or converse node of conduct or end-state of existence."
He distinguished between two types of values—terminal and instrumental.
Terminal values are worth achieving for their own sake. *Instrumental values* are
desirable because they contribute to achieving terminal values. "A knowledgeable, skilled employee" is valued by a supervisor for the employee's instrumentality; "an effective, growing firm" is valued for its own sake (Rokeach 1973, 5).

Talent Development activities are usually valued for their instrumentality.
They lead to changes in individual or group performance or capabilities that are,
in turn, associated with desirable ends. Talent Development is thus a means to an
end of achieving the organization's desired strategic objectives. (For individuals, of
course, Talent Development has more to do with achieving career goals and realizing potential.) Managers favor a Talent Development effort when they believe it
leads to improved job performance, increased compliance with organizational
policies and procedures, greater profits, or other measures of results. Individuals
favor participating in Talent Development activities when they believe their participation will lead them down a path toward realizing their personal or career goals.

Why Are Values Important?

The answer to this question should be readily apparent. Managers evaluate the
Talent Development effort relative to its perceived contribution to fostering the
values they prize in employees and realizing desired organizational goals. Of
course, matters are rarely this simple. There are several reasons why. First, individual values and desired organizational goals vary. Second, perceptions about
what is important vary across levels of management. As a result, WLP practitioners have to begin evaluative efforts by defining values and goals that are most
prized in the organization, and then determining how much they are prized at
each level. By doing so, they can identify bottom-line concerns by level and gear
their evaluation to assessing how much Talent Development contributes to the
concerns of the key stakeholders they serve.

From a list of organizational goals based on one classic research study
(Schmidt and Posner 1982), managers preferred *effectiveness and high productivity* the most. (*Effectiveness* means accomplishing desired results.) However, not all

managers value these goals to the same degree. Generally, executives feel they are more important than supervisors do. Supervisors value *high morale* and *efficiency* more than executives. (*Efficiency* means getting more done with fewer resources.)

Why Is Evaluation Worthwhile?

In the most general sense, evaluation of Talent Development is worthwhile:

I It provides information that can be used to improve planned learning, making it more effective in meeting needs, solving past performance problems, and anticipating future opportunities for performance improvement.

I It sheds light on problems stemming from lack of individual knowledge or skill and other causes.

I It makes people accountable for Talent Development activities.

I It points out results of Talent Development activities, demonstrating how well they are working.

I It stimulates improvement generally, providing feedback that triggers additional plans and actions.

What Are Some Ways of Thinking about Evaluation?

In evaluating planned learning, WLP practitioners should begin by thinking about six fundamental questions: (1) Who wants to know? (2) Who is doing the evaluating? (3) What is the real focus of interest? (4) When should evaluation be carried out? (5) Why is evaluation necessary? and (6) How will the evaluation be conducted? These questions have to do with the stakeholders, evaluator, content, timing, purpose, and method of evaluation.

Stakeholders. To be useful, an evaluation must meet the needs of stakeholders, those decision-makers and interested groups or individuals who want the results of an evaluation and who intend to make decisions based on those results. However, needs of different stakeholder audiences vary substantially, as Exhibit 12-1 illustrates. Generally, the broader the audience of stakeholders whose interests are to be addressed by an evaluation, the more complex the evaluation needs to be. Broad audiences vary in interests, and an evaluation needs to be comprehensive to answer the questions of more people.

Evaluator. Who will conduct the evaluation? This question is important because no matter how carefully designed and executed an evaluation, stakeholders inevitably consider the source. Credibility is essential: Evaluation results are discounted when evaluators are perceived to be biased or poorly qualified. It is essential to choose evaluators who are credible in assessing the subject, capable in assessing instruction, and competent in using methods selected for collecting and analyzing data.

Exhibit 12-1: Interests of Stakeholders

Stakeholders	Interests
Top managers	▪ Is Talent Development contributing to the bottom line? ▪ Is Talent Development producing an adequate supply of talent from within the organization, and is it building bench strength? ▪ Are Talent Development efforts helping the organization achieve a competitive advantage and helping realize strategic objectives?
Middle managers	▪ Is Talent Development contributing to the bottom line? ▪ Are Talent Development efforts making the department more productive?
Supervisors	▪ Are Talent Development efforts making the work unit more productive? ▪ Are Talent Development efforts helping solve operational problems? ▪ Are Talent Development efforts improving morale?
Workers	▪ Are Talent Development efforts contributing to improved work performance? ▪ Are Talent Development efforts leading to better appraisals? Raises? Improved prospects for professional or organizational advancement?
WLP practitioners	▪ Are Talent Development efforts improving performance at present? ▪ Are Talent Development efforts contributing to the realization of the organization's strategic objectives? ▪ Are Talent Development efforts contributing to learning in the organization and for individuals? ▪ Do people participating in the Talent Development efforts enjoy them?

Content. What do evaluators want to know about? This question focuses on *content*. Unlike research, which is carried out to create new knowledge, evaluation is carried out to provide information for subsequent decision-making. This means that evaluation has to be judged according to *usefulness or practicality,* rather than *form* or *rigor of research design and execution.* By way of contrast, research is judged more by its form than by its usefulness.

Many content issues can be examined (see Exhibit 12–2). Generally, the more issues that are included in an examination, the more comprehensive, costly, and time-consuming the evaluation must be.

Timing. When is evaluation appropriate? This question focuses on *timing*. If evaluation is to provide information for decision-making, then appropriate timing depends on what decisions are to be made. For example, it is important to have information about problems before deciding whether learning needs exist distinct from other needs. Likewise, information about the value of training materials is needed before they are used on a broad scale.

Evaluation may be conducted before, during, or after decisions are made about planned learning. The essential point is to determine *when* that information is needed, depending on the purpose of the evaluation.

Purpose. Why is evaluation conducted? This question is undoubtedly the single most important one. There are, of course, several major reasons why an organization decides to undertake an evaluation:

❘ The organization wants to know if formal instruction is the most appropriate strategy for meeting a need.

❘ The organization wants to know if instructional materials will produce desired results.

❘ The organization wants to know if instruction is worth continuing or is worth repeating.

❘ The organization wants to assess how instruction is being delivered and how well learners are mastering desired knowledge/skills or building essential competencies as measured through behavioral indicators or behavioral anchors during instruction.

Exhibit 12–2: Content Issues for Evaluation

Issue	Brief Description of Issue	Key Questions
Purpose of Instruction	The reason for offering the instruction	▪ What performance problem is to be solved by the training? ▪ What career objectives are to be met by employee education? ▪ What organizational objectives are to be supported by developmental activities?
Linkage to needs	The relationship between training, education, or development and the needs to be met by them	▪ Are instructional objectives clearly linked to identified needs? ▪ Are objectives for training linked to job performance problems? ▪ Are objectives for education linked to staffing plans? Individual career plans? ▪ Are objectives for development linked to long-term organizational strategy?
Marketing	The way the instruction is promoted/communicated to stakeholders	▪ Are stakeholders clearly identified? ▪ Are their interests clear? ▪ Is instruction promoted to them based on their interests and needs?
Objectives/Goals	▪ The general outcomes to be met by instruction ▪ The specific outcomes to be met by a training course, educational experience, or developmental intervention	▪ Are the instructional goals of the program stated? ▪ Are instructional objectives for each program, lesson, and unit clearly stated?
Desirable Outcomes	The desired impact of training on the job; the desired impact of education on career mobility; the desired impact of development on a part of the organization, the culture, or a stakeholder group	▪ Are the desired on-the-job effects of instruction clarified? ▪ Is someone held accountable for transfer of learning from the instructional setting to the work setting?
Assessment of Outcomes	The way the outcomes of training, education, or development will be measured	▪ Is it clear how participant reactions to instruction will be measured? ▪ Is it clear how learning outcomes will be measured? ▪ Is it clear how behavior will be measured? ▪ Is it clear how on-the-job effects will be measured?

Exhibit 12-2: *(continued)*

Issue	Brief Description of Issue	Key Questions
The setting	Where instruction will be carried out; where evaluation will be carried out	❚ What is special about the instructional setting? ❚ What is special about the evaluation setting?
The learners	The people for whom the instruction is intended	❚ What assumptions are made about the learners? ❚ What prerequisite skills are needed?
Instruction	The subject matter to be delivered	❚ Does the subject matter match instruction? ❚ Is the subject matter selected/prepared appropriately?
Provision for differences	Planning for differences between learners	❚ How are differences between learners recognized? ❚ How are differences between learners dealt with during instruction?
Logistics	Planning for delivering the instruction	❚ Are the resources available for carrying out instruction? Planned for?
Testing of instruction	How learning will be measured at the end of instruction	❚ Are test items clearly linked to instructional objectives? ❚ Have tests been tested?
Implementation of instruction	How the instruction will be carried out	❚ Do presentation methods match objectives, and are they appropriate for them?
Application	How instruction will be applied on the job	❚ What on-the-job application is desired? ❚ How will on-the-job application be measured?
Effects	The results of instruction in improved productivity, cost savings, improved quality of work life, improved morale	❚ What effects are possible? ❚ What effects are desired? ❚ What effects are being achieved?
Use of information about the effects	How information about the effects of instruction will be used	❚ Who wants to know about training? Education? Development? ❚ What decisions will be made based on the information?

Method. How will the evaluation be carried out? This question has to do with planning the evaluation. An *evaluation plan* sets forth precisely what to evaluate and how to evaluate it. An evaluation plan resembles a research plan. A typical evaluation plan consists of five parts: (1) problem, (2) hypothesis or objectives, (3) research design, (4) sample, and (5) methods for analyzing and interpreting data.

The *problem component* of an evaluation plan sets forth the question that the evaluation study is designed to answer. It is a purpose statement phrased as a question. As we shall see later in this chapter, differences exist between evaluations of training, education, development, and the entire Talent Development effort. Nevertheless, a common problem is to measure how much and what kind of change occurred before and after planned learning experiences.

The *hypothesis* is appropriate only when evaluators seek statistical evidence that some change occurred as a result of instruction. An *evaluation hypothesis* sets forth what evaluators expect to find and why they expect to find it. A *null hypothesis* is what evaluators actually test. It is an arbitrary convention proposing that changes did *not* occur or, if they did, that they are attributable to chance or some other variable out of the researcher's direct control. When evaluators seek evidence different from that yielded by statistics, they establish objectives instead of hypotheses. Objectives describe what results are to be achieved by the evaluation study.

An evaluation design is a description of procedures to be followed in the evaluation study. Its meaning is similar to that for the term *research design,* which sets forth the procedures to be used in testing a hypothesis. Evaluation designs, like research designs, fall into three general categories: (1) descriptive, (2) quasi-experimental, and (3) experimental. The choice of which one to use depends on what is to be evaluated, evaluator purposes, and the working environment.

Descriptive evaluation designs, as the name implies, are set up to describe existing phenomena. They cannot be used to test hypotheses. No attempt is made to control conditions. Evaluators simply describe what they see.

Quasi-experimental evaluation designs are more rigorous than descriptive evaluation. They are appropriate for imposing at least partial control over experimental conditions and the assignment of individuals to groups. Other differences between groups are held constant. The idea is to set up, for comparative purposes, two groups that are essentially the same. Change through planned learning is sought in one group but not in the other. Evaluators then compare groups to find differences in attitudes, learning, behavior, or results before the change effort is begun and after it has been administered.

In quasi-experimental designs, evaluators make every effort to preserve existing work groups, but select at least two that are essentially the same but perhaps not identical. Baseline measurements of both groups are taken. These measurements can come from results of attitude surveys, pre-tests, structured observations of on-the-job behavior, examinations of production data, or some combination. Attitude surveys measure feelings; pre-tests measure knowledge; behavioral observations measure what people do; and examinations of production data focus on work outputs. Members of one group are then provided with planned learning experiences, while members of another group are not. After planned learning events—so-called *experimental treatments*—measures are again taken of attitudes, knowledge, behavior, or results. Statistically significant differences in measures of the groups are attributed to the learning events.

Experimental designs are more rigorous. Participants in each group are assigned at random; all other conditions affecting performance are held constant. Baseline measurements are taken of both groups before learning events. Only the experimental group receives planned learning. Then measurements are taken again. Differences are attributed to learning events.

It is possible to use other, more sophisticated, quasi-experimental or experimental designs. More sophisticated designs remove threats to *internal validity* ("In this situation, did instruction make a difference that is not attributable to such possible problems as unplanned events before and after training, the aging of participants, etc.?") and *external validity* ("Can the results of this evaluation study be reasonably generalized as true for other similar groups?").

Practically speaking, experimental rigor is rare in organizational settings. Practical considerations, such as the need to make all workers maximally productive, make it difficult to offer learning experiences to some people while not offering it to others. Differential treatment can also create morale problems. People who do not receive the benefit of learning experiences may feel slighted. In fact, such feelings can influence performance and thus distort evaluation results. Participants in evaluation must not feel they are being manipulated like puppets.

The *sample* is the fourth component of an evaluation plan. It describes a group to be studied. Sampling is used when a large group is to be studied—perhaps the entire organization. Sampling economizes effort so that a relatively small group can be studied and the results can apply to all people affected. Sampling also reduces bias. *Random sampling*—assigning participants to control or experimental groups on a random basis—holds differences between participants constant.

Sampling is not always used in evaluation studies. For example, in a case study of a training program, the evaluator might describe the entire organization, one department, one work group, or one individual. In descriptive studies of this kind, however, the evaluator is obliged to clarify the *unit of analysis*—literally, the person, group, or structural component of an organization to be analyzed.

When using sampling in quasi-experimental and experimental designs, evaluators find some kinds of samples more appropriate than others. *Simple random sampling* is common with relatively small populations. People are assigned to control and experimental groups through random number tables or random number generators. *Stratified random sampling* is appropriate for larger populations or those in which wide variations exist among participants. The aim is to ensure representativeness in the sample to preserve the distribution of such variables as age, location, and educational background found in the population. *Systematic random sampling* is appropriate for the largest populations. All employees are listed and chosen on some systematic basis, such as including every sixth person in the study. Finally, *simple cluster sampling* is also appropriate for the largest populations. Prospective participants in the evaluation are clustered by operating unit, location, supervisor, or other means. Only some "clusters" are used for drawing a sample.

Methods to be used in analyzing and interpreting data are described in the last section of an evaluation plan. It is important before data collection to specify how information will be organized and subsequently examined. In fact, it helps if evaluators think ahead to the time when results will be presented to decision-makers. By doing so, they can anticipate questions and the kind of information they will need to answer those questions.

If statistical methods will be used for analysis, evaluators should clarify in advance of data collection precisely what statistical tests they will apply to the data. In this way, evaluators can make sure they collect the data necessary for performing those tests. Nothing is more embarrassing than to have to backtrack to collect data because no advance thought was given as to how the data would later be analyzed.

If non-statistical, qualitative research methods are used for analysis and interpretation, then evaluators still need to think ahead. How will descriptive information be organized and presented? These questions must be answered before information is collected.

Evaluating Training

What should be evaluated? Training is traditionally designed to produce immediate change in employee job performance. Its focus is on the job. The purpose of training is to narrow gaps between what job incumbents should know or do and what they actually know or do. Training is a very short-term change effort.

Evaluation pervades all aspects of training. It guides decisions to use training to correct a performance problem, rather than use some other improvement strategy. This is called front-end analysis. It influences the preparation of test items matched to instructional objectives. It is used in field-testing instruction before and after widespread adoption, and even during instruction. However, evaluation is perhaps most often associated with post-instructional assessment.

Front-End Evaluation: The Traditional Approach. Front-end evaluation bridges the need and the action taken to meet it. It is thus intended to correct the most glaring human performance problems in the most cost-effective manner. Typical questions asked during front-end evaluation include the following:

❘ Who has the problem? Who first noticed that it was a problem, and how did they notice?
❘ What is the problem?
❘ When was the problem first noticed?

▌ Where is the problem evident?

▌ Why is it a problem?

▌ How has the problem been addressed so far? Has corrective action been attempted, and with what result?

▌ How much is the problem worth to the organization? How could its effects be made measurable?

In sorting out instructional from noninstructional needs, WLP practitioners should apply four acid tests by examining:

1. *Management commitment.* Do managers view a problem as important enough to warrant attention?

2. *Resources.* Are adequate resources available to meet the need? If not, are managers willing to provide funds, staff, time, and materials?

3. *Skills.* Do WLP practitioners possess necessary skills to meet the need? If not, can they identify people who do possess the skills from inside or outside the organization? Are they free to contract for needed skills?

4. *Costs versus benefits.* Will costs of solving a problem produce greater benefits than alternatives such as taking no action or selecting a different solution?

Of these tests, cost-benefit analysis is the most important and the most difficult. It is important because WLP practitioners are often faced with the necessity of convincing managers that training is worth the costs associated with it. A cost is understood to mean both (1) *direct* expenditures such as funding required to analyze a problem or develop, deliver, and evaluate instruction, and (2) *indirect* expenditures on salaries, lost production time, and rental of facilities. Benefits are estimates of increased production or cost savings. They can be calculated per employee and then multiplied over the number of trainees. Calculating cost-benefit ratios is difficult because they are simple estimates that are easily challenged. It is not all that clear what cost or benefit categories should be used.

If the results of front-end analysis reveal that training is an appropriate and cost-beneficial solution to a performance problem, then WLP practitioners can complete an intensive needs assessment and begin instructional design.

Front-End Evaluation: The Strategic Approach. One major problem exists with the traditional approach to front-end evaluation, or FEE: It assumes that any performance problem can be judged using information about *present* conditions and *present* cost-benefits. That assumption is not always valid. Changes inside or outside an organization may gradually increase or decrease the importance of a performance problem, or even alter the nature of it.

Consider a simple example. Suppose that production output is below standard in one work group. Upon further analysis, WLP practitioners determine that the problem is attributable to lack of employee skills. For simplicity's sake, assume that new machines are being introduced gradually. Even experienced workers do not know how to use them. A simple front-end analysis of this problem may or may not demonstrate a present need for training. However, common sense dictates that production levels will probably remain below standard until all new machines are introduced and, assuming no formal training is provided, workers learn through trial and error how to use the machines.

In this example, a traditional approach to FEE does not tell the whole story. The performance problem is not severe at present, but it might well become more severe as new machines are introduced. Experience is not an adequate gauge for judging how long it will take for production levels to reach or exceed normal levels, unless similar machines were introduced on a similar production line at another company facility some time before.

If WLP practitioners wait around for this performance problem to reveal itself, valuable production output will be lost. Nor will it be easy to estimate how much output will be lost. Even supervisors may not be convinced under present conditions that training is necessary.

What then? Are the workplace learning and performance professionals forced into a reactive mode, unable to respond until the performance problem is apparent to everyone and managers are willing to support organized instruction on new machines?

Not at all. The WLP practitioner has to demonstrate beforehand that the problem will exist, will affect production, and will lend itself to a solution through training.

How is this accomplished? There are several ways: The first is *through direct persuasion*. WLP practitioners can go to the people affected by the problem (the production manager, the foreperson, and workers) to discuss the problem. The second is *through indirect persuasion*. Practitioners can find analogous situations, remind managers of historical events, and point out similarities between them and the problem at hand. *Simulation* can also be used. Practitioners can set up a demonstration and show supervisors or managers what the problems are (if this is not possible, they can shoot a videotape and show it to key decisionmakers).

The purpose of future-oriented front-end evaluation is to anticipate future performance problems before they come up and determine the most effective means of averting them. To undertake a future-oriented FEE, WLP practitioners must do these things:

1. Scan trends in work flow and work methods at the operational level.
2. Isolate areas in which changes are likely to occur.
3. Pinpoint changes that are likely to be most costly in the future.
4. Separate noninstructional from instructional needs.
5. Consider alternative strategies for averting a performance problem.
6. Isolate root causes of anticipated problems, such as changes in technology, job, or work group redesign, new products, or job duties.
7. Point out the likely problem to managers and supervisors, gaining their support to avert future performance problems.

If these steps are followed, WLP practitioners will find that their mode of operation is proactive. Planned learning activities will anticipate and help avert problems before they arise.

Testing: The Traditional Approach. Traditionally, a major purpose of testing is to measure how well trainees achieved terminal objectives upon course completion. It can also be used to screen trainees to ensure that they possess the necessary prerequisite skills to receive training or to measure their progress during training.

Criterion-referenced tests are, however, most important because they measure trainee mastery of course objectives. They take their name from explicit linkage to objectives. Objectives are stated in measurable terms, and achievement of them is intended to close a performance gap. Test items are prepared from objectives and linked to them.

There are numerous types of test items, such as true-false, multiple choice, essay, matching, and many others. Each is more appropriate for measuring some objectives than others. Recall that objectives can be classified in three broad domains: affective or feeling-oriented, cognitive or knowledge-oriented, and psychomotor or movement-oriented.

Testing: The Strategic Approach. There are two major problems with traditional testing. First, it tends to focus solely on terminal *course* objectives. When tests are geared to measuring end-of-unit (enabling) objectives or end-of-course (terminal) objectives alone, trainees are held accountable only for formal instruction. Testing that focuses on objectives of this kind no doubt makes trainers accountable for doing a good job, but testing does not really hold trainees accountable for *applying* on the job what they learned in training.

A more useful approach is to express instructional objectives on several levels, including not just end-of-course mastery, but also on-the-job behaviors and results. Testing is sometimes carried out back on the job. In this way, trainees are held accountable for making sure that change occurs on the job, where it really counts.

The second problem with traditional testing is that it does not take into account changes in job conditions occurring over time. In fact, most training is purely maintenance-oriented, intended to bring the performance of inexperienced workers in line with experienced ones. WLP practitioners look at historical standards and tried-and-true methods. This technique works well in settings where job conditions do not change much. It is not, however, appropriate under fast-paced, rapidly-changing conditions. In such cases, practitioners should prepare instructional objectives based on *predictions* of future job conditions. When that is done, test items have to be prepared accordingly.

This is admittedly risky business, because job conditions may not change as expected. But in fast-paced, dynamic settings, it is more appropriate than waiting around to design tests until some future time when conditions become more settled.

The format of future-oriented test items need not differ much from its traditional counterparts. However, it might be more appropriate under some conditions to rely on experiential exercises such as case studies, role plays, simulations, and critical incidents instead of paper-and-pencil testing to assess how well trainees will fare in expected future job conditions. Testing should be handled longitudinally, with pre-programmed follow-ups on the job to assess performance under future conditions.

Formative Evaluation: The Traditional Approach. Michael Scriven (1967) was the first to suggest rigorous, advance testing of instructional content and presentation methods before widespread use of them. Formative evaluation takes its name from using evaluation to *form* instruction (Gagné and Briggs 1979).

Formative evaluation is conducted in many different ways and is often carried out rather informally. Think of it as a special kind of market test in which the product (the instructional materials) is tried out on all its possible consumers (instructors, trainees, supervisors, and perhaps others). A whole range of issues may be considered in this process.

Formative evaluations can be as complicated or as uncomplicated as WLP practitioners wish them to be. However, extensive testing is probably worthwhile under the following conditions: (1) when opinions on the issue are sharply divided within the organization, within the occupation/discipline, or between managers or supervisors or prospective trainees; (2) when WLP practitioners are using methods or media with which they are unfamiliar; (3) when targeted trainees vary widely in skills, knowledge, or attitudes; or (4) when the instruction is a first attempt to satisfy a need.

Exhibit 12-3 describes some ways of conducting a formative evaluation. Any or all may be used, depending on preferences of evaluators and time and money available.

Formative Evaluation: The Strategic Approach. One problem with the traditional approach to formative evaluation is that it is based on the fundamental assumption that instructional materials can be made more effective in the future if they are revised on the basis of tests in the present or past. If requirements are stable, this assumption is valid enough. If they are unstable, however, results of past tests will do nothing to improve instruction, especially when the subject matter itself is also past-oriented.

Exhibit 12-3: Methods of Conducting Formative Evaluation

Method	When?	Description
Individualized Testing	Upon completion of the training materials	Treat the instructional materials to intensive field-testing with only one person. Go through the materials with the individual, attempting to identify anything that is unclear.
Small-Group Testing	Upon completion of individualized testing	Go through the instructional materials in a small-group setting. Identify any problems with the material.
Field Testing	Upon completion of small-group testing	Offer instruction under real conditions—but on an experimental basis.
Expert Testing	Upon completion of field-testing	Ask subject experts/supervisors to review the instructional materials.

A simple example should illustrate this point. Suppose a WLP practitioner is orienting entry-level auditors to their job requirements. The auditors possess appropriate entry-level knowledge of accounting basics. What they do not possess is organization-specific knowledge of policies and procedures. They know from college courses what a work paper or white paper is; they do not know the kind of white-paper requirements that exist in one public accounting firm. On the latter issue, they need training. WLP practitioners can design a program to teach them organizational requirements for preparing such authoritative reports. If white-paper requirements in the organization do not change, then the results of formative evaluation will be appropriate for revising instruction to increase its effectiveness.

But suppose that policymakers decide to change the organization's policies on white paper reports, perhaps as a result of attending a rehearsal of training on present policies. Then what? Will training have to be redesigned and retested accordingly? The answer is yes, particularly if the change in policy is a radical departure from past practices.

In some instances, however, WLP practitioners are aware that such a change is likely. When they are, it makes no sense for them to develop and test instructional materials based on a white-paper policy about to be changed. Some practitioners will argue that, in such a case, the sensible course of action is to wait around until a new work-paper policy has been formalized. Then training can be designed and tested.

The trouble is that this wait-and-see method makes WLP practitioners purely reactive. When the policy changes, instruction lags long after. By that time, many otherwise unnecessary on-the-job mistakes have been made.

The point is that formative evaluation should be carried out under conditions that closely match the conditions expected to exist when trainees are ready to apply what they learned. If radical changes are expected, then WLP practitioners should simulate those conditions when they test instructional materials. Admittedly, that might be easier said than done. But if formative evaluation is to be effective, it has to be carried out in this way. If not, trainees will be instructed the wrong way, and future job performance will not be as effective as it could have been.

Summative Evaluation: The Traditional Approach. Michael Scriven (1967) considered formative evaluation only a first step in testing instructional materials. He believed that it should be followed at a later time by summative evaluation, which takes its name from using *summed effects* of instruction for evaluative purposes.

To conduct a traditional summative evaluation, a WLP practitioner must

1. *Examine all instructional materials* after they have been revised in light of formative evaluation results. Do they appear to do what they are supposed to do?

2. *Observe an instructor* delivering the materials. Do learners respond as expected? Does the instructor adequately present the material?

3. *Administer a post-test* to measure trainee achievement of objectives.

4. *Administer an attitude survey* to find out how well participants liked the course and whether or not they think it met their needs.

5. *Compare subsequent job performance* of people who received the training and people who did not receive the training (or who benefited from a different kind of performance-improvement strategy).

Summative Evaluation: The Strategic Approach. The same problem that plagues formative evaluations also affects their summative counterparts. Will present or past evaluation results be appropriate for judging the future? Traditionally it is assumed they will be.

As in formative evaluations, this assumption is valid only when job conditions and learners' entry characteristics or skills remain stable. If work methods or organizational policies change, then the results of *past* summative evaluations will be inappropriate for judging instruction based on *present* conditions or *present* needs. Likewise, if entry characteristics of learners change because the organization recruits workers with different backgrounds, then summative evaluations carried out in the past will no longer be valid.

What can be done, then? Will new summative evaluations have to be carried out? Perhaps. It all depends on *how much* future conditions will change. WLP practitioners have to scan the environment to foresee changes likely to have a future impact either on trainees selected for instruction or on job requirements. Consider: Is there a chance that the kind of workers recruited in a job class will differ significantly from those entering that class in the past? Is there a chance that work methods, technology, company policy, or some other characteristic will change substantially?

If the answer to either question (or both) is yes, then WLP practitioners will have to (1) identify what changes they expect, (2) predict what impact they expect those changes to have on work methods and corresponding training needs, (3) modify present training in line with predictions, and (4) test the training under simulated conditions like those expected on the job in the future.

Concurrent Evaluation: The Traditional Approach. A concurrent evaluation is undertaken during training delivery. It is thus *concurrent* with the instruction it is intended to evaluate. It can be undertaken as part of a summative study, or it can stand alone.

A third-party evaluator, someone other than the instructor, can call a time-out during a course or at the end of a course unit. An attitude survey is then administered to trainees to assess their feelings at that point. They are asked to describe their reactions to the instructor, presentation methods, progress to that point, and group interaction.

Tests may also be administered during a training course to measure trainee achievement relative to enabling objectives. In this way, trainee progress can be assessed during the training. If test results reveal inadequate progress, individuals can then be targeted for remedial attention, or training methods can be altered when group progress collectively falls below expectations.

Structured observation by a third party, another method of concurrent evaluation, is typically carried out by a peer or supervisor who sits in on training. The evaluator does not rely on vague, subjective impressions about the quality of delivery; rather, the evaluator completes a structured observation form during the presentation. This form, developed in advance, lists critical dimensions of instructor performance and corresponding behaviors along a continuum. The evaluator notes how often these behaviors are exhibited by the instructor. The results are later discussed as a starting point to improve delivery.

Unstructured naturalistic observation also requires a third-party evaluator. However, the evaluator does not record observations on a form prepared in advance. Instead, the evaluator is the instrument of inquiry and relies on observation of the classroom setting, personal impressions, and perhaps follow-up interviews with instructor and/or participants to arrive at conclusions about strengths and weaknesses of the instructor's presentation methods. These are, in turn, fed back to the instructor as a stimulant for improvement.

Electronically enhanced feedback is a fancy phrase for something simple: using videotapes to show the instructor precisely what behaviors are being exhibited during delivery. There are two kinds: (1) simultaneous feedback, occurring during delivery, and (2) delayed feedback, occurring after delivery. Imagine aiming a television camera on an instructor during delivery with a television monitor placed so that the instructor can see it. Feedback occurs as the delivery is made. The instructor who is simultaneously the observed and the observer can then modify behavior as events occur. (For some instructors, this creates stage fright that was not apparent before.) Delayed feedback occurs after delivery: the instructor watches the presentation, noting behaviors and their effects on participants. This feedback is the starting point for self-modeling, in which the instructor notes areas for future improvement in delivery methods.

Concurrent Evaluation: The Strategic Approach. It is difficult to anticipate conditions in group training before they occur. Each group has its own chemistry, stemming from the individual group members and from interactions between people.

One approach that helps anticipate problems that may occur in a group setting is to poll participants in advance. At the beginning of the training session, read through the returned surveys as a "warm-up." In this way, the hidden agenda of an individual is revealed and dealt with up front. While this approach does not always work, it sometimes serves as a lightning rod for releasing pent-up feelings or problems.

The best advance preparation for delivery of instruction is, of course, practice: it never hurts any presenter, even the most experienced, to rehearse an entire training program before delivery. Dry-runs have beneficial side effects, especially if interested parties such as supervisors or executives are invited to attend. The instructor benefits from their suggestions, while supervisors are exposed to the training their subordinates receive and are thus informed enough to later hold subordinates accountable for on-the-job application.

Post-Instructional Evaluations: Traditional Approaches. Post-instructional evaluations are conducted, as their name suggests, after a training course or program has been delivered. They overlap with other forms of training evaluation that have already been discussed.

Donald Kirkpatrick (1959; 1960; 1998) conceptualized a classic way of viewing post-instructional evaluations by arranging possible results of training on a four-level hierarchy of change (see Exhibit 12–4). In ascending order, these levels are

1. *Reactions.* How much did trainees like a course? How much do they feel it will help them improve their job performance?

2. *Learning.* How much knowledge or skill change resulted from a course? How well did participants achieve the terminal objectives of the course?

3. *Behaviors.* What changes in job behaviors resulted from training? How much are workers applying what they learned in a way that is measurable and observable?

Exhibit 12–4: Donald Kirkpatrick's Evaluation Hierarchy

Reactions	Learning	Behavior	Results
How well do learners like the training?	How well do learners score on tests at the end of training?	How well do learners apply the behaviors they learned in training on the job?	How well does the productivity of the learners improve on the job?

4. *Results.* What changes in job results are attributable to training? How much more productive are trained than untrained workers? What differences in productivity levels stem from training?

Reactions are probably measured more frequently than the other three levels, often by means of attitude surveys or so-called participant evaluations that are handed out at the end of courses or sessions. While reaction surveys can indicate *feelings*, they do not really address bottom-line *results*.

Another way to evaluate reactions is to send trainees a survey about one to six months after their participation in a training program. Sometimes their views change as they acquire more experience or reflect on course content.

Learning, the second step in Kirkpatrick's hierarchy of change, is measured by tests. During instructional design, one or more test items are written to correspond to each instructional objective. After test items are developed, instructional content (subject matter) and delivery methods (means of presentation) are chosen. The result is a direct link between intentions for end-of-course change as expressed in terminal objectives and test items for measuring them.

Most people think of *written* tests, which are sometimes called paper-and-pencil tests. However, tests can also be administered orally or through demonstration of knowledge or skills. What could be a better way to prove mastery of learning objectives than to perform what was learned? Frequently, demonstration involves assembling or disassembling machinery or some other physical object. To demonstrate skill or knowledge mastery with data (as in mathematics), trainees may be asked to solve a problem. To demonstrate skill or knowledge mastery with people, trainees may be asked to participate in an experiential exercise simulation, a role play, or a case study.

Tests need not be administered only at the end of a course, though that is appropriate if the intent is to measure *end-of-course* learning. They can also be given to trainees before instruction in order to measure entry knowledge or skills. Sometimes *pretests* are used for screening purposes to make sure that learners possess adequate entry skills and thus have satisfied prerequisites. Tests can also be given periodically during a course to determine how well learners are progressing.

Behaviors, the third level in Kirkpatrick's hierarchy of change, are measured *on the job* rather than *at the end of a course.* This distinction is important, because trainee job behavior is affected by much more than instruction. It is also affected by individual motivation, peer pressure exerted by co-workers, expectations of supervisors, and much more. It is possible for a trainee to complete training successfully and never change behavior on the job.

There are several ways to assess changes in job behaviors produced by training, what some call simply *transfer of learning.* To list a few: (1) Ask the learners, their co-workers, supervisors, or subordinates if training has influenced job behavior. (2) Show up at the work site and ask former trainees to demonstrate how they are using what they learned in training. (3) Observe former trainees at work both before and after training, noting any changes in observable work methods. (4) Compare job behaviors of former trainees and a control group of similar but randomly selected non-trainees using predetermined criteria. To phrase it another way, behavioral change on the job can be measured through the opinions of trainees or other people, through tests of learning conducted at the job site, through work sampling of behaviors, or through evaluation design. Obviously, the first method is the easiest, but it is the least valid and reliable, because opinions are not necessarily accurate. The fourth method is most valid and reliable, but is also the most costly and time-consuming.

Results, the fourth level of Kirkpatrick's hierarchy of change, are also (like behaviors) measured on the job rather than at the end of instruction. Results are the real bottom-line: Did training change on-the-job output or quality? To address this difficult question, WLP practitioners must identify before training (1) *what results* they will attempt to change, (2) *how much change* they will try to achieve, and (3) *how they will analyze and interpret* change.

Depending on the performance problem that training is intended to solve, *the results* that are sought can vary. Spitzer and Conway (2002) note that fewer than 3 percent of all training programs are evaluated for business impact.

Post-Instructional Evaluations: The Strategic Approach. It is difficult to predict post-instructional outcomes of training. For this reason, practitioners should improve an area they have too often neglected during instructional design–analysis of the work content.

Before training is delivered and during needs assessment, practitioners should carefully examine the work setting. Just what are the accepted norms of behavior? What does a supervisor believe his or her employees need to know? What rewards or punishments are likely to affect application of new methods on the job?

Once these questions have been addressed, practitioners should gear their efforts as closely as possible to conditions likely to exist when trainees return to the job. If barriers to application exist, they should be identified during training. Trainees will have to be furnished with methods to help them eliminate the barriers or apply instruction *despite* barriers. While this is quite difficult (especially when trainees attend from a cross-section of work groups, rather than only one), it is not impossible. WLP practitioners should enlist the support of others back on the job site, such as experienced workers who have attended training in the past, or supervisors who have a stake in performance improvement. These supporters serve as on-the-job coaches who facilitate application of training.

Comprehensive Reviews of Training. There is little point in distinguishing between traditional and future-oriented approaches to comprehensive reviews of all training courses. There are two good reasons why. First, few organizations develop a long-term learning plan or training curriculum by job class. Second, evaluation is relatively rare. In short, there is no training curriculum and little evaluation.

Before a comprehensive review of training can be conducted in an organization, several preconditions must be met. First, a curriculum must exist. That means that WLP practitioners have succeeded in planning for long-term training needs in each job class. Second, the purpose of the training curriculum must be stated. Why does it exist? Third, the goals must also be stated. What results are sought from training for each job class and for all job classes taken together? Fourth, each training program must be systematically planned and evaluated.

Fifth, each training program should simultaneously reflect (a) job requirements for its targeted learners, (b) organizational requirements and priorities, and (c) organizational strategy for Talent Development. Sixth and finally, the evaluation results of each training program should be collected and stored (a) program-by-program, (b) learner-by-learner, and (c) job class-by-job class.

Perhaps the most important preconditions are the first, fourth, and sixth. A curriculum must exist before a comprehensive review of training can be carried out. Each training course or other planned instructional event must be planned and evaluated so that information is available about each program. This information must be recorded in a way that allows data to be compared and aggregated over time.

To carry out a comprehensive review of training, practitioners should begin by setting a policy that such reviews will be conducted at periodic intervals—every year or two. A training advisory committee, composed of representatives from the WLP department, line management, top management, and trainees, can be especially useful. This committee directs studies, participates in them, and/or receives results and makes recommendations for corrective action.

Regardless of who is involved, however, it will be necessary to (1) clarify the purpose, goals, and objectives of the review, (2) select people who possess the skills necessary to carry it out, (3) establish an evaluation plan, and (4) clarify precisely what will be done with the results once they are received.

In most respects, a comprehensive training review is approached like any evaluation study. The only key difference between it and most studies has to do with focus. A comprehensive training review focuses on the overall training plan for each job class or all job classes in the organization.

Evaluating Employee Education

What should be evaluated? Employee education grooms individuals for specific future jobs, keeps people current and up-to-date in their fields, and stimulates new ideas by exposing people to practices in other organizations. Each of these purposes and end-results is somewhat different. Hence, evaluation of education varies in methods and approaches, depending on purpose.

Evaluative methods for employee education are similar to those used for train-ing, but there are differences. The methods include front-end analysis for employee education, advance counseling, evaluation of educational materials, concurrent evaluation, post-educational follow-up, and comprehensive reviews of employee education.

Front-End Analysis (FEA) for Employee Education. Front-end analysis for employee education is different from its training counterpart. Its purpose, from a manager's standpoint, is to plan for future staffing needs. From an individual's standpoint, its purpose is to plan for realizing immediate career objectives—advancement to a higher position, transfer to a different career line, or some other objective. The idea is to negotiate these objectives so that the supervisor and the employee share a common goal for the employee's next career step.

The essence of FEA for education is best summarized through a series of questions. Supervisors should ask (1) What will be the most critical future staffing needs of the unit, department, or organization? (2) How can those needs be met in the most cost-effective means? Through external education? External recruitment? Internal transfer? Internal education and transition into the new position? Or external contracting? (3) If external education is selected, what is the best source or group of sources of education to meet future staffing needs?

Individuals should consider these questions: (1) What skills or competencies are essential in a targeted future position? (2) What skills or competencies does the individual possess at present? (3) What differences exist between the individ-ual's present skills or competencies and those needed in the future for the targeted position? and (4) How can needed skills or competencies be acquired? What sources are available to meet needs?

When supervisors and individuals negotiate answers to these questions, then they can arrive at a plan for employee education that will satisfy or at least strike a balance between both individual and organizational needs. It is wise to express this plan in terms of educational objectives, which can be negotiated through a Management by Objectives plan or a learning contract.

Evaluation of Educational Sources. There are, of course, many ways to meet an educational need. Individuals can be sent to external seminars, directed through externally produced materials, sent to college courses, or sent to programs delivered by external consultants but presented in-house.

Each alternative should be considered according to cost, convenience, and relevance to educational objectives, as well as constraints on time, funding, and available information. Once a prospective source is chosen, it should be evaluated carefully in advance. Methods of doing that may vary, depending on the source.

If an external seminar or college course is a possible source, the WLP practitioner should research it carefully before sending people to it. A good place to start is with the course brochure. What does it say about the course? What objectives are stated for it? For what kind of people is it intended? Is an outline available and, if so, what subject matter will be covered? By what methods? It also helps to contact past participants (the vendor should be willing to give that information). What do past participants say about the course's strengths and weaknesses? What is the general reputation of the vendor? If these questions yield satisfying answers, then consider how many people in the organization share the same educational need. If many do, it might be worthwhile for the WLP practitioner to attend the course and/or send a few experienced employees to attend and bring back a report.

If the educational source is a package available for purchase, WLP practitioners can request it on a trial basis. They can look it over. They should ask subject matter experts in the organization to do likewise.

If an external consultant is to be hired, practitioners should check out his or her education and experience in advance. What about recommendations from previous clients?

If WLP practitioners consider meeting educational needs in-house, they should be as rigorous in their up-front assessments as they are in evaluating external sources. Does the WLP department possess the resources and expertise to meet a specific educational need? If not, can these resources be acquired? Can expertise be obtained through temporary transfers from other departments? Will the in-house costs of meeting needs be cheaper *and* more effective than alternatives?

Advance Counseling. Before sending employees through educational experiences, advance counseling is crucial and is essential to success. Employees should understand why they are going through an experience, what they should be able to do upon completion, and why the experience is important. It is helpful to counsel individuals prior to their participation in education. Such counseling sessions can be handled by the WLP practitioner, the employee's supervisor, or both.

Concurrent Evaluation. Some educational experiences take a long time. A college course may last up to sixteen weeks, for example. Some in-house programs may last even longer.

Concurrent evaluation is performed during educational experiences. On the simplest level, the WLP practitioner arranges to speak with employees periodically as they progress through education. These sessions are usually informal, intended to check on progress. If an individual is experiencing difficulties, this is the time to discuss them and arrange for help.

Post-Educational Follow-up. Each educational experience should be evaluated after the individual has completed it. Much like training, an employee educational experience can be judged according to (1) *reactions* (Do employees feel that the experience contributed to preparing them for career advancement? Do supervisors believe the experience contributed to meeting future staffing needs?); (2) *learning* (Can employees demonstrate the skills or competencies they learned during the educational experience?); (3) *behavior* (Can employees apply, upon promotion, the skills or competencies they learned through employee education?); and (4) *results* (How well are employees able to perform under future conditions in their new position?). Reactions are measured through surveys and interviews; learning is measured by tests; behavior is measured by observation, employee appraisals, and long-term follow-up; and results are measured by availability of talent and/or expressions of individual satisfaction with career progress.

Comprehensive Reviews of Employee Education. A comprehensive review of employee education is similar to a comprehensive review of training, except that its focus is on the entire range of educational offerings sponsored by an organization. The purpose for carrying out such a review is precisely the same as it is for reviewing training comprehensively. It helps managers consider the value of employee education in contributing to the achievement of goals pertinent to business strategy, staff strategy, individual career mobility, organizational profitability, Talent Development strategy, and quality of work life.

Several preconditions are necessary before a comprehensive review of employee education can be carried out:

1. Employee education must be planned according to a formal, deliberate process.
2. The purpose(s) of employee educational efforts must be stated.
3. The goals of employee education must be stated. What results are sought?
4. Each educational effort must be related to a personalized, negotiated plan for each individual.
5. Each educational effort must be formally planned and evaluated.
6. Each educational activity should simultaneously reflect (a) career objectives of individuals; (b) staffing requirements of the organization, department, or work unit; and (c) the organizational strategy for Talent Development.
7. Evaluation results, by individual, should be maintained in a Human Resource Information System.

Perhaps the most appropriate way to approach a comprehensive review of employee education is from the standpoint of formal career planning for individuals (on one hand) and formal HR planning for the organization (on the other hand). Consider the following:

1. *Evaluation of paths.* Have decision-makers in the organization clarified educational, experience, and other requirements for each position and for movement between positions?
2. *Evaluation of staff planning.* Have decision-makers clarified the organization's future staffing needs?
3. *Evaluation of educational sourcing.* How well is the organization identifying sources for meeting educational needs? Does the WLP department systematically collect and store such information?
4. *Evaluation of educational management.* How well is the organization managing employee educational efforts and tracking them?
5. *Meta-evaluation.* How is the organization evaluating educational efforts?

A comprehensive review of employee education is carried out much like a comprehensive review of training. In fact, they can be carried out together as well as separately.

Evaluating Development

What should be evaluated? Development is a long-term change effort carried out to change the collective competencies of people in group settings.

Employee development activities are difficult to plan, let alone evaluate, because the odds are stacked against them: Supervisors have trouble defining the mix of employee competencies needed to match up to group needs; and top managers tend to assume that human skills are acquired easily enough externally (so long-term internal development efforts will not be necessary).

Organization development (OD) is valued by managers at all levels, once they know what it is. Most experienced managers know how difficult it is to overcome resistance to change. Top managers realize that changes in organizational direction or strategy grow more difficult as they run counter to past tradition, culture, and group norms. OD encourages cultural change, but is by no means a "quick fix."

Nonemployee development is rarely approached systematically through organized Talent Development activities. Managers sometimes have difficulty recognizing immediate payoffs from these activities. In the United States, however, business leaders can hardly overlook increasing pressure on business to take an active role in improving community life. Nor can leaders easily dismiss the fact that products and services are becoming more technologically complex in response to consumer demand, so there is more need to help consumers learn how to use the sophisticated goods and services they buy. Indeed, lack of knowledge among consumers might be the greatest barrier to future sales growth for some high-technology firms.

While methods of development vary, evaluation methods are somewhat similar to those used in employee education or training. Evaluation can be done before, during, or after the implementation of a development strategy. When it is done beforehand, it is front-end analysis or field testing; when it occurs during implementation, it is concurrent evaluation; when it occurs at the end, it is post-developmental follow-up. Since development is long-term, however, after-the-fact evaluation is not as useful as it is in training or education. Objectives should be articulated for each type of development and then used as a basis for evaluation.

Front-End Analysis of Development. To conduct front-end analysis for employee development, the WLP practitioner must work in tandem with other managers in the organization to decide on long-term objectives to satisfy the staffing needs for each work unit. The purpose of front-end analysis for employee development is to pinpoint the most critical long-term staffing needs of each work group in line with strategic business plans.

To carry out front-end analysis (FEA) for employee development, WLP practitioners should begin with information about organizational staffing plans. In concert with other managers in the organization, they should deliberate over such questions as these: (1) What skills will be needed over three to five years to meet needs of the organization? (2) What skills or competencies are presently available? and (3) How can gaps between skills or competencies needed in the future and those available at present be narrowed?

Once supervisors answer these questions, they need to consider sources. How can individuals be groomed over the long term for the benefit of the work group? Sources include long-term mentoring programs; transfer or exchange programs; special job assignments; field trips; professional conferences; behavior modeling; and "think-tank" experiences. Each must be weighed not so much for cost as for effectiveness: How useful will it be in meeting the long-term staffing needs of the work unit?

When is an organizational development (OD) intervention appropriate? This question has to do with front-end analysis for OD. OD is appropriate when someone desires change, because conditions are not meeting expectations, top managers support change, problems stem from interactions between individuals or groups, cultural norms are at odds with desired change, and there is sufficient time and other resources to enact change. Unlike most WLP or Talent Development activities, OD facilitates group learning and group change.

When OD practitioners are asked to lend assistance, they begin by collecting information about the problem that prompted the call for help. In OD, data about problems is provided to those doing data collection and to decision-makers in order to stimulate problem-solving and decision-making. In WLP, data is used to separate training needs from non-training needs.

In OD, managers and employees set objectives for change. With the help of a consultant (typically from outside the unit or organization experiencing trouble), they then choose an appropriate OD intervention.

When is community and/or stakeholder development appropriate? This question has to do with front-end evaluation for nonemployee development. Progressive decision-makers believe nonemployee development efforts are *always* appropriate, because business firms should strive for improved relations with the communities in which their facilities are located and with the society in which they do business. Improved relations with suppliers, consumers, distributors, and other key stakeholder groups produce significant advantages to the firm. The more that stakeholders understand the unique needs of the business, the more effectively the firm will be able to sell its products or services, obtain necessary supplies, and produce goods or deliver services.

To conduct front-end evaluation for community/stakeholder development, WLP practitioners need to work with managers in the organization. There are four questions to ask: First, what future relationships are desirable with each external stakeholder group? Second, what is the nature of the present relationships between the organization and each major group outside it? Third, how can Talent Development efforts improve relations between the organization and external groups? Fourth and finally, what efforts stand the best chance of improving relations over time?

By systematically addressing these questions, managers and WLP practitioners establish a unified direction for nonemployee development efforts.

Field-Testing Development. The old adage "start small but think big" is appropriate for any development effort. It is a way of field testing. To field test employee development, start with one work group or department in the organization. Establish a model for employee development in the department or work group that is appropriate to it. Enlist the support of managers, supervisors, and employee opinion-leaders in planning, implementing, and periodically following up on it.

Once a model of employee development has been successfully used in one work group or department, it can be extended gradually into the remainder of the organization.

Use exactly the same approach with OD and nonemployee development. Start with one group, devise a successful means of developing the group, scan the environment for changes, and implement the development effort gradually.

Concurrent Evaluation of Development. Concurrent evaluation controls development efforts against initial objectives to ensure that activities are in line with intentions.

The WLP department should hold periodic meetings for interested parties to assess the progress of developmental efforts and identify areas requiring corrective action. Group meetings can be held for those participating in employee development programs or OD interventions. Advisory groups, much like marketing focus groups, can be assembled to represent external stakeholders, and meetings can be held with these groups to evaluate nonemployee development activities.

Post-Development Follow-up. Use post-development follow-up only when there is a need to *change* employee, organization, or nonemployee development initiatives. Change is appropriate when there is a major shift in strategic business plans, environmental conditions, staffing strategy, or organizational strategy for Talent Development.

Post-development follow-up begins with data collected through surveys or interviews. Results are then presented in meetings, along with information about the successes and failures of each development effort. This information sets the stage for establishing new development objectives and new action plans to meet them.

Evaluating the Talent Development Effort

Definition of Strategic Evaluation. Strategic evaluation (SE) of the Talent Development effort may be understood to mean monitoring the following:

▎ *Results match intentions.* Have the consequences of an organization's strategy for Talent Development been working as desired?

▎ *Organizational strategy for Talent Development is being implemented in line with long-term objectives.* Is the organization practicing operationally what was preached strategically?

I   *Organizational strategy for Talent Development is attuned to environmen-*
     tal conditions as the future unfolds in the present. Were expectations about
     the future accurate, and do they still furnish a reliable guide for Talent
     Development activities?

Strategic evaluation of the Talent Development effort is a comprehensive examination of how well human resources in the organization have been, are being, and
will be developed over time. It is the culmination of separate but comprehensive
reviews of training, education, and development. Its purpose is to take stock of
how well the organization's strategy has worked, is working, and will probably
work in the future.

When is strategic evaluation appropriate? Strategic evaluation (SE) is
appropriate before, during, and after implementation of organizational strategy.
When a proposed Talent Development strategy is examined before implementation, it is instrumental in making a *strategic choice;* when the chosen strategy is
evaluated during implementation, it is called *strategy review* or *concurrent evalu-*
ation; when the strategy is evaluated as decision-makers are contemplating a
change, it is called *summative evaluation.*

Strategic Evaluation Prior to Strategic Choice. Strategic evaluation is helpful in choosing organizational strategy for Talent Development. To carry out
strategic evaluation prior to strategic choice, decision-makers should address five
key issues in line with five key issues that should be regarded for organizational
strategy (Schendel and Hofer 1979):

1.   *Goal consistency.* How much are the goals/objectives of the existing or
     proposed organizational strategy for Talent Development internally
     consistent? In short, is the direction unified across proposed activities
     and integrated with strategic business plans and HR plans?

2.   *Design process.* How well designed was the process used to formulate the
     organizational strategy for Talent Development?

3.   *Strategy implementation.* How well can the organizational strategy be
     implemented? Will operating managers do their share? Will the WLP
     department do its share? How well-matched to proposed organizational
     strategy are structure, leadership, policies, and rewards?

4. *Early indicators.* How well has this organizational strategy been working? Have indicators been established to provide feedback about the effectiveness of the Talent Development strategy in the early stages of implementation? Will time allow tentative, small-scale tests of strategy in some plants or regions without committing all resources to an unproven strategy?

5. *Strategy content.* How well does the existing or proposed organizational strategy for Talent Development meet the needs and conform to the values of key stakeholders inside and outside the organization? How well does it meet tests for completeness, consistency, resource requirements, environmental accuracy, and goodness of fit with environmental assumptions?

By addressing these questions, decision-makers can choose a strategy that is appropriate to the organization and its environment.

Strategy Review. Once a unified organizational strategy has been chosen and implemented, decision-makers need some way to find out whether it is working out as intended.

A *strategy review* is a periodic examination of how well the strategy is working out. It can be included as an item on the agenda of a strategic business planning review meeting, or it can be the topic of a meeting all its own. Meetings of this kind should be scheduled on some regular basis—monthly, quarterly, semiannually, or annually. Often the frequency of review meetings is a function of hierarchical level. Corporate officers might meet only once or twice a year; business, functional, and divisional officers usually meet more frequently.

What issues are appropriately addressed during a review of organizational strategy? First, consider *progress to date.* Assuming that long-term objectives have been established to measure achievement, how well is organizational strategy contributing to organizational learning and adaptation, to preparation of individuals for movement to future jobs, and to performance improvement in present jobs? Second, review *responsiveness to stakeholders.* How well is organizational strategy meeting needs and conforming to the values of top managers, middle managers, first-line supervisors, nonsupervisory employees, and customers, suppliers, distributors, and community members? Third, review the *adequacy of original assumptions*. As the future unfolds, assumptions may remain valid, but strategy implementation may not necessarily follow the original course charted for it. On the other hand, assumptions may prove faulty and need to be reconsidered. Are assumptions still valid? Are they congruent with implementation? Fourth, review *realism*. Was the original organizational strategy realistic? In short, was it ever capable of being implemented, or did it call for too much change in too short a period of time? Fifth and finally, check the *availability of skills*. Are the skills needed to implement organizational strategy available to the organization? Do line managers, supervisors, and WLP staff members possess the necessary skills or competencies to do what is required of them? By addressing these questions periodically, decision-makers control actions against intentions and pinpoint areas needing correction or attention.

Summative Evaluation. For most WLP practitioners, summative evaluation is backward-looking because it judges the value of past instruction; it is forward-looking because these judgments are used to make decisions about adopting a planned learning experience on a broader scale.

When applied to strategic evaluation, the summative approach aims to identify and underscore the need for a change in the organization's strategy for Talent Development. In this sense, it closes the circle begun when the purpose, goals, and objectives of an organization's Talent Development effort were established.

What issues are appropriately addressed during a summative evaluation of organizational strategy? First, does the purpose match up to strategic business plans, HR plans, and the needs and expectations of key stakeholders inside and outside the organization? Changes in business strategy, major HR plans, and leadership of the organization each might require alterations to the purpose of the Talent Development effort. Second, does the existing organizational strategy match up to the external environment of the organization? Major changes outside the firm may require a complete review of organizational strategy so that people are being developed in line with present and future needs. Third and finally, does the existing organizational strategy build on strengths within the firm and minimize weaknesses?

The most appropriate time to carry out a summative evaluation is during strategic business planning. Future organizational initiatives imply human skills or competencies to carry them out. When these skills or competencies are *not* already available, decision-makers should think twice before choosing a strategy calling for them; when untapped human skills or competencies *are* available, decision-makers should think about how this organizational strength can be put to best competitive use. The development of human resources from within the organization is only one way to meet future skill needs. Others are recruitment from outside, short-term and long-term outside contracting, and transfer from inside. It is clear, however, that the Talent Development effort should support all strategic business plans. Evaluation helps determine how much it fits in with strategic plans and just when a new organizational strategy for Talent Development will be needed.

Activity 12–1: Importance of Goals in Instructional Evaluation

Directions: Use this activity to do some brainstorming to set priorities. For each job group shown in the left column, make some notes about what goals you believe should be most important in evaluating the results of Talent Development efforts for that group. There are no right or wrong responses.

Job Group				Goals and priorities
Top managers	Middle managers	Supervisors	Employees	
1.				
2.				
3.				
4.				
5.				

Activity 12–2: Fundamental Issues to Consider in Instructional Evaluation

Directions: Reflect on instructional evaluation in your organization. Use this activity to brainstorm on evaluation. Answer the questions that follow.

Stakeholders

1. Who are the primary stakeholders of planned learning activities in your organization? Who are the primary stakeholders of instructional evaluation?

Evaluators

2. Who are the primary evaluators of instruction in your firm? Why are they the evaluators?

Content

3. What is the primary focus of instructional evaluation in your organization? Describe it.

Activity 12–2: *(continued)*

Timing

---

4.   Is timing of evaluation important? Is it particularly important that the results of evaluation be compiled and communicated at any specific time?

Purpose

---

5.   Why is instructional evaluation carried out in your organization?

Method

---

6.   How is instructional evaluation carried out in your organization? (Describe the methods that are used.)

Activity 12–3: Strategic Front-End Analysis of Training

Directions: Use this activity to structure your thinking about the need for training. Answer in the right column each question posed in the left column.

Questions	Responses
1. What trends in work flow and work methods are most likely to be felt over the next year?	
2. In what specific work areas is change most likely to occur?	
3. What changes are likely to be most costly in the future?	
4. What knowledge/skills can help employees prepare for changes in the future?	
5. What methods other than formal, classroom-based training can help prepare employees for changes in the future?	
6. What will be the causes of anticipated future problems?	
7. How can supervisors and managers be convinced of the need to prepare for anticipated future problems?	

Activity 12–4: Reviewing Organizational Strategy for the Development of Talent

Directions: Use this activity to structure your thinking about organizational strategy for the development of talent in your organization. Answer the following questions in the space provided.

Progress to Date

1.   How well is organizational strategy for the development of talent contributing to

    a.   organizational learning and adaptation?

    b.   the preparation of individuals for movement to future jobs?

    c.   improving performance on jobs at present?

Responsiveness to Stakeholders

2.   How well is organizational strategy for the development of talent conforming to the values of

    a.   top managers?

    b.   middle managers?

    c.   supervisors?

    d.   nonsupervisory employees?

    e.   other stakeholders?

Activity 12–4: *(continued)*

Adequacy of Assumptions

---

3. Have the original assumptions on which organizational strategy for the development of talent was based remained valid?

---

4. Was the original organizational strategy for the development of talent realistic?

---

5. Are the skills needed to implement organizational strategy for the development of talent available in the organization? Do managers, supervisors, and Talent Development staff members possess the necessary skills to implement the strategy?

APPENDICES

Appendix I: A Template to Formulate Organizational Strategy for the Development of Talent

Directions: Use this template to help you formulate an organizational strategy for the development of talent in your organization. For the questions appearing in the left column below, prepare notes for your organization in the right column. Share the results of this activity with key stakeholders in your organization.

Questions	Responses/Notes
1. What is your vision of strategy for the development of talent in your organization? Describe it in words. What should it look like?	
2. What is the purpose or mission of the Talent Development effort in your organization? Explain who it serves, what it does, when it helps people, where it helps people, why it is done, how it aligns with the organization's strategic business plan, and how it can be measured.	
3. Over the next year, what are the general goals and the specific, measurable objectives of the Talent Development effort?	

Appendix I: *(continued)*

Questions	Responses/Notes
4. What is the organization doing now in its Talent Development efforts that is especially good? What is the organization doing now that can (and probably should) be improved?	
5. What external environmental issues/ trends are likely to affect the organization in the future? What are the likely consequences of those issues/trends, and how are they likely to affect the Talent Development effort? What threats and opportunities will the organization face, in general, and what threats and opportunities are likely to affect efforts to develop talent in the organization?	
6. What Grand Strategy should be chosen for the Talent Development effort in your organization, and why should it be chosen?	
7. What needs to be done to establish an effective action plan that will align the Grand Strategy for Talent Development with the organization's strategy? What should be done about ▪ Policies of the organization relevant to Talent Development? ▪ Leadership of the organization relevant to Talent Development? ▪ The organization of Talent Development effort within the organization? ▪ Rewards and incentives of the organization relevant to the Talent Development effort?	

Appendix I: *(continued)*

Questions	Responses/Notes
8. What role should be played by each functional strategy in the implementation of the Talent Development effort? Address specifically how each of the following should help to achieve the organization's Talent Development objectives: ▮ Organization development ▮ Nonemployee development ▮ Employee development ▮ Employee education ▮ Training	
9. How should the relative success of the organizational strategy for the development of talent be measured?	

Appendix II: An Instrument to Assess the Competencies of Stakeholders in the Talent Development Effort

Directions: Use this instrument to assess how well you are able to demonstrate the competencies essential for success in formulating, implementing, and evaluating an organizational strategy for the development of talent. For each competency listed in the left column below, rate your own perceived level of competence in the center column. Use this scale:

1 = Lacks essential knowledge, skills, and attitudes
2 = Possesses some essential knowledge, skills, and attitudes
3 = Possesses adequate essential knowledge, skills, and attitudes to function professionally
4 = Possesses greater-than-adequate essential knowledge, skills, and attitudes to function professionally

In the right column, make notes to yourself about what you believe you should do to increase your competence. *When you finish, summarize the key areas/competencies in which you feel a need to build your competence.*

Competencies	Your rating				Notes
How well can you demonstrate each competency listed below?	Lacks 1	 2	 3	Possesses greater-than-adequate 4	What do you believe you should do to increase your competence?
Visioning					
1. Formulates a clear, compelling vision of what the Talent Development effort should do and what results it should achieve in the organization	1	2	3	4	
2. Works with others to establish buy-in and ownership for the vision of the Talent Development effort	1	2	3	4	
Establishing Purpose, Goals, and Objectives					
3. Formulates a clear purpose statement for the Talent Development effort that is aligned to achieving the organization's strategic objectives	1	2	3	4	

Appendix II: *(continued)*

Competencies	Your rating				Notes
	Lacks			Possesses greater-than-adequate	
How well can you demonstrate each competency listed below?	1	2	3	4	*What do you believe you should do to increase your competence?*
4. Works with others to establish buy-in and ownership for the purpose statement of the Talent Development effort	1	2	3	4	
5. Formulates clear goals for the Talent Development effort	1	2	3	4	
6. Works with others to establish buy-in and ownership for the goals of the Talent Development effort	1	2	3	4	
7. Formulates clear, measurable objectives for the Talent Development effort	1	2	3	4	
8. Works with others to establish buy-in and ownership for the objectives to be achieved	1	2	3	4	
Conducting Internal Appraisal					
9. Identifies areas of the Talent Development effort that are stronger than others	1	2	3	4	
10. Identifies areas for improvement for the Talent Development effort	1	2	3	4	

Appendix II: *(continued)*

Competencies	Your rating				Notes
	Lacks			Possesses greater-than-adequate	
How well can you demonstrate each competency listed below?	1	2	3	4	What do you believe you should do to increase your competence?
11. Summarizes present strengths and weaknesses	1	2	3	4	

Conducting External Environmental Scanning

12. Identifies areas of the Talent Development effort that are stronger than others	1	2	3	4	
13. Identifies areas for improvement for the Talent Development effort	1	2	3	4	
14. Summarizes present strengths and weaknesses	1	2	3	4	
15. Formulates clear goals for the Talent Development effort	1	2	3	4	
16. Works with others to establish buy-in and ownership for the goals of the Talent Development effort	1	2	3	4	
17. Formulates clear, measurable objectives for the Talent Development effort	1	2	3	4	
18. Works with others to establish buy-in and ownership for the objectives to be achieved	1	2	3	4	

Appendix II: *(continued)*

Competencies	Your rating				Notes
	Lacks			Possesses greater-than-adequate	
How well can you demonstrate each competency listed below?	1	2	3	4	What do you believe you should do to increase your competence?
Conducting Internal Appraisal					
19. Identifies areas of the Talent Development effort that are stronger than others	1	2	3	4	
20. Identifies areas for improvement for the Talent Development effort	1	2	3	4	
21. Summarizes present strengths and weaknesses	1	2	3	4	
Conducting External Environmental Scanning					
22. Identifies external environmental issues/ trends that may create future opportunities for Talent Development	1	2	3	4	
23. Identifies external environmental issues/ trends that may create future threats for Talent Development	1	2	3	4	
24. Summarizes future threats and opportunities	1	2	3	4	

Appendix II: *(continued)*

Competencies	Your rating				Notes
	Lacks			*Possesses greater-than-adequate*	
How well can you demonstrate each competency listed below?	1	2	3	4	*What do you believe you should do to increase your competence?*
Choosing Organizational Strategy for the Development of Talent					
25. Selects organizational strategy for the development of talent based on a comparison between present strengths/ weaknesses to future threats/opportunities	1	2	3	4	
Implementing Organizational Strategy for the Development of Talent					
26. Aligns the organization's policies, leadership, rewards, organizational structure, and other issues essential to implement the organizational strategy for the development of talent	1	2	3	4	
Implementing Organizational Strategy for the Development of Talent					
27. Evaluates the results of the organizational strategy for the development of talent	1	2	3	4	

REFERENCES

Abdalla, H., and Amin, S. (1995). Corporate executives and environmental scanning activities: An empirical investigation. *S.A.M. Advanced Management Journal, 60*(2), 41–47.

Abell, D. (1978, July). Strategic windows. *Journal of Marketing*, 42, 21–26.

Abels, E. (2002). Hot topics: Environmental scanning. *Bulletin of the American Society for Information Science, 28*(3), 16–17.

Ackerman, R. (1975). *Managing Corporate Responsibility*. Boston: Harvard University Press.

Agor, W. (1989). Intuition and strategic planning: How organizations can make productive decisions. *Futurist, 23*(6), 20–23.

Aguilar, F. (1967). *Scanning the business environment*. New York: Macmillan.

Ahituv, N., Zif, J., and Machlin, I. (1998). Environmental scanning and information systems in relation to success in introducing new products. *Information and Management, 33*, 201–211.

Akin, G., and Palmer, I. (2000). Putting metaphors to work for change in organizations. *Organizational Dynamics, 28*(3), 67–77.

Alpander, G. (1982). *Human resource management planning*. New York: Amacom.

Archer, S., Kelly, C., and Bisch, S. (1984). *Implementing change in communities: A collaborative process*. St. Louis: C. V. Mosby Company.

Argyris, C. (1962). *Interpersonal competence and organizational effectiveness*. Homewood, Ill. : Dorsey Press.

Argyris, C. (1970). *Intervention theory and method*. Reading, Mass. : Addison-Wesley.

Argyris, C. (1982). How learning and reasoning processes affect organizational change. In P. Goodman and Associates (eds.), *Change in organizations: New perspectives on theory, research, and practice*. San Francisco: Jossey-Bass.

Argyris, C., and Schön, D. (1974). *Theory in practice.* San Francisco: Jossey-Bass.

Argyris, C., and Schön, D. (1978). *Organizational learning: A theory of action perspective.* Reading, Mass. : Addison-Wesley.

Arthur, J. (2000). Staying on top. *Human Resource Executive, 14*(7), 65–68.

Arthur, J. (1999). No secrets. *Human Resource Executive, 13*(7), 34–36.

Atwater, L., and Waldman, D. (1998). Accountability in 360-degree feedback. *HR Magazine, 43*(6), 96–104.

Bailey, R. (1982). *Human performance engineering: A guide for system designers.* Englewood Cliffs, N.J. : Prentice-Hall.

Baird, L., and Meshoulam, I. (1984, January). Strategic human resource management: Implications for training human resource professionals. *Training and Development Journal,* 76–78.

Bandura, A. (1971). *Psychological modeling: Conflicting theories.* Chicago: Aldine-Atherton.

Bandura, A. (1977). *Social learning theory.* Englewood Cliffs, N.J. : Prentice-Hall.

Bandura, A., and Walters, R. (1963). *Social learning theory and personality development.* New York: Holt, Rinehart, and Winston.

Bartlett, C., and Ghosal, S. (1998). Beyond strategic planning to organization learning: Lifeblood of the individualized corporation. *Strategy and Leadership, 26*(1), 34–39.

Bates, A. (2002). Improving profitability. *Industrial Distribution, 91*(4), 61–64.

Beal, R. (2000). Competing effectively: Environmental scanning, competitive strategy, and organizational performance in small manufacturing firms. *Journal of Small Business Management, 38*(1), 27–47.

Bechet, T. (2002). *Strategic staffing: A practical toolkit for workforce planning.* New York: Amacom.

Beckhard, K. (1967). The confrontation meeting. *Harvard Business Review, 45*(2), 149–155.

Bedeian, A. (1984). *Organizations: Theory and analysis* (2nd ed.). Chicago: The Dryden Press.

Benne, K., and Sheats, P. (1948). Functional roles of group members. *Journal of Social Issues, 4,* 41–49.

Bennett, N., Ketchen, D., and Schultz, E. (1998). An examination of factors associated with the integration of human resource management and strategic decision-making. *Human Resource Management, 37*(1), 3–16.

Bibeault, D. (1982). *Corporate turnaround.* New York: McGraw-Hill.

Bidwell, S. (1997a). *Helping teachers connect academics to the workplace: An implementation guide for teacher worksite externships.* Columbus, Ohio: The Ohio State University.

Bidwell, S. (1997b). *Helping students connect academics to the workplace: An implementation guide for student worksite learning experiences.* Columbus, Ohio: The Ohio State University.

Bierema, L., Bing, J., and Carter, T. (2002). The global pendulum. *Training and Development, 56*(5), 70–78.

Blancett, R. (2002). Learning from productivity learning curves. *Research Technology Management, 45*(3), 54–58.

Bloom, B., et al. (1956). *Taxonomy of educational objectives, Handbook I: Cognitive domain.* New York: David McKay.

Bloom, B., Hastinga, J., and Madaus, G. (1971). *Handbook on formative and summative evaluation of student learning.* New York: McGraw-Hill.

Bobbitt, F. (1918). *The curriculum.* Boston: Houghton Mifflin.

Booth, R. (1998). The measurement of intellectual capital. *Management Accounting, 76*(10), 26–28.

Bossidy, L. (2001). The job no CEO should delegate. *Harvard Business Review, 79*(3), 46–49.

Boyatzis, R. (1982). *The competent manager.* New York: Wiley-Interscience.

Boyd, B. (1980). Developing case studies. *Training and Development Journal, 34*(6), 113–117. (Reprinted from a 1964 article).

Boyd, B., and Fulk, J. (1996). Executive practices and perceived uncertainty: A multidimensional model. *Journal of Management, 22*(1), 1–21.

Briggs, L. (1970). *Handbooks of procedures for the design of instruction.* Pittsburgh, Pennsylvania: American Institutes for Research.

Briskin, A. (1996). *The stirring of soul in the workplace.* San Francisco: Jossey-Bass.

Brookfield, S. (1980). Independent adult learning. (Doctoral dissertation, University of Leicester).

Brookfield, S. (1986). *Understanding and facilitating adult learning.* San Francisco: Jossey-Bass.

Brown, M. (1998). Improving your organization's vision. *Journal for Quality and Participation, 21*(5), 18–20.

Bruner, J. (1960). *The process of education.* New York: Vintage Books.

Burke, W. (1997). The new agenda for organization development. *Organizational Dynamics, 26*(1), 6–20.

Burke, W. (1982). *Organization development: Principles and practices.* Boston: Little, Brown and Co.

Burton, T. (2000). Mutually inclusive. *People Management, 6*(2), 48–50.

Bushe, G. (1995). Advances in appreciative inquiry as an organization development intervention. *Organization Development Journal, 13*(3), 14–22.

The business of training: How Halliburton's "I-learn" strategy links to its business mission. (2002). *IOMA's Report on Managing Training and Development, 2*(2), 1, 7, 10.

Byars, L. (1984). *Strategic management: Planning and implementation.* New York: Harper and Row.

Byrne, J. (1996, August 26). Strategic planning. *Business Week, 3490*, 46–52.

Camillus, J., Sessions, R., and Webb, R. (1998). Visionary action: Strategic processes in fast-cycle environments. *Strategy and Leadership, 26*(1), 20–24.

Campbell, A. (1999). Tailored, not benchmarked: A fresh look at corporate planning. *Harvard Business Review, 77*(2), 41–50.

Campbell, A., and Alexander, M. (1997). What's wrong with strategy? *Harvard Business Review,* 75(6), 42–51.

Caster, M. (2001). Survivor: How HR can survive and thrive in the organization. *Organization Development Journal,* 19(2), 79–92.

Caudron, S. (1996). Rebuilding employee trust. *Training and Development,* 50(8), 18–21.

Chandler, A. (1962). *Strategy and structure: Chapters in the history of American industrial enterprise.* Cambridge, Mass. : M.I.T.

Chin, R., and Benne, K. (1969). General strategies for effecting changes in human systems. In W. Bennis, K. Benne, and R. Chin (eds.), *The planning of change* (2nd ed.). New York: Holt, Rinehart and Winston.

Choo, C. (1998a). *Information management for the intelligent organization: The art of scanning the environment* (2nd ed.). Medford, N.J. : Information Today, Inc.

Choo, C. (1998b). *The knowing organization: How organizations use information to construct meaning, create knowledge, and make decisions.* New York: Oxford University Press.

Choo, C. (1999). The art of scanning the environment. *Bulletin of the American Society for Information Science,* 25(3), 21–24.

Christensen, C. (1997). Making strategy: Learning by doing. *Harvard Business Review,* 75(6), 141–156.

Clark, C. (1978). *The Crawford slip writing method.* Kent, Ohio: Charles H. Clark.

Cloke, K., and Goldsmith, J. (1997). *Thank God it's Monday! 14 values we need to humanize the way we work.* Chicago: Irwin Professional Publishing.

Conhaim, W. (1999). Futurist Resources. *Link Up,* 16(6), 5–6.

Cooperrider, D. L., and Srivastva, S. (1987). Appreciative inquiry in organizational life. In R. Woodman and W. Pasmore (eds.), *Research in organizational change and development: Volume 1* (pp.129–169). Greenwich, Conn. : JAI Press.

Coppard, L. (1976). Gaming simulation and the training process. In R. Craig (ed.), *Training and development handbook* (2nd ed.). New York: McGraw-Hill.

Corboy, M., and O'Corrbui, D. (1999). The seven deadly sins of strategy. *Management Accounting,* 77(10), 29–33.

Cross, R., and Israelit, S. (eds.). (2000). *Strategic learning in a knowledge economy: Individual, collective, and organizational learning process.* Boston: Butterworth-Heinemann.

Cummings, L., and Schwab, D. (1973). *Performance in organizations: Determinants and appraisal.* Glenview, Ill. : Scott, Foresman and Co.

Cummings, T., and Worley, C. (2001). *Organization development and change* (7th ed.). Cincinnati, Ohio: South-Western Publishing.

Cyert, R., and March, J. (1963). *A behavioral theory of the firm.* Englewood Cliffs, N.J. : Prentice-Hall.

Dahlgaard, S., Dahlgaard, J., and Edgeman, R. (1998). Core values: The precondition for business excellence. *Total Quality Management,* 9(4/5), S51–S55.

Dalton, J. (2002). Strategic score-keeping. *Association Management, 54*(6), 53–57.

Danis, C., and Tremblay, N. (1985). *Critical analysis of adult learning principles from a self-directed learner's perspective*, No. 26. Tempe, Arizona: Arizona State University.

DeBono, E. (1970). *Lateral thinking: Creativity step by step.* New York: Harper and Row.

Deegan, A. (1986). *Succession planning: Key to corporate excellence.* New York: John Wiley.

DeFeo, J., and Janssen, A. (2001). Strategic deployment: A key to profitable growth: Matching capabilities and plans to customer needs. *Measuring Business Excellence, 5*(2), 4–5.

Delahoussaye, M. (2002). Licking the leadership crisis. *Training, 39*(1), 24–29.

Delbecq, A. (1967, December). The management of decision-making within the firm: Three strategies for three types of decision-making. *Academy of Management Journal,* 334–335.

DeNisi, A., and Kluger, A. (2000). Feedback effectiveness: Can 360-degree appraisals be improved? *Academy of Management Executives, 14*(1), 129–139.

Desatnick, R. (1984, February). What makes the human resource function successful? *Training and Development Journal,* 41–44, 46.

Dewey, J. (1938). *Experience and education.* New York: Collier Books.

DiFonzo, N., and Bordia, P. (1998). A tale of two corporations: Managing uncertainty during organizational change. *Human Resource Management, 37*(3 and 4), 295–303.

Dubois, D. (1993). *Competency-based performance improvement: A strategy for organizational change.* Amherst, Mass. : Human Resource Development Press.

Dubois, D. (ed.). (1998). *The competency casebook.* Amherst, Mass. : Human Resource Development Press.

Dubois, D. (1996). *The executive's guide to competency-based performance improvement.* Amherst, Mass. : Human Resource Development Press.

Dubois, D., and Rothwell, W. (2000). *The competency toolkit* (Vols. 1–2). Amherst, Mass. : Human Resource Development Press.

Dyer, L. (1977). *Team building: Issues and alternatives.* Reading, Mass. : Addison-Wesley.

Earl, M. (2001). Knowledge management strategies: Toward a taxonomy. *Journal of Management Information Systems, 18*(1), 215–233.

Egan, K. (1978). What is curriculum? *Curriculum Inquiry, 8*(1), 65–72.

Eilington, H. (1985). *Producing teaching materials: A handbook for teachers and trainers.* New York: Nichols Publishing.

Eisenhardt, K. (1999). Strategy as strategic decision-making. *Sloan Management Review, 40*(3), 65–72.

Eisenhardt, K., and Sull, D. (2001). Strategy as simple rules. *Harvard Business Review, 79*(1), 106–116.

Erickson, E. (1959). *Identity and the life cycle.* New York: International Universalities Press.

Evan, M. (1982). Adapting cognitive style theory in practice. *Lifelong Learning: The Adult Years, 5*(5), 14–16, 27.

Fahey, L. (1997). Using scenarios to beat out the competition. *National Productivity Review, 16*(4), 39–50.

Fahey, L., King, W., and Narayanan, V. (1981, February). Environmental scanning and forecasting in strategic planning: The state of the art. *Long Range Planning, 14*(1), 32–39.

Fahey, L., and Narayanan, V. (1983). The politics of strategic decision making. In K. Albert (ed.), *The strategic management handbook.* New York: McGraw-Hill.

Fahey, L., and Randall, R. (1998). *Learning from the future: Competitive foresight scenarios.* New York: John Wiley and Sons.

Fiedler, F. (1972, Autumn). How do you make leaders more effective? *Organizational Dynamics,* 3–8.

Fischer, G. (1981). When oracles fail: A comparison of four procedures for aggregating subjective probability. *Organizational Behavior and Human Performance,28*(1), 96ff.

Fister, S. (2000). At your service. *Inside Technology Training, 4*(4), 30–38.

Flores, L., and Fadden, J. (2000). How to have a successful strategic planning meeting. *Training and Development, 54*(1), 31–34.

Flynn, G. (1997). It takes values to capitalize on change. *Workforce, 76*(4), 27–34.

Ford, L. (1970). *Using the case study in teaching and training.* Nashville, Tenn. : Broadman.

Fordyce, J., and Weil, R. (1971). *Managing with people.* Reading, Mass. : Addison-Wesley.

Frady, M. (1997). Get personal to communicate coming change. *Performance Improvement, 36*(7), 32–33.

French, W., and Bell, C., Jr. (1984). *Organization development: Behavioral science interventions for organization improvement* (3rd ed.). Englewood Cliffs, N.J. : Prentice-Hall.

Friedman, S. (2001). Leadership DNA: The Ford Motor Story. *Training and Development, 55*(3), 22–29.

Fuld, L. (1995). *The new competitor intelligence: The complete resource for finding, analyzing, and using information about your competitors.* New York: John Wiley and Sons.

Fuller, J. (1998). Planning is dead, long live planning. *Across the Board, 35*(3), 35–38.

Fulmer, R. (2001). Johnson and Johnson: Frameworks for leadership. *Organizational Dynamics, 29*(3), 211–220.

Fulmer, R., Gibbs, P., and Goldsmith, M. (2000). Developing leaders: How winning companies keep on winning. *Sloan Management Review, 42*(1), 49–59.

Gagné, R., and Briggs, L. (1979). *Principles of Instructional Design* (2nd ed.). New York: Holt, Rinehart and Winston.

Galagan, P. (1997). Strategic planning is back. *Training and Development, 51*(4), 32–37.

Galbraith, J., and Nathanson, D. (1979). The role of organizational structure and process in strategy implementation. In D. Schendel and C. Hofer (eds.), *Strategic management: A new view of business policy and planning.* Boston: Little Brown.

Galosy, J. (1983). Curriculum design for management training. *Training and Development Journal, 37*(1), 48–51.

Garrett, D. (1999). Crossing the channel. *Training, 36*(9), L14–L20.

Gay, G. (1980). Conceptual models of the curriculum planning process. In R. Foshay (ed.), *Considered action for curriculum improvement.* Alexandria, Va. : Association for Supervision and Curriculum Development.

Gebelein, S., Stevens, L., Skube, C., Lee, D., Davis, L., and Hellervik, L. (2000). *Successful manager's handbook: Development suggestions for today's managers* (6th ed.). Minneapolis, Minnesota: Personnel Decisions, Inc.

Ghemawat, P. (2002). Competition and business strategy in historical perspective. *Business History Review, 76*(1), 37–74.

Ghemawat, P. (2001). *Strategy and the business landscape: Core concepts.* Englewood Cliffs, N.J. : Prentice-Hall.

Ghosal, S. (1988). Environmental scanning in Korean firms: Organizational isomorphism in action. *Journal of International Business Studies, 18*(1), 69–86.

Gibson, J., Ivancevich, J., and Donnelly, J., Jr. (1997). Organizations: Behavior, structure, processes (9th ed.). Plano, Texas: Business Publications.

Gilbert, T. (1967, Fall). Praxeonomy: A systematic approach to identifying training needs. *Management of Personnel Quarterly,* 20.

Gilbert, T. (1978). *Human competence: Engineering worthy performance.* New York: McGraw-Hill.

Giles, W. (1991). Making strategy work. *Long Range Planning, 24*(5), 75–91.

Gilley, J., and Maycunich, A. (2000). *Organizational learning performance and change: An introduction to strategic human resource development.* Cambridge, Mass. : Perseus Publishing.

Gilley, J., and Maycunich, A. (1998). *Strategically integrated HRD: Partnering to maximize organizational performance.* Reading, Mass. : Addison-Wesley.

Glueck, W. (1980). *Business policy and strategic management* (3rd ed.). New York: McGraw-Hill.

Glueck, W., and Jauch, L. (1984). *Business policy and strategic management* (4th ed.). New York: McGraw-Hill.

Godet, M. (2001). *Creating futures: Scenario planning as a strategic management tool.* (K. Radford, Trans.). Paris: Economica.

Gordon, J., and Zemke, R. (2000). The attack on ISD. *Training, 37*(4), 42–53.

Graham, J. (2000). Is your company threatened by the killer curve? *Air Conditioning, Heating, and Refrigeration News, 210*(4), 5.

Grant, J., and Gnyawali, D. (1996). Strategic process improvement through organizational learning. *Strategy and Leadership, 24*(3), 28–33.

Gratton, G. (1999). Linking individual performance to business strategy: The people process model. *Human Resource Management, 38*(1), 17–31.

Gratton, L. (2000). A real step change. *People Management, 6*(6), 26–30.

Grayson, C., and O'Dell, C. (1998). Mining your hidden resources. *Across the Board, 35*(4), 23-28.

Greene, M. (1977). The artistic-aesthetic curriculum. *Curriculum Inquiry,* 6, 283-284.

Grensing-Pophal, L. (2000). Follow me. *HR Magazine, 45*(2), 36-41.

Guffey, W., and Nienhaus, B. (2002). Determinants of employee support for the strategic plan of a buisiness unit. *S.A.M. Advanced Management Journal, 67*(2), 23-30.

Guidelines and ethical considerations for assessment center operations. (2000). *Public Personnel Management, 29*(3), 315-331.

Gupta, A., and Govindarajan, V. (1984, March). Build, hold, harvest: Converting strategic intentions into reality. *Journal of Business Strategy,* 34-47.

Gupta, K. (1998). *A practical guide to needs assessment.* San Francisco: Pfeiffer and Co.

Hacker, M., and Akinyele, A. (1998). Focusing on visible management at a USPS distribution center. *National Productivity Review, 17*(4), 45-52.

Hackman, J., and Oldham, G. (1975). Development of the job diagnostic survey. *Journal of Applied Psychology,* 60, 150-170.

Hagen, A., Hassan, M., and Amin, S. (1998). Critical strategic leadership components: An empirical investigation. *S.A.M. Advanced Management Journal, 63*(3), 39-44.

Hale, J. (2000). *Performance-based certification: How to design a valid, defensible, cost-effective program.* San Francisco: Jossey-Bass.

Hamel, G., and Prahalad, C. (1994). *Competing for the future.* Boston, Mass. : Harvard Business Press.

Haney, D. (2002). Assessing organizational readiness for e-learning: 70 questions to ask. *Performance Improvement, 41*(4), 8-13.

Hanpachern, C., Morgan, G., and Griego, O. (1998). An extension of the theory of margin: A framework for assessing readiness for change. *Human Resource Development Quarterly, 9*(4), 339-350.

Harless, J. (1975). *An ounce of analysis (is worth a pound of objectives).* Newman, Georgia: Harless Performance Guild, Inc.

Harrison, D. (1999). Assess and remove barriers to change. *HR Focus, 76*(7), 9-10.

Harvey, L. (1983, October). Effective planning for human resource development. *Personnel Administrator,* 46-48, 50, 52, 112.

Hegstad, C. (1999). Formal mentoring as a strategy for human resource development: A review of research. *Human Resource Development Quarterly, 10*(4), 383-390.

Heifetz, R., and Laurie, D. (1997). The work of leadership. *Harvard Business Review, 75*(1), 124-134.

Hennings, D. (1975). *Mastering classroom communication.* Pacific Palisades, California: Goodyear Publishing.

Higgins, R., and Diffenbach, J. (1989). Communicating corporate strategy: The payoffs and the risks. *Long Range Planning, 22*(3), 133-139.

Hilton, A. (1999, January). Have I got news for you. *Management Today,* 28-32.

Hofer, C., and Schendel, D. (1978). *Strategy formulation: Analytical concepts*. St. Paul, Minnesota: West Publishing.

Horan, J., and Shaw, R. (1997). *The one page business plan: Start with a vision, build a company*. One Page Business Plan Co.

Houle, C. (1972). *The design of education*. San Francisco: Jossey-Bass.

Houle, C. (1961). *The inquiring mind*. Madison, Wisconsin: University of Wisconsin Press.

Huczynski, A. (1983). *Encyclopedia of management development methods*. London: Gower.

Huff, A., and Reger, R. (1987). A review of strategic process research. *Journal of Management, 13*, 211–236.

Hulett, D., and Renjilian, J. (1983). Strategic planning demystified. In S. Sherwook, ed., *Organization development: Present practice and future needs*. Washington, D. C.: American Society for Training and Development.

Hultman, K., with B. Gellerman. (2001). *Balancing individual and organizational values: Walking the tightrope to success*. San Francisco: Jossey-Bass/Pfeiffer.

Hultman, K. (1998). *Making change irresistable: Overcoming resistance to change in your organization*. Palo Alto, California: Davies-Black.

Hunkins, F. (1980). *Curriculum development: Program improvement*. Columbus, Ohio: Charles E. Merrill.

Huse, E. (1982). *Management* (2nd ed.). St. Paul, Minnesota: West Publishing.

Inamdar, N., Kaplan, R., and Bower, M. (2002). Applying the balanced scorecard in healthcare provider organizations. *Journal of Healthcare Management, 47*(3), 179–196.

Ireland, D., and Hitt, M. (1999). Achieving and sustaining strategic competitiveness in the 21st century: The role of strategic leadership. *Academy of Management Executives, 13*(1), 43–57.

Ishoy, K., and Swan, P. (1992). Creating a mission statement for your work group: A guide for managers and supervisors. *Performance and Instruction, 31*(10), 11–15.

Jackson, J., and Greller, M. (1998). Decision elements for using 360-degree feedback. *Human Resource Planning, 21*(4), 18–28.

Jacobs, R., and McKeown, F. (2000). Real-time strategic change. *Executive Excellence, 17*(2), 13.

Jain, S. (1984). Environmental scanning in U.S. corporations. *Long Range Planning, 17*(2), 117–128.

Janis, I. (1971, November). Group think. *Psychology Today, 5*, 43–46.

Janis, I. (1973). *Victims of group think: A psychological study of foreign policy decisions and fiascos*. Boston: Houghton Mifflin.

Johnson, S. (1983). Critical incident. In F. Ulschak (ed.), *Human resource development: The theory and practice of need assessment*. Reston, Virginia: Reston Publishing.

Joinson, D. (1982). Using checklists as an aid to transfer of training. *Adult learning in your classroom*. Minneapolis, Minnesota: Lakewood Publications. (Reprinted from a June 1977 training article.)

Jonassen, D., Hannum, W., and Tessmer, M. (1989). *Handbook of task analysis procedures.* New York: Praeger.

Kaeter, M. (1994). Customer training: More than a sales tool. *Training, 31*(3), 33–38.

Kahaner, L. (1996). *Competitive intelligence: From black ops to boardrooms: How businesses gather, analyze, and use information to succeed in the global marketplace.* New York: Simon and Schuster.

Kaplan, R., and Norton, D. (1996). *The balanced scorecard.* Boston: Harvard Business School Press.

Kapp, K. (2000). Moving training to the strategic level with learning requirements planning. *National Productivity Review, 19*(4), 27–33.

Katz, D., and Kahn, R. (1978). *The social psychology of organizations* (2nd ed.). New York: John Wiley.

Kaufman, R. (1998). *Strategic thinking: A guide to identifying and solving problems.* Alexandria, Virginia: The American Society for Training and Development.

Kay, E. (1999, May). Supply-side training. *Inside Technology Training,* 10–12.

Keegan, W. (1974, September). Multinational scanning. *Administrative Science Quarterly,* 441–21.

Kerr, S. (1975). On the folly of rewarding A, while hoping for B. *Academy of Management Journal,* 18, 796–83.

Khandwalla, P. (1977). *The design of organizations.* New York: Harcourt, Brace, and Jovanovich.

Kim, W., and Mauborgne, R. (2002). Charting your company's future. *Harvard Business Review, 80*(6), 76–83.

King, S., King, M., and Rothwell, W. (2000). *The complete guide to training delivery: A competency-based approach.* New York: Amacom.

Kinsella, K., and Velkoff, V. (2001). *An aging world: 2001.* Washington, D. C. : U.S. Government Printing Office.

Kirkpatrick, D. (1959). Techniques for evaluating training programs. *Journal of the American Society of Training Directors,* 13, 3–9; 21–26.

Kirkpatrick, D. (1960). Techniques for evaluating training programs. *Journal of the American Society of Training Directors,* 14, 13–18; 28–32.

Kirkpatrick, D. (1998). *Evaluating training programs: The four levels* (2nd ed.). San Francisco: Berrett-Koehler.

Kleiner, A., Roth, G., and Kruschwitz, N. (2001). Should a company have a noble purpose? *Across the Board, 38*(1), 18–24.

Klemp, G., Jr. (1979). Identifying, measuring and integrating competence. In P. Pottinger and J. Goldsmith (eds.), *Defining and measuring competence.* San Francisco: Jossey-Bass.

Knowles, M. (1986). *Using learning contracts: Practical approaches to individualizing and structuring learning.* San Francisco: Jossey-Bass.

Knowles, M. (1980). *The modern practice of adult education: From pedagogy to andragogy* (Revised ed.). Chicago: Association Press.

Knowles, M. (1984). *The adult learner: A neglected species* (3rd ed.). Houston, Texas: Gulf Publishing.

Kolb, D. (1984). *Experiential learning: Experience as the source of learning and development.* Englewood Cliffs, N.J. : Prentice-Hall.

Krathwohl, D., Bloom, B., and Masia, B. (1964). *Taxonomy of educational objectives, Handbook Two: Affective domain.* New York: David McKay.

Krattenmaker, T. (2002). Write a mission statement that your company is willing to live. *Harvard Management Communication Letter, 5*(3), 8–9.

Kravetz, D. (1995). *The directory for building competencies.* Bartlett, Ill. : Kravetz and Associates.

Krell, E. (2001). The knowledge race. *Training, 38*(7), 40–43.

Kruger, M. (1983). How to make a management advisory committee work for you. *Training and Development Journal, 37*(6), 86–90.

Kuchinke, K. (2002). Institutional and curricular characteristics of leading graduate HRD programs in the United States. *Human Resource Development Quarterly, 13*(2), 127–143.

Kumar, K., Subramanian, R., and Strandholm, K. (2001). Competitive strategy, environmental scanning, and performance: A context-specific analysis of their relationship. *International Journal of Commerce and Management, 11*(1), 1–33.

Lado, A., and Wilson, M. (1994). Human resource systems and sustained competitive advantage: A competency-based perspective. *The Academy of Management Review, 19*(4), 699.

Laird, D. (1985). *Approaches to training and development* (2nd ed.). Reading, Mass. : Addison-Wesley.

Lang, J., Calantone, R., and Gudmundson, D. (1997, January). Small firm information-seeking as a response to environmental threats and opportunities. *Journal of Small Business Management,* 11–23.

Langeler, G. (1992). The vision trap. *Harvard Business Review, 70*(2), 46–55.

Lawler, E., III. (1977). Reward systems. In J. Hackman and J. Suttle (eds.), *Improving life at work.* Santa Monica, California: Goodyear.

Levy, A., and Merry, V. (1986). *Organizational transformation: Approaches, strategies, theories.* New York: Praeger.

Lewin, K. (1951). *Field theory in social science.* New York: Harper.

Lewin, K. (1947, June). Frontiers in group dynamics: Concept, methods, and reality in social science. *Human Relations,* 1, 5–41.

Lewis, A., and Miel, A. (1972). *Supervision for improved instruction.* Belmont, California: Wadsworth.

Liedtka, J. (1998). Linking strategic thinking with strategic planning. *Strategy and Leadership, 26*(4), 30–35.

Likert, R. (1967). *The human organization*. New York: McGraw-Hill.

Linkow, P. (1985). HRD at the roots of corporate strategy. *Training and Development Journal*, *39*(5), 85–87.

Linkow, P. (1999). What gifted strategic thinkers do. *Training and Development, 53*(7), 34–37.

Lombardo, M., and Eichinger, R. (1989). *Eighty-eight assignments for development in place: Enhancing the developmental challenge of existing jobs*. Greensboro, North Carolina: The Center for Creative Leadership.

Lombardo, M., and Eichinger, R. (2000). High potentials as high learners. *Human Resource Management, 39*(4), 321–329.

Ludeman, K. (2000). How to conduct self-directed 360°. *Training* and *Development, 54*(7), 44–47.

McCord, B. (1976). Job instruction. In R. Craig (ed.), *Training and development handbook: A guide to human resource development* (2nd ed.). New York: McGraw-Hill.

McCracken, M., and Wallace, M. (2000). Towards a redefinition of strategic HRD. *Journal of European Industrial Training, 24*(5), 281ff.

McDowell, C. (1996). Achieving workforce competence. *Personnel Journal, 75*(9), 1, 4, 6, 8, 10.

McGehee, W., and Thayer, P. (1961). *Training in business and industry*. New York: John Wiley.

McLagan, P. (1999). As the HRD world churns. *Training and Development, 53*(12), 20–30.

Macmillan, I. (1978). *Strategy formulation: Political concepts*. St. Paul, Minnesota: West Publishing.

Mager, R. (1997). *Goal analysis* (3rd ed.). Atlanta, GA: The Center for Effective Performance.

Mager, R. (1997). *How to turn learners on...without turning them off* (3rd ed.). Atlanta, Georgia: The Center for Effective Performance.

Mager, R. (1997). *Measuring instructional results* (3rd ed.). Atlanta, Georgia: The Center for Effective Performance.

Mager, R. (1997). *Preparing instructional objectives* (3rd ed.). Atlanta, Georgia: The Center for Effective Performance.

Mager, R., and Pipe, P. (1997). *Analyzing performance problems, or 'you really oughta wanna'* (3rd ed.). Atlanta, Georgia: The Center for Effective Performance.

Manzini, A., and Gridley, J. (1986). *Integrating human resources and strategic business planning*. New York: Amacom.

Marquardt, M., King, S., and Koon, E. (2001). *The 2001 ASTD International Comparisons Report*. Alexandria, Virginia: The American Society for Training and Development.

Marx, R. (1999). *The ASTD media selection tool for workplace learning*. Alexandria, Virginia: The American Society for Training and Development.

Mascarenhas, B., Baveja, A., and Mamnoon, J. (1998). Dynamics of core competencies in leading multinational companies. *California Management Review, 40*(4), 117–132.

Mason, R., and Mitroff, E. (1981). *Challenging strategic planning assumptions: Theory, cases, and techniques.* New York: Wiley.

Maurer, R. (1997). Transforming resistance. *HR Focus, 74*(10), 9–10.

Miles, R., and Snow, C. (1984, Summer). Designing strategic human resources systems. *Organizational Dynamics*, 36–52.

Mintzberg, H. (1979a). *The structuring of organizations.* Englewood Cliffs, N.J. : Prentice-Hall.

Mintzberg, H. (1979b). Organizational power and goals: A skeletal theory. In C. Hofer and D. Schendel (eds.), *Strategic management: A new view of business policy and planning.* Boston: Little Brown.

Mintzberg, H. (1994). The fall and rise of strategic planning. *Harvard Business Review, 72*(1), 107–14.

Mintzberg, H., Raisinghani, D., and Theoret, A. (1976, June). The structure of 'unstructured' decision process. *Administrative Science Quarterly, 21*(2), 246–75.

Mirabile, R. (1997). Everything you wanted to know about competency modeling. *Training and Development, 51*(8), 73–77.

Mirabile, R., Caldwell, D., and O'Reilly, C. (1986, September). Designing and linking human resource programs. *Training and Development Journal, 60*, 63.

Mitroff, I., and Denton, E. (1999). *A spiritual audit of corporate America: A hard look at spirituality, religion, and values in the workplace.* San Francisco: Jossey-Bass.

Moravec, M. (1995). Readiness to change. *Executive Excellence, 12*(10), 16.

Morrisey, G. (1976). *Management by objectives and results in the public sector.* Reading, Mass. : Addison-Wesley.

Morrow, C., and Fredin, B. (1999). *Worksite mentoring guidebook: Practical help for planning and implementing quality worksite learning experiences.* Columbus, Ohio: The Ohio State University.

Moser, M. (2001). Calibrating Texas Instruments: Business effectiveness regulates training solutions. *New Corporate University Review, 9*(2), 17, 20–21.

Nadler, L. (1979). *Developing human resources* (2nd ed.). Austin, Texas: Learning Concepts.

Neary, D., and O'Grady, D. (2000). The role of training in developing global leaders: A case study at TRW, Inc. *Human Resource Management, 39*(2 and 3), 185–193.

Nerney, C. (1997). Getting to know knowledge management. *Network World, 14*(39), 101.

Newman, P., and Mahmoud, S. (1993). Strategic management of emerging human resource issues. *Human Resource Development Quarterly, 4*(1), 81ff.

Nickolson, D. (2002). Envisioning an enriched future. *Association Management, 54*(5), 52–57.

Nkomo, S. (1986). The theory and practice of planning: The gap still remains. *Personnel Administrator, 31*(8), 71–84.

Noble, C. (1999). The eclectic roots of strategy implementation research. *Journal of Business Research, 45*, 119–34.

Norton, R. (1997). *DACUM handbook* (2nd ed.). Columbus, Ohio: The Center on Education and Training for Employment, The Ohio State University College of Education.

Odiorne, G. (1984). *Strategic management of human resources: A portfolio approach.* San Francisco: Jossey-Bass.

Oliver, R. (2000). The real-time toolbox. *The Journal of Business Strategy, 21*(2), 7–10.

Oliver, R. (2001). Real-time strategy: What is strategy, anyway? *The Journal of Business Strategy, 22*(6), 7–10.

Olson, E., and Eoyang, G. (2001). *Facilitating organizational change.* San Francisco: Jossey-Bass/Pfeiffer.

Opening Doors. (2000). *Human Resource Executive, 14*(12), A1–A34.

Orr, B. (2002). Six strategic roles HR to fill. *Canadian HR Reporter, 15*(3), 7.

Osborn, A. (1953). *Applied imagination.* New York: Charles Scribner and Sons.

Oster, S. (1999). *Modern competitive analysis* (3rd ed.). New York: Oxford University Press.

Paine, E., and Naumes, W. (1974). *Strategy and policy formation: An integrative approach.* Philadelphia, Pennsylvania: W. B.

Pattan, J. (1986, March). The strategy in strategic planning. *Training and Development Journal, 40*(3), 30–33.

Pearce, J., and Robinson, R., Jr. (1985). *Strategic management: Strategy formulation and implementation* (2nd ed.). Homewood, Ill. : Richard D. Irwin.

Peiperl, M. (2001). Getting 360-degree feedback right. *Harvard Business Review, 79*(1), 142–47.

Peterson, D., and Hicks, M. (1995). *Development first: Strategies for self-development.* Minneapolis, Minnesota: Personnel Decisions, Inc.

Phillips, J. (ed.). (1999). *In action: Effective leadership programs.* Alexandria, Virginia: The American Society for Training and Development.

Picken, J., and Dess, G. (1997). Out of (strategic) control. *Organizational Dynamics, 26*(1), 35–48.

Pigors, P. (1987). Case method. In R. Craig (ed.), *Training and development handbook* (3rd ed.). New York: McGraw-Hill.

Pope, S. (2002). Form a successful strategy. *e-learning, 3*(2), 34–37.

Porter, M. (1980). *Competitive strategy: Techniques for analyzing industries and competitors.* New York: The Free Press.

Prahalad, C., and Hamel, G. (1990, May-June). The core competence of the corporation. *Harvard Business Review,* 79–91.

Pratt, D. (1980). *Curriculum: Design and development.* New York: Harcourt, Brace, Jovanovich.

Pritchett, P., and Pound, R. (2000). *A survival guide to the stress of organizational change.* Plano, Texas: Pritchett Rummler-Brache.

Pulley, M., Sessa, V., and Malloy, M. (2002). E-leadership: A two-pronged idea. *Training and Development, 56*(3), 34–47.

Raimy, E. (1998). Precious moments. *Human Resource Executive, 12*(11), 1, 26–29.

Reichers, A., Wanous, J., and Austin, J. (1997). Understanding and managing cynicism about organizational change. *Academy of Management Executives, 11*(1), 48–59.

Revans, R. (1971). *Developing effective managers.* New York: Praeger.

Rieley, J., and Rieley, M. (1999). Is your organization addicted to change? *National Productivity Review, 18*(3), 63–68.

Robin, M. (2000). Learning by doing. *Knowledge Management, 3*(3), 44–49.

Rokeach, M. (1973). *The nature of human values.* New York: The Free Press.

Romiszowski, A. (1981). *Designing instructional systems: Decision-making in course planning and curriculum design.* New York: Nichols Publishing.

Rosenberg, S. (1983, August). The power of team play. *Management World,* 26–28.

Rosse, J., and Levin, R. (2001). *Talent flow: A strategic approach to keeping good employees, helping them grow, and letting them go.* San Francisco: Jossey-Bass.

Rothschild, W. (1976). *Putting it all together: A guide to strategic thinking.* New York: Amacom.

Rothwell, W. (1984). Strategic needs assessment. *Performance and Instruction Journal, 23*(5), 19–20.

Rothwell, W. (1995). Assessing the training needs of supervisors-turned-team-leaders: The Americana insurance company case. In J. Phillips and E. Holton (eds.), *In action: Needs assessment* (pp. 410-450). Alexandria, Virginia: The American Society for Training and Development.

Rothwell, W. (1996). *The self-directed on-the-job learning workshop.* Amherst, Mass. : Human Resource Development Press.

Rothwell, W. (1999a). *The action learning guidebook: A real-time strategy for problem-solving, training design, and employee development.* San Francisco: Jossey-Bass/Pfeiffer.

Rothwell, W. (1999b). Planning for self-directed learning. In W. Rothwell and K. Sensenig (eds.), *The sourcebook for self-directed learning* (pp. 191-194). Amherst, Mass. : Human Resource Development Press.

Rothwell, W. (1999c). The case study method reinvented for self-directed learning. In W. Rothwell and Kevin Sensenig (eds.), *The sourcebook for self-directed learning* (pp. 157-162). Amherst, Mass. : Human Resource Development Press.

Rothwell, W. (1999d). The role play reinvented for self-directed learning. In W. Rothwell and Kevin Sensenig (eds.), *The sourcebook for self-directed learning* (pp. 163-164). Amherst, Mass.: Human Resource Development Press.

Rothwell, W. (2002). *The workplace learner.* New York: Amacom.

Rothwell, W. (2000). *Effective succession planning: Ensuring leadership continuity and building talent from within* (2nd ed.). New York: Amacom.

Rothwell, W., Donahue, W., and Park, J. (2003). *Creating effective in-house sales training and development programs.* Westport, Conn. : Quorum Books.

Rothwell, W., Hohne, C., and King, S. (2000). *Human performance improvement: Building practitioner competence.* Woburn, Mass. : Butterworth-Heinemann.

Rothwell, W., and Kazanas, H. C. (2000). *Building in-house leadership and management development programs: Their creation, management, and continuous improvement.* Westport, Conn. : Quorum Books.

Rothwell, W., and Kazanas, H. (1994). *Improving on-the-job training.* San Francisco: Jossey-Bass.

Rothwell, W. and Kazanas, H. (2002). *Planning and managing human resources: Strategic planning for human resource management* (2nd ed.). Amherst, Mass. : Human Resource Development Press.

Rothwell, W. and Kazanas, H. (1998). *Mastering the instructional design process: A systematic approach* (2nd ed.). San Francisco: Jossey-Bass.

Rothwell, W., and Lindholm, J. (1999). Competency identification, modeling, and assessment in the USA. *International Journal of Training and Development, 3*(2), 90–105.

Rothwell, W., Lindholm, J., and Wallick, W. (2003). *What CEOs expect from corporate training.* New York: Amacom.

Rothwell, W., Prescott, R., and Taylor, M. (1998). *Strategic HR leader: How to help your organization manage the six trends affecting the workforce.* Palo Alto, California: Davies-Black Publishing.

Rothwell, W., Sanders, E., and Soper, J. (1999). *ASTD models for workplace learning and performance: Roles, competencies, outputs.* Alexandria, Virginia: The American Society for Training and Development.

Rothwell, W., and Sensenig, K. (eds.). (1999). *The sourcebook for self-directed learning.* Amherst, Mass. : Human Resource Development Press.

Rothwell, W., and Sredl, H. (2000). *The ASTD reference guide to workplace learning and performance* (3rd ed.). (Vols.1–2). Amherst, Mass. : Human Resource Development Press.

Rothwell, W., Sullivan, R., and McLean, G. (eds.). (1995). *Practicing organization development: A guide for consultants.* San Francisco: Jossey-Bass/Pfeiffer.

Rowley, K., Bunker, E., and Cole, D. (2002). Designing the right blend. *Performance Improvement, 41*(4), 24–34.

Rowntree, D. (1982). *Educational technology in curriculum development* (2nd ed.). New York: Harper and Row.

Rummler, G. (1976). The performance audit. In R. Craig (ed.), *Training and development handbook: A guide to human resource development* (2nd ed.). New York: McGraw-Hill.

Salopek, J. (2002). Trend watch. *Training and Development, 56*(1), 68–70.

Sawyerr, O., Bahman, E., and Thibodeaux, M. (2000). Executive environmental scanning, information source utilisation, and firm performance: The case of Nigeria. *Journal of Applied Management Studies, 9*(1), 95–115.

Saylor, J., Alexander, W., and Lewis, A. (1981). *Curriculum planning for better teaching and learning* (4th ed.). New York: Holt, Rinehart and Winston.

Schein, E. (1978). *Career dynamics: Matching individual and organizational needs.* Reading, Mass. : Addison-Wesley.

Schein, E. (1984). The coming awareness of organization culture. *Sloan Management Review, 25*(2), 3–16.

Schein, E. (1985). *Organizational culture and leadership: A dynamic view.* San Francisco: Jossey-Bass.

Schendel, D., and Hofer, C. (1979). Strategy evaluation. In D. Schendel and C. Hofer (eds.), *Strategic management: A new view of business policy and planning.* Boston: Little, Brown and Co.

Schmidt, W., and Posner, B. (1982). *Managerial values and expectations: The silent power in personal and organizational life.* New York: AMA Membership Publications Division.

Schoemaker, P. (1992). How to link strategic vision to core capabilities. *Sloan Management Review, 34*(1), 67–81.

Schrage, M. (2001). That's a brilliant business plan—but is it art? *Fortune, 143*(5), 226.

Scott, G. (2001). Strategic planning for technology products. *R and D Management, 31*(1), 15–26.

Scriven, M. (1967). The methodology of evaluation. In R. Stake (ed.), *Perspectives on curriculum evaluation.* Aera Monograph. Chicago: Rand McNally.

Senge, P. (1990). *The fifth discipline: The art and practice of the learning organization.* New York: Doubleday/Currency.

Sensenig, K. (1998). *A single-site descriptive analysis of managers' perceptions concerning the value-added of linking leadership development efforts to strategic corporate objectives.* (Doctoral dissertation, University Park: The Pennsylvania State University.)

Sharplin, A. (1985). *Strategic management.* New York: McGraw-Hill.

Shaw, G., Brown, R., and Bromiley, P. (1998). Strategic stories: How 3M is rewriting business planning. *Harvard Business Review, 76*(3), 41–50.

Sherman, H., and Schultz, R. (1999). Questions they never asked. *Across the Board, 36*(1), 13.

Showkeir, J. (1999). The power of large group events. *Journal for Quality and Participation, 22*(4), 52–55.

Simpson, E. (1969). *Psychomotor domain: A tentative classification.* Urbana, Ill. : University of Illinois.

Spencer, L., and Spencer, S. (1993). *Competence at work: Models for superior performance.* New York: Wiley.

Spitzer, D., and Conway, M. (2002). Linking training to your bottom line. *Info-Line,* No. 250201. Alexandria, Virginia: The American Society for Training and Development.

Spychalski, A., et al. (1997). A survey of assessment center practices in organizations in the United States. *Personnel Psychology, 50*(1), 71–90.

Staunton, M., and Giles, K. (2001). Age of enlightenment. *People Management, 7*(15), 30–33.

Stewart, Thomas A. (1999) Rate your readiness to change. *Fortune, 129*(3), 106–110.

Stonich, P. (1990). Time: The next strategic frontier. *Planning Review, 18*(6), 4–7, 46–48.

Stover, J., and Gordon, T. (1978). Cross-impact analysis. In J. Fowles (ed.), *Handbook of futures research*. Westport, Conn. : Greenwood Press.

Strategies for building individual competencies through self-directed learning. (1999). In W. Rothwell and K. Sensenig (eds.), *The sourcebook for self-directed learning* (pp. 195–232). Amherst, Mass. : Human Resource Development Press.

Strong leadership navigates bumpy road to profits: Best Buy: Specialty Retailer of the Decade (2001). *Retailing Today, 40*(1A), 8.

Sullivan, R., Fairburn, L., and Rothwell, W. (2002). The whole-system transformation conference: Fast change for the 21st century. In S. Herman (ed.), *Rewiring organizations for the networked economy: Organizing, managing, and leading in the information age* (pp. 115–142). San Francisco: Jossey-Bass/Pfeiffer.

Tannenbaum, R., and Schmidt, W. (1973, May–June). How to choose a leadership pattern. *Harvard Business Review*, 162–180.

Tanner, D., and Tanner, L. (1980). Curriculum development: Theory into Practice (2nd ed.). New York: MacMillan.

Tarley, M. (2002). Leadership development for small organizations. *Training and Development, 56*(3), 52–55.

Thompson, J. (1997). *Lead with vision: Manage the strategic challenge.* Boston: International Thomson Business Press.

Tichy, N. (1983). *Managing strategic change.* New York: John Wiley.

Titcomb, T. (1998). Chaos and complexity theory. *Info-Line*, No. 9807. Alexandria, Virginia: The American Society for Training and Development.

Topchik, G. (1998). Attacking the negativity virus. *Management Review, 87*(8), 61–64.

Tough, A. (1979). *The adult's learning projects* (2nd ed.). Toronto: Ontario Institute for Studies in Education.

Trahant, B., and Burke, W. (1996). Creating a change reaction: How understanding organizational dynamics can ease reengineering. *National Productivity Review, 15*(4), 37–46.

Tregoe, B., and Zimmerman, J. (1984). Needed: A strategy for human resource development. *Training and Development Journal, 38*(5), 78–80.

Tregoe, B., and Zimmerman, J. (1985). The new strategic manager. In J. Ryans, Jr., and W. Shanklin (eds.), *Strategic planning: Concepts and implementation.* New York: Random House.

Van Buren, M., and Erskine, W. (2002). *The 2002 ASTD state of the industry report.* Alexandria, Virginia: The American Society for Training and Development.

Van De Ven, A., and Delbecq, A. (1972, June). Nominal versus interacting group processes for committee decision-making effectiveness. *Academy of Management Journal*, 203–12.

Van De Ven, A., and Delbecq, A. (1974). The effectiveness of nominal, delphi, and interacting group decision-making processes. *Academy of Management Journal, 17*, 605–21.

Van Gundy, A. (1981). *Techniques of structured problem-solving.* New York: Van Norstrand Reinhold.

Venkatraman, N., and Ramanujam, V. (1986). Measurement of business performance in strategy research: A comparison of approaches. *Academy of Management Review, 11*, 801–814.

Verespej, M. (1998). Formal training: 'Secondary' education? *Industry Week, 247*(1), 42–44.

Wah, L. (1998). Welcome to the edge. *Management Review, 87*(10), 24–29.

Wall, J. (1974, November-December). What the competition is doing: Your need to know. *Harvard Business Review, 52*(6), 22–24, 28, 30, 32, 36, 38.

Wall, S. (1997). Creating strategists. *Training and Development, 51*(5), 75–79.

Wall, S., and Wall, S. (1995). The evolution (not the death) of strategy. *Organizational Dynamics, 24*(2), 6–19.

Walton, R. (1969). *Interpersonal peacemaking: Confrontations and third party consultation.* Reading, Mass. : Addison-Wesley.

Ward, L. (1982). Eight steps to strategic planning for training managers. *Training, 19*(11), 22–23, 25, 28–29.

Watkins, J., and Mohr, B. (2001). *Appreciative inquiry: Change at the speed of imagination.* San Francisco: Jossey-Bass/Pfeiffer.

Webb, J., and Gile, C. (2001). Reversing the value chain. *The Journal of Business Strategy, 22*(2), 13–17.

Weiss, D. (2002). How to fail at strategic alignment. *Canadian HR Reporter, 15*(4), 7.

Weiss, R. (2002). Crisis leadership. *Training and Development, 56*(3), 28–33.

Wells, S. (1999). A new road: Traveling beyond 360-degree evaluation. *HR Magazine, 44*(9), 82–91.

Wenger, E. (1999). *Communities of practice: Learning, meaning, and identity.* New York: Cambridge University Press.

Werther, W., and Davis, K. (1985). *Personnel management and human resources* (2nd ed.). New York: McGraw-Hill.

Willmore, J. (1998). Scenario planning. *Info-Line*, No. 9809. Alexandria, Virginia: The American Society for Training and Development.

Wohlking, W., and Weiner, H. (1981). Structured and spontaneous role-playing. *Training and Development Journal, 35*(6), 111–112, 120–121.

Wright, P., et al. (1998). Strategy, core competence, and HR involvement as determinants of HR effectiveness and refinery performance. *Human Resource Management, 37*(1), 17–29.

Young, M. (2002). *Holding on: How the mass exodus of retiring baby boomers could deplete the workforce; How employers could stem the tide: A white paper.* Lexington, Mass. : The Center for Effective Performance.

Zack, M (ed.). (1999). *Knowledge and strategy*. Boston: Butterworth-Heinemann.

Zemke, R. (1999). Don't fix that company. *Training, 36*(6), 26–33.

Zemke, R. (1981). Curriculum development as strategic planning. *Training, 18*(4), 29.

Zemke, R., and Kramlinger, T. (1982). *Figuring things out: A trainer's guide to needs and task analysis*. Reading, Mass. : Addison-Wesley.

Zemke, R., and Rossett, A. (2002). A hard look at ISD. *Training, 39*(2), 26–34.

Zenger, J., Ulrich, D., and Smallwood, N. (2000). The new leadership development. *Training and Development, 54*(3), 22–27.

ABOUT THE AUTHORS

William J. Rothwell is professor of human resource development on the University Park Campus of The Pennsylvania State University. He is also president of Rothwell and Associates Inc., a private consulting firm specializing in a comprehensive approach to human performance improvement, which has a client list that includes 32 multinational corporations. Previously assistant vice president and management development director for the Franklin Life Insurance Company in Springfield, Illinois, and training director for the Illinois Office of Auditor General, Dr. Rothwell has worked full-time in human resource management and employee training and development since 1979, combining real-world experience with academic and consulting experience.

Rothwell's most recent published work includes *What CEOs Expect from Corporate Training* (with J. Lindholm and W. Wallick, 2003); *The Workplace Learner* (2002); *Building Effective Technical Training* (with J. Benkowski, 2002); *Planning and Managing Human Resources* (2nd ed., with H. C. Kazanas, 2002); *The Manager and Change Leader* (2001); *Effective Succession Planning* (2nd ed., 2000); *The Complete Guide to Training Delivery: A Competency-Based Approach* (with M. King and S. King, 2000); *The Competency Toolkit* (with D. Dubois, 2000); *Human Performance Improvement: Building Practitioner Competence* (with C. Hohne and S. King, 2000); *The ASTD Reference Guide to Workplace Learning and Performance: Present and Future Roles and*

Competencies (3rd ed., Vols. 1–2, with H. Sredl, 2000); *The Analyst* (2000); *The Evaluator* (2000); *The Intervention Selector, Designer and Developer, and Implementor* (2000); *ASTD Models for Human Performance Improvement* (2nd ed., 2000); *Building In-House Leadership and Management Development Programs* (with H. C. Kazanas, 2000); *ASTD Models for Workplace Learning and Performance* (with E. Sanders and J. Soper, 1999); *The Action Learning Guidebook: A Real-Time Strategy for Problem-Solving, Training Design, and Employee Development* (1999); *The Sourcebook for Self-Directed Learning* (with K. Sensenig, 1999); *Creating, Measuring, and Documenting Service Impact: A Capacity Building Resource; Rationales, Models, Activities, Methods, Techniques, Instruments* (1998); *In Action: Improving Human Performance* (with D. Dubois, as editors, 1998); *Strategic Human Resource Leader: How to Help Your Organization Manage the Six Trends Affecting the Workforce* (with R. Prescott and M. Taylor, 1998); *In Action: Linking HRD and Organizational Strategy* (as editor, 1998); and *Mastering the Instructional Design Process: A Systematic Approach* (2nd ed., with H. C. Kazanas, 1998).

Dr. Rothwell can be reached at wjr9@psu.edu, or at www.rothwell-associates.com (Web site).

H. C. Kazanas is professor emeritus of education at the College of Education at the University of Illinois, Urbana-Champaign. He received his B.Sc. and M.Ed. from Wayne State University in industrial education and his Ph.D. in education from the University of Michigan.

Dr. Kazanas's current professional interests as a consultant are in the areas of management development, on-the-job employee training, and the effects of work values on productivity. He has been an active member of several professional organizations, including the American Society for Training and Development (ASTD) and the International Society for Performance Improvement. He has served and held leadership positions on numerous committees, including the National Association of Industrial and Technical Teacher Educators, of which he was president. He has received several awards for outstanding service, and has published 80 articles in 20 different journals on education and human resource development. Kazanas has been the author of several book chapters and monographs, and has either authored or co-authored 11 books relating to technical training in manufacturing and human resource development. One of his technical books has been translated into Spanish and Arabic. With William J. Rothwell, he co-authored *Human Resource Development: A Strategic Approach* (1994); *Improving On-the-Job Training* (1994); and *Planning and Managing Human Resources: Strategic Planning for Human Resource Management* (2nd ed., 2002).

Dr. Kazanas worked for 10 years in the manufacturing industry as a machinist and production supervisor, and was for 30 years an educator in human resource development. He has done human resource development consulting for such national and international organizations and agencies as the U.S. Department of Labor, the U.S. Department of Education, the U.S. Agency for International Development, Motorola, Westinghouse, the World Bank, the United Nations Development Program, the International Labor Office, and UNESCO. He has worked in Asia, Africa, Europe, and South America, and taught at Eastern Michigan University, the University of Missouri-Columbia, and the University of Illinois. He was graduate program coordinator at the University of Missouri-Columbia and department chair at the University of Illinois. During his academic career, he coordinated and directed research studies in such areas as work values, attitudes and productivity; strategic human resource planning; on-the-job training; management job rotation programs; and individualizing instruction.

INDEX

360-degree assessment, 38
3M, 204

Ability
  of future learners, 442
  training and, 406
Absenteeism, career planning and,
  364
Academic approach to curriculum,
  192, 193
Acquisitions, 229
Action learning projects,
  336–337, 346
Action plans, 328, 512
Action research, 204–205, 224,
  263–265, 274
Active environmental scanning
  strategy, 121. *See also*
  Environmental scanning
Activity-oriented learners, 234
Administrative employees, 97
Adult basic education, 386–387
Adult learners, classification of,
  234
Advance counseling, 493–494
Advancement, 97
Advance reading, 419–420
Advertising, 100–101, 237

Advisory committee, 104,
  240–243
  management-development,
  334–335
Affective learning domain, 222
Affirmative action goals, career
  planning and, 365
Allen, C. R., 425
Allied Signal, 40
American Management
  Association, 33
American Society for Training and
  Development, 338
Analysis
  business definition, 9
  career path, 369, 370–373
  cross-impact, 441, 449
  customer, 52–53
  data, 476–477
  environmental, 122. *See also*
    Environmental scanning
  force field, 448
  front-end, 492, 496, 497–498
  individual, 91
  job, 33, 150, 152
  morphological, 450
  organization, 91
  scenario, 449–450

situation, 90
strategic business, 443-444
SWOT, 167-169, 172-174
tactics, 92
task, 103, 105-106, 150, 152, 413
unit of, 476
work, 91, 369-373, 413, 443-444
workforce, 373-376
WOTS-UP, 167-169, 172-174
Androgogy, 212
Appreciative inquiry, 277
Argyris, Chris, 259, 265
Articles (journal), 225, 394
Artificial experience approach to talent
    development, 54, 55, 61-62, 79
Aspen Institute, 149
Aspiration, workforce analysis
    and, 374
Assessment
    360-degree, 38
    competency, 35, 38
    See also Needs assessment;
        Performance appraisal
Assessment centers, 38, 103, 104,
    107-108
    future-oriented, 150, 153
Attitude surveys, 104, 237, 270-271,
    475, 484, 485
Authority hierarchy, geographical scope,
    external groups, and, 289
Awareness, in lateral thinking, 451
Awareness of results, 234

Background, workforce analysis and
    employee, 374
Balanced scorecard, 7, 467
BARS. *See* Behaviorally anchored rating
    scales
Batelle-bildmappen brainwriting,
    446

Behavior
    vs. competency, 209
    evaluation of training and, 487, 489
    vs. performance, 402
    post-educational, 494
    structure and, 228
Behavioral anchors, 37, 38, 210
Behavioral-event interviews, 37
Behaviorally anchored rating scales
    (BARS), 107
Behavioral objectives, 222
Behavioral observations, 475
Behavior modeling, 339-340, 346, 424,
    497
Blended learning, 132
Board of directors, 18
Books, as self-study texts, 394
Bossidy, Larry, 40
Bottom-up strategy for needs assessment,
    102
Brainstorming, 61, 300, 445-446
    exercise, 349
Brainwriting, 446-447
    pool approach, 446
British Petroleum, 52
Bruner, Jerome, 213
Budgeting/budgets, 19, 20, 21, 236, 250
Bulletin boards, 237
Business, role in society, 294
Business competencies, 188
Business Plan Pro software, 11
Business planning/plans, 60
    environmental scanning and, 122-123
    organizational strategy for
        development of talent and, 187
    organizational structure, human
        resource plans, and, 25-26
    talent development, human resource
        plans, and, 29
Buzz groups, 421

California, social monitoring in, 295
Career, defined, 363
Career advancement
  horizontal, 362
  vertical, 361–362
Career anchors, 378
Career counseling, 363
Career development, defined, 363
Career education, 387–388
  defined, 363
Career management, 363
Career market, 98–99
Career path
  defined, 370
  establishing formal, 371
Career path analysis, 369, 370–373
Career planning/plans, 363–380
  analyzing work, 369–373
  analyzing workforce, 373–376
  defined, 363
  developing climate conducive to,
    365–366
  education on, 387–388
  employee education and, 369, 495
  establishing career policy, 366–369
  identifying future needs, 376–378
  individual issues in, 378–380
  long-term, 380
  in organization, 364–365
  purposes of, 378
Career planning approach to talent
  development, 54, 55, 59–60, 79
Career policy, 366–369
Career program, 145, 362–363
  employee education and, 362–363
Career stage, planning educational efforts
  by, 384
Case studies, 62, 422
  on employee development, 360
  on employee training, 463

on environmental scanning for talent
  development, 159
on implementing organizational
  trategy for development of talent,
  252–253
on organizational strategy for
  development of talent, 216–218
on purpose of talent development
  effort, 85
role plays and, 423
on strengths and weaknesses of
  organization's talent development
  effort, 118
Cause, determining, 170–171
CEOs. *See* Chief executive officers
Certification, 389
Chairpersons, 241
Change
  assessing pressures favoring, 279–280
  assessing pressures impeding, 280
  bringing about through learning, 205
  comparing forces impeding and
    favoring, 280, 284
  culture, 99, 107, 434
  curriculum planning and, 196
  deciding what should occur, 299–300
  direction of, 223
  first-order, 433
  identifying organizational forces
    favoring, 282
  identifying organizational forces
    impeding, 283
  instructional objectives and effecting,
    222–224
  learning and, 259
  mobilizing support for, 206
  organizational, 265
  overcoming resistance to, 276
  perception of needed, 263
  readiness to, 276

second-order, 433
selecting facilitator, 274
stress caused by, 276
types sought through talent
    development effort, 314
See also Organization development
Change champion, 279
Chaos theory, 276
Checklists, 450–451
    on organizational strategy for
        development of talent, 41–47
    on reconsideration of work
        activities/job tasks, 462
Chief executive officers (CEOs)
    Grand Strategy and, 18
    HR Grand Strategy and, 26
    leadership and, 226
    role in talent development efforts, 40
    selecting business strategy, 14
    visioning and, 50
Civic groups, talent development policies
    and serving in, 225
Clark, Charles, 446
Classification scheme
    creating, 287–291
    organizational analysis and, 144, 147
Classroom training, 407
    alternatives to, 407–408, 457
Clerical support, 97
Client, defined, 94
Closed-ended questions, 150, 453, 454
Closed-ended surveys, 105
Coaching, 439
Coercion, 258
Cognitive learning domain, 222
Cohesiveness, 260
College course, external, 493
Collier, John, 263
Combination organizational strategy,
    45

Committees
    advisory or oversight, 104, 240–243,
        334–335
    curriculum, 240
    employee, 341–342
    talent development, 240–243
Communication
    during change efforts, 276
    about organizational strategy, 251
    of reasons for employee development,
        343–344
    work group stage and, 261, 262
Communication channels, 237–238
    about organizational strategy for
        development of talent, 46, 237–243
Community
    community education efforts, 100,
        302–303
    issues and concerns of, 292
    key institutions, 306
    needs of, 289–290, 297, 298
Community colleges
    community education, 302
    external instruction sponsored by,
        391–392
Community development efforts, 303,
    304–305, 498
Community of practice, 390
Community polls, 293
Community service seminars, 302–303
Company newsletters, 237
Compensation/benefits, 27, 58, 188, 190
Competency
    core, 9, 346
    defined, 35, 209
    employee development and, 324
    identifying department, 357
    identifying organizational, 356
    identifying work group, 345–346,
        357

inventorying, 375–376
organizational, 346
strategic development of talent and, 30,
    33
Competency assessment, 38
    defined, 35
Competency-based career path analysis,
    372–373
Competency-based curriculum planning,
    209–211
Competency identification, 35, 36–38,
    370
Competency modeling/models, 34, 36,
    370
    defined, 35
    strategic development of talent and,
        34–40
Competitive advantage
    human resource planning and, 21–22
    sustainable, 9
Competitors, 135, 288. *See also* External
    stakeholders; Stakeholders
Complexity theory, 276
Comprehensive Employment and
    Training Act (1973), 364
Comprehensive human resource
    information system, 326
Comprehensive reviews
    of employee education, 494–496
    of training, 490–491
Computer-based/assisted instruction,
    231, 393–394, 430
Computer simulations, 27, 62
Concentration strategy, 177, 180
Concentric diversification, 177, 181
Concurrent evaluation, 485–486, 494
    employee development and, 496, 499,
        500
    strategic, 487
Condition, 103, 140–141

Conferences, professional, 338–339,
    346
Conflict
    constructive, 267
    interpersonal peacemaking and
        destructive, 267
    law of interorganizational, 273
    in organization, 272–273
    organizational mirror and, 271–274
Confrontation, organization development
    interventions and, 265
Confrontation meetings, 341, 342
Conglomerate diversification, 177,
    179–180
Consensus groups, 153–154
Constructive conflict, 267
Consultant inventory, 392
Consumers, 288, 290
    analyzing trends, 135
    company responsibility to, 133
    education of, 100
    task analysis and, 105
    testing, 301
    See also External stakeholders;
        Stakeholders
Content, evaluation issues, 471,
    472–473
Content analysis, 37
Content preparation, 427–432, 453
Context shifting, 208, 213
Contingency planning, 190–191
Contingency scenarios, 191
Continuing education, 388, 396
Contracting for talent, 57
Coordinative needs, 102
Coordinative planning, 19
Core competency, 9, 346
Core values, 40
Corporate issues, talent development
    and, 188–189

Corporate-level plans, organizational
　　strategy for development of talent and,
　　187
Corporate open house, 293
Corporate social responsibility, 133, 294
Corporate strategy, 17–18
Corporation
　　pinpointing strengths/opportunities
　　　　in relations with external groups,
　　　　313
　　pinpointing weaknesses/threats in
　　　　relations with external groups, 312
　　planning methods used by, 19–20
　　public, stakeholders, and, 291–293,
　　　　308
　　structure, 17
Cost-benefit analysis, training evaluation
　　and, 478
Costs
　　choosing data collection method and,
　　　　110
　　content development and, 427
　　of needs assessment, 410
　　of rewards, 234
　　trends in, 135
Course-centered curriculum planning,
　　199, 202–204
Courses, 428, 430, 493
Course titles, 202
Crawford slip writing, 446–447
Creation, work group stage, 261, 262
Creative needs, 171
Creativity
　　confrontation meetings and, 342
　　questioning and, 347–348
　　strategic business planning and, 15
Crisis
　　external, 279
　　as impetus for learning, 205
　　internal, 279

perception change needed and, 263
　　strategic business plans and, 185
Criteria, 103, 140–141
　　present vs. future, 440
Criterion-referenced tests, 480–481
Critical incidents, 62
　　activity, 353
　　future-oriented, 150, 154
Critical incident technique, 103, 108,
　　422–423
Critical needs, 171
Critical success factors, 9
Cross-impact analysis, 441, 449
Culture. defined, 72. *See also*
　　Organizational culture
Culture audit, 73–74, 81–84
Curriculum, 164, 191–196
　　approaches to, 192–193
　　defined, 191
　　design, 194, 199, 461
　　development, 113, 194–196
　　educational, 113
　　history, 192–193
　　needs assessment, 125
　　nonemployee development, 113
　　perceived vs. formal, 205–206
　　selecting for instruction aimed at
　　　　external groups, 301–304
　　sequencing, 231–233
　　spiral, 233
　　training, 113, 428, 430
Curriculum committees, 240
Curriculum matrix, 200–201
Curriculum planning, 196–213
　　alternative approaches, 199–213
　　course-centered approach, 199,
　　　　202–204
　　experience-centered approach, 199,
　　　　204–206
　　goal-centered approach, 199, 206–211

learner-centered approach, 199, 212–213
process, 196–199
results, 213–214
strategic-centered approach, 202
Customer representatives, 98
Customers
analysis of, 9, 52–53
loyalty of, 135
satisfaction of, 7
strategic business strategy and, 12
training directed to, 143, 285
See also External stakeholders;
Stakeholders

DACUM. *See* Developing a Curriculum
Data analysis, 476–477
Data collection methods, 103–110
selecting, 110–111
strategic training needs assessment,
440–441
Deadwood, 99
DeBono, Edward, 451
Debriefing, 334, 344
Decision aids, 408
Decision-making, 61, 379
Deficiencies, in performance, 140
Degree programs, external, 392–393
Delayed feedback, 486
Delivery methods, 172
articles, 394
behavior modeling, 424
books, 394
brainstorming, 445–446
brainwriting, 446–447
buzz groups, 421
case studies, 422
checklists, 450–451
computer-based and
computer-assisted, 393–394
Crawford slip writing, 446–447

cross impact analysis, 449
Delphi procedure, 448
demonstration, 424–425
devil's advocate, 451–452
for employee educational programs,
389–395
employee training, 418–427
exercises, 421–422
external degree programs, 392–393
for external groups, 318
external instruction sponsored by
community colleges, 391–392
external instruction sponsored by
universities, 391
external instruction sponsored by
vendors, 392
force field analysis, 448
group debate method, 452
incident process, 422–423
independent reading, 419–420
in-house, formal group instruction,
389–390
in-house, informal group instruction, 390
in-house-sponsored, externally
developed instruction, 390–391
for instruction aimed at external
groups, 304
lateral thinking, 451
lectures, 418–419
microsimulations, 451
morphological analysis, 450
nominal group technique, 448
off-the-shelf training packages, 393
panels, 420–421
Phillips 66 technique, 447–448
role play, 423–424
scenario analysis, 449–450
selecting, 426–427
simulations/games, 425–426
speakers' bureaus, 394

strategic training, 445–453
tuition reimbursement programs,
    394–395
Delivery of training, 453–454
Delphi procedure, 61, 103, 109, 150,
    154–155, 439, 441, 448
    role analysis technique and, 267
Demonstration, 424–425, 488
Department
    environmental context of, 138
    identifying competencies in, 357
    organizational mirror and, 271
    strategic employee development for, 345
    structure of, 228
    turnaround efforts in, 332
    workforce analysis by, 375–376
    in WOTS-UP analysis, 173
Department market, 99–100
Derailment competency models, 36
Descriptive career path analysis, 370–371
Descriptive evaluation design, 474
Desired results, 146
Detailed outlining, 431
Developing a Curriculum (DACUM), 376
Development curriculum, 113
Devil's advocate, 451–452
Dewey, John, 28, 213
Dialogues, 431
Diary
    conference, 339
    field trip, 338
    think-tank experience, 342
Directive training, 444–445, 453
Direct mail, 237
Discrepancy method of career path
    analysis, 372
Distance education, 339, 392–393
Distributors, 287, 290
    analyzing trends, 135
    assessing needs of, 298

education of, 100
testing, 301
See also External stakeholders;
    Retailers; Stakeholders
Distributor sector, 126, 136
Diversification strategy, 45, 172, 174, 177
    concentric, 177, 181
    conglomerate, 177, 179–180
Divestiture, 176, 177, 179
Divestment, 229
Division, workforce analysis by, 375–376
Dixon, Pam, 392–393
Domain experts, 123
Double-loop learning, 278
Doughnut sequencing method, 418
Downward channels of communication, 237
Dual-career couples, 134
Dual career ladders, 371–372
Dual-career pathing method, 381–382
Dual labor market theory, 364
Duties, 146

EAPs. See Employee assistance programs
Economic development, 141
Economic sector, 126, 129–130
Education, xxiv, 64, 124
    adult basic, 386–387
    career, 387–388. *See also* Career
        planning/plans
    change and, 258
    continuing, 388, 396
    curriculum, 113
    distance, 339, 392–393
    functional strategies and, 244
    needs, 108
    occupational, 388–389, 397–398
    proficiency and, 103
    tied to training, 64–65
    trends in, 141
    See also under Employee education

Educational approach to talent
development, 54, 55, 64–65, 80
Educational management, 495
Educational sources, 492–493, 495
Effectiveness, value of, 468
Efficiency, value of, 469
e-learning, 39, 132, 285, 407
Employee appraisal, 103, 106–107
future-oriented, 150, 152–153
planning educational efforts by,
384–385
workforce analysis and, 374
Employee assessment, competency
models and, 38
Employee assistance, 58
human resource plans, 188
Employee assistance programs (EAPs),
383
Employee committees, 341–342
Employee development, xxi, xxiii, 31,
124, 186, 323–360
action learning projects, 336–337
assessing developmental climate, 354
behavior modeling, 339–340
case study, 360
critical incidents, 353
defined, 323–324
vs. employee training, 402
field trips, 337–338
functional strategies and, 244
identifying efforts in organization, 358
identifying employee development
needs, 324–328
identifying organizational
competencies, 356
identifying problems/issues in work
groups, 355
identifying work group/department
competencies, 357
mentoring programs, 328–330, 349

needs, 108
objectives, 415
problems with traditional, 343–345
professional conferences, 338–339
proficiency and, 103
resources to meet needs of, 359
rotation programs, 333–335, 350–352
specialized methods for, 328–343
specialized to meet long-term
organizational needs, 346–348
special job assignments, 335–336
strategic, 345–346
think-tank experiences, 340–342
transfer programs, 330–332
Employee development evaluation, 496–499
concurrent evaluation of development,
499
field-testing, 498–499
front-end analysis, 497–498
post-development follow-up, 499
Employee education, 31, 186, 361–400
career plans and, 369
career program and, 362–363
comprehensive reviews of, 494–496
defined, 361–362
delivery methods, 389–395
vs. employee training, 402
human resource plans and, 369
individual performance and, 98
kinds of programs, 386–389
objectives, 415
organization development
interventions and, 265
organization strategy for development
of talent, 369
planning individual component,
384–386
planning organizational component,
381–384
strategic business plans and, 368

tying to organizational strategy for
    development of talent, 395, 399–400
vertical market and, 441
Employee education evaluation, 491–496
    advance counseling, 493–494
    comprehensive reviews, 494–496
    concurrent evaluation, 494
    evaluation of educational sources,
        492–493
    front-end analysis, 492
    post-educational follow-up, 494
Employee education programs, 386–389
    adult basic education, 386–387
    career education, 387–388
    continuing education, 388
    occupational education, 388–389
Employee evaluation, talent development
    and, 32. *See also* Performance appraisal
Employee expectations, work setting and,
    412
Employee families, 288, 290. *See also*
    External stakeholders
Employee performance appraisals. *See*
    Performance appraisal
Employee retreats, 341
Employees, 132
    classifying, 59
    evaluation interests, 470
    identifying what should be doing in
        future, 437–439
    new, 410
Enabling training objectives, 414, 415,
    444
Enterprise Resource Programs (ERPs), 7
Enterprise strategy, 18
    human resource, 26–27
Entrepreneurial thinking, strategic
    business strategy and, 11–12
Environment, performance-based
    curriculum and problems in, 207

Environmental analysis, 122
Environmental change database, 165
Environmental diagnosis, 122
Environmental scanning, xxiii, 9,
    119–159
    anticipating effects of environmental
        changes, 136–139
    in business planning, 122–123
    case study, 159
    classifying external environment, 126
    competency identification and, 37
    curriculum needs assessment and, 125
    deciding on time horizon, 126–129
    defined, 122
    description of, 120–122
    examining environmental sectors,
        129–136
    identifying future learning needs,
        140–147
    methods, 150–155
    reassessing learning needs by market
        or market segment, 155–156
    sources of information for, 148–150
Environmental sectors, 126–128
    examining, 129–136
Environmental uncertainty, organizational
    strategy for development of talent and,
    183
Erickson, Erik, 384
ERPs. *See* Enterprise Resource Programs
Espoused theory, 206, 278
Estimating human resource needs, 327–328
Evaluation
    of business strategy, 15
    choosing method of, 319
    defined, 467–468
    designs, 474–475
    formative, 482–484
    hypothesis, 474
    of individual learning contract, 385

instructional, 504, 505–506
of organizational strategy, 518
of organizational strategy for talent
    development, 47
value of, 469
See also Employee development
    evaluation; Employee education
    evaluation;
Evaluation of talent development;
    Strategic evaluation; Training
    evaluation
Evaluation of talent development,
    467–469, 499–503
content, 471
content issues, 472–473
evaluator, 470
method, 474–477
purpose, 471
stakeholders and, 469–470
timing, 471
value of, 469
Evaluation plan, 475
Evaluator, 470, 485, 486
Event, 14
Exchange programs, 330–331, 346, 497
Executive in residence program, 330–331
Executives, 97. *See also* Top
    management/managers
Exemplars, 106
Exercises, 421–422
Exit interviews, 104
Experience
    long-term planning of related, 346–347
    organizational culture and, 262–263
    talent development and, 29–30
Experience-centered curriculum, 231
Experience-centered curriculum
    planning, 199, 204–206
Experiential approach to curriculum,
    192, 193

Experiential learning, 265
Experimental evaluation design, 475, 476
Experimental treatments, 475
Expert testing, 483
External change agent, 269–270
External consultants
    to facilitate change effort, 263,
        269–270
    to offer instruction, 391
    organization development and,
        257–258
    strategic business planning and, 20
    study of external groups and, 293
External crisis, 279
External degree programs, 392–393
External environment
    anticipating effects of, 136–139
    classifying, 126
    instructional objectives and
        influencing, 222
    scanning. *See* Environmental
        scanning
    strategic business planning and, 5–6
    strategic orientation and, 285
External groups, 140
    authority hierarchy, geographical
        scope, and, 289
    choosing delivery methods for
        instruction, 318
    choosing instruction to offer, 317
    long-term learning needs and, 186
    methods for assessing needs of,
        296–299
    nonemployee development and, 186
    organizational strategy for
        development of talent and, 169
    pinpointing strengths/opportunities in
        relations with corporations, 313
    pinpointing weaknesses/threats in
        relations with corporations, 312

in WOTS-UP analysis, 174
See also External stakeholders;
  Stakeholders
External instruction
  sponsored by community colleges,
    391–392
  sponsored by universities, 391
  sponsored by vendors, 392
External labor market, 364
External market, 100–101
External opportunities, 279
External stakeholders, 18, 120–121, 132,
  143–144, 287–291, 307. *See also*
  Stakeholders
External suppliers of talent, 178
External validity, 475
Extrinsic rewards, 233, 234

Face-to-face group discussion, in role
  analysis technique, 267
Fact-finding, 337
Families, employee, 288, 290. *See also*
  External stakeholders
Family group, 259
Fastcompany, 11
Fast-cycle environments, 7
Feedback
  in action research, 264
  concurrent evaluation and, 486
  delayed, 486
  from external groups, 293
  noninstructional needs and, 296
  organization development
    interventions and, 265
  in process consultation, 268
  role message and, 266
  simultaneous, 486
  training and, 406
Field operations chief, 230
Field testing, 483, 496, 498–499

Field trips, 337–338, 346, 497
  conferences and, 338–339
Financial analysis, 9
Financial forecasting, 21
Financial performance, 7
First-generation planning, 5
First-line managers, 19, 20
First-line supervisors, 97
First-order change, 433
Fixation, work group stage, 261, 262
Flexibility, in reward systems, 234
Focused panel format, 421
Focus groups, 104, 155, 292
Follow-up
  on developmental experience, 348
  on instructional needs, 304–305
  phone calls, 293
  post-educational, 494
Force field analysis, 448
Formal curriculum, vs. perceived, 205–206
Formal organization, 265
Formative evaluation
  methods, 483
  strategic, 482–484
  traditional, 482
Fourth-generation planning, 7
Frequency, of rewards, 234
Front-end analysis
  of employee development, 496, 497–498
  of employee education, 492
Front-end evaluation
  strategic approach, 479–480
  traditional, 477–478
Functional strategy, 18
  human resource, 27
  for talent development, 46, 243–244,
    513
Future
  competency identification and, 37–38
  competency models and, 39–40

focus on in training, 432–433
identifying what employees should be
doing in, 437–439
scanning for workforce needs, 377
Web site resources on, 149
Future criteria, 140–141
Futures Group International, 149
Futuring, defined, 60
Futuring approach to talent development,
54, 55, 60–61, 79

Games, 425–426
General Electric, 40
General instruction, 95
General public, 120, 132, 287, 288
assessing needs of, 298
education of, 100
learning needs of, 141–142
stakeholders, corporation, and,
291–293, 308
Geographic scope, external groups,
authority hierarchy, and, 289, 290
Geographic sector, 126, 135–136
Georgia Tech, 393
Gilbert, Thomas, 92
Goal-centered curriculum planning, 199,
206–211, 231
Goal-oriented learners, 234
Goals, 13
conflict over, 273
formulating for curriculum, 197
in instructional evaluation, 504
selecting, 8
Government
influence on business, 130–131
top management and, 288
Grand Strategy, 17–18, 163, 512
effect on talent, 229
functional strategy and, 243
human resource, 26

human resource planning and, 21,
22–23
integrating with instruction for external
groups, 320
organizational strategy for
development of talent and, 244
strategy choices, 176, 177–178
Grand Strategy Selection Matrix,
175, 176
Group debate method, 452
Group discussions, 103, 108
environmental scanning and, 150,
153–154
Group dynamics, 259
Group instruction, in-house
formal, 389–390
informal, 390
Group interviews, 108
Group-learning plan, 186
Group norms, 406, 412, 443
Group process, 60
Groups
generating in curriculum planning, 197
learning and, 259
norms, 259, 260, 406, 412, 443
organizational strategy for
development of talent and key, 183
organization development
interventions and, 268, 269
planning educational efforts by,
382–383
Groupthink, 261
Group training, 439
Growth strategy, 44, 172, 174
Guided questioning approach,
431–432

Hay/McBer, 33
Hewlett-Packard, 40
Horizontal career advancement, 362

Horizontal market, 441
Hospitals, community education,
    301–302
HRD. *See* Human resource development
HR Guide to the Internet, 33
HRP. *See* Human resource planning
HRPs. *See* Human resource plans
Hudson Institute, 149
Human performance improvement, xix.
    See also Strategic business planning
Human performance problems, 455–456
Human resource audit, 326
Human resource development (HRD),
    xix, 4. *See also* Strategic business
    planning
Human resource enterprise strategy, 26–27
Human Resource Executive's Desk
    Reference, 25
Human resource functional strategy, 27
Human resource Grand Strategy, 26
Human resource information system, 326
Human resource management, Web
    resources, 33
Human resource planning (HRP), 21–28
    assumptions of, 23–25
    defined, 21
    employee education and, 495
    estimating human resource needs,
        327–328
    levels of, 25–27
    methods of, 27–28
    model of, 22–23, 24
    planning for future learners and, 442
    vs. strategic business planning, 24
    strategic training and, 435
    training and, 403
    value of, 25
Human resource plans (HRPs)
    career policy and, 367
    employee development and, 325

employee education and, 369
organizational strategy for
    development of talent and, 187
talent development, business plans,
    and, 29
talent development, strategic business
    plans, and, 54–68, 79–80
Human Resources Planning Society, 25
Human resource supplies, 327–328
Hypothesis, 474

Identity, clarifying personal, 379
Ideology, development of, 272
IDPs. *See* Individual development plans
Illiteracy, 134
Implementation, 219–220
    of business strategy, 14
    of organizational strategy, 518
    programs, 239
    of strategic business plan, 20
Implementation of organizational strategy
    for development of talent, 31, 219–250
    budgeting, 250
    case study, 252–253
    communicating about strategy,
        237–243, 251
    creating talent development policies,
        224–225, 246–247
    developing functional strategies for
        talent development, 243–244
    establishing operational objectives,
        220–224, 245
    examining leadership, 226–227, 248
    obtaining resources, 236
    reviewing reward systems, 233–236,
        249
    reviewing structure, 227–233
Incidental learning, 39
Incident process, 422–423
Independent learning projects, 335–336

Independent reading, 419–420

Individual analysis, 91

Individual career, instructional objectives and influencing, 223

Individual career planning/plans, 188, 362, 378–380

Individual development plans (IDPs), 35, 39, 186, 386

Individual development programs, 60

Individualized instruction, 408

Individualized testing, 483

Individual learning, vs. organizational learning, 262

Individual learning contract, 385–386, 492

Individual market, 98–99

Individual performance, future trends and, 153

Individuals
classifying, 117
educational efforts and socialization stage of, 383–384
experience-centered approach to curriculum planning and, 205
future learning needs of, 145–146
learning and, 259
long-term learning needs and, 186
organization development interventions and, 265
organization strategy for development of talent and, 169
performance-based curriculum and problems in, 207
relation with organization, 259–260
self-initiated learning by, 325
training needs of, 106
workforce analysis by, 373–374
in WOTS-UP analysis, 174

Informal learning, 39

Informal organization, 265

Information collecting, 309

Information sources, for talent development scanning, 148–150

In-house
formal group instruction, 389–390
informal group instruction, 390
instruction, 95
organizational strategy for development of talent and, 184–185

In-house-sponsored, externally developed instruction, 390–391

Innovation, 7

Innovation strategy, 178, 180–181

Inquiry-oriented instruction, 213

Inside-outside approach to strategy formulation, 64

Institutional memory, 261–262

Instruction, 194
directed to external groups, 299
general, 95
in-house, 95, 389–390
innovative, 315
inquiry-oriented, 213
methods. *See* Delivery methods
programmed, 231
specific, 95

Instructional design, 300–301

Instructional evaluation
goals in, 504
issues in, 505–506

Instructional needs, 91–92
follow-up on, 304–305
microtraining vs. macrotraining, 92
movements of people and, 97
vs. noninstructional, 91–92, 296–299

Instructional objectives, 211, 221–222, 414–415
alternative to course development from, 431–432
content development and, 427–431

strategic, 444
test item, job task, and, 415
Instructional plan, 213–214
Instructional programs/packages, 65, 430
Instructional setting, 412–413, 460
    evaluation and, 472
    future, 443
Instructional structure, 228
Instructor's guide, 430
Instrumental values, 468
Integration, 45
Integration strategy, 174
Intellectual capital, 4, 20
Intention, 50
Interdependence, conflict and, 273
Interest groups, 295
Interlocking conference, 271
Internal appraisal, conducting, 515–516, 517
Internal crisis, 279
Internal groups, 140
    long-term learning needs and, 186
    See also Groups; Work groups
Internal labor market, 364
Internal opportunities, 279
Internal validity, 475
Interpersonal approach to talent development, 55, 65–66, 80
Interpersonal peacemaking, 267–268, 274
Interviews, 103–104
    behavioral-event, 37
    environmental scanning, 150–152
    ethnographic techniques, 74
    exit, 104
    group, 108
    guide, 103
    schedule, 103
Intrinsic rewards, 233–234
Intuition, strategic business strategy and, 12

Investors, 288, 290. See also External stakeholders; Stakeholders
Issue-based strategic management, 67

JIT. See Job instruction training
Job
    defined, 96, 413
    future learning needs and, 146–147
Job aids, 407, 439
Job analysis, 33
    future-oriented, 150, 152
Job categories, 146–147
    defined, 96
    experience-centered approach to curriculum planning and, 205
    learning plan, 199
    long-term learning needs and, 186
    organizational strategy for development of talent and, 169
    performance-based curriculum and problems in, 207
    in WOTS-UP analysis, 174
Job class, 96, 199, 428
Job description, 35, 443
Job family, 96
Job groupings, 116, 429
Job/group orientation, 97
Job incumbents, 441
Job instruction training (JIT), 425
Job market, 96–98
Job performance
    defined, 402
    instructional objectives and influencing, 223
    training and, 401, 402
Job redesign, 57, 58
Job rotation, 333–335
Job skills, 134
Job specifications, 35
Job titles, classifying, 97

Job Training Partnership Act (1983), 364
Job transfers, 331–332, 346
Johnson & Johnson, 40
Joint venture, 176, 177, 181
Journal of Business Strategy, 11
Journals, 394

Kirkpatrick, Donald, evaluation hierarchy,
  487, 488
Knowledge, 209
  comparing actual to desired, 101–112
Knowledge management, 4, 20
Knowles, Malcolm, 212

Labor agreements, 382
Labor markets, 364
Labor relations, 58, 188, 190
Laird, Dugan, 92
Large-scale group event (LSGE), 277
Lateral thinking, 451
Law of interorganizational conflict, 273
Layoffs, 179–180
Leadership, 12
  competence, 35
  talent development and, 4, 40, 46,
    226–227, 248
  training and, 406
  work group behavior and, 260
Learner-centered curriculum, 231
Learner-centered curriculum planning,
  199, 212–213
Learners
  activity-oriented, 234
  assessing needs of, 408–410
  characteristics, 410–412, 459
  classifying, 43
  classifying by market segment, 95–101
  defined, 94
  evaluation and, 472
  future characteristics of, 441–442

goal-oriented, 234
identifying, 42, 93, 94–95, 114–115,
  117
learning-oriented, 234
types of, 193
Learning
  blended, 132
  change through, 205
  crisis as impetus for, 205
  double-loop, 278
  e-, 39, 132, 285, 407
  evaluation of training, 487, 488–489
  experiential, 265
  incidental, 39
  informal, 39
  innovation and, 7
  lifelong, 388
  objectives, 333
  post-educational, 494
  rewards and, 234
  self-directed, 212
  single-loop, 278
  situated, 39
  strategies, xxiii
  talent development and, 4
  transfer of, 489
  See also Organizational learning
Learning contract, 385–386, 492
Learning domains, 222
Learning hierarchy, 232
Learning Navigator, 343
Learning needs
  change in organizational structure and,
    228–229
  curriculum planning and, 197–198
  of external stakeholders, 143–144
  of general public, 141–142
  identifying by market or market
    segment, 112–113
  identifying future, 140–147

individual, 145–146
jobs and, 146–147
of learners, 408–410
organization's future, 144–145
present, 169
See also Needs assessment
Learning-oriented learners, 234
Learning plan, 199
Legal requirements, planning educational
efforts and, 382
Legislators, training directed to, 286
Lessons, 428, 430
objectives, 222
plan, 428, 430
Lewin, Kurt, 263, 448
Life cycle stages
classifying employees by, 99
classifying individuals and, 117
of work groups, 261, 262
Lifelong learning, 388
Likert, Rensis, 270
Liquidation, 176, 177, 179, 229
Listservs, for human resource planning,
25
Literacy, education for, 386–387
Local level, 289–290.
See also Community
Log
conference, 339
field trip, 338
think-tank experience, 342
Long-range planning, 5
Long-term, formalized transfer programs,
330–332, 346
Long-term, formal mentoring program,
329–330, 346
Long-term, informal mentoring program,
328–329, 346
Long-term needs, 171
Long-term objectives, 222

Long-term planning of related
experience, 346–347
Long-term strategy, 14
Lower-level managers
effects of trends on, 137
environmental scanning and, 123
leadership and, 227
time perspective of, 128
See also Management/managers
LSGE. *See* Large-scale group event

Macrotraining need, 92, 405
Mager, Robert, 206–207
Maier, Norman R. F., 423
Maintenance subsystem, 28–29
Management/managers, 132
career planning for, 366
first-line, 19, 20
middle, 19, 20, 97, 470
role in effecting change, 279
trainees, 334
See also Lower-level managers; Top
management/managers
Management by objectives (MBO), 107,
153, 221, 336, 385, 492
Management commitment, evaluation of
training and, 478
Management-development advisory
committee (MDAC), 334–335
Management requests, 104, 440–441
Management retreats, 341
Manpower Development and Training
Act (1962), 364
Manual workers/jobs
observation and, 105
task analysis and, 105, 413
training for, 233
Market
defined, 95
identifying learning needs by, 112–113

reassessing learning needs by,
    155–156
Market development, 176, 177, 180
Market-driven approach to talent
    development, 54, 55, 57–59, 79
Marketing, evaluation and, 472
Market sector, 43, 126, 134–135
    analyzing concerns relating to, 297
    classifying learners by, 95–101
    defined, 95
    identifying learning needs by, 112–113
    reassessing learning needs by,
        155–156
Mary Kay Inc., 52
Massachusetts, social monitoring in, 295
Mass media
    perception of relations with public and
        stakeholders and, 292
    top management and, 288
Matrix structure, 230, 261
MBO. *See* Management by objectives
McLagan, Patricia, 194
MDAC. *See* Management-development
    advisory committee
Meaningfulness, of rewards, 234
Media models, 427
Media selection, 426–427. *See also*
    Delivery methods
Medium-sized companies, strategic
    business planning and, 20
Meetings
    to communicate about strategy,
        237, 238–239
    confrontation, 341, 342
    process consultation and, 268
    staff, 342
    strategic training needs assessment, 441
Megatrends, 149
Memos, 237
Mentees, 329

Mentoring, 497
    career planning and, 363
    long-term, formal program, 329–330,
        346
    long-term, informal program, 328–329,
        346
Mergers, 229
Meta-evaluation, 495
Metaphors, for business planning, 7–8
Method, evaluation, 474–477
Microsimulations, 451
Microsoft, 18
Microtraining need, 92, 405
Middle managers, 19, 20, 97, 470.
        See also Management/managers
Minorities
    planning educational efforts for, 382
    in workforce, 134
Mission, 50, 189, 511
Mission statement, 50
Mobility
    career planning and, 363
    upward, 381
Modeling
    behavior, 339–340, 346, 424, 497
    competency, 34–40, 370
Morale, value of, 469
Morphological analysis, 450
Motivation
    career planning and, 364–365
    of future learners, 442
    job performance and, 402
    noninstructional needs and, 296
    training and, 406
Motive, 209
Multiple scenario analysis, 450
Multisource assessment, 38

Naisbitt, John, 149
Narrative competency model, 37, 38

National Technical University, 393
Needs
    collecting information on
        future-oriented, 157–158
    coordinative, 102
    creative vs. noncreative, 171
    critical and not-so-critical, 171
    identifying future workforce,
        376–378
    long-term and short-term, 171
    macrotraining, 405
    microtraining, 405
    nonrepetitive, 171
    nontraining, 405–406, 438
    operational, 102
    organizational, 346–348
    planning educational efforts by,
        382–383
    repetitive and nonrepetitive, 171
    strategic, 102
    strategic employee-development, 359
    strategic training, 438
    See also Instructional needs; Learning
        needs; Training needs
Needs assessment, xxii, 89–118, 458
    approaches to instructional, 104
    background issues, 91–93
    classifying learners by market segment,
        95–101, 116
    comparing actual to desired knowledge
        and skills, 101–112
    data collection methods, 103–110
    defined, 90–91
    description, 90–91
    environmental scanning and
        curriculum, 125
    finding strengths and weaknesses via,
        63
    identifying learners, 93, 94–95,
        114–115, 117

identifying present learning needs by
    market or market segment, 112–113
involving others in data collection and
    analysis, 111–112
levels of, 102–103
relation with public and stakeholders
    and, 291
selecting data collection methods,
    110–111
selecting strategy for, 102–103
talent development and, 42
Negotiated strategy for needs assessment,
    102
Network sequencing method, 418
New employees, learner characteristics,
    410
New York state, social monitoring in, 295
NGT. See Nominal group technique
Nominal group technique (NGT), 61,
    103, 109–110, 150, 154–155, 439,
    441, 448
Noncreative needs, 171
Nondirective training, 444–445, 453
Nonemployee development, xxi, xxiii, 31,
    100, 186, 285–321, 496
    analyzing present and future criteria,
        294–295, 309
    analyzing relationships among
        corporation, public, stakeholders,
        291–293, 308, 312–313
    creating classification schemes, 287–291
    curriculum, 113
    deciding what changes should occur,
        299–300, 314, 316
    designing instruction, 300–301, 317
    following up on instructional needs,
        304–305, 319
    front-end analysis of, 498
    functional strategies and, 244
    needs, 108

pinpointing discrepancies, 296
proficiency and, 103
relation between organizational
    strategy for development of talent
    and talent development for external
    groups, 305, 320–321
selecting content and delivery
    methods, 301–304, 318
separating instructional from
    noninstructional needs, 296–299
steps in, 286–305
Noninstructional needs, 92
vs. instructional, 296–299
Nonrecurring problems, 211
Nonrepetitive needs, 171
Nontraining needs, 405–406
future, 438
Norms
changing, 265
group, 259, 260, 406, 412, 443
identifying norms that should exist,
    278–279
Null hypothesis, 474

Objectives, 13, 106
assessing in stakeholders, 514–515
behavioral, 222
employee development, 415
employee education, 415
enabling, 444
establishing operational for talent
    development effort, 220–224
evaluation and, 472
instructional. *See* Instructional
    objectives
learning, *333*
lesson, 222
organizational, 221
selecting, 8
sequencing, 417–418

setting for implementing organizational
    strategy for development of
    talent, 245
strategic, 8
strategic business, 224
strategic instructional, 444
talent development, 224, 511
terminal, 444
training, 414–415
unit, 222
Observation, 103, 105
behavioral, 475
structured, 486
unstructured naturalistic, 486
Occupation, defined, 96, 413
Occupational certification, 389
Occupational competency models, 36
Occupational education, 388–389, 397–398
Occupational group
planning educational efforts by, 381–382
workforce analysis by, 375
OD. *See* Organization development
Off-the-shelf training packages, 393
On-the-job training (OJT), 231, 408, 424
Open book management, 323
Open-ended questions, 150, 272, 347,
    453–454
Open-ended surveys, 105
Open forums, 108
Operational needs, 102
Operational planning, 19
Operation analysis, 91
Opinion polls, 293
Opportunities
analyzing future, 9, 14, 16
environmental scanning and, 121,
    155–156
external, 279
internal, 279
WOTS-UP analysis and, 167–169

Oral test, 415–416, 488
Organization
     career planning in, 364–365
     changes in, 265
     conflict in, 272–273
     environmental sectors and, 127
     experience-centered approach to
          curriculum planning and, 205
     future learning needs, 144–145
     instructional objectives and
          influencing, 222
     performance-based curriculum and
          problems in, 207
     relation with individual, 259–260
Organizational career programs, 362
Organizational climate, career planning
     and, 365–366, 368
Organizational competencies, 35, 346
     core, 35
     identifying, 356
Organizational culture
     assessment of, 73–74, 76, 81–84
     business planning and, 20
     change in, 99, 107, 222, 223, 434
     effect on purpose of talent
          development effort, 72–74
     experience and, 262–263
     long-term learning needs and, 186
     organization development and change
          in, 258
     selecting needs assessment strategy
          and, 102–103
     survey-guided development and
          change in, 270–271
Organizational development intervention,
     497–498
Organizational learning, 261–263
     organization development and,
          258–263
Organizational mirror, 271–274, 275

Organizational needs, employee-develop-
     ment methods for meeting long-term,
     346–348
Organizational objectives, 221
Organizational offering, planning
     educational efforts by, 386
Organizational paradigm, strategic
     training and, 434
Organizational performance, strategic
     business planning and, 15
Organizational philosophy, effect on
     purpose of talent development
     effort, 72
Organizational purpose. See Purpose
Organizational strategy
     implementing, 518
     long-term objectives and, 499
     selecting, 518
Organizational strategy for development
     of talent, 31, 163–218
     attitudes about risk and, 184
     available skills, 187
     case study, 216–218
     choosing, 44–45, 175–181
     considering possible solutions, 174–175
     curriculum, 191–196
     curriculum planning, 196–213
     definition, 163–164
     dependence on key groups and, 183
     employee education and, 369
     environmental uncertainty and, 183
     finding problems, 167–169
     formulating, 511–513
     formulating problems, 169–170
     identifying way to look at problem,
          170–174
     implementing. See Implementation of
          organizational strategy for
          development of talent
     importance of, 164–165

in-house politics and, 184–185

integrating with instruction for external groups, 321

need for special focus, 185–187

past strategy and, 182–183

planning for contingencies, 190–191

problem framing, 215

process of choosing, 166–181

relation to other plans, 187–190

results of curriculum planning for, 213–214

reviewing, 508–509

rewards and changes in, 234–236

special issues to consider in choosing, 182–190

strategic training and, 434–435

suggestions for choosing, 165–166

talent development efforts aimed at external groups and, 305

timing, 185

training and, 403

Organizational structure

business plans, human resource plans, and, 25–26

dramatic changes in, 229–230

learning needs and change in, 228–229

work groups and, 260

Organization analysis, 91

Organization development (OD), xxi, xxiii, 27, 31, 187, 257–284, 496

culture change and, 99

defined, 257–258

functional strategies and, 244

methods, 263–275

organizational learning and, 258–263

vs. other change methods, 258

problems associated with interventions, 275

proficiency and, 103

recent themes, 276–277

strategic, 277–281

Organization development interventions, 263, 265–275

defined, 265

Orientation, 97

job rotation and, 335, 350–352

programs, 239

Outcomes, training, 472

Outlining, 431

Outside-inside approach to strategy formulation, 64

Oversight committees, 240–243

Panels, 420–421

Passive environmental scanning strategy, 121

Past-oriented competency models, 36

Past tradition, employee development and perpetuation of, 344

Pay, skill-based, 235

Paycheck notices, 237

Peacemaking, interpersonal, 267–268

People with disabilities, planning educational efforts for, 382

Perceived curriculum, vs. formal, 205–206

Performance, 106

vs. competency, 209

stable, 97

Performance appraisal, 103, 106–107

future-oriented, 150, 152–153

planning educational efforts by, 384–385

workforce analysis and, 374

Performance-based curriculum planning, 207–209, 211

Performance diagnosis approach to talent development, 54, 55, 63–64, 80

Performance documents, 104

Performance/productivity measures, 103

Performance test, 415, 488
Personal performance contract (PPC),
    336
Personal strengths/weaknesses, 379
Personal values, 379
Personnel handbooks, 237
Persuasion, 258, 480
Phillips 66 technique, 447–448
Philosophy
    of instructional setting, 413
    of sequencing, 418
    of talent development, 72
Physical condition, of setting, 412, 413
    future, 443
Planned learning experiences, 101
    organizational plan and, 31–32
Planning/plan
    for contingencies, 190–191
    coordinative, 19
    general training on, 239
    history of, 5–7
    long-range, 5
    objectives for talent development, 165
    operational, 19
    program, 195
    programmed, 191
    strategic, 6, 19
    strategic training and, 434
    training and, 402–403
Planning gap, 444
Plato, 431
Policies, 5
    future, 443
    training and company, 405
Policy analysis, 92
Political sector, 126, 130–131
Politics, organizational strategy for devel-
    opment of talent and in-house,
    184–185
Popcorn, Faith, 149

Position
    defined, 96
    workforce analysis by, 374–375
Post-developmental follow-up, 497, 499
Post-educational follow-up, 494
Post-instructional evaluation, 487–490
    strategic, 490
Post-test, 484
Power, 184
PPC. See Personal performance contract
Pragmatic approach to curriculum, 192–193
Prereading, 419–420
Prescriptive career path analysis, 370
Present learning need, 169
Present-oriented competency models, 36
Pre-socialization, 97
Pressure groups, 295, 298
Pretests, 475, 489
Primary labor market, 364
Priority matrix, 154
Problem
    action learning projects and, 336
    defining, 264
    evaluation and, 474
    finding, 167–169, 436, 439
    formulating, 169–170
    identifying way to look at, 170–174
    nonrecurring, 211
    performance-based approach to
        curriculum planning and, 207
    recurring, 211
Problem employees, 98–99
Problem framing, 215
Problem-solving
    creative, 315
    impromptu groups, 341, 342
    skills, 15
Process, vs. work methods, 268
Process consultation, 268–269, 275
Process efficiency, 7

Product development, 176, 178, 180
Product-development life cycle, 58–59
Production, work group stage, 261, 262
Production workers, 97
Productivity
    measures, 106
    value of, 468
    work group stage and, 261
Product users, assessing needs of, 297, 298. *See also* Consumers
Professional conferences, 338–339, 346, 497
Professionals, 97
Professional societies, talent development policies and serving in, 225
Proficiencies, 103
Profit maximization, 179
Programmed instruction, 231
Programmed plan, 191
Program planning, 195
Progress to date, 501
Project structure, 230–231, 261
Proteges, 329 **COMP: Please add accent marks**
Provocative methods, 451
Psychomotor learning domain, 222
Public education, 101
Public image of business, 288, 294
Public relations, 291–292
Public seminars, 304
Public speaking, 453
Pulse-taking approach to talent development, 54, 55, 62–63, 79
Purpose, 50–53
    changing group, 279
    clarifying, 8, 13, 15
    evaluation of, 471, 472
    importance of, 54

talent development efforts and, 30, 41, 85, 511
    work groups and, 325, 326
Purpose statement, 12–13, 49, 50, 51–52
    drafting, 78
    organizational culture and, 73
    strategic planning and, 165
    for talent development effort, 31, 41, 68–70, 71
Pyramid model for planned education, 381
Pyramid sequencing method, 418

Qualitative research methods, 477
Quasi-experimental evaluation designs, 474–475, 476
Question-and-answer sessions, 421
Questioning, 347–348, 453
Questions, 453–454
    future-oriented, 347
    long-term planning for talent development, 53
    open-ended, 272, 347
    strategic, 9

Rand Corporation, 109, 340
Random sampling, 476
RAT. *See* Role analysis technique
Reactions
    evaluation, 494
    to training, 487
Reaction surveys, 488
Reading, independent, 419–420
Realism, 502
Reality shock, 383
Real-time strategic thinking, 6–7
Record review, 441

Recruitment, 27, 57, 58, 97, 176
    exchange programs with universities
        and, 331
    human resource plans, 188, 189, 190
Recurring problems, 211
Regulatory requirements, planning
    educational efforts and, 382
Reorganization, 228–229
Repetitive needs, 171
Replacement planning, 374
Research and development, 131–132
Research design, 474–475
Resources
    evaluation of training, 478
    implementing organizational strategy
        for development of talent and, 236
    of instructional setting, 412–413
    for strategic employee-development
        needs, 359
Responsibility, 234
Results
    awareness of, 234
    evaluation of training and, 488,
        489–490
    intentions and, 499
    post-educational, 494
Retailers, 290
    training directed to, 286
    trends in, 136
    See also Distributors; External
        stakeholders; Stakeholders
Retention, 33
Retreats, 341
Retrenchment, 45, 172, 174, 176, 179
Return on investment, employee
    development and, 324
Rewards
    extrinsic, 233, 234
    intrinsic, 233–234
    learning and, 234

reviewing, 233–236
talent development and, 6, 249
training and, 405–406
types of, 233–234
Rifle approach to talent development, 55,
    67, 80
Risk, organizational strategy for
    development of talent and, 184
Role analysis technique (RAT), 266–267,
    274
Role messages, 266
Role models, 339
Role of corporation in society, 310
Role plays, 62, 423–424
Roles, work group, 260–261, 266–267
Rotation programs, 333–335, 346
Rummler, Geary, 92

Sales personnel, 97, 290
Sample, 476
SBU. See Strategic business unit
Scaled surveys, 105
Scenario analysis, 6, 449–450
Scenarios
    contingency, 191
    development of, 61, 441
    defined, 61–62
Scriven, Michael, 482, 484
SDT. See Strategic development
    of talent
Secondary labor market, 364
Second-generation planning, 6
Second-order change, 433
Segmentation, 287
Selection, 97, 190
Self-appraisals, 153
Self-criticism, 272–273
Self-development, mentoring and, 329
Self-directed learning, 212
Self-schema, 209

Seminars
  community service, 302–303
  external, 493
  public, 303, 304
  training, 300, 301
  university, 391
  Webinars, 339
Senior managers, 97
Sequencing curriculum, 198–199, 231
Sequencing instruction, 231–233
Sequencing objectives, 417–418
  strategic, 444–445
Service line users, assessing needs of,
  297, 298
Service workers, 97
Setting
  instructional, 412–413, 443, 460,
    472
  work, 412, 443, 460
Short-term needs, 171
Short-term objectives, 222
Significance, of rewards, 234
Simple cluster sampling, 476
Simple random sampling, 476
Simulations, 62, 425–426, 480
  designing, 426
  programs, 239
Simultaneous feedback, 486
Single-loop learning, 278
Situated learning, 39
Situation analysis, 90
Skeletal outlining, 431
Skill-based pay, 235
Skills, 209
  availability of, 187, 502
  blocks of, 235
  comparing actual to desired, 101–112
  evaluation of training, 478
  of future learners, 442
  inventory of, 326

  obsolescence in, 388
  tests of, 104
Small companies, strategic business
  planning and, 20
Small-group testing, 483
Social audit, 293
Social issues, employee education and, 383
Social learning theory, behavior modeling
  and, 340, 424
Social monitoring, 295, 311
Social responsibility, corporate, 294
Social sector, 126, 132–134
Social trends, 133
Society for Human Resources
  Management, 25
Sociopolitical forecasting, 295
Socratic method, 431–432
Software, Business Plan Pro, 11
Solutions, 170, 171–172, 174–175
Souder, William, 393
Sources
  evaluation of educational, 492–493
  for talent development scanning,
    148–150
Speakers' bureau, 394
Special interest groups, 288
Special job assignments, 335–336, 346, 497
Specification, 443
Specific instruction, 95
Speeches, talent development policies
  and, 225
Spiral concept for planned education, 381
Spiral curriculum, 233
Spirituality, in workplace, 276
Spontaneous role play, 423–424
Stable performance, 97
Staff meetings, 342
Stakeholders
  assessing competencies of, 514–518
  audit of, 290–291

development of, 498
evaluation and, 469–470
external, 18, 120–121, 132, 143–144, 287–291, 307
instructional objectives and influencing key, 223
public, corporation, and, 291–293, 308
responsiveness to, 501–502
strategic development of talent and, xxii
Stars, 98
Start-up efforts, 332
State-of-the-art developments, 131
Statistical methods, 477
Status, 260
Stereotyping, 272
Stockholders
company responsibility to, 133
training directed to, 285–286
Strategic business objectives, 224
Strategic business planning, 5–20
assumptions of, 15–16
history of, 5–7
vs. human resource planning, 24
interventions, 274–275
key terms, 9
levels of planning, 17–19
metaphor and, 7–8
methods, 19–20
model of, 8–15
organization development and, 258–259
questions to understand, 8
reemergence of, xix–xx
strategic development of talent and, 33
strategic training and, 435
summative evaluation and, 503
training and, 403
value of, 16–17
visioning and, 50

Strategic business plans
career policy and, 367
employee education and, 368
human resource plans, talent development, and, 54–68
improving relationships with HR plan and talent development effort and, 79–80
meeting to communicate, 238
work group and, 145
Strategic business strategy
business planning process, 8–10
diversification, 172, 174
evaluating, 10
growth, 172, 174
implementing, 10
long-term, 10
retrenchment, 172, 174, 176
turnaround, 172, 175, 176
Strategic business unit (SBU), 18
Strategic-centered curriculum planning, 202
Strategic choice, 163, 167
strategic evaluation prior to, 500–501
Strategic concurrent evaluation, 487
Strategic development of talent (SDT), xx–xxi, 28–40
assumptions of, 31–33
background issues, 3–4
checklist for, 41–47
competency identification, modeling, and assessment and, 34–40
defined, xxii, 4, 28
formal planning and, 32–33
importance of, 33–34
leadership development programs for, 40
learning and, 4
model of, 30–31
business planning and, xx

Strategic employee development,
  345–346
  conceptualizing, 345–346
  needs, 359
Strategic evaluation
  defined, 499–500
  prior to strategic choice, 500–501
  strategy review, 501–502
  summative evaluation, 502–503
Strategic formative evaluation, 482–484
Strategic front-end analysis, of employee
  training, 507
Strategic front-end evaluation, of training,
  479–480
Strategic instructional objectives, 444
Strategic management, 6
  issue-based, 67
Strategic needs, 102
Strategic objectives, 8
Strategic organization development,
  277–281
  assessing existing pressures that
    impede change, 280
  assessing future pressures favoring
    change, 279–280
  carrying out interventions, 280–281
  comparing pressure favoring and
    impeding change, 280
  conceptualizing, 277
  identifying norms that should exist,
    278–279
Strategic orientation, external environ-
  ment and, 285
Strategic post-instructional evaluation,
  490
Strategic question, 9
Strategic readiness, seven Ss, 9
Strategic staffing, 23
Strategic summative evaluation, 485
Strategic testing, 481–482

Strategic thinking, 7, 64, 442
Strategic training, 436–454
  content preparation, 453
  delivery methods, 445–453
  future learner characteristics,
    441–442
  future-oriented work analysis, 443–444
  future setting, 443
  human resource planning and, 435
  occasions to use approach, 437–439
  organizational strategy for
    development of talent and,
    434–435
  planning and, 434
  sequencing objectives, 444–445
  strategically oriented tests, 444
  strategic business planning and, 435
  strategic instructional objectives, 444
  vs. traditional, 432–433
  training delivery, 453–454
  training needs, 438, 439–441
  See also Training
Strategic work analysis, 443–444
Strategy
  defined, 5
  enterprise, 18
  functional, 18, 243–244
  HR enterprise, 26–27
  HR functional, 27
  HR Grand Strategy, 26
  long-term, 14
  needs assessment, 102–103
  trends in, 135
Strategy analysis, 92
Strategy formulation, 60
  curriculum development and, 194
  inside-outside approach, 64
  outside-inside approach, 64
Strategy review, 500, 501–502
Stratified random sampling, 476

Strengths
  assessing personal, 379
  identifying organizational, 9, 13–14,
    15–16
  talent development and assessing, 30,
    42, 43
  WOTS-UP analysis and, 167–169
Strengths/weaknesses, comparing to
  threats/opportunities, 10, 14, 31, 44
Stress, change efforts and, 276
Structure
  corporate, 17
  instructional, 228
  matrix, 230
  project, 230–231
  reviewing, 227–233
  See also Organizational structure
Structured role play, 423
Structure panel format, 420–421
Subject-centered curriculum, 231
Subject matter, type of, 193
Succession, 189
Succession planning, 22, 326–327
  mentoring and, 330
  workforce analysis and, 374
Suggestion systems, 237
Summative evaluation, 484, 500
  strategic, 485
  strategic evaluation and, 502–503
Supervisors
  career planning role, 366
  evaluation interests, 470
  first-line, 97
  organization development intervention
    and, 269
Supervisory expectations, work setting
  and, 412
Suppliers, 287, 290
  analyzing trends, 135
  assessing needs of, 298

education of, 100
training directed to, 286
See also External stakeholders;
  Stakeholders
Supplier sector, 126, 136
Survey-guided development, 270–271,
  275
Surveys, 103, 104–105
  attitude, 104, 237, 270–271, 475, 484,
    485
  Delphi procedure and, 109
  environmental scanning, 152
  opinion, 293
  in organizational mirror, 271–272
  reaction, 488
Sustainable competitive advantage, 9
SWOT analysis, 9, 14, 167–169,
  172–174. *See also* WOTS-UP analysis
Syllabus, 428
Systematic random sampling, 476

Tactics analysis, 92
Takeovers, 229
Talent
  distributors/suppliers of, 178
  value of, 12
Talent development
  business plans, human resource plans,
    and, 29
  corporate issues, 188–189
  human resource plans, strategic
    business plans, and, 54–68
  information for, 114–115
  See also Environmental scanning
Talent development committee, 240–243
Talent development effort
  career policy and, 367
  case study on purpose of, 85
  changing purpose statement, 71
  effect of organizational culture on, 72–74

establishing operational goals for, 220–224

evaluation of, 499–503

formulating purpose of, 68–70

improving relationships with strategic business plan and human resource plan and, 79–80

purpose activity, 75–78

strengths and weaknesses of, 118

Talent development functions, 188

Talent development objectives, 224

Talent development policies, 224–226

Talent development strategies, 54–67

choosing approach, 68

Talent planning, 21

Task analysis, 103, 105–106, 150, 152, 413

Task forces, 341

Tasks, 462

defined, 96, 413

test item, instructional objective, and, 415

Team, virtual, 336

Team building, 269–270, 274–275

Team development, 269–270

Technical approach to curriculum, 192, 193

Technical training, 233

Technological innovation, 132

Technological sector, 126, 131–132

Template, to formulate organizational strategy for talent development, 511–513

Terminal objectives, 414, 444

Terminal values, 468

Testing, 472

expert, 483

field, 483

formal, 300–301

individualized, 483

small-group, 483

strategic, 481–482

traditional, 480–481

Test items, 481

job task, instructional objective, and, 415

Tests

creating, 415–417

criterion-referenced, 480–481

to evaluate learning, 488–489

oral, 488

performance, 488

strategically oriented, 444

types of, 415

written, 488

Texas Instruments, 40

Theory, espoused, 278

Theory-in-use, 206, 278

Thinking, lateral, 451

Thinking skills, of future learners, 442

Think-tank experiences, 340–342, 346, 497

Third-generation planning, 6

Third party, concurrent evaluation and, 485–486

Threats

analyzing future, 9, 14, 16

changes in external environment and, 121

environmental scanning and, 155–156

talent development and identifying future, 43

WOTS-UP analysis and, 167–169

Threats/opportunities, comparing with strengths/weaknesses, 10, 14

Time frames

choosing data collection method and, 110

curriculum planning and, 196

environmental scanning for talent
    development and, 126–129
for individual learning contract, 385,
    386
using alternatives to classroom training
    and, 407
for talent development, 43
Timing
    of evaluation, 471
    organizational strategy for
        development of talent and, 185
Timeline assessment, 9
Tools
    future, 443
    of setting, 412
Top corporate executives, strategic
    planning and, 19, 20
Top-down approach to talent
    development, 54, 55, 56–57, 58, 79
Top-down strategy for needs assessment,
    102
Top management/managers
    effects of external trends on
        organization and, 137
    environmental scanning and, 123
    evaluation interests, 470
    external stakeholders and, 288
    increasing interaction with, 65–66
    organizational strategy for
        development of talent and, 164
    team building and, 270
    time perspective of, 127–128
    See also Management/managers
Trainee guide, 430
Trainees, 441
Training, xxi, xxiv, 27, 31, 57, 58, 65, 96,
    124, 186, 401–463
    alternatives to classroom-based, 457
    analyzing human performance
        problems, 455–456

case study, 463
classroom, 407
comprehensive reviews of, 490–491
computer-based, 231
content preparation, 427–432, 461
defined, 401–402
delivery methods, 418–427
design and delivery model, 403–408
directive, 444–445, 453
education tied to, 64–65
vs. employee education and employee
    development, 402
on environmental scanning, 138–139
to facilitate implementing
    organizational strategy, 239–240
vs. forecasting, 138
functional strategies and, 244
human resource plans, 188, 189
job performance and, 402
learner characteristics, 410–412, 459
learner needs, 408–410
needs assessment for, 458
nondirective, 444–445, 453
on-the-job, 231
organization development
    interventions and, 265
problems with traditional model,
    432–434
proficiency and, 103
restricting access to, 412
sequencing objectives in, 417–418
setting, 412–413, 460
strategic. See Strategic training
strategic front-end analysis of, 507
talent development policies and, 225
tests and, 415–417
training and, 402–403
training objectives, 414–415
work analysis and, 370, 413, 462
See also Strategic training

Training and development, xix. *See also* Strategic business planning
Training catalogs, 237
Training curriculum, 113, 196, 428, 430
Training delivery, 453–454
Training design, 239–240
Training evaluation, 477–491
  comprehensive reviews of training, 490–491
  concurrent evaluation, 485–487
  formative evaluation, 482–484
  front-end evaluation, 477–480
  post-instructional evaluation, 487–490
  summative evaluation, 484–485
  testing, 480–482
Training needs, 108, 198
  strategic, 438, 439–441
Training objectives, 414–415
Training packages, 393
Trait, 209
Trait ratings, 107
Transfer of learning, 489
Transfer programs, 330–332, 346, 497
Trends, 14
  assessing future, 379–380
  social, 133
Trust
  change efforts and, 276
  employee development and, 328
TRW, 40
Tuition reimbursement programs, 225, 394–395
Turnaround, 45, 172, 175, 176, 179, 229
Turnover, 330, 364

U.S. Postal Service, 40
Unit objectives, 222
Unit of analysis, 476
Units, 428, 430

Universities
  exchange programs with, 330–331
  external instruction sponsored by, 391
University of Alabama, 393
University of Phoenix, 393
Unskilled workers, 97–98
Upward channels of communication, 237–238
Upward mobility, 381

Validity, 475
Value chain analysis, 9
Values
  clarifying personal, 379
  core, 40
  defined, 467–468
  importance of, 468–469
  instrumental, 468
  terminal, 468
  in workplace, 276
Value system analysis, 9
Vendors, external instruction sponsored by, 392
Vertical career advancement, 361–362
Vertical integration, 176, 177, 178
Vertical market, 441
Virtual teams, action learning projects and, 336
Visibility
  career planning and, 363
  of rewards, 234
Vision, 12
  defined, 49–50
  strategic planning and, 165
  talent development effort, 30, 511
Visioning, 12, 49–50, 278
  assessing in stakeholders, 514
  for the future, 128
Vision statements, 52–53

Visual awakening, 50
Visual communication, 50
Visual exploration, 50
Visual strategy, 50

Weaknesses
  assessing personal, 379
  identifying organizational, 9, 13–16
  talent development and assessing, 30,
    42, 43
  WOTS-UP analysis and, 167–169
Web-based courses, 430
Webinars, 339
Web site, company, 292
Web site resources
  for finding information about the
    future, 149
  for human resource planning, 25
  for strategic business planning, 11
  for strategic development of
    talent, 33
  for visioning, 51
  for WOTS-UP analysis, 168
Whole person, educating, 383
Wholesales, trends in, 136
Whole-systems change, 277
WLP. *See* Workplace learning and
  performance
Women, planning educational efforts for,
  382
Word-of-mouth, talent development
  scanning and, 148
Work activities, 462
  career paths and, 371–372
Work analysis, 91, 369–373
  employee training and, 413
  future-oriented, 443–444
Work assignments
  employee development and, 324
  special, 335–336, 346

Work behavior, career paths and,
  371–373
Work duties, allocation of, 405
Workers, disadvantaged, 301
Workforce, identifying future needs,
  376–378
Workforce analysis, 373–376
  by department, division, or work
    group, 375–376
  by individual, 373–374
  by occupational group, 375
  by position, 374–375
Workforce Investment Act (1998), 364
Workforce Magazine, 25
Workforce planning, 21
Work group market, 99–100
Work groups
  assessment centers and, 108
  characteristics, 260–261
  classifying, 279–280
  creating alternative, 279
  defined, 99
  determining people available,
    326–328
  development efforts and phase of
    group, 262
  employee development action plans,
    328
  environmental context, 138
  human resource supplies, 327–328
  identifying, 325
  identifying competencies, 345–346,
    357
  identifying problems/issues
    confronting, 355
  identifying purpose, activities, 325
  learner characteristics of, 410–411
  life cycle stages, 261, 262
  norms, 259, 260, 406, 412, 443
  organizational mirror and, 271

organizational strategy for
development of talent and, 169
organization development and, 257,
259–261
organization development
interventions and, 265
organized learning efforts, 144
plan changes in purpose/activities, 326
roles, 260–261, 266–267
strategic employee development for, 345
workforce analysis by, 375–376
in WOTS-UP analysis, 173
Workhorses, 98
Work method, 146
future, 443
vs. process, 268
Work perceptions, career paths and, 371
Workplace learning and performance
(WLP), xix, 4. *See also* Strategic
business planning
Workplace learning and performance
(WLP) department
change in organizational structure and,
230
organizational strategy for
development of talent and, 164
skills in, 187
Work results, competencies and, 35
Work setting, 412, 460
future, 443

Worksharing, 57
Worksheets
collecting information on future-
oriented needs, 157–158
comparing forces impeding and
favoring change, 284
identifying competencies in
organization, 356
identifying employee-development
efforts, 348
identifying forces favoring change in
organization, 282
identifying forces impeding change in
organization, 283
identifying work group/department
competencies, 357
problem framing, 215
social monitoring, 311
Work simplification, 439
Work standards, 106, 404
Work unit, instructional objectives and
influencing, 223
World Future Society, 149
WOTS-UP analysis, 167–169,
172–174
Written test, 415–416, 488

Xerox, 40

YES!, 149